Cognitive Neuroscience Studies
of the Chinese Language

Cognitive Neuroscience Studies of the Chinese Language

Edited by

Henry S. R. Kao,
Che-Kan Leong,
Ding-Guo Gao

香港大學出版社

HONG KONG UNIVERSITY PRESS

Hong Kong University Press
14/F Hing Wai Centre
7 Tin Wan Praya Road
Aberdeen
Hong Kong

© Hong Kong University Press 2002

ISBN 962 209 568 2

A CIP catalogue record for this book is available from the British Library.

Secure On-line Ordering
http://www.hkupress.org

Printed and bound by Condor Production Ltd., Hong Kong, China

Contents

Preface

Chinese is one of the oldest and the most widely used languages in the world. The unique properties of the Chinese writing system, its phonology, morphology and semantics are critical to an understanding of the universal as well as culturally specific aspects of language processing. Research into Chinese has fundamental significance for developing general theories of language processing through the exploration of the cognitive and neural mechanisms underlying Chinese reading, writing and speech.

The last two decades have witnessed a growing interest in the scientific study of Chinese from the perspectives of psychology, linguistics, neuroscience, computer science and speech and hearing science. Greater interdisciplinary endeavours are needed from these and allied disciplines to foster future research into the development for methods and technology for language learning and communication. To date, the University of Hong Kong has played an instrumental role in this research as well as in promoting academic activities in this emerging field.

As a concrete step taken to foster future research efforts among scholars within the university as well as across academic institutions, the University of Hong Kong and the Chinese Academy of Sciences established in 1997 the HKU-CAS Chinese Language-Cognitive Science Research Centres as a joint venture dedicated to this cause. The actual operation of these centres has been carried out through the Beijing Laboratory of Cognitive Science in Beijing and the Department of Psychology of the University of Hong Kong in Hong Kong.

The inaugural function of the Joint HKU-CAS Chinese Language-Cognitive Science Research Centres was the organization of the International Symposium on Cognitive Processes of the Chinese Language, held from August 29 to September 2, 1997 in Hong Kong and sponsored by the University of Hong Kong. 'An Advanced Study Institute: Advances in Theoretical Issues and Cognitive Neuroscience Research of the Chinese Language', a conference sponsored by the Croucher Foundation, Hong Kong, followed this academic activity and was held in Hong Kong and Beijing from November 23 to December 2, 1998. The former event placed its primary focus on various cognitive issues while the latter concentrated on neuroscience perspectives of Chinese language processing. Both conferences were highly successful and yielded a large number of high-quality presentations. A representative selection of these papers forms the basis of this edited volume.

The publication of this book has benefited from the generous sponsorship of University of Hong Kong and the Croucher Foundation, Hong Kong. The Department of Psychology of the University of Hong Kong provided needed logistics and staff support during both conferences. The Croucher Foundation also provided funds to finance the preparation of this edited volume. We gratefully acknowledge the sustained support of Anthony Tsui, Director of the Croucher Foundation.

The preparation of this volume was facilitated by a conscientious reviewer who made critical and constructive comments and suggestions, which have been adopted broadly in the final selection of the papers. The untiring support of the Hong Kong University Press was instrumental to our continuing effort to assure a high-quality book. In this regard, the patience and co-operation of all the authors of this book have been the key to the efforts of the three editors. To all these friends and colleagues, we owe them our deepest appreciation and gratitude. To my fellow editor C. K. Leong, we are indebted to his enthusiasm, diligence, hard work and professional rigour displayed throughout the preparation of this volume. Without his dedication and commitment, this book would not have been a reality.

In appreciation of its long-standing cause in the promotion of science and scientific research in Hong Kong, as well as its vision in support of the development of the emerging field of scientific research in the Chinese language, we take pleasure in dedicating this volume to the noble cause of the Croucher Foundation, Hong Kong.

Henry S. R. Kao

List of Contributors

CHEN, May Jane, School of Psychology, Australian National University, Canberra, ACT 0200 Australia.

CHEN, Xuefeng, Department of Psychology, South China Normal University, Guangzhou 510631, China.

CHEN, Yi-Ping, CTSU, Nuffield Department of Clinical Medicine, University of Oxford, Harkness Bldg., Radcliffe Infirmary, Oxford 0X2 6HE, UK.

DAVIES, Robert, Laboratory of Experimental Psychology, School of Biological Sciences, University of Sussex, Falmer, Brighton BN1 9QG, UK.

FU, Shimin, Department of Experimental Psychology, University of Oxford, South Parks Road, Oxford 0X1 3UD UK.

GAO, Ding-Guo, Institute of Logic and Cognition, and Department of Psychology, School of Education, Sun Yat-Sen University, Guangzhou, 510275, China.

GUTHRIE, John T., School of Human Development, University of Maryland, Benjamin Building, College Park, MD 20742, USA.

HAN, Buxin, Institute of Psychology, Chinese Academy of Sciences, Beijing 100101, China.

HOOSAIN, Rumjahn, Department of Psychology, The University of Hong Kong, Pokfulam Road, Hong Kong.

IVERSEN, Susan, Department of Experimental Psychology, University of Oxford, South Parks Road, Oxford, 0X1 3UD UK.

KAO, Henry S. R., Chinese Language Cognitive Science Research Centre and Department of Psychology, The University of Hong Kong, Pokfulam Road, Hong Kong.

KWAN, Anna S. F., Centre for the Enhancement of Learning & Teaching (CELT), City University of Hong Kong, Tat Chee Avenue, Kowloon Tong, Hong Kong.

LAM, Agnes S. L., English Language Centre, The University of Hong Kong, Pokfulam Road, Hong Kong.

LEONG, Che-Kan, Department of Educational Psychology and Special Education, University of Saskatchewan, 28 Campus Drive, Saskatoon, Saskatchewan, Canada S7N 0X1 and Department of Educational Psychology, The Chinese University of Hong Kong, Shatin, New Territories, Hong Kong.

LI, Ping, Department of Psychology, University of Richmond, Richmond, VA 23175, USA.

LIU, Godfrey K. F., Language Information Sciences Research Centre, City University of Hong Kong, Tat Chee Avenue, Kowloon Tong, Hong Kong.

LIU, Ying, Learning Research and Development Centre and Department of Psychology, University of Pittsburgh, Pittsburgh, PA 15260, USA.

MATSUNAGA, Sachiko, Department of Modern Languages and Literatures, California State University, Los Angeles, CA 90032, USA.

MATTHEWS, Paul M., Centre for Functional Magnetic Resonance Imaging of the Brain, and Department of Clinical Neurology, University of Oxford, John Radcliffe Hospital, Headley Way, Headington, Oxford, 0X3 9DU UK.

PERFETTI, Charles A., Learning Research and Development Centre and Department of Psychology, University of Pittsburgh, Pittsburgh, PA 15256, USA.

TAN, Li-Hai, Laboratory for Language Neuroscience and Cognition, Department of Linguistics, The University of Hong Kong, Pokfulam Road, Hong Kong.

T'SOU, Benjamin K. Y., Language Information Sciences Research Centre, City University of Hong Kong, Tat Chee Avenue, Kowloon Tong, Hong Kong.

WANG, Judy Huei-Yu, Center for New Constructs, Educational Testing Service, Rosedale Road, MS16R, Princeton, NJ 08541, USA.

WEEKES, Brendan, Laboratory of Experimental Psychology, School of Biological Sciences, University of Sussex, Falmer, Brighton BN1 9QG, UK.

'Cognitive Conjunction' Analysis of Processing Chinese

Che-Kan Leong

In as much as any one person can be so credited, Nobel laureate Herbert Simon is usually regarded as the founder of cognitive science. He explained the field as 'the study of intelligence and its computational processes in humans (and animals), in computers, and in the abstract' (Simon & Kaplan, 1989, p. 2). Intelligence systems in this context are identified with adaptability, with learning, problem solving and evolution. Simon and Kaplan discussed from a computational standpoint the contributions to cognitive science from psychology, artificial intelligence, linguistics, philosophy and neuroscience to explain the architecture of intelligence systems and different levels of abstraction. Just as they considered neuroscience as important in 'providing hypotheses about fruitful architectures for machine intelligence (and presumably also human intelligence)' (p. 6), so Sejnowski and Churchland (1989, p. 343) emphasized the brain and cognition connection in that 'neurobiological data provide essential constraints on computational theories'. In their elegant paper Sejnowski and Churchland discussed neural and connectionist models to the late 1980s and stressed that knowledge of brain architecture could explain the problem solving level and the algorithmic level of analyses of human cognition. They detailed different anatomical and physiological techniques, including imaging technology, to buttress their argument that integration should consist of intertwined theories such that phenomena at one level are explained by those from another level.

More recently, Price and Friston (1997) introduced the concept of *cognitive conjunction* as a new approach to designing and analysing cognitive experiments. Price and Friston explained that, 'Cognitive conjunction studies are designed such that two or more distinct task pairs each share a common processing difference. The neural correlates of the process of interest are then associated with the common areas of activation for each task pair ...' (1997, p. 261). While these scientists' interest is in brain activation and cognitive components, together with their statistical considerations, it may not be inappropriate to borrow both the concept and the term *cognitive conjunction* for this edited volume on cognitive neuroscience studies of the Chinese language.

As is well known, an edited volume suffers from some diffusion of conceptual underpinnings and methodological sophistication, but gains from enrichment of ideas from diverse schools of thoughts. This volume is no exception. It contains cutting edge papers discussing research into the processing of Chinese from connectionist and functional neuroimaging perspectives and the acquisition of lexical meaning and semantic structures from computational viewpoints. It has insightful papers on phonological, orthographic and semantic strategies in reading two character Chinese words and picture naming and recognition of Chinese words. It has critical psycholinguistic analyses in mapping phonology and meaning of Chinese words and early phonological activation in processing the Japanese kanji, which is derived basically from Chinese characters. It has clear exposition of a psycho-geometric theory with supporting data in explaining the analysis of visual spatial patterns of Chinese characters. It also has succinct papers in the spirit of corpus linguistics on the development of vocabulary in Chinese secondary school students. Thus the fifteen chapters span from the basic to the more applied research and all are based on current theories in explicating the processing of Chinese.

From the set of rather diverse papers as outlined above, it is the aim of this commentary to show some 'common processing difference', to borrow from the neuroscientists Price and Friston (1997). We attempt to provide some moderate coverage on the cognitive processing of Chinese characters and words to show what the linguist DeFrancis (1989) calls the 'diverse oneness' even in dealing with one-language systems such as Chinese. We are conscious of the lack of coverage of other key areas in processing Chinese, such as the parsing of sentences and discourse processing. It is hoped this selective coverage with its diverse topics, methods and research findings will further stimulate the cognitive and neuroscience study of Chinese and other language systems.

Cognitive Neuroscience Approaches

The pioneering work by Tzeng, Hung and Wang (1977) on speech recoding in reading Chinese characters nearly thirty years ago may be said to provide the impetus to enhance further systematic studies of information processing of the Chinese language system. In the intervening years there have been investigations of inter-related issues of cognitive processing of Chinese as reported in edited volumes (Chen & Tzeng, 1992; Kao & Hoosain, 1984, 1986; Leong & Tamaoka, 1998; Liu, Chen, & Chen, 1988; Peng, Shu, & Chen, 1997; Wang, Inhoff, & Chen, 1999), books (e.g., Hoosain, 1991), in addition to cumulative research papers from laboratories in Pittsburgh (e.g., Perfetti & Tan, 1998; Tan & Perfetti, 1998, 1999), in Sydney (e.g., Taft & Zhu, 1997), in London (e.g., Zhou & Marslen-Wilson, 1995), in Taiwan (e.g., Liu, Wu, & Chou, 1996), in Beijing (e.g., Peng, Liu, & Wang, 1999), among other sources. Some of the authors in these research studies are represented in this volume.

Process-oriented approach

Careful reading of the above works suggests several trends. One is the process-oriented approach to explore the general properties of language systems within the framework of human cognition (Alegria, Holender, Morais, & Radeau, 1992). This information processing approach has been applied with considerable success to show fine-grained differences in cognitive processing of alphabetic language systems. Take for example the Romance languages such as Spanish and Portuguese. These language systems are syllable-timed with phonemic constraints operating on syllables, and provide easier access to phonology as compared with the stress-based English (Morais, 1995). For the highly regular Dutch alphabetic language system, research findings with children indicate that grapheme-phoneme conversion can go on in parallel with the lexical look-up in cascading processes (see Leong & Joshi, 1997).

The same information processing approach to understanding lexical access to the non-alphabetic Chinese and Japanese language systems has provided theories and research findings into the cognitive analysis of these systems. Take the biscriptal (kanji and kana), or more correctly, the tri-scriptal (kanji, hiragana and katakana) Japanese syllabary as an example. The processing of kanji symbols (basically Chinese characters) with their On- and Kun-reading to represent meaning, and of kana (basically phonetic) symbols with their moraic segments to represent subsyllabic and timing units, may involve different cognitive structures (Inagaki, Hatano, & Otake, 2000; Leong & Tamaoka, 1998). In the case of the morphosyllabic Chinese, the phonological basis in analytic character and word reading has been shown in psychological studies (e.g., Perfetti & Zhang, 1995) and this phonological activation occurs 'at lexicality' or 'lexically' (Perfetti, Liu, & Tan, chapter 2; Perfetti, Zhang, & Berent, 1992, p. 228). Thus some of the critical and interesting research questions are the extent to which recognition and naming Chinese characters and words is aided by phonological representation.

Cross-language studies

The other trend is the need for cross-language studies to examine underlying mechanisms of processing shallow or transparent and deep or opaque alphabetic language systems and the morphosyllabic Chinese. While this volume is concerned almost solely with Chinese, we should bear in mind that the morphosyllabic nature of Chinese entails a phonetic component of Chinese characters (DeFrancis, 1989). This term is preferred over the earlier term of 'phonosemantic' proposed by Boodberg (1937), which stresses the meaning part as important over the syllabic aspect of Chinese characters. Noted linguists such as Yuen Ren Chao (1968, 1976) and Michael Halliday (1981) all emphasize the shape-sound-meaning interrelationship of the 'complex of character-syllable morpheme' characteristic of Chinese characters (Halliday, 1981).

All these linguists emphasize from diachronic and synchronic Chinese linguistics the underlying phonological nature of the language system. Chao (1968), for example, carefully distinguishes in Chinese the *zi* 'sociological word' from the *ci* 'syntactic word'. He states: 'By the "sociological word" I mean that type of unit, intermediate in size between a phoneme and a sentence, which the general, non-linguistic public is conscious of, talks about, has an everyday term for, and is practically concerned with in various ways. It is the kind of thing which a child learns to say, which a teacher teaches children to read and write in school' (Chao, 1968, p. 136). Halliday (1981) also emphasizes this syllabic nature of Chinese. He suggests that 'the phonology [for Chinese] remained a phonology of the syllable, always analysed into initial and final, with the initials classified by place and manner of articulation and the finals by rhyme, vowel grade, labialisation and tone' (Halliday, 1981, p. 137).

This paradigmatic process is explained in terms of analogies made between members of a set of utterances sharing speech characteristics in a slot-filling 'network of relationships' (Spencer, 1991, p. 417). The emphasis on the paradigmatic analysis of Chinese characters and words is important for at least two reasons. One reason is that in the current phonetic system (*Pin*[1]*yin*[1] in China or *Zhu*[4]*yin*[1] *Fu*[2]*hao*[4] in Taiwan) for beginning reading, what constitutes a syntactic word will determine the way that word is transcribed phonetically. The other reason is that in real classroom practices, learning to read Chinese integrates the phonological and orthographic components in parallel in building a network of related shape, sound and meaning components (Leong, 1997). It is this paradigmatic nature in linking speech to reading print that seems to be important in learning to read Chinese (Leong, 1997) and one that should be exploited, as shown in two studies with *Pu*[3]*tong*[1]*hua*[4] speaking Chinese children in Beijing (Leong & Tan, 2002). The Leong and Tan work, which highlights the main vowel in the rime part of the intrasyllabic segments of Chinese characters and the involvement of speech-sound segments retrieval and repetition, points to phonological processing skills common to and modulated by language systems. These common and specific phonological representations investigated cross-linguistically should further advance our knowledge of reading as cognitive development and also developmental dyslexia in different language systems (Goswami, 2000).

This discussion on phonological processing and the specific nature of such processing in Chinese in relation to early reading is within the context of the *universal phonological principle* and especially the Interactive Constituency Model (Perfetti, Liu, & Tan, chapter 2; Perfetti & Tan, 1999; Tan & Perfetti, 1999) of visual word identification. The Interactive Constituency Model specifies that the orthographic-phonological form-form mapping at the character or word level is stronger and faster acting than the form-meaning mapping. However, the model also provides for the activation of orthographic units, which should include stroke complexity, printed frequency of characters (e.g., Leong, Cheng, & Mulcahy, 1987) and 'higher' orthographic units of 'stroke patterns' as shown by Chen (chapter 7; Chen, Allport, & Marshall, 1996) and other contributors to this volume. We shall return to these issues in subsequent sections.

Cognitive neuroscience architecture of language

While phonological processing modulated by psycholinguistic consideration of different language systems provides a locus of reading processes, a much more powerful framework should link the cognitive, behavioural and biological levels. This neuro-developmental aspect with emphasis on functional neuroimaging is an important scientific advance to delineate more clearly the basic architecture of cognitive and linguistic operations and their mapping onto neural substrates in different language systems and specific and interrelated domains within each system (Matthews, Fu, Chen, & Iversen, chapter 3; Perfetti, Liu, & Tan, chapter 2).

William James' (1890) reference to changes in cortical blood flow during mental operations and Sherrington's (1940) vision of large-scale visualization of physiological activities can now be tested with the advent of new theories and functional neuroimaging techniques to study the neurocognition of language. Non-invasive neuroimaging technology such as *magnetic resonance imaging* (MRI) with its high anatomic resolution permits in vivo search for subtle and mild changes in geometric configurations of the human brain. *Functional magnetic resonance imaging* (fMRI) provides a measure of the hemodynamic responses in the brain during the performance of cognitive and linguistic tasks; and *positron emission tomography* (PET) allows the measurement of changes in neural activities by measuring changes in regional cerebral blood flow (for details, see Brown & Hagoort, 1999; Eden & Zeffiro, 1997).

These neuroimaging techniques combined with careful experimental strategies of cognitive psychology have led to a more refined understanding of the organization of language in normal human brains and the complexity of brain structure. Some of the advances in addition to what is described in Perfetti et al. (chapter 2) and Matthews et al. (chapter 3) can be outlined. Neuroimaging techniques have led to the observations that there are different routes between word perception in visual cortices and speech production from motor cortices and that practice blocks or novelty would need different neural circuitry for responses (Posner & Raichle, 1994; Raichle, Fox, Videen, MacLeod, Pardo, Fox, & Petersen, 1994). Neuroimaging studies have also led to the observations that the cerebellum plays a role in the cognitive aspects of single word processing in addition to the motor aspects of speech (Leiner, Leiner & Dow, 1993; Posner & Raichle, 1994)

Following a well specified model of processing visual word forms

(Petersen, Fox, Snyder & Raichle, 1990) and that of working memory (Baddeley, 1986), Friedman, Kenny, Wise, Wu, Stuve, Miller, Jesberger & Lewin (1998) used fMRI to study 11 healthy adults during their covert word generation beginning with particular letters in the *Controlled Oral Word Association Task* (COWAT). These researchers constructed from their fMRI results a 'brain-area by cognitive function' matrix based on the co-ordinate systems of Talairach and Tournoux (1988), which can be translated into Brodmann areas. To grossly over-simplify this elegant study, Friedman et al. (1998, p. 248) found that the covert generation of words was associated with the following areas of the left hemisphere: '(1) Brodmann areas 44 and 45 in the inferior frontal gyrus, (2) Brodmann areas 21 and 37 in the caudal portion of the middle and inferior temporal gyri, and (3) striate and/or extrastriate areas (Brodmann areas 17 and/or 18).' While one may speculate on possible results from different brains based on three-dimensional analysis such as Roland and Zilles (1994), these findings are generally consistent with those of other neuroimaging studies. What is important is that these researchers showed that individual brain areas subserve multiple cognitive functions and that individual cognitive functions activate multiple brain areas.

Interrelated Issues of Orthographic and Phonological Forms and Meaning in Processing Chinese

The necessarily succinct discussion above suggests that cognitive activities such as reading and language are typically studied in cognitive science as components in terms of millisecond reaction times to measure the time course of cognitive operations. The advent of neuroscience technology such as functional imaging techniques enables the testing of where these operations are localized in specific areas of the brain. What is important is that the fine-grained latency measures, the visualization of fairly precise brain areas from fMRI and the recording of brain activation from electrophysiological measures such as *event-related potentials* (ERP), all require well-defined theories for the integration of these different levels of component operations. Simon and Kaplan (1989, p. 26) put this *sine qua non* clearly and succinctly: 'What is a reaction time without a theory relating time to amount of processing? What is an image from a microscope without the optical theory that explains what a microscope does?'

Activation models and neural substrates

The various chapters in this volume demonstrate how these deceptively simple questions of Simon and Kaplan (1989) are answered in some ways with reference to the processing of Chinese. **Perfetti, Liu, and Tan** in their *tour de force* paper (chapter 2) reiterate the need for cross-language and cross-writing studies of reading and discuss their updated orthographic-phonological activation model to explain the general components of reading. This Interactive Constituency Model emphasizes that in visual word identification the orthography to phonology activation (form-form mapping) is stronger and faster acting than the orthography to meaning activation (form-meaning mapping). In earlier papers, Perfetti and Tan (1999) and Tan and Perfetti (1999) have demonstrated how this model explains the primacy of phonology to orthography activation over the orthography to meaning activation in the visual recognition of two-character Chinese words. The current model consisting of a network of linked units with spreading activation should also apply to other language systems. Perfetti, Liu and Tan are modest in their findings: 'phonology is rapid, probably automatic, and perhaps universal'.

In addition to their accumulated experimental results from various priming, forward and backward masking experiments, Perfetti et al. educe two further lines of converging evidence to support the general framework of their multi-level representations and interactions amongst the levels as mapped out in their Interactive Constituency Model. One line of research is electrophysiological from event-related potentials (ERP). The other line of work is from functional neuroimaging (fMRI).

In their ERP studies Perfetti et al. ask if the time course of the interference effect in judging characters with the same meaning and the same pronunciation might be associated with the negative wave form N400. The N400 amplitude usually shows a large negative effect when a subject is presented with a final word (especially an open-class word) semantically incongruous in a sentence whereas congruous endings show a positive going wave (Kutas & Van Patten, 1988). In a detailed review of event-related brain potentials in 'electrifying psycholinguistics', Kutas and Van Patten (1994) discuss the significance of peaks, amplitude and polarity of ERP waveforms; the advantages (e.g., large amounts of data, freedom from extraneous task demands, providing a topographic map of the brain in magnetic ERP) and disadvantages (e.g., experimental constraints, overlapping components elicited by the same stimulus) in using ERPs to study language processing.

The approach taken by Perfetti et al. in their ERP study of the time course, when there is a conflict in form-meaning in Chinese characters and words, is analogous to the electrophysiological study of the interactions in amplitude and latency between rhyme and orthographic similarity judgment by Polich, McCarthy, Wang, and Donchin (1983). Similar to Perfetti et al., Polich et al. also found from their ERP recordings that both orthographic and phonological information is accessed early and continues to interact as reflected by P300 latency and response time. The finding by Polich et al. that conflict of English word orthography with phonology produces large reaction time effects adds support to the cascading style of English phonology activated with orthography, as explicated by Perfetti et al. (chapter 2).

Perfetti, Tan and their colleagues provide further converging evidence from fMRI studies to show extensive activities of the neural systems in processing Chinese characters and words with vague and precise meanings (Tan, Spinks, Gao, Liu, Perfetti, Xiong, Stofer, Pu, Liu, & Fox, 2000). The Tan et al. results suggest that linguistic complexity in terms of semantic vagueness and precision modulates brain activation and also challenge the belief that reading single Chinese characters is right lateralized and reading two-character words is left lateralized.

The significance of the Tan et al. (2000) study in challenging the conventional view of dissociation in neural substrates in processing single Chinese characters and two-character words is commented on by **Matthews, Fu, Chen and Iversen** (chapter 3). Matthews et al. provide a clear explication of the nature and characteristics of functional magnetic resonance imaging and positron emission tomography (PET) studies of the organization of language in the brain. Consonant with the earlier views expressed by Simon and Kaplan (1989), they reiterate the need for a 'firm psychological model' and discuss the complexity in teasing out confounds from specific language aspects. They also point to such exciting aspects as brain plasticity in early and late second language acquisition and effects of gender.

Matthews et al. report an imaging study in which native Mandarin or Putonghua speaking Chinese subjects make semantic judgment by first accessing the phonology of stimulus Chinese characters and stimulus Pinyin symbols sounding or not sounding like real Chinese words. Consistent with other studies they found the involvement of Brodmann areas (BA) 44/45 and BA47 in the left inferior frontal areas in both the character and Pinyin reading and further suggest that the right hemisphere may be involved in processing 'phonological units larger than a single phoneme'. Matthews et al. discuss other intricate and significant aspects of their study such as the finding of the involvement of stronger left cerebellum activation for character reading relative to the Pinyin reading in their novel semantic judgment task based on phonological characteristics rather than visual forms of the stimulus materials. They suggest that patterns of brain activation result from phonological, orthographic and meaning processing of Chinese characters and words, and not so much from their 'surface forms'. This notion finds support in Chee, Caplan, Soon, Sriram, Tan, Thiel, and Weekes (1999), who carried out one of a small number of neuroimaging studies characterizing Mandarin Chinese and English sentence processing in fluently bilingual Chinese subjects. Chee et al. demonstrated that their fluently bilingual Singaporean Chinese subjects, exposed early to both language systems, show an overlap of activations of prefrontal regions. They argued that the overlap of common neuronal networks reflects conceptual and syntactic processing of written Chinese and English, rather than surface language forms of these disparate systems.

Very recently, Tan, Feng, Fox and Gao (2001) used event-related fMRI to study the neural substrates subserving the automatic processing of sublexical phonological information in reading aloud regular and exception (irregular) Chinese words by ten subjects. They find a large neural network activated by reading the two types of Chinese stimulus words with the involvement of 'left inferior frontal regions (BAs 44/9, 45/47), left (pre-)motor cortex including supplementary motor area, and left superior temporal lobe' (Tan et al., 2001, p. 85). They show that BA9 and BA47 are important in the orthography to phonology transformation process and also the heavy involvement of the right hemisphere because of the unique square-shaped Chinese characters demanding fine-grained analyses of spatial features. The Tan et al. (2001) event-related fMRI study is important in elucidating the neural involvement in analysing the inter-related sub-processes of phonological, tonal processing and the articulation of Chinese words. Corroborative results are provided by Tan, Liu, Perfetti, Spinks, Fox and Gao (2001) in their recent fMRI study of pairs of semantically related and pairs of homophones of Chinese characters to show the distributed neural system in reading Chinese.

In all the excitement about the use of functional neuroimaging techniques in cognitive neuroscience, we should bear in mind the cautionary note by Rugg (1999, p. 30) that neuroimaging effects 'can only be informative about how cognitive processing is instantiated in the brain if the functional role of the neural activity reflected by the effect can be identified.' Rugg points out several unresolved issues. One is that functional accounts of cognition can take different forms, just as Sejnowski and Churchland (1989) have discussed different levels of investigation of brain-cognition relationship. The other issue is the 'correlational' nature of neuroimaging data in providing neural correlates of one or more cognitive operations. The third issue is the establishment of a causal relationship between the neural activity and the cognitive operations. Rugg makes the innovative suggestion of reversing the role of neuroimaging experiments by manipulating neural systems instantiating cognitive operations and observing the functional consequences, but this manipulation is made difficult in the absence of an animal model of language processing. In a recent study of semantic judgment with two groups of Chinese-English bilinguals, Chee, Hon, Lee and Soon (2001) find changes in the spatial distribution and magnitude of blood oxygenation level dependent (BOLD) imaging commensurate with language proficiency. Their findings of linkage between or among longer processing time, greater BOLD signal change in the left prefrontal and parietal areas and language proficiency suggest the importance of task requirement and cognitive load in imaging studies. With all these cautionary notes, Posner and DiGirolamo (2000) are optimistic that the mapping of cognitive functions in the human brain provides a means of better understanding of human cognition including reading, language, attention and emotion.

Within the framework of neural networks and activation Li (chapter 4) has provided a dynamic and developmental account from connectionist and computational perspectives to explain the acquisition of semantic structures in Chinese. At the risk of over-simplification, we can say that connectionist models emphasize the learning of associative pairs of patterns without reference to explicit rules. These patterns in our context can be the phonological or orthographical form of a word as input and the read or spelled form of a word as output. A connectionist network consists of a large number of computational units behaving in manners resembling those of neurons. For each unit there is an activation level and a weighted connection communicates the activation of one unit to another. The level of activation of a unit is a function of all the activation (total learning experience or weighted sum) received by that unit over a threshold value. In general, the size of activation of a unit and the strength of its connection with another unit determine the amount of influence one unit has over the other. The essential feature of a connectionist network is that it learns about the associations between pairs of patterns through iterative processes by modifying connection strengths and produces the correct output pattern in response to input. A good example is the influential connectionist model by Seidenberg and McClelland (1989) which learns to pronounce 3,000 monosyllabic words from input representations of orthographic forms and pronunciation representation based on phoneme triples. Another example is the extension by Plaut, McClelland, Seidenberg and Patterson (1996) to understand normal reading acquisition and impaired reading following brain injury.

This learning property and the computational aspect, particularly the abstraction of statistical structure of connectionist models, underpin Li's work. He first discusses some cross-language issues (see Li & MacWhinney, 1996) of how children focus on semantic properties of lexical items, especially meanings of verbs and the connection with grammatical tense-aspect morphology in a 'semantic space'. Specifically, he asks the question of how learners extract from their linguistic input the co-occurrences of lexical information in connectionist networks. He argues for a 'high-dimensional input space' and focuses on global rather than local lexical co-occurrences to accommodate the complex semantic relationships in lexical aspects of verbs. Li explains that global co-occurrences of a word are the sum total of the learning experience of that word in the context of other words in certain grammatical structures which include covert, subtle meaning categories termed *cryptotypes*. Local co-occurrences, according to Li, pertain to the immediate lexical environment, such as the form classes of words.

Li proposes a dynamic, self-learning or self-organizing connectionist network in a two-dimensional feature map ('implicit in the multi-dimensional input space') as a more powerful learning mechanism for the organization and reorganization of the abstract, internal lexicon. He shows how the application of this self-organizing network with the pairing of a phonological map and a semantic map successfully models the acquisition of lexical and grammatical aspects. He further demonstrates, from 509 lexical items extracted from a large corpus of nearly 4 million token words, the derivation of more precise lexical semantic representation (89% accuracy). This precision results from the statistical structure inherent in connectionist models in general and the learning experience of the connectionist network (as shown in the clustering and distances from various clusters of different kinds of meanings in the vector space of his self-organizing two-dimensional map) in particular. As Li has shown in his powerful dynamic two-dimensional feature map, the precision of semantic representation is expected to increase when learners are further provided with linguistic and extra-linguistic cues in language acquisition *in situ*. It may be pointed out that the class of 'unsupervised learning' in mapping inputs and outputs in high-dimensional space was shown earlier by Small, Hart, Nguyen and Gordon (1995) in the learning of topographical space of semantic features.

Working within the broad, general framework of connectionist networks, Perfetti, Liu and Tan (chapter 2) have also provided a computational instantiation of multi-level representations and interactions among different levels (orthographic, phonological and semantic) in recognizing 204 Chinese characters. Perfetti et al. have summarized the main features of the computational instantiation of their Interactive Constituency Model and have shown how the activation of cohorts of similar orthographic, phonological and semantic features explains the learning of Chinese characters in a 'threshold style' and as 'phonological diffusion'. Perfetti et al. focused on the more direct and faster acting phonological linkage to orthographic forms of words and deal with phonological and semantic linkages only in an 'indirect implementation'. In contrast, Li has explicated the theory and computation in the acquisition of lexical semantic representations in his topographical two-dimensional map of network learning. Both sets of authors have amply demonstrated, from different learning algorithms and from localized and global representations, the force and precision from connectionist network models of learning Chinese and other languages. The interplay between network architectures and learning algorithms (both *supervised learning* with training sets of input/output pairs to be associated and *unsupervised learning* with no external teaching except the exposure of the network to inputs to build internal representations) explains a great deal of cognitive and linguistic phenomena. What is more, connectionist models provide a link to neural structures in computing cognitive and linguistic functions.

Interfacing orthographic, phonological and semantic processing

From different perspectives of activation models, **Weekes, Davies and Chen** (chapter 5) use the picture-word interference paradigm (naming picture and ignoring accompanying word or *distractor*) to investigate semantic interference and graphemic-phonological facilitation effects in picture naming and Chinese word recognition. They exploit the rather unique property in Chinese of a large number of visually dissimilar homophones or heterographic homophones to study the locus of semantic decision level interference and the name or lexical retrieval level and raise the possibility of the intermediate *lemma* level (Levelt, 1989). The lemma level focuses on the semantic and syntactic properties of words but not on their conceptual and phonological properties. Specifically, a lexical entry in the abstract, internal lexicon consists of a lemma and a morpho-phonological form and this metaphorical partitioning of the mental lexicon into meaning and form is particularly useful in explaining language production. Levelt (1989) states that speakers use syntactic information in addition to semantic information in retrieving lexical items to build up a framework of utterance. He defines this non-phonological part of an item's lexical information as the item's 'lemma information' or lemma. Levelt's distinction between the functional level (from conceptualization to formulation) and the positional level (from formulation to articulation) explains well a number of phenomena such as the 'slips of the tongue' phenomenon (e.g., 'Chomsky and Halle' becomes 'Homsky and Challe').

Weekes et al., in three reaction-time experiments, show reliable results of a semantic interference effect and a graphemic and phonological facilitation effect in picture naming in Chinese. The categorical interference is due to shared category membership between target and distractor; an orthographic facilitation effect is due to shared orthographic information between target and distractor; and a phonological facilitation effect is due to homophony between target and distractor. Of interest is that they found no significant difference between the amount of graphemic and phonological facilitation and that there was a lack of interaction between graphemic and phonological facilitation, which is considered a 'unique' result. Weekes et al. argue for an additional lemma level of representation between the semantic and name retrieval levels to account for their data. This level is seen by these authors to represent grammatical information for the large number of polysemous words in spoken Chinese and as the locus of graphemic facilitation in picture naming in Chinese. In a broader cross-language perspective, the recent theory of lemma access model (Levelt, Roelofs, & Meyer, 1999) provides a comprehensive account for a wide range of reaction time results in the production lexicon.

Parenthetically, in an important study, Vandenberghe, Price, Wise, Josephs, and Frackowiak (1996) measured neural activation by means of positron-emission tomography in semantic or non-semantic judgment tasks of triplets of either pictures or words. Vandenberghe et al. showed that semantic tasks activate a distributed semantic processing system shared by both pictures and words, as compared with baseline, and these areas are distributed widely in the left frontal, parietal, temporal and occipital cortices. Furthermore, there are some specific areas activated by either pictures or words. This important study also brings up the question of the need to examine different semantic categories and how they are organized in the brain. In a broad sense, some of the physical structures of the lexical system in the brain are also captured in the high-density, self-organizing global feature map reported by Li (chapter 4). With such a map it would be possible to verify the underlying fine neural structure and pathways in the form of connected groups of neurons (see Miikkulainen, 1997; Plaut et al., 1996).

The interface among semantic, orthographic and phonological processing in reading Chinese is further explored by Hoosain (chapter 6) and Y. P. Chen (chapter 7). **Hoosain**'s opening remarks in his chapter about the 'myth' that single Chinese characters have been reported in functional cerebral laterality studies to be right lateralized and two-character words to be left lateralized have been demystified with current functional neuroimaging techniques (see Matthews et al., chapter 3; Perfetti et al., chapter 2; Tan et al., 2000). Tan et al. demonstrate clearly from their fMRI study of tasks requiring semantic analysis and word retrieval that processing single Chinese characters and two-character words does not bring about a significant difference in cerebral laterality and that there is a shared neural network across these lexical items. Tan et al. (2001) have provided corroborative evidence from event-related functional magnetic resonance imaging to show how the human brain processes phonology and transforms a word's orthographic form into a phonological form in reading Chinese.

Hoosain then goes on to discuss some 'working hypotheses' in the speed of processing Chinese and casts his argument in a cross-language context (Chinese and English). He examines the speed of processing meaning of Chinese and English words; accessing phonology and meaning of English words; accessing phonology of Chinese words as compared with accessing phonology of English words; and situational variables affecting accessing phonology and meaning of Chinese words. The issue of time course in the activation of phonology and meaning is addressed by Perfetti and his colleagues (e.g., Perfetti & Tan, 1999; Tan & Perfetti, 1999). Hoosain points out some of the inherent problems in these experiments, such as the more restricted range of pronunciation for a character as compared with denotative and connotative aspects of word meaning, and the need to specify the level of meaning to be activated. His closing remarks about discourse processing is not addressed directly in this volume and is an area that needs further attention.

Chen (chapter 7) investigates in adult Mandarin speaking Chinese readers their differential and selective use of activated orthographic, phonological and semantic information (termed *reading strategies*) in lexical decision of two-character Chinese words. *Reading efficiency* is explained in terms of overall mean latency of the subject in responding to the differential processing of the words. Her data from regression analyses show that there are individual differences in reading strategies, as can be expected, but also there are variations for the same individual over time and contexts. The developmental and contextual aspects have been commented on by Hoosain in his chapter; and as a means to reinforcing unsupervised learning in connectionist models as emphasized by Li in his chapter. Chen takes the more conservative approach, as compared with other authors in this volume and in the literature, that 'phonological decoding strategy' is an 'optional strategy' in segmenting lexical items into constituents. However, her statement that orthographic knowledge such as knowledge of radical patterns may play an important role in Chinese word recognition 'only in so far as phonological decoding is involved' is in accord with the position of Perfetti and his colleagues and related connectionist literature.

Toward the end of chapter 6, Hoosain raises the issue of eye movement studies during text processing. With more refined instrumentation to record eye movements interfaced with the computer and more sophisticated theories of language processing, eye movement data are very useful in studying fined-grained cognitive processes in reading. In particular, the findings of relatively small area of effective vision and word fixation and of no appreciable eye-mind span have helped in the moment-to-moment studies of reading in such areas as word ambiguity and sentential parsing and inferencing (for review, see Rayner, 1999). But there are considerable individual differences between subjects and within subjects and there are task effects such as text difficulty and syntactic complexity. When texts are more difficult, fixations get longer, saccades get shorter and regressions increase (Rayner, 1999). The general findings in the literature of eye movements during reading of Chinese and Japanese sentences are that the perceptual spans are smaller as compared with reading English because of the densely packed Chinese and Japanese (kanji) scripts (Inhoff & Liu, 1998; Osaka, 1992; Rayner, 1999).

In her eye tracking study of native Japanese adult readers reading two versions of newspaper text (the error free version by control subjects and the other containing homophonic or non-homophonic kanji errors by target subjects), **Matsunaga** (chapter 8) addresses the question of the time course of phonological processing in reading natural Japanese text materials. Her general logic is that if there is early phonology (see also Perfetti, Liu, & Tan, chapter 2) there should be *homophonic interference effects* (experimental subjects having more difficulties in noticing homophonic errors). There should be shorter *first fixation durations* and *gaze durations*. First fixation durations are defined as durations of first fixation on a word and gaze durations are the sum of all fixations on a word before moving on to another word (Rayner, 1999). Matsunaga's data show that there was homophonic interference effect on first fixation and gaze fixation durations and difficulty in noticing non-homophonic errors, thereby confirming her hypothesis. Her eye-tracking results add to the recent important study on eye movements in Chinese character identification by Pollatsek, Tan and Rayner (2000).

In three experiments, Pollatsek et al. (2000) provide strong evidence of the early involvement of both lexical and sublexical phonological codes in identifying Chinese characters. They show that phonological information was extracted parafoveally from a target Chinese character and this early phonological information helped the identification of that character when it was subsequently fixated. Furthermore, there was a regularity effect in that high frequency phonetically regular characters were named faster than high frequency phonetically irregular characters, and orthographic information was also involved in integrating information in Chinese characters across saccades. Pollatsek et al. caution against equating their view of 'sublexical phonology' with 'prelexical phonology' and suggest these as matters for further investigation. We are thus brought back to the careful statement of Perfetti et al. (chapter 2) on this empirical issue for further study.

Structural relationship of components of Chinese characters

Thus far, much of the research literature on the cognitive processing of the Chinese language focuses on character and word recognition and with less work on sentence parsing and discourse process. There is a paucity of research studies of Chinese handwriting or calligraphy as a cognitive process. The findings in character and word recognition can be utilized in experimental studies of Chinese calligraphy. The visual search stage model of character recognition of Huang and Wang (1992) in terms of non-accidental visual properties of symmetry, parallelism and collinearity forms a good basis for the analysis of Chinese handwriting. These two-dimensional structural properties, found in the intersections of strokes, have been studied in relation to character recognition by Chen and Huang (1999), Peng and Zhang (1984), Yu, Zhang and Pan (1997), among others. Corresponding roles of structural spatial properties in brush writing Chinese, however, have only slowly received their due share of attention.

Recently, Kao and his associates (see Chen & Kao, chapter 9; Gao & Kao, chapter 10) have conducted a series of experiments on Chinese handwriting, especially brush writing, as a dynamic calligraphic process. In their research program, Kao and his colleagues studied cognitive changes including memory, digit span and perceptual tasks during Chinese handwriting as functions of variations of such structural spatial properties as linearity, closure, symmetry and orientation. Earlier, Wong and Kao (1991) studied the development and skills in the processing of characters including the execution of strokes, their shaping, spacing and framing in internal, cohesive relationships. Kao and his colleagues (Kao, 2000) discussed a systematic psycho-geometric theory of Chinese character brush writing to explain the relationship between writing as a cognitive process, the motor act in executing the calligraphy and accompanying psychophysiological changes such as heart rate, EEG and skin resistance. This theory forms the basis of this line of research and Kao and colleagues reported some preliminary ERP data to substantiate the neural basis of cortical activation during Chinese handwriting.

Although originally developed as a conceptual basis of Chinese character writing, Kao's structural geometric theory is also concerned with the effect of non-accidental properties, such as the intersections of strokes, along with their structural relationship within the character in character identification. **Chen and Kao** (chapter 9) report two experiments with Chinese primary school children, in which the psycho-geometric nature of the compositionality of Chinese characters was the theoretical framework in character recognition, latency and error measures were the dependent variables. Their first experiment found that non-accidental geometric properties facilitated the orthographic processing of Chinese characters. Their second experiment showed the cumulative effects of these orthographic properties in reading Chinese. These results largely confirm the classical Gestalt principle of *Pragnanz* or 'the goodness of forms' as a parsimonious way of organizing two-dimensional patterns, which are the salient orthographic characteristics of Chinese scripts.

Largely as a result of the encouraging findings of Chen and Kao and several other related experiments, Kao and his colleagues have further analysed thoroughly a set of commonly used Chinese characters from the psycho-geometric perspective. **Gao and Kao** (chapter 10) report on the preliminary results of this major exercise in analysing the perceptual and orthographic features of nearly 5,000 most commonly used Chinese characters. Their results show that the Pragnanz properties of connectivity, linearity, symmetry and visual balance are important elements in the compositionality of Chinese characters and lend further support to Kao's psycho-geometric theory.

The issue of goodness of form in recognizing Chinese characters is approached in a different way by **Han** (chapter 11). Han explains components as functional units akin to the stroke patterns of Chen (chapter 7) and component combinations as intermediate between components and characters. Frequency pertains to type, token frequency and position frequency, and is based on Han's corpus linguistic research into the frequency database of some 567 components and 7583 component combinations. He shows from latency and error data in his experiments the left-right component combination effects and their interaction with frequency and the general structure of the character as a whole. His interpretation of positional effects of component combinations in facilitating or inhibiting Chinese character recognition will need to be reconciled with the functional approach such as that studied by Feldman and Siok (1999), who emphasized the functional roles of the phonetic and semantic components of characters and not so much the left-right positions. In particular, Han's study will also need to accommodate at least two broad groups of activation models of Chinese character recognition. One is the multi-level hierarchical interactive model such as that of Taft and Zhu (1997), who stress the activation of information of submorphemic components. The other is the Interactive Constituency Model with phonology as a main constituent along with orthographic and semantic components in Chinese word identification (Perfetti, Liu, & Tan, chapter 2; Perfetti & Tan, 1999; Tan & Perfetti, 1999).

Learning Chinese characters and words

In the discussion of relevant cognitive neuroscience literature and the summary of the different chapters on the cognitive and neural bases of interfacing orthographic, phonological and semantic components of

Chinese characters and words, some pertinent applied research questions relate to how readers acquire words accurately, rapidly and with precision. These are the empirical issues of making explicit what beginning readers know from their language to make contact with print; the reading of two Chinese scripts: the traditional or complex script as used in Taiwan and Hong Kong and the simplified script as used in mainland China and Singapore; strategies used by skilled and less skilled young Chinese students in reading Chinese characters and words; and the acquisition and development of vocabulary for pedagogical purposes. These issues are addressed in this volume by the five sets of authors: Leong; Lam; Wang and Guthrie; T'sou, Kwan, and Liu; and Kwan and T'sou.

From a cross-language perspective (see Leong & Joshi, 1997), **Leong** (chapter 12) discusses the central issue of the involvement of phonological and orthographic processes and their interplay in reading the alphabetic English and the morphosyllabic Chinese. Cumulative research findings have shown that sensitivity to speech sounds and their mapping to script is a precursor to learning to read and in preventing reading difficulties (Leong, 1991; Snow, Burns, & Griffin, 1998). In learning to read English, children need to be sensitive to the morpho-phonemic nature of the system, which is represented by phonemes, syllables with their onsets and rimes and other sublexical units. In learning to read the kana script of Japanese, children need to be sensitive to the subsyllabic and timing unit of *morae* (Leong & Tamaoka, 1998). In learning to read Chinese, children need to be sensitive to the internal structure of the syllable with its *onset* (initial in the Chinese syllable) and *rime* (final in the Chinese syllable).

Leong's proposal (Leong, 1997) of paradigmatic analysis emphasizes a network of linguistic connections as a potent approach to learning to read Chinese characters and words. These are the basic psychological issues of what constitutes a word and word boundaries in Chinese (Hoosain, 1992); and the linguistic issues of a word being a free form entailing syntactic relation with other similar units as explicated by the noted linguist Yuen Ren Chao (1968, 1976). The underlying psycholinguistic principle is the unit of processing or the size of speech segment to be recognized as a word and the mapping between the speech unit and print. Leong discusses relevant research studies on segmental and syllabic analysis of Chinese characters and words; and emphasizes explicit, systematic teaching of more precise Chinese word knowledge in schools.

In the modern Chinese writing system in use from 1949, there are in fact two slightly different scripts with the same pronunciation. The traditional script with complex characters is used in Taiwan and Hong

Kong and the simplified script (simplified from, and orthographically very similar to, the traditional script) is used in mainland China, in Singapore and in Chinese courses taught in many universities in the USA. What is the ease or difficulty for Hong Kong learners trained in the traditional script learning these two scripts, and, conversely, for Beijing students trained in the simplified script? These are the psycholinguistic issues explored by **Lam** (chapter 13), who focuses on the context effects of reading these two scripts with the same pronunciation. She first outlines the linguistic principles of character simplification and discusses two studies, one with Hong Kong university students and the other with Beijing university students, on the nature of phonetic and semantic activation in reading character lists and text materials. Using reading time per character and percentage error as her metrics, she found the response time and difficulty of reading the unfamiliar script for the two different groups to be considerably reduced when the characters were embedded in texts. Moreover, her prediction that different types of character simplification would result in different degrees of difficulty in reading was also upheld.

The issue of ease or difficulty in reading Chinese by elementary school students in Taiwan was explored by **Wang and Guthrie** (chapter 14). In three studies they focused on the strategies and cues used by skilled and less skilled fifth grade readers, selected by their teachers, in identifying unknown Chinese characters. The first study used a verbal report protocol from reading aloud a story, in which the students reported how they read the characters and if they knew the meaning and function of the left-right radicals constituting the characters. The different errors of pronunciation of the characters were taken as different reading strategies. From this study and the subsequent two studies, Wang and Guthrie found that skilled and less skilled readers differed in their reading strategies in recognizing and pronouncing unknown characters, and that skilled readers used more linguistic cues, especially phonetic cues. Moreover, their skilled readers were able to differentiate phonetic cues from semantic cues inherent in the orthographic information in the characters. While there may be a caveat in the teacher selection of skilled and unskilled readers, the Wang and Guthrie analysis highlights the need to examine the fine-grained aspects of Chinese character compositionality, as discussed in the chapters by Chen, Chen and Kao, Gao and Kao, Han and others. Furthermore, their statement of greater use of phonetic cues by skilled readers may be better understood in the broader context of the Interactive Constituency Model of reading Chinese, as instantiated with both regular and exception Chinese characters and words at different frequency ranges.

Continuing the theme of learning words and acquiring word knowledge, the two chapters by T'sou and his colleagues should be read within the context of Chinese corpus linguistics. Current studies of corpus linguistics are usually defined in terms of a collection of electronic texts selected according to certain linguistic criteria (Atkins, Clear, & Ostler, 1992). The general idea is to extract linguistic data so as to reflect the behaviour of a language in general at a particular time, such as the well-known Brown corpus of English (Kučera & Francis, 1967). From this extraction linguists can form theoretical hypotheses, verify them and further apply them for computational purposes. Grammatical categories or 'tags' help to provide structure for the linguistic data. The rationale of tagging is 'basically syntactic, with some morphological distributions' (Francis & Kučera, 1982, p. 9).

This raises the question of what constitutes a word in Chinese, as alluded to earlier (Chao, 1968, 1976; Hoosain, 1992). There is also the relationship between word-syntax and sentence-syntax in Chinese compound words. Take as examples the case of reduplication in Chinese compound words (e.g., reduplication of *look/ see*, or of *beautiful*). Leong (1995, 1998) treats these reduplicated compound Chinese words as morphological constraints, and Tang (1994) as syntactic manifestations of aspect and degree intensification. Linguists Di Sciullo and Williams (1987) discussed the different senses or forms of a 'word' in English. There is the morphological form in terms of a set of 'atoms' or morphemes; the syntactic form in terms of syntactic atoms; and the memorized lists of language objects termed *listemes* or 'frozen expressions' (e.g., *red herring*). The fourth sense of the word — the phonological form — is barely discussed by Di Sciullo and Williams. Just as Di Sciullo and Williams (1987) argued for the close relationship between English phrases and sentences, it is reasonable to say that in Chinese there is a parallel between morphological structure and syntactic structure in Chinese compound words, especially in compound verbs, verb phrases and sentences (Tang, 1994).

The above succinct discussion underpins the rationale and methods of the large-scale Chinese corpus linguistics investigation known as Linguistic Variation in Chinese Communities (LIVAC, 1995–1997) conducted in China, Taiwan, Singapore and Hong Kong by T'sou and his team. Chinese newspapers were used as the database because newspaper texts are available on-line and easily lend themselves to computational linguistic analyses, and also because newspapers typically contain all genres of literary styles. Within this broad framework and using words derived from the LIVAC corpus, **T'sou, Kwan and Liu** (chapter 15) studied the passive or receptive and active or productive vocabulary knowledge and general and academic vocabulary in 856 Hong Kong secondary students. They also related these different levels of vocabulary knowledge to student characteristics such as education level, general ability and Chinese language proficiency. T'sou et al. suggested that successful vocabulary learning requires the conditions of need or motivation, frequent encounter in different contexts and active usage. **Kwan and T'sou** (chapter 16) selected 12 typical students out of the subgroup of 90 from the nearly 900 secondary students in T'sou et al. (chapter 15) to further explore their 'decoding' strategies. Kwan and T'sou used the term *decoding* to denote getting meaning from very low frequency and almost unknown multi-character Chinese words and employed the talking aloud protocol as the source of data collection. These naturalistic data throw light on the way that secondary students in Hong Kong grapple with the meaning of difficult and obscure words and provide a window to their lexical development. The two chapters by T'sou and his colleagues have also raised the issue of assessing word meaning and vocabulary knowledge. The typical approach as used by Anglin (1993) and in the literature is to ask for definitions, then usage of words in sentences so as to explain their meanings and also in the multiple-choice format or all these different approaches. However, knowing the meanings of words also involves knowing the situations in which words are used (see Anglin, 1993; Li, chapter 4) and of acquiring different levels of word meanings (Leong, 1998).

One of the ways in vocabulary development that T'sou and his colleagues allude to is the process of collocation. This refers to the phenomenon that lexical items which consistently co-occur and which are semantically transparent (e.g., 'heavy smoker' but not * 'heavy thinker') are learned easier than others. In computational linguistics the notion of collocation can be defined statistically in probabilistic terms of mutual information to determine which words are collocated according to syntactic and semantic criteria (Church & Hanks, 1990; Sinclair, 1991). The mutual information between linguistic elements, expressed as a unidimensional log function in relation to the size of the corpus and of the linguistic window selected, is in some contrast to the high-density two-dimensional self-organizing map in learning word meaning that Li (chapter 4) has explicated.

There is another aspect of word meaning and vocabulary development that is more typical of the Chinese language. There are non-transparent or semantically opaque expressions of idioms or listemes (Di Sciullo & Williams, 1987) that are distinguishable from collocations and that form stumbling blocks to learning Chinese. These frozen expressions, or listemes (e.g., 'to break the axe and sink the boat'), are not easily decipherable without knowing the historical context. There are also familiar phrases, which convey propositional forms (e.g., 'mud Buddha crossing the river' with the implication that not even Buddha can save himself). Study of Chinese vocabulary development should include these two-, three- and four-character words in frozen forms because they figure prominently in text reading and in literacy development. The interrelated issues of word meaning, vocabulary acquisition and development provide rich sources of study in psychology and psycholinguistics.

Making Connections

We began this integrative commentary with the assertion of Simon and Kaplan (1989) that cognitive science is concerned with the study of intelligent behaviour and its computational processes and also with the explication of Sejnowski and Churchland (1989) that knowledge of brain architecture could explain human cognition. The different chapters in this volume have provided theoretical and research perspectives of the cognitive conjunction approach of Price and Friston (1997) in showing the analyses of psychological and psycholinguistic data on the Chinese language system and their interpretation within a cognitive neuroscience framework. Our contributors have shown, from different theoretical and research paradigms, the complex nature of the interfacing of orthographic, phonological and semantic processing of Chinese. We are enjoined by Brown and Hagoort (1999) to take a more integrative approach toward languages in terms of their core characteristics, their different levels and representational systems, their measurements and the use of different psychological, psycholinguistic and neural techniques for their fuller understanding. We are further reminded by Gazzaniga (2000) to understand the mind and the brain as 'cognitive thinking', and by Perfetti et al. (chapter 2) and other contributors how the mind can meet the brain in language processing, which can help to ensure that we are studying challenging and interesting constructs and topics.

References

Alegria, J., Holender, D., Morais, J. J. D., & Radeau, M. (Eds.). (1992). *Analytic approaches to human cognition.* Amsterdam: North-Holland.

Anglin, J. M. (1993). Vocabulary development: A morphological analysis. *Monographs of the Society for Research in Child Development, 58* (10, Serial No. 238).

Atkins, S., Clear, J., & Ostler, N. (1992). Corpus design criteria. *Literary and Linguistic Computing, 7,* 1–16.

Baddeley, A. D. (1986). *Working memory.* New York: Oxford University Press.

Boodberg, P. A. (1937). Some proleptical remarks on the evolution of archaic Chinese. *Harvard Journal of Asiatic Studies, 2,* 320–372.

Brown, C. M., & Hagoort, P. (Eds.). (1999). *The neurocognition of language.* New York: Oxford University Press.

Chao, Y. R. (1968). *A grammar of spoken Chinese.* Berkeley, CA: University of California Press.

Chao, Y. R. (1976). *Aspects of Chinese sociolinguistics.* Stanford, CA: Stanford University Press.

Chee, M. W. L., Caplan, D., Soon, C. S., Sriram, N., Tan, E. W. L., Thiel, T., & Weekes, B. (1999). Processing of visually presented sentences in Mandarin and English studied with fMRI. *Neuron, 23,* 127–137.

Chee, M. W. L., Hon, N., Lee, H. L., & Soon, C. S. (2001). Relative language proficiency modulates BOLD signal change when bilinguals perform semantic judgments. *NeuroImage, 13,* 1155–1163.

Chen, C. F., & Huang, X. T. (1999). Research on characteristics of visual recognition to symmetrical structural Chinese characters. *Acta Psychologica Sinica, 31,* 154–161 (in Chinese).

Chen, H. C., & Tzeng, O. J. L. (Eds.). (1992). *Language processing in Chinese.* Amsterdam: North-Holland.

Chen, Y. P., Allport, D. A., & Marshall, J. C. (1996). What are the functional orthographic units in Chinese word recognition: The stroke or the stroke pattern? *The Quarterly Journal of Experimental Psychology, 49A,* 1024–1043.

Church, K., & Hanks, P. (1990). Word association norms, mutual information, and lexicography. *Computational Linguistics, 16,* 22–29.

DeFrancis, J. (1989). *Visible speech: The diverse oneness of writing systems.* Honolulu: University of Hawaii Press.

Di Sciullo, A. M., & Williams, E. (1987). *On the definition of word.* Cambridge, MA: MIT Press.

Eden, G. F., & Zeffiro, T. A. (1997). PET and fMRI in the detection of task-related brain activity: Implications for the study of brain development. In G. R. Lyon, R. W. Thatcher, J. Rumsey, & N. A. Krasnegor (Eds.), *Developmental neuroimaging: Mapping the development of brain and behavior* (pp. 77–90). London: Academic Press.

Feldman, L. B., & Siok, W. W. T. (1999). Semantic radicals in phonetic compounds: Implications for visual character recognition in Chinese. In J. Wang, A. W. Inhoff, & H.-C. Chen (Eds.), *Reading Chinese script: A cognitive analysis* (pp. 19–35). Mahwah, NJ: Lawrence Erlbaum.

Francis, W. N., & Kučera, H. (1982). *Frequency analysis of English usage: Lexicon and grammar.* Boston: Houghton Mifflin.

Friedman, L., Kenny, J. T., Wise, A. L., Wu, D., Stuve, T. A., Miller, D. A., Jesberger, J. A., & Lewin, J. S. (1998). Brain activation during silent word generation evaluated with functional MRI. *Brain and Language, 64,* 231–256.

Gazzaniga, M. S. (Ed.). (2000). *Neuroscience: A reader.* Oxford: Blackwell Publishers.

Goswami, U. (2000). Phonological representations, reading development and dyslexia: Towards a cross-linguistic theoretical framework. *Dyslexia, 6*(2), 133–151.

Halliday, M. A. K. (1981). The origin and early development of Chinese phonological theory. In R. E. Asher, & E. J. A. Henderson (Eds.), *Towards a history of phonetics* (pp. 123–140). Edinburgh: Edinburgh University Press.

Hoosain, R. (1991). *Psycholinguistic implications for linguistic relativity: A case study of Chinese.* Hillsdale, NJ: Lawrence Erlbaum.

Hoosain, R. (1992). Psychological realities of the word in Chinese. In H. C. Chen, & O. J. L. Tzeng (Eds.), *Language processing in Chinese* (pp. 111–130). Amsterdam: North-Holland.

Huang, J.-T., & Wang, M.-Y. (1992). From unit to Gestalt: Perceptual dynamics in recognizing Chinese characters. In H. C. Chen, & O. J. L. Tzeng (Eds.), *Language processing in Chinese* (pp. 3–35). Amsterdam: North-Holland.

Inagaki, K., Hatano, G., & Otake, T. (2000). The effect of kana literacy acquisition on the speech segmentation unit used by Japanese young children. *Journal of Experimental Child Psychology, 75,* 70–91.

Inhoff, A. W., & Liu, W. (1998). The perceptual span and oculomotor activity during the reading of Chinese sentences. *Journal of Experimental Psychology: Human Perception and Performance, 24,* 20–34.

James, W. (1890). *Principles of psychology.* New York: Henry Holt.

Kao, H. S. R. (Ed.). (2000). *Chinese calligraphy therapy.* Hong Kong: Hong Kong University Press (in Chinese).

Kao, H. S. R., & Hoosain, R. (Eds.). (1984). *Psychological studies of the Chinese language.* Hong Kong: The Chinese Language Society of Hong Kong.

Kao, H. S. R., & Hoosain, R. (Eds.). (1986). *Linguistics, psychology, and the Chinese language.* Hong Kong: Centre of Asian Studies, the University of Hong Kong.

Kučera, H., & Francis, W. N. (1967). *Computational analysis of present-day American English.* Providence, RI: Brown University Press.

Kutas, M., & Van Patten, C. K. (1988). Event-related brain potential studies of language. In P. K. Ackles, J. R. Jennings, & M. G. H. Coles (Eds.), *Advances in psychophysiology* (pp. 139–187). Greenwich, CT: JAI Press.

Kutas, M., & Van Patten, C. K. (1994). Psycholinguistics electrified: Event-related brain potential investigations. In M. A. Gernsbacher (Ed.), *Handbook of psycholinguistics* (pp. 83–143). New York: Academic Press.

Leiner, H. C., Leiner, A. L., & Dow, R. S. (1993). Cognitive and language functions of human cerebellum. *Trends in Neurosciences, 16,* 444–447.

Leong, C. K. (1991). From phonemic awareness to phonological processing to language access in children developing reading proficiency. In D. J. Sawyer, & B. J. Fox (Eds.), *Phonological awareness in reading: The evolution of current perspectives* (pp. 217–254). New York: Springer-Verlag.

Leong, C. K. (1995). Orthographic and psycholinguistic considerations in developing literacy in Chinese. In I. Taylor, & D. J. Olson (Eds.), *Scripts and literacy: Reading and learning to read alphabets, syllabaries and characters* (pp. 163–183). Dordrecht: Kluwer Academic Publishers.

Leong, C. K. (1997). Paradigmatic analysis of Chinese word reading: Research findings and classroom practices. In C. K. Leong, & R. M. Joshi (Eds.), *Cross-language studies of learning to read and spell: Phonologic and orthographic processing* (pp. 379–417). Dordrecht: Kluwer Academic Publishers.

Leong, C. K. (1998). On knowing words: A lexicalist hypothesis. In B. Asker (Ed.), *Teaching language and culture* (pp. 86–108 + ref.). Hong Kong: Longman.

Leong, C. K., Cheng, P. W., & Mulcahy, R. (1987). Automatic processing of morphemic orthography by mature readers. *Language and Speech, 30,* 181–197.

Leong, C. K., & Joshi, R. M. (Eds.). (1997). *Cross-language studies of learning to read and spell: Phonologic and orthographic processing.* Dordrecht: Kluwer Academic Publishers.

Leong, C. K., & Tamaoka, K. (Eds.). (1998). *Cognitive processing of the Chinese and the Japanese languages.* Dordrecht: Kluwer Academic Publishers.

Leong, C. K., & Tan, L. H. (2002). Phonological processing in learning to read Chinese: In search of a framework. In E. Hjelmquist, & C. von Euler (Eds.), *Dyslexia and literacy: A tribute to Ingvar Lundberg.* London: Whurr Publishers.

Levelt, W. J. M. (1989). *Speaking: From intention to articulation.* Cambridge, MA: MIT Press.

Levelt, W. J. M., Roelofs, A., & Meyer, A. S. (1999). A theory of lexical access in speech production. *Behavioral and Brain Sciences, 22,* 1–38.

Li, P., & MacWhinney, B. (1996). Cryptotype, overgeneralization and competition: A connectionist model of the learning of English reversive prefixes. *Connection Science, 8,* 3–30.

Liu, I.-M., Chen, H.-C., & Chen, M. J. (Ed.). (1988). *Cognitive aspects of the Chinese language* (Vol. 1). Hong Kong: Asian Research Service.

Liu, I.-M., Wu, J.-T., & Chou, T. L. (1996). Encoding operation and transcoding as the major loci of the frequency effect. *Cognition, 59,* 149–168.

Miikkulainen, R. (1997). Dyslexic and category-specific aphasic impairments in a self-organizing feature map model of the lexicon. *Brain and Language, 59,* 334–366.

Morais, J. (Ed.). (1995). Literacy onset in Romance language [Special issue]. *Reading and Writing: An Interdisciplinary Journal, 7*(1).

Osaka, N. (1992). Size of saccade and fixation duration of eye movements during reading: Psychophysics of Japanese text processing. *Journal of the Optical Society of America, A9,* 5–13.

Peng, D., Liu, Y., & Wang, C. (1999). How is access representation organized? The relation of polymorphemic words and their morphemes in Chinese. In J. Wang, A. W. Inhoff, & H.-C. Chen (Eds.), *Reading Chinese script: A cognitive analysis* (pp. 65–89). Mahwah, NJ: Lawrence Erlbaum.

Peng, D., Shu, H., & Chen, H.-C. (Eds.). (1997). *Cognitive research on Chinese language.* Shandong: Shandong Education Publishing (in Chinese).

Peng, R. X., & Zhang, W. T. (1984). Some characteristics in tachistoscopic recognition of Chinese characters. *Acta Psychologica Sinica, 1,* 49–54 (in Chinese).

Perfetti, C. A., & Tan, L. H. (1998). The time-course of graphic, phonological, and semantic activation in Chinese character identification. *Journal of Experimental Psychology: Learning, Memory, and Cognition, 24,* 1–18.

Perfetti, C. A., & Tan, L. H. (1999). The constituency model of Chinese word identification. In J. Wang, A. W. Inhoff, & H.-C. Chen (Eds.), *Reading Chinese script: A cognitive analysis* (pp. 115–134). Mahwah, NJ: Lawrence Erlbaum.

Perfetti, C. A., & Zhang, S. (1995). Very early phonological activation in Chinese reading. *Journal of Experimental Psychology: Learning, Memory, and Cognition, 21,* 24–33.

Perfetti, C. A., Zhang, S., & Berent, I. (1992). Reading in English and Chinese: Evidence for a 'universal' phonological principle. In R. Frost, & L. Katz (Eds.), *Orthography, phonology, morphology, and meaning* (pp. 227–248). Amsterdam: North-Holland.

Petersen, S. E., Fox, P. T., Snyder, A. Z., & Raichle, M. E. (1990). Activation of extrastriate and frontal cortical areas by visual words and word-like stimuli. *Science, 249,* 1041–1044.

Plaut, D. C., McClellend, J. L., Seidenberg, M., & Patterson, K. E. (1996). Understanding normal and impaired word reading: Computational principles in quasi-regular domains. *Psychological Review, 103,* 56–115.

Polich, J., McCarthy, G., Wang, W. S., & Donchin, E. (1983). When words collide: Orthographic and phonological interference during word processing. *Biological Psychology, 16,* 155–180.

Pollatsek, A., Tan, L. H., & Rayner, K. (2000). The role of phonological codes in integrating information across saccadic eye movements in Chinese character identification. *Journal of Experimental Psychology: Human Perception and Performance, 26,* 607–633.

Posner, M. I., & DiGirolamo, G. J. (2000). Cognitive neuroscience: Origins and promise. *Psychological Bulletin, 126,* 873–889.

Posner, M. I., & Raichle, M. E. (1994). *Images of mind.* New York: W. H. Freeman.

Price, C. J., & Friston, K. J. (1997). Cognitive conjunction: A new approach to brain activation experiments. *NeuroImage, 5,* 261–270.

Raichle, M. E., Fox, J. A., Videen, T. O., MacLeod, A.-M. K., Pardo, J. V., Fox, P. T., & Petersen, S. E. (1994). Practice-related changes in human brain functional anatomy during nonmotor learning. *Cerebral Cortex, 4,* 8–26.

Rayner, K. (1999). What have we learned about eye movements during reading? In R. M. Klein, & P. A. McMullen (Eds.), *Converging methods for understanding reading and dyslexia* (pp. 23–56). Cambridge, MA: MIT Press.

Roland, P. E., & Zilles, K. (1994). Brain atlases — A new research tool. *Trends in Neurosciences, 17,* 458–467.

Rugg, M. D. (1999). Functional neuroimaging in cognitive neuroscience. In C. M. Brown, & P. Hagoort (Eds.), *The neurocognition of language* (pp. 15–36). Oxford: Oxford University Press.

Seidenberg, M. S., & McClelland, J. L. (1989). A distributed, developmental model of word recognition and naming. *Psychological Review, 96.* 523–568.

Sejnowski, T. J., & Churchland, P. S. (1989). Brain and cognition. In M. I. Posner (Ed.), *Foundations of cognitive science* (pp. 301–356). Cambridge, MA: MIT Press.

Sherrington, C. S. (1940). *Man and his nature.* Cambridge, UK: Cambridge University Press.

Simon, H. A., & Kaplan, C. A. (1989). Foundations of cognitive science. In M. I. Posner (Ed.), *Foundations of cognitive science* (pp. 1–47). Cambridge, MA: MIT Press.

Sinclair, J. M. (1991). *Corpus, concordance, collocation.* Oxford: Oxford University Press.

Small, S. L., Hart, J., Nguyen, T., & Gordon, B. (1995). Distributed representations of semantic knowledge in the brain. *Brain, 118,* 441–453.

Snow, C. E., Burns, M. S., & Griffin, P. (Eds.). (1998). *Preventing reading difficulties in young children.* Washington, DC: National Academy Press.

Spencer, A. (1991). *Morphological theory: An introduction to word structure in generative grammar.* Oxford: Blackwell Publishers.

Taft, M., & Zhu, X. (1997). Submorphemic processing in reading Chinese. *Journal of Experimental Psychology: Learning, Memory, and Cognition, 23,* 761–775.

Talairach, J., & Tournoux, P. (1988). *Co-planar stereotactic atlas of the human brain: 3-dimensional proportional system: An approach to cerebral imaging*. Stuttgart: Georg Thieme Verlag.

Tan, L. H., Feng, C.-M., Fox, P. T., & Gao, J.-H. (2001). An fMRI study with written Chinese. *NeuroReport, 12*, 83–88.

Tan, L. H., Liu, H.-L., Perfetti, C. A., Spinks, J. A., Fox, P. T., & Gao, J.-H. (2001). The neural systems underlying Chinese logograph reading. *NeuroImage, 13*, 836–846.

Tan, L. H., & Perfetti, C. A. (1998). Phonological codes as early sources of constraint in Chinese word identification: A review of current discoveries and theoretical accounts. *Reading and Writing: An Interdisciplinary Journal, 10*, 165–200.

Tan, L. H., & Perfetti, C. A. (1999). Phonological activation in visual identification of Chinese two-character words. *Journal of Experimental Psychology: Learning, Memory, and Cognition, 25*, 382–393.

Tan, L. H., Spinks, J. A., Gao, J. H., Liu, A., Perfetti, C. A., Xiong, J., Stofer, K. A., Pu, Y., Liu, Y., & Fox, P. T. (2000). Brain activation in the processing of Chinese characters and words: A functional MRI study. *Human Brain Mapping, 10*, 16–27.

Tang, T. C. (1994). On the relation between word-syntax and sentence-syntax: A case study in Chinese compound verb. In M. Y. Chen, & O. J. L. Tzeng (Eds.), *Interdisciplinary studies of language and language change: In honor of William S.-Y. Wang*. (pp. 495–530). Taipei, Taiwan: Pyramid Press.

Tzeng, O. J. L., Hung, D. L., & Wang, W. S.-Y. (1977). Speech recoding in reading Chinese characters. *Journal of Experimental Psychology: Human Learning and Memory, 3*, 621–630.

Vandenberghe, R., Price, C., Wise, R., Josephs, O., & Frackowiak, R. S. J. (1996). Functional anatomy of a common semantic system for words and pictures. *Nature, 383* (6597), 254–256.

Wang, J., Inhoff, A. W., & Chen, H.-C. (Eds.). (1999). *Reading Chinese script: A cognitive analysis*. Mahwah, NJ: Lawrence Erlbaum.

Wong, T. H., & Kao, S. R. H. (1991). The development of drawing principles in Chinese. In J. Waan, A. M. Wing, & N. Sovik (Eds.), *Development of graphic skills* (pp. 93–112). London: Academic Press.

Yu, B. L., Zhang, S. L., & Pan, Y. J. (1997). Effects of stroke type on identification of upright and tilted Chinese characters. *Acta Psychologica Sinica, 29*, 23–28 (in Chinese).

Zhou, X., & Marslen-Wilson, W. (1995). Morphological structure in the Chinese mental lexicon. *Language and Cognitive Processes, 10*, 545–601.

Author Note

Preparation of this paper is assisted in part by the Social Sciences and Humanities Research Council of Canada (SSHRC) Research Grant No. 410–2001–0059. The different drafts were completed during my tenure as Visiting Professor at the Chinese University of Hong Kong and at my home institution, the University of Saskatchewan. I am grateful for all the assistance. I also thank all the contributors to this volume, and my two co-editors for the privilege of editing this volume. I am indebted to Michael Chee, Charles Perfetti and Li Hai Tan for their insightful comments. Any shortcomings are necessarily my own.

Part 1

Neurocognitive Architecture of Language

2

How the Mind Can Meet the Brain in Reading: A Comparative Writing Systems Approach

Charles A. Perfetti, Ying Liu and Li-Hai Tan

Reading is at once both simple and rich — simple enough for cognitive research to have gained an increasingly clear picture of how it works; rich enough to yield important lingering questions to be addressed by the convergence of cognitive and neurocognitive methods. One particular characteristic of reading can illustrate this simplicity and richness: it begins with a reader looking at marks that are encoded in a system — a writing system. We have to take into account that the world has different writing systems if we want to achieve a full understanding of the reading processes. In what follows, we will highlight some of the issues that have been informed by taking a writing system approach and to point to some possibilities for how neuroscience methods will add to the picture.

To be clear, it is the cognitive-behavioral approach that has dominated our own research and it has produced the most information on reading, including how writing systems make a difference. Thus, our treatment of the cognitive neuroscience approach is in proportion to its relative contribution to our thinking about the general questions of reading. One way the cognitive approach forms the foundation for other approaches is that it establishes a heuristic architecture for reading.

A Cognitive Architecture for Reading

Figure 1 shows an overall cognitive architecture, according to more or less standard views that have emerged from research. Although generally it reflects a consensus, there is one way in which this architecture might be controversial. The assumption that word identification includes a routine early phase of mutual orthographic-phonological activation — as opposed to a one-direction route from orthography with an optional route for phonology — is probably not a consensus view. It reflects a hypothesis that visual processing of writing system units immediately initiates phonological processing. The representation of word meaning is immediate but, typically, slightly lagged with this orthographic-phonological activation.

Figure 1 reflects the question of how writing systems influence reading in a most general way, representing the fact that the orthographic units are provided by the writing system. The details of this influence are an empirical matter. A basic constraint on these details provided by the relationship between writing systems and the spoken language is critical: that all writing systems encode spoken languages in one way or another (DeFrancis, 1989). The Chinese writing system has some important differences from alphabetic and true syllabic systems that allow it to make more direct contact with meanings, certainly linguistic meanings and perhaps non-linguistic meanings as well. But its characters ultimately are connected to language at the level of the syllable-morpheme, giving them both a phonological and semantic correspondence.

The standard way to consider the connection between writing system and language is as follows: each system has a basic writing unit that is mapped onto one unit of the language system. Alphabetic systems map phonemes; syllabary systems map syllables, and logographic systems map words. It is interesting to note that the only example of a currently used logographic system is Chinese (and the Japanese adaptation of Chinese characters). And it is questionable whether one ought to accept this designation even for Chinese. Certainly the mapping of single characters onto syllables gives it a syllabic aspect. It fails to be essentially syllabic because the character is not taken to be a unit that is used productively to represent pronunciations but rather a unit of spoken language that has a meaning as well as a pronunciation. Rather than logographic, however, the system can be considered morphemic (e.g., Leong, 1973) or even morphosyllabic (e.g., DeFrancis, 1989; Mattingly, 1992). This is because the character often contains components that provide information about pronunciation or meaning. In any case, the direct expression of

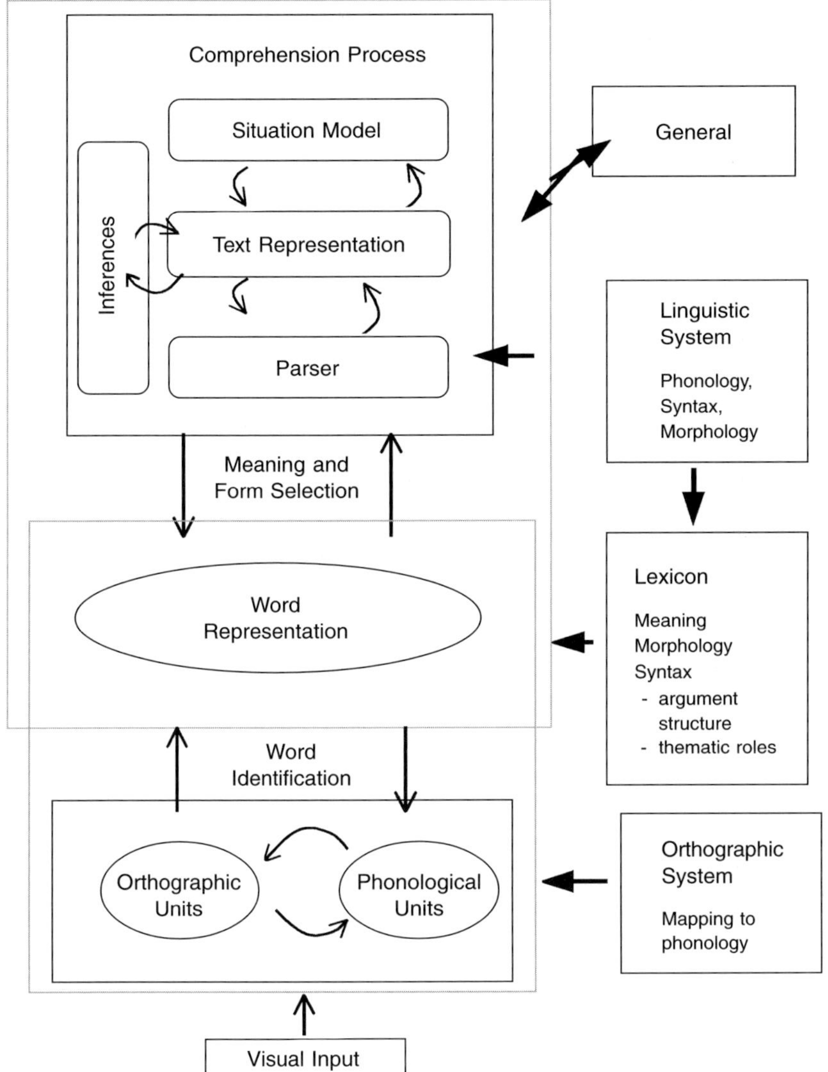

Figure 1.   A schematic blueprint showing the general components of reading. Arrows indicate flow of information or direction of influence. Linguistic knowledge informs the components of phonology, morphology, and syntax that are used in word reading and sentence comprehension. General (nonlinguistic) knowledge informs the lexicon and the comprehension process. Word identification is represented as a process that establishes phonological-orthographic identities. Other views of word reading may not share this assumption. However, in most respects, the blueprint makes no commitment to particular architectural assumption. In particular whether bidirectional arrows are needed everywhere, is an empirical question.

morphemes in the writing system — as units of meaning and form (grammatical and phonological) — give characters a status that is unique among the world's writing systems.

Comparisons of Reading English and Chinese

Given the important differences between an alphabetic and a logographic system, one expects to see equally profound differences in the way reading works in the two systems. Differences are apparent immediately at the script level, the conventions for displaying the graphic units of a writing system. Indeed, the visual display differences are quite dramatic. For example, Chinese not only builds its simple graphic units (radicals) out of independent ordered stroke sequences, it also builds its compound graphic units out of compositional units (simple characters) in a number of different ways: left and right; top and bottom; inside and outside. English, and most alphabetic systems, compose all complex units out of linear arrays of basic units (letters). Korean is an exception, demonstrating clearly that linear arrays are not defining characteristics of alphabetic writing. As a second example, the equal spacing of Chinese characters, and the resulting ambiguity about word boundaries, stands in contrast to the word-based spacing in English and most other examples of an alphabetic system. However, in all cases the question is not merely whether there are differences in the visual expression of the systems, but also what differences in reading follow from each difference in visual display. For example, does the linear composition of English compared with the non-linear composition of a single character (compound) word lead to relatively holistic perception of characters and more serial processing of letters?

It is not only differences that are important, however, but also similarities. If all writing systems encode language, then language based reading is a likely process in all writing systems.

Phonology: Some Similarities Between Chinese and English Reading

We have been especially interested in the universal hypothesis that spoken language provides a basis for reading in all writing systems, even when a system such as Chinese allows other possibilities. Could not the phonological word forms of the spoken language be an intrinsic part of reading in Chinese as well as English? Contrarily, could it be that in neither system do spoken language forms play anything more than an incidental role? Both possibilities for finding similarity have seemed plausible at some point.

Indeed, there is an interesting parallel in research on English and Chinese reading. In both systems, there has existed the potential for readers to bypass phonology while accessing only meaning. In both systems, the conclusion that readers did exactly this has been modified in the light of further research. Earlier, it seemed reasonable, even in English, to suppose that skilled readers, with much practice at word reading, used mainly a visual form-to-meaning process, with phonology limited to lending support for difficult reading. Research on alphabetic writing systems, however, has led to the conclusion that phonology is involved in a broad range of ordinary word processing tasks (Berent & Perfetti, 1995; Frost, 1998). This generalization now is incorporated into a variety of models of word reading, including Dual Route (Coltheart, Curtis, Atkins, & Haller, 1993) and distributed non-symbolic models (Harm & Seidenberg, 1999; Plaut, McClelland, Seidenberg, & Patterson, 1996; van Orden, Pennington & Stone, 1990).

In the case of Chinese, it seemed even more reasonable to suppose that Chinese worked as a visual form-to-meaning system. After all, the Chinese writing system has been viewed as meaning-based rather than speech based. But the research has forced a new understanding of Chinese reading: As summarized in a recent review by Tan and Perfetti (1998), the evidence is that Chinese reading involves phonology at the word level as well as at the text level (Tzeng, Hung, & Wang, 1977; Zhang & Perfetti, 1993). The explanation for these discoveries seems to require highly general, perhaps universal, processes, even with constraints imposed by writing systems.

The morphemic nature of Chinese writing led easily to the assumption of a close connection between graphic form and meaning. First, simple Chinese characters (pictographs and their derivatives), according to some, were encoded as images that vividly signal meaning (Liu, 1995; Wang, 1973). Second, in compound characters, one or more semantic components may suggest the character's meaning. About 80% of compounds have a degree of semantic validity: some aspect of their meaning is suggested by a semantic component (Fan, 1986). Some compound characters have two semantic components; others have one semantic and one phonetic component (phonetic compounds). About 85% of present-day characters are phonetic compounds (Perfetti & Tan, 1998; Zhu, 1988). However, the validity of the phonetic component — whether the phonetic component, when pronounced as a stand-alone character, actually is the pronunciation of the whole character — is estimated at about 38% (Zhou, 1978), higher with different computational assumptions. Interestingly, both semantic validity and phonetic validity increase with decreasing printed frequency of the compound character (Perfetti, Zhang, & Berent, 1992). Most important for comparisons with alphabetic writing systems is that a phonetic component always maps to a syllable, never a phoneme. Whereas the *b* in *beech* maps to a segment of the spoken word, a phonetic maps not to a piece of the word but to a syllable that may (or may not) be the whole word. Thus, Chinese writing does not reflect the segmental structure fundamental to alphabetic systems (Mattingly, 1987; Leong, 1997).

Another important property of Chinese is its extensive homophony. Modern-day usage includes about 4,574 characters according to the *Modern Chinese Frequency Dictionary* (Beijing Language College, 1986) and 420 distinct syllables (disregarding tone). Thus, on average, 11 characters share a pronunciation. Context plays a big role in selecting a spoken word from among its phonetically similar cohorts (Li & Yip, 1996). In reading, characters with the same pronunciation are disambiguated by their graphic forms. A graphic form serves, in principle, to select meaning and escape homophony.

It is easy to see why a writing system with these properties encourages the hypothesis that reading is strictly a visual-form-to-meaning process (e.g., Baron & Strawson, 1976; Chen, Yung & Ng, 1988; Hoosain & Osgood, 1983; Tzeng & Hung, 1978; Wang, 1973; Zhou & Marslen-Wilson, 1996). However, the evidence now clearly is otherwise (e.g., Cheng & Shih, 1988; Hung, Tzeng, & Tzeng, 1992; Lam, Perfetti, & Bell, 1991; Perfetti & Zhang, 1991, and other studies reviewed in Tan & Perfetti, 1998). The *identification-with-phonology* hypothesis (Perfetti & Zhang, 1995, Perfetti & Tan, 1998, 1999; Tan & Perfetti, 1997) places phonology as a constituent of word recognition (rather than a by-product), a characterization earlier applied to alphabetic writing (Perfetti, Bell, and Delaney, 1988). Thus, across writing systems, phonology may provide an early source of constraint in word reading (van Orden et al., 1990). Based on experimental results, Perfetti and Tan (1998) suggest that phonology is activated at the moment of orthographic recognition — the point at which the identification system distinguishes a given graphic representation from other (similar and partly activated) representations. Thus, although graphic information initiates identification, phonological activation does not lag behind; rather it is part of a *psychological moment of identification.*

This hypothesis has received support form many studies (see Tan & Perfetti, 1998 for a review), including recent studies by Xu, Pollatsek & Potter (1999) and Chua (1999), who independently report evidence for phonological activation in a semantic categorization task. In addition, Weekes, Chen, and Lin (1998) report effects in lexical decision tasks, where such effects are not always found (Zhou & Marslen-Wilson, 1996.)

This places alphabetic and non-alphabetic reading much closer together on one point than one might have supposed. Phonology has a role in word identification in both systems. This is not to say that role is identical in the two systems.

Phonology: Some Differences Between Chinese and English Reading

The research to date has established that phonology is rapid, probably automatic, and perhaps universal. It emerges in less than 90 ms in semantic tasks (Perfetti & Zhang, 1995) and less than 60 ms in naming (Perfetti & Tan, 1998) and brief exposure masked identification tasks (Tan, Hoosain & Peng, 1995). The research also has exposed some differences that arise from the writing systems. A summary of some of these is shown in Figure 2, based on experimental results from our current or previous work, along with analyses of the writing systems.

Orthography-phonology process

The first difference is the most interesting and the most tentative because it rests on the data from one published study by Perfetti and Tan (1998). In a primed naming task, they found that briefly presented graphic primes first facilitated and then inhibited the naming of a target. This inhibition lasted for about 28 ms before returning to baseline. At the same time that graphic facilitation turned to inhibition, phonological facilitation occurred from a homophone prime to a target. Thus, there was an oscillation phasing effect due to graphic form that was correlated with a phonological effect. No similar situation has been reported for English. Figure 2a shows the effect of Perfetti and Tan (1998), while Figure 2b shows an effect of Perfetti and Bell (1991), who used primed identification with masking rather than naming, and pseudo-word primes instead of real word primes. Although this makes for an imprecise comparison, there is little reason to suppose that a different state of affairs would be found with primed naming in English.

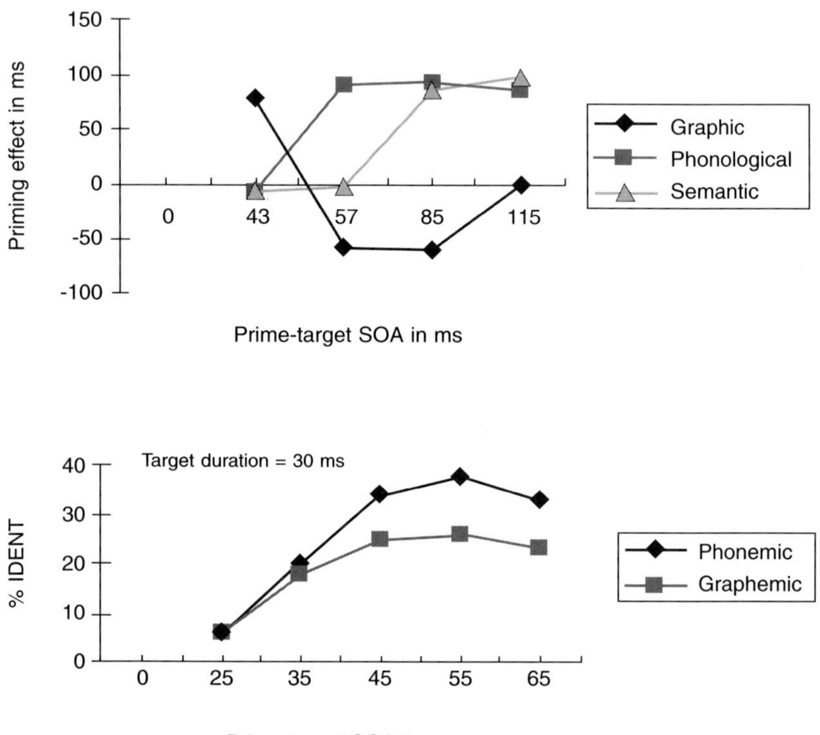

Figure 2.   Figure 2a shows data adopted from Perfetti & Tan (1998), who varied the relationship between a prime and a target across several short SOAs (stimulus onset-asynchrony). An early graphic facilitation effect turned into an inhibition effect at the same SOA at which a phonological prime produced facilitation. This bi-phasic alternation of graphic and phonological effects contrasts with English, shown in Figure 2b, based on data in a brief exposure task (with non-word primes) adapted from Perfetti & Bell (1991).

Table 1 summarizes this difference as one between cascade-style and threshold style activation of phonology. The idea is that in an alphabetic system, the word level units do not wait for a complete specification of all letter units prior to activating word level phonology — hence, *cascade* style. In Chinese, the word-level phonology is not activated prior to a full orthographic specification of the character — hence, *threshold* style. Inhibition from visually similar characters occurs upon reaching the threshold of the target because these characters have received activation. Prior to threshold this activation is facilitative, but once a character has been identified (activated at threshold) it is inhibitory.

Table 1
A Comparison of Phonological Aspects of Alphabetic and Non-alphabetic Word Reading

Alphabetic (English)	Logographic (Chinese)
Phonology activated with orthography — cascade style	Phonology activated with orthography — threshold style
Sublexical units: proper parts	Sublexical units: wholes are parts
Phonology can be 'pre-lexical'	'Pre-lexical' is not a coherent concept
Phonology can 'mediate' meaning (but phonological coherence more apt)	'Mediation' is a dubious concept phonological diffusion more apt

Sublexical units

This difference is inherent in the writing system comparison. In English the letters are at a lower level than the words and become constituent parts (wholly contained within) of the whole word. In Chinese, the components themselves are characters. Thus they participate in the system at the higher word level and are not contained wholly within a lower constituent level. The question is whether this matters for processing. Indeed it does. It could be the main difference responsible for the cascade vs. threshold difference described above. The threshold feature of Chinese identification may derive from the fact that a component of a character (e.g., a semantic radical) activates all characters that contain it in addition to activating its own character representation. The inhibition of highly activated competitors then follows as a means for the identification system to secure a lexical identity (including its phonology).

Pre-lexical phonology

This difference follows from the basic differences in sublexical units. The phonology that is activated in a Chinese character may include that of its components as well as the character as a whole. Because the component is not 'pre-lexical', its phonology, whether activated before that of the character as a whole or not, cannot be pre-lexical in the same sense it can be in an alphabetic system.

Mediation

Because a Chinese character typically has so many homophones, the pronunciation of the character — by itself — is not adequately constraining. It will not pick out a unique morpheme. This means that using the phonology to access the meaning — the usual sense of phonological mediation — would be maladaptive process. Indeed, it would be an indeterminate process. Although one might want to say this a basic difference in the two systems — thus allowing mediation in this sense for alphabetic reading — we think there is a lesson to apply from this analysis of Chinese to alphabetic systems. In both systems, one can think of phonology, not as an instrument to meaning, but rather as a constituent of a word that constrains the identification process. The triple constituents of graphic form, phonological form and meaning uniquely constrain the identification of a word, or at least a lexical root. This is a concept of phonological mediation that can replace the instrumental sense in all writing systems.

The Interactive Constituency Model of Chinese Reading

Perfetti and Tan (1998, 1999) and Tan and Perfetti (1997) described a model of character identification that incorporates multi-level representations and interactions among the levels. Taft and Zhu (1997) describe a model that is similar in its use of multi-level representations, while differing in other respects, including the treatment of radicals. Here we want to illustrate a computational instantiation of this model.

Currently, the model is a network of linked units across which activation spreads. The radical input and the phonological levels of the model can be considered distributed representations, whereas the orthographic and semantic representations can be considered localized representations. An illustration and a description of the model are presented in Figure 3.

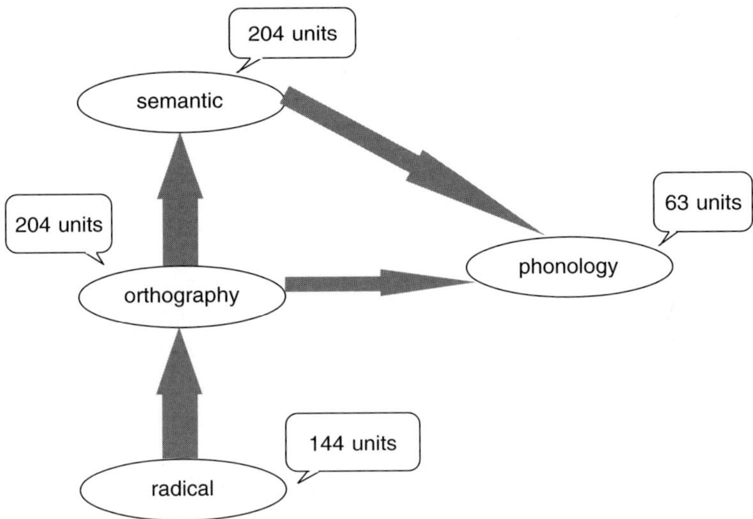

Figure 3.   The constituency model. The input units are 144 radicals that begin activation in a three-constituent system. The three constituent levels — orthography, phonology, and semantic — combine to produce a three-constituent identification event.

The model in its current version is a mix of localist and distributed representations with limited scope. It is designed to recognize 204 characters, but we believe it can be easily expanded within the general design principles. Its goal is modestly to capture some of the naming data in experiments. We summarize briefly the main features of the model.

Model framework

Input (radical) level

The 144 input units represent radicals, the basic components of Chinese characters, distributed across 9 slots × 16 binary-code units per slot. Each slot is one radical, assigned according to writing sequence within a character. Because no character in the National Standard Chinese Character Set (GB2312–80) has more than 9 radicals according to the *Chinese Character Information Dictionary* (Beijing Science Publishers, 1988), 9 slots can represent all characters in our simulation set. The 16 binary-code units match the 16 binary codes of the Chinese National Character Component Standard for Information Processing (GB2312–80), and with slots to represent the writing sequence, this system is sufficient to represent the shared radical structure between almost any two Chinese characters. (Two characters sharing all radicals with same writing sequence, but in different positions such as one left-right and one top-down, a rare occurrence, are not distinguished in this system.)

Orthography level

This is a localized representation of the abstract orthography of characters. Each unit of this level represents one of 204 characters.

Phonology level

This distributed representation uses the Chinese national standard Pinyin system, with each syllable coded across 3 units — onset, vowel and tone. To represent the syllables of Mandarin, 23 onsets, 34 vowels and 5 tones are sufficient. With the addition of one additional unit to represent null onsets, the phonological level consisted of 63 units. Because this level is a distributed representation, there are no within-level linkages, in contrast to the orthography and semantic levels.

Semantic level

This is a localized representation of 204 units, each corresponding to a unique meaning of a character. Meaning precision is represented by connection weights between orthographic and semantic levels. The semantic level currently does not represent meaning components.

Connections within orthographic level

There are negative (inhibitory) connections between each pair of orthographic units, reflecting competition between characters at the input level.

Connections within semantic level

Two related meanings are connected at a weight of .5, arbitrarily reflecting the assumption that semantic relations are not perfectly determinate, hence <1. Other connections are set at 0.

Connections between radical level and orthographic level

The radical level is fully connected to the orthography level, sending activation to the 204 character units along hand-adjusted weighted connections. The weights reflect the presence of input radicals in specific characters.

Connections between orthography and phonology

Each orthographic unit has three connections weighted 1: one to its onset, one to the vowel and one to the tone. All other weights are set to 0.

Connections between orthography and semantics

A precise meaning character is connected to one semantic unit with weight 1. A vague meaning character connects to one semantic unit at weight .9 and to all other 203 semantic units at randomly distributed weights summed .1.

Connections between semantic and phonology levels

Each semantic unit is connected with its three phonology units (onset, vowel, and tone) at weight 1.

Similarity representation

A key idea of the model is to represent similarity along graphic, phonological, and semantic dimensions, implemented as follows: Graphic similarity results from shared radicals. A given radical input activates a cohort of similar characters. Phonological similarity results from shared phonological activation patterns. Homophones have identical patterns; lower levels of similarity result from shared onsets, vowels, or tones. Related meanings arise from connections between the semantic units of characters that are semantically related. For example, semantically related primes and targets are linked with connection weights .5.

Threshold

Each unit in all three levels has a threshold below which the unit cannot send output to another level. For example, below threshold, orthographic units send no output to phonology. The threshold of a character is lowered by the presentation of an orthographically similar prime.

Simulation

Certain assumptions of the model — especially a threshold setting for orthographic units — turn out to be useful for simulating Perfetti and Tan's (1998) time course results for graphic, phonological, and semantic priming effects. Of special interest is the oscillation effect for orthographically similar primes and the rise of phonological priming, co-incident with orthographic inhibition. The simulation of this effect is shown below in Figure 4. (The X axis shows processing cycles; the Y axis shows activation level, <0 reflects inhibition.)

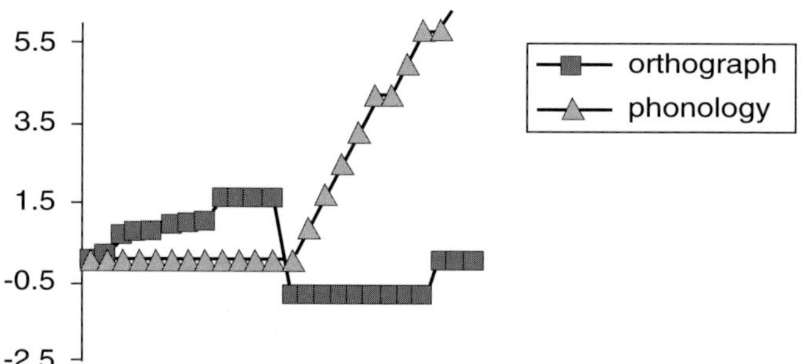

Figure 4. A simulation of the oscillation effect for graphic and phonological priming (Perfetti & Tan, 1998).

What the simulation captures clearly is the pattern of graphic oscillation, with the onset of inhibition coinciding with the onset of phonological facilitation. This occurs because visually similar orthographic units are activated by the same radical. If one of these activated units turns out to be the target, its activation level is nearer to threshold than it would be otherwise; hence, graphic facilitation at first. But when an orthographic unit reaches threshold, it sends its activation to the phonological unit, immediately allowing a phonological priming effect if the activated unit happens to be a homophone — i.e., a pronunciation shared with the target.

At the same time, inhibition results from this longer presentation of a prime, because it reaches threshold and begins to compete with other orthographic units — including the target. For a few processing cycles, the target actually supports activation of the prime character through their shared orthographic units. This competition delays identification of the target.

Phonological priming effects are successfully simulated based on pre-activation of phonological units, which occurs as the orthographic unit reaches threshold and activates its connected phonological unit. Semantic priming results also from an orthographic unit that reaches threshold and sends its output to its semantic unit, which can activate related orthographic units, especially the target. However, this priming is not as rapid as phonological priming, because the link between a target's semantic unit and that of a related prime is not as strong as the link between the target's orthographic unit and its phonological units.

This difference in semantic and phonological linkages is an indirect implementation of the assumption of differential determinacy of semantics and phonology, given an orthographic form. It might equivalently be characterized as capturing the idea that while forms can be identical (homophones), meanings cannot. At the present these two related assumptions are not distinguished.

The model also simulates the meaning precision effect — faster priming for precise primes, but only for meaning-related primes. This is because the system doesn't care about semantics at the phonological or graphic level; a vague homophone prime is not different from a precise homophone prime. But at the semantic level, precision is represented directly in the distribution of meaning activation across the semantic units.

A further implication of the model

Important to the model's ability to simulate the graphic-phonological oscillation effect is the role of the orthographic level and its relation to the radical input level. In particular, the important assumption is that both phonology and similarity-based orthographic competition arise from an orthographic character when its threshold is reached. An implication of the model, then, is that the orthographic interference effect requires character-level competition and will not occur based on visual similarity at the radical level. An unpublished experiment carried out by Liu and Perfetti gives some support for this prediction. When the primes were pseudo-characters, composed of legal radicals and made to be visually similar to the target, there was no interference observed across three short SOAs (54 to 140 ms). Real character primes with visual similarity showed interference at 86 ms in error rates, an SOA at which pseudo-characters produced facilitation. Although the interference effect for visually similar primes was somewhat less than that observed by Perfetti and Tan (1998), the pattern of facilitation-without-interference by pseudo-characters, and facilitation then interference from actual characters, is consistent with that study and with the implemented Interactive Constituency Model.

The significance of the modeling effort lies not so much in its specific implementation, which will undergo further development, as in the instantiation of the principles that are central to the Interactive Constituency Model. The basic principle is the organization of word identity as a triple of its three constituents, all of which are activated in normal reading processes. This entails rapid phonology through direct connections between orthographic word forms and phonological word forms. When a character maps to a spoken word-syllable, the spoken syllable is automatically activated. The evidence is that this activation applies to semantic tasks as well, although the simulations have been concerned only with naming. It also entails rapid semantics. But semantic processes at the word level are less constrained, less deterministic, than phonological processes.

Finally, we note that the implemented model, but not the general framework of the Interactive Constituency theory, privileges whole characters over components. It seems likely, based on a variety of results, that whole character forms control output from the orthographic level. This does not mean that character components do not play a role in this, and, in fact they do. For example, a dissertation by Yang (1999) on the role of components in the time course of priming effects of the sort modeled here showed that the phonology of both whole character primes and their phonologically valid components affected the naming times of related targets. Such multiple unit effects are consistent with the general model, and particular implementations could incorporate the connections needed to produce them.

What Can Cognitive Neuroscience Methods Add?

The development of neuroimaging techniques, especially fMRI, has led to a dramatic surge in research aimed at identifying the functional neuroanatomy of reading. (For reviews, see Fiez & Petersen, 1998; Price, Indefrey, & van Turennout, 1999.) This goal does not supplant, but rather complements, the identification of components of reading that have been the fruit of cognitive behavioral studies. However, there have been some inconsistencies in the results from neuroimaging studies within English, and it may be fair to say that more studies and perhaps new techniques (Horwitz, Rumsey, & Donohue, 1998) are needed before such studies actually add clearly to the cognitive understanding of how reading works.

Cross language and cross-writing systems comparisons may actually help with this problem because such comparisons may expose those shared functional mappings that are robust enough to survive the profound differences in both the principles and the visual appearance of the world's writing systems. Unlike the question of trying to identify 'the phonological decoder' or the 'semantic access network', the cross systems comparison seeks the answer to a simpler question that may produce leads to the more detailed goals. Thus, the question of 'same process' vs. 'different process' can be directly cast onto neuroanatomy: Do the same neuroanatomical networks involved in reading an alphabetic writing system also function in the reading of Chinese?

There is already an indication that *within* the class of alphabetic writing systems, the depth of the orthography makes a difference in the procedures used for reading words (Paulesu, McCrory, Fazio, Menoncello, Brunswick, Cappa, Cotelli, Cossu, Corte, Lorusso, Pesenti, Gallagher, Perani, Price, Frith, & Frith, 2000). In the case of Chinese-English comparisons, one might expect more profound differences, based on the traditional understanding of Chinese. However, considering the cognitive research showing pervasive phonology in Chinese reading, perhaps any differences will be accompanied by critical similarities that reflect the universal appearance of word-level phonology in reading.

To illustrate how a neuroimaging approach can help in a specific case, consider the question of hemispheric specialization for Chinese character reading. Based on behavioral methods that control bilateral processing (e.g., hemifield visual presentation), a number of studies suggested that processing of single Chinese characters is right lateralized (Cheng & Yang, 1989; Tzeng, Hung, Cotton, & Wang, 1979). From such studies arose the *Chinese character-word dissociation hypothesis*, reviewed in Fang (1997). The idea is that a single character is processed in the right hemisphere (by perceptual and semantic processes), whereas two characters (always a word) are processed in the left hemisphere, evoking the spoken language systems. Support for this dissociation hypothesis has not been consistent, however, with some studies finding no right hemisphere advantage for single characters (Besner, Daniels, & Slade, 1982; Fang, 1997; Leong, Wong, Wong, & Hiscock, 1985). Data from neuroimaging might be helpful.

Such data come from a recent study by Tan, Spinks, Gao, Liu, Perfetti, Xiong, Stofer, Pu, Liu, and Fox (2000). In this fMRI study, subjects performed a word generation task in which they implicitly produced a word semantically related to a visually presented target. This task, which requires semantic analysis and implicit word retrieval, was performed for one-character words with either vague or precise meanings, and two-character words (precise meanings). Activation was compared across these stimulus types and with a fixation control. The results clearly exposed a shared neural network across the one and two character tasks. This network included strong left-lateralized components in frontal (BAs 9, 46, and 47) and temporal (BA 37) cortices along with right-lateralized components in the visual (BAs 17–19) and parietal areas (BA 3), as well as the cerebellum. The left frontal regions showed peak activation patterns that were nearly identical for one- and two-character words and for vague as well as precise-meaning characters. In addition, left frontal activations were more pronounced for vague compared with precise meanings.

The fMRI results thus converge with one hypothesis from the cognitive research and contradict another. They suggest that the distinction between vague and precise meanings, which is functional in cognitive studies of naming and brief exposure identification, has a neuro-anatomical correlate. Approximately speaking, vague-meaning characters require more effort after meaning, and this is reflected in left frontal cortical regions. The contradiction is that the study provides no evidence for the dissociation hypothesis. It appears that the neuroanatomical networks that support one character processes are the same ones that support two character processes, at least in implicit semantic association tasks. These networks overlap substantially with those identified in English word reading.

Of course, what one wants is converging evidence. And there are other studies suggesting that the dissociation hypothesis is wrong. A neuroimaging study of Chinese single character processing by Chee, Tan and Thiel (1999) showed peak activations in the left hemisphere regions (e.g., BA 44/45, BAs 46/9 and 37) and strong activations in bilateral occipital and bilateral parietal regions (BA 7). This result and the Tan et al. (2000) result are in substantial agreement. In addition, clinical studies of selective impairments with Japanese patients indicate similar neural pathways support both Japanese Kanji and Kana reading (Koyama, Kakigi, Hoshiyama, & Kitamura, 1998; Sugishita, Otomo, Kabe, & Yunoki, 1992). Although there is much to learn about the differences in processes that are associated with different writing systems, and even within systems (Paulesu et al., 2000), it appears that there may be some shared functional neuroanatomy that is responsible for reading. We should expect this shared structure to reflect reading's dependence on shared visual processes and language processes, both of which appear to be intrinsic and hence universal to reading.

One thing that even event-related fMRI is unlikely to provide is temporal information on processes that is comparable to the temporal grain that our models of cognitive processes have developed. For example, the timing of semantic and phonological outcomes is a matter of milliseconds, as are the even smaller differences between them. For such timing observations, event-related potentials (ERP) are promising, and indeed have been very informative on issues of language processing (Hagoort, Brown, & Osterhout, 1999). Of special interest in language processing has been the N400, a mid-latency endogenous component related to subjects' semantic and pragmatic expectations. Kutas and Hillyard (1980), who first described this component, found a larger N400 when a sentence ended with a semantically anomalous word. Furthermore, the more consistent or predictable the sentence endings, the smaller the N400 (Kutas, Lindamood, & Hillyard, 1984). The N400 amplitude also is influenced by the characteristics of single words. Repeated words, high frequency words, and concrete words elicit smaller N400s than do novel, low frequency, and abstract words (Kutas, Federmeier, & Sereno, 1999; Kutas & Van Petten, 1994). Interestingly, a phonological prime prior to a target word reduces the N400 latency (Radeau, Besson, Fonteneau, & Castro, 1998).

ERP data can help inform some of the comparative issues we have raised. One particular example is the role of phonology as reported by Perfetti and Zhang (1995) for meaning judgments and by Xu, Pollatsek and Potter (1999) and Chua (1999) for semantic categorization. In the meaning judgment experiments, the critical finding is that when subjects judge whether two characters have the same meaning, interference (in decision times and error rates) is observed if they instead happen to have the same pronunciation. And inversely, when subjects judge whether the characters have the same pronunciation, there is interference when they have the same meaning. The time course of these interference effects suggested phonological interference before semantic interference. In an

ERP version of this experiment, we can ask whether interpretable ERP components are associated with the various tasks and conditions. For example, the N400 might be associated with processing the second word as a function of its relationship to the first word.

Our preliminary data show ERP components vary in interesting ways in this task. For example, the N400 component during the second stimulus is reduced when the reader is judging meaning compared with pronunciation (homophony). This is consistent with the semantic interpretation of the N400. Additionally, the subject's processing mode is seen in the N400. When the task is meaning judgment, a second stimulus that is semantically similar to the first stimulus produces a reduced N400 compared with one that is unrelated. This too is to be expected on the semantic interpretation of the N400. However, when the task is homophone judgment and the second stimulus is indeed a homophone, the N400 is also reduced compared with when the second stimulus is unrelated. Thus in a homophone task, the homophone is congruent with the task and the N400 reflects this fact. In English rhyme judgments, similar results have been reported (reduced N400 for rhymes compared with controls; Rugg, 1984).

Beyond these processing mode effects, the interesting questions concern the 'out-of-mode' effects — when a homophone occurs during semantic judgments and when a synonym occurs during homophone judgments. The general picture is that reduced P200 components are produced by homophones during meaning judgment and reduced N400 by synonyms during homophone judgment. It appears we can identify task dependent and strictly word (form and meaning) effects in either P200 or N400 (Barnea & Breznitz, 1998). In particular, P200 may signal early phonological activation in word identification across languages. This encourages the belief that ERP data will prove to be informative on questions of the time course of the form and meaning constituent of words and that cross writing system comparisons will be useful.

Conclusion

A cross-writing systems approach to reading is important to an understanding of the basic universal processes in reading. The cognitive behavioral research has pointed to the possibility of a universal linguistic underpinning to reading. Results that we've reviewed point to both universal and writing-system specific processes when Chinese is compared with English. The Interactive Constituency Model gives a general account of the components of reading, and its computational implementation can simulate some specific results. Further understanding of how reading processes are expressed in different writing systems and different languages can benefit from the convergence of neuroimaging and electrophysiological methods with cognitive behavioral methods; progress probably depends on studies using different methods. Despite its complexity at some levels, the relative simplicity of reading at the word level makes it a particularly good problem to see how the mind meets the brain. The comparative approach helps to expose the most general function-structure relations in reading.

References

Baron, J., & Strawson, C. (1976). Use of orthographic and word-specific knowledge in reading words aloud. *Journal of Experimental Psychology: Human Perception and Performance, 2*, 386–393.

Barnea, A., & Breznitz, Z. (1998). Phonological and orthographic processing of Hebrew words: Electrophysiological aspects. *Journal of Genetic Psychology, 159*, 492–504.

Beijing Language College (1986). *Modern Chinese character frequency dictionary.* Beijing: Beijing Language College Press (in Chinese).

Beijing Science Publishers (1988). *Chinese character information dictionary (Hanzi Xinxi Zidian).* Beijing: Author (in Chinese).

Berent, I., & Perfetti, C. A. (1995). A rose is a REEZ: The two-cycles model of phonology assembly in reading English. *Psychological Review, 102*, 146–184.

Besner, D., Daniels, S., & Slade, C. (1982). Ideogram reading and right hemisphere language. *British Journal of Psychology, 73*, 21–28.

Chee, M., Tan, E., & Thiel, T. (1999): Mandarin and English single word processing studies with functional magnetic resonance imaging. *Journal of Neuroscience, 19*, 3050–3056.

Chen, M. J., Yung, Y. F., & Ng, T. W. (1988). The effect of context on the perception of Chinese characters. In I. M. Liu, H.-C. Chen, & M. J. Chen (Eds.), *Cognitive aspects of the Chinese language*, pp. 27–39. Hong Kong: Asian Research Service.

Cheng, C. M., & Shih, S. I. (1988). The nature of lexical access in Chinese: Evidence from experiments on visual and phonological priming in lexical judgment. In I. M. Liu, H.-C. Chen, & M. J. Chen (Eds.), *Cognitive aspects of the Chinese language*, pp. 1–14. Hong Kong: Asian Research Service.

Cheng, C. M., & Yang, M. J. (1989). Lateralization in the visual perception of Chinese characters and words. *Brain and Language, 36,* 669–689.

Chua, F. (1999). Phonological recoding in Chinese logograph recognition. *Journal of Experimental Psychology: Learning, Memory, and Cognition, 25,* 876–891.

Coltheart, M., Curtis, B., Atkins, P., & Haller, M. (1993). Models of reading aloud: Dual-route and parallel-distributed-processing approaches. *Psychological Review, 100,* 589–608.

DeFrancis, J. (1989). *Visible speech: The diverse oneness of writing systems.* Honolulu: University of Hawaii Press.

Fan, K. Y. (1986). Graphic symbols of Chinese characters. Paper presented at the Symposium on Chinese Character Modernization, Beijing, China.

Fang, S. P. (1997): Morphological properties and the Chinese character-word difference in laterality patterns. *Journal of Experimental Psychology: Human Perception and Performance, 23,* 1439–1453.

Fiez, J. A. & Petersen, S. E. (1998). Neuroimaging studies of word reading. *Proceedings of the National Academy of Sciences, USA, 95,* 914–921.

Frost. R. (1998). Toward a strong phonological theory of visual word recognition: True issues and false trails. *Psychological Bulletin, 123*(1), 71–99.

Hagoort, P., Brown, C., & Osterhout, L. (1999). The neurocognition of syntactic processing. In C. M. Brown & P. Hagoort (Eds.), *The neurocognition of language,* pp. 273–318. New York: Oxford University Press.

Harm, M. W., & Seidenberg, M. S. (1999). Phonology, reading acquisition, and dyslexia: Insights from connectionist models. *Psychological Review, 106*(3), 491–528.

Hoosain, R., & Osgood, C. E. (1983). Information processing times for English and Chinese words. *Perception and Psychophysics, 34,* 573–577.

Horwitz, B., Rumsey, J. M., & Donohue, B. C. (1998). Functional connectivity of the angular gyrus in normal reading and dyslexia. *Proceedings of the National Academy of Sciences, USA, 95,* 8939–8944.

Hung, D. L., Tzeng, O. J. L., & Tzeng, A. K. Y. (1992). Automatic activation of linguistic information in Chinese character recognition. In R. Frost, & L. Katz (Eds.), *Orthography, phonology, morphology, and meaning,* pp. 119–130. Amsterdam: North-Holland.

Koyama, S., Kakigi, R., Hoshiyama, M., & Kitamura, Y. (1998): Reading of Japanese Kanji (morphograms) and Kana (syllabograms): a magnetoencephalographic study. *Neuropsychologia, 36,* 83–98.

Kutas, M., Federmeier, K. D., & Sereno, M. I. (1999). Current approaches to mapping language in electromagnetic space. In C. M. Brown, & P. Hagoort (Eds.), *The neurocognition of language,* pp. 359–393. New York: Oxford University Press.

Kutas, M., & Hillyard, S.A. (1980). Reading senseless sentences: Brain potentials reflect semantic incongruity. *Science, 207,* 203–205.

Kutas, M., Lindamood, T. E., & Hillyard, S. A. (1984). Word expectancy and event-related brain potentials during sentence processing. In S. Kornblum & J. Requin (Eds.), *Preparatory states and processes*, pp. 217–237. Hillsdale, NJ: Erlbaum.

Kutas, M., & Van Petten, C.K. (1994). Psycholinguistics electrified: Event-related brain potential investigations. In M. A. Gernsbacher (Ed.), *Handbook of psycholinguistics*, pp. 83–143. San Diego, CA: Academic Press.

Lam, A., Perfetti, C.A., & Bell, L. (1991). Automatic phonetic transfer in bidialectal reading. *Applied Psycholinguistics, 12,* 299–311.

Leong, C. K. (1973). Reading in Chinese with reference to reading practices in Hong Kong. In J. Downing (Ed.), *Comparative reading: Cross-national studies of behavior and processes in reading and writing*, pp. 383–402. New York: Macmillan.

Leong, C. K. (1997). Paradigmatic analysis of Chinese word reading: Research findings and classroom practices. In C. K. Leong & R. M. Joshi (Eds.), *Cross-language studies of learning to reading and spell: Phonological and orthographic processing*, pp. 379–417. Dordrecht: Kluwer Academic Publishers.

Leong, C. K., Wong, S. Wong, A., & Hiscock, M. (1985). Differential cerebral involvement in perceiving Chinese characters: Levels of processing approach. *Brain and Language, 26,*131–145.

Li, P., & Yip, C.W. (1996). Lexical ambiguity and context effects in spoken word recognition: Evidence from Chinese. In G. Cottrell (Ed.), *Proceedings of 18th Annual Conference of the Cognitive Science Society*, pp. 228–232. Hillsdale, NJ: Lawrence Erlbaum Associates.

Liu, I.-M. (1995). Script factors that affect literacy: Alphabetic vs. logographic languages. In I. Taylor & D. R. Olson (Eds.), *Scripts and literacy*, pp. 145–162. Netherlands: Kluwer Academic Publishers.

Mattingly, I. G. (1987). Morphological structure and segmental awareness. *Cahiers de Psychologie Cognitive/Current Psychology of Cognition, 7*(5), 488–493.

Mattingly, I. G. (1992). Linguistic awareness and orthographic form. In R. Frost & L. Katz (Eds.), *Orthography, phonology, morphology, and meaning*, pp. 11–26. Amsterdam: Elsevier.

Paulesu, E., McCrory, E., Fazio, F., Menoncello, L., Brunswick, N., Cappa, S. F., Cotelli, M., Cossu, G., Corte, F., Lorusso, M., Pesenti, S., Gallagher, A., Perani, D., Price, C., Frith, C. D., & Frith, U. (2000). A cultural effect on brain function. *Nature Neuroscience, 3,* 91–96.

Perfetti, C. A., & Bell, L. (1991). Phonemic activation during the first 40 ms of word identification: Evidence from backward masking and masked priming. *Journal of Memory and Language, 30,* 473–485.

Perfetti, C. A., Bell, L., & Delany, S. (1988). Automatic phonetic activation in silent word reading: Evidence from backward masking. *Journal of Memory and Language, 27,* 59–70.

Perfetti, C. A. & Tan, L. H. (1998). The time-course of graphic, phonological, and semantic activation in Chinese character identification. *Journal of Experimental Psychology: Learning, Memory, and Cognition, 24*, 1–18.

Perfetti, C. A. & Tan, L. H. (1999). The constituency model of Chinese word identification. In J. Wang, A. W. Inhoff et al. (Eds.), *Reading Chinese script: A cognitive analysis*, pp. 115–134. Mahwah, NJ: Lawrence Erlbaum.

Perfetti, C. A., & Zhang, S. (1991). Phonological processes in reading Chinese characters. *Journal of Experiment Psychology: Learning, Memory, and Cognition, 17*, 633–643.

Perfetti, C. A., & Zhang, S. (1995). Very early phonological activation in Chinese reading. *Journal of Experimental Psychology: Learning, Memory, and Cognition, 21*, 24–33.

Perfetti, C. A., Zhang, S., & Berent, I (1992). Reading in English and Chinese: Evidence for a 'universal' phonological principle. In R. Frost, & L. Katz, (Eds.), *Orthography, phonology, morphology, and meaning*, pp. 227–248. Amsterdam: North-Holland.

Plaut, D. C., McClelland, J. L., Seidenberg, M. S., & Patterson, K. (1996). Understanding normal and impaired word reading: Computational principles in quasi-regular domains. *Psychological Review, 103*, 56–115.

Price, C., Indefrey, P., & van Turennout, M. (1999). The neural architecture underlying the processing of written and spoken word forms. In Brown, M. and Hagoort, P. (Eds.), *The neurocognition of language*, pp. 211–240. New York: Oxford University Press.

Radeau, M., Besson, M., Fonteneau, E., & Castro, S. L. (1998). Semantic, repetition, and rime priming between spoken words: Behavioral and electrophysiological evidence. *Biological Psychology, 48*, 183–204.

Rugg, M. D. (1984). Event-related potentials and the phonological processing of words and non-words. *Neuropsychologia, 22*, 435–443.

Sugishita, M., Otomo, K., Kabe, S., & Yunoki, K. (1992): A critical appraisal of neuropsychological correlates of Japanese ideogram (kanji) and phonogram (kana) reading. *Brain, 115*, 1563–1585.

Taft, M., & Zhu, X. (1997). Submorphemic processing in reading Chinese. *Journal of Experimental Psychology: Learning, Memory, and Cognition, 23*, 761–775.

Tan, L. H., Hoosain, R., & Peng, D.-L. (1995). Role of early presemantic phonological code in Chinese character identification. *Journal of Experimental Psychology: Learning, Memory, and Cognition, 21*, 43–54.

Tan, L. H., & Perfetti, C. A. (1997). Visual Chinese character recognition: Does phonological information mediate access to meaning? *Journal of Memory and Language, 37*, 41–57.

Tan, L. H., & Perfetti, C. A. (1998). Phonological codes as early sources of constraint in Chinese word identification: A review of current discoveries and theoretical accounts. *Reading and Writing: An Interdisciplinary Journal, 10*, 165–200. Reprinted in C. K. Leong, & K. Tamaoka (Eds.).

(1998). *Cognitive processes of the Chinese and the Japanese languages.* Series (pp. 11–46). Dordrecht: Kluwer Academic Publishers.

Tan, L. H., Spinks, J. A., Gao, J. H., Liu, H., Perfetti, C. A., Xiong, J., Stofer, K. A., Pu, Y. L., Liu, Y., & Fox, P. T. (2000). Brain activation in the processing of Chinese characters and words: A functional MRI study. *Human Brain Mapping, 10,* 16–27.

Tzeng, O. J. L., & Hung, D. L. (1978). Reading the Chinese character: Some basic research. *Acta Psychologica Taiwanica, 20,* 45–49 (in Chinese).

Tzeng, O., Hung, D. L., Cotton, B., & Wang, W. S-Y. (1979): Visual lateralization effect in reading Chinese characters. *Nature, 282,* 499–501.

Tzeng, O. J. L., Hung, D. L., & Wang, W. S.-Y (1977). Speech recoding in reading Chinese characters. *Journal of Experimental Psychology: Human Memory and Learning, 3,* 621–630.

Van Orden, G. C., Pennington, B., & Stone, G. (1990). Word identification in reading and the promise of subsymbolic psycholinguistics. *Psychological Review, 97,* 488–522.

Wang, W. S.-Y. (1973). The Chinese language. *Scientific American, 228,* 50–60.

Weekes, B. S., Chen, M. J., & Lin, Y. B. (1998). Differential effects of phonological priming on Chinese character recognition. *Reading and Writing, 10,* 201–222.

Xu, Y., Pollatsek, A., & Potter, M. (1999). The activation of phonology during silent Chinese word reading. *Journal of Experimental Psychology: Learning, Memory, and Cognition, 25,* 838–857.

Yang, H. (1999). *How to access phonology of Chinese phonetic-compound-characters: Phonological activation and interaction of the whole characters and their phonetics.* Paper based on Ph.D. dissertation, Beijing Normal University.

Zhang, S., & Perfetti, C. A. (1993). The tongue twister effect in reading Chinese. *Journal of Experimental Psychology: Learning, Memory, and Cognition, 19,* 1082–1093.

Zhou, X., & Marslen-Wilson, W. (1996). Direct visual access is the only way to access the Chinese mental lexicon. In G. Cottrell (Ed.), *Proceedings of 18th Annual Conference of the Cognitive Science Society,* pp. 714–719. Hillsdale, NJ: Lawrence Erlbaum.

Zhou, Y. (1978). To what degree are the 'phonetics' of present-day Chinese characters still phonetic? *Zhongguo Yuwen, 146,* 172–177(in Chinese).

Zhu, X. (1988). Analysis of cueing function of phonetic components in modern Chinese. In X. Yuan (Ed.), *Proceedings of the Symposium on the Chinese Language and Characters.* Beijing: Guang Ming Daily Press (in Chinese).

Author Note

Some of the research summarized in this chapter was supported by grant SBR-9223125 from the National Science Foundation to Charles Perfetti.

Functional Magnetic Resonance Imaging: A Promising Tool for Defining the Organization of Chinese Language in the Brain

Paul M. Matthews, Shimin Fu, Yi-Ping Chen and Susan Iversen

A fundamental problem in language studies is to determine whether the written form of a language influences the way in which information is encoded in the brain. Study of the Chinese language offers a potentially powerful strategy for addressing this question. Chinese is unique relative to English and other alphabetic languages because, with the introduction of Pinyin, spoken language used can be represented in two distinct forms, one with a morphographic script and the other with a phonetic-based language.

Chinese characters convey information by virtue of the organization of lines in space. They have a structure and their interpretation depends on its configuration relative to the local environment. In contrast, the alphabetic symbols of Pinyin are interpreted in terms of the translated sound, in common with other phonetic languages. These fundamental differences suggest that the underlying brain representations during reading of the two languages may be distinct.

Functional magnetic resonance imaging (fMRI) provides a method for mapping the organization of cognitive processes in the brain (Matthews, Clare, & Adcock, 1999; Ogawa, Lee, Kay, & Tank, 1990). It offers the advantages of being a non-invasive, widely diffused technology. Because it does not employ radioactive tracers or pose other significant risks, subjects can be studied on many occasions. In this brief review chapter, we will outline the principals of fMRI, briefly review the application of this technique to language studies, and then discuss a new application to the study of the Chinese language.

Functional Magnetic Resonance Imaging of the Brain

Work of Charles Sherrington over 100 years ago demonstrated that increased local blood flow accompanies neuronal activity. The increased blood flow results from higher energy utilization at the synapse with either excitatory or inhibitory transmission (Villringer & Dirnagl, 1995). The increase in blood flow delivers more oxygen to an activated area of brain than the enhanced metabolism requires. In consequence, the blood in the capillaries serving the area and in the veins draining from it show a relatively greater oxygenated to deoxygenated haemoglobin ratio.

Magnetic resonance imaging (MRI) relies on detection of signal from the protons of water molecules in the tissue. The precise amount of signal that comes from any part of the tissue depends both on the water content and also on factors which control what is known as the 'relaxation' of the protons in water. When water protons are placed in an area of local, rapidly changing magnetic field strengths, their relaxation rate ($1/T_2{}^*$) is enhanced, giving rise to greater signal loss by the time that it is observed (Thulborn, Waterton, Matthews, & Radda, 1982).

Deoxyhaemoglobin is paramagnetic, i.e. it bends a magnetic field towards it. Thus, water protons that are near a blood vessel containing a higher proportion of deoxyhaemoglobin will experience a rapidly changing local magnetic field, which gives rise to signal loss. In contrast, when the proportion of oxygenated haemoglobin rises, the local magnetic field effects are smaller and there is less signal loss. Thus, when an area of brain becomes activated and local blood flow increases (increasing the ratio of oxygenated to deoxygenated haemoglobin in the capillaries of the tissue and in the draining veins) there is a small increase in signal intensity. This small signal change — on the order of only about 1% — can be measured if many images are acquired and compared using statistical methods (Ogawa et al., 1990).

An fMRI examination is performed most typically by imaging the brain of the subject many times while in a 'rest' comparison state and then in a state of active cognitive processing. For example, images might be acquired first while a subject is viewing a crosshair on a screen and then when the subject is reading. As this paired cycle is repeated many times and the signal change in images taken during the active reading period relative to the rest period are averaged, the signal-to-noise increases and meaningful signal detection is possible.

This can be done on a pixel-by-pixel basis across the entire brain image. Those areas that show significant change in comparing the two states then can be identified. Their localization establishes the specific regions involved in the cognitive process of interest.

What distinguishes the fMRI mapping from that of PET is that *relative* signal changes are measured, rather than *absolute* values of blood flow. What distinguishes the fMRI measurement from mapping based on the electroencephalogram (EEG) or magnetoencephalography is that the haemodynamic consequences of neuronal activation are mapped rather than the neuronal depolarization event itself. The time course of the changes is thus much slower (typically the haemodynamic time course lags at least a second or more behind the neuronal depolarization event itself). The issues of the precise spatial localization remain a matter of debate, but it appears as though an effective spatial resolution on the order of a few millimetres in any dimension is possible routinely. Moreover, using special techniques in some areas of the brain, mapping even of volumes as small as a cortical column appears possible (Kim, Duong, & Kim, 2000).

Functional Magnetic Resonance Imaging Studies of Language Organization in the Brain

Functional magnetic resonance imaging has already begun to make a significant contribution to our understanding of the organization of language in the brain. It is of particular importance technically that there is sufficient sensitivity for the analysis of activations in single subjects. In the future, the ability to study subjects with a broad range of paradigms containing many contrasts also likely should prove to be particularly important.

It was clear from the earliest language imaging studies with positron emission tomography (PET) that language processing engages a wide network in the brain, particularly in the left hemisphere (Petersen, Fox, Posner, Mintun, & Raichle, 1995). It therefore may be useful to consider the regional activations in three categories as suggested by Damasio and Damasio (1992). Functional sub-divisions defined by them include those for language 'implementation' and 'concept formation', with a distinct neural substrate for 'mediation' of the interactions between the two. A key idea here is that there is a final common implementation pathway that conveys information or concepts of a very wide range of types and that is accessed through multiple sensory pathways. This expresses the idea that meaningful language can be expressed in many forms, e.g., sign vs. pictographic vs. phonetic language — a concept possibly fundamental to understanding brain representations of different written forms of the Chinese language.

In the normal brain, the language-specific pathways are being refined from models developed on the basis of lesion studies, but they remain essentially consistent. The study of language using functional imaging follows on in general concept from the principles established by Petersen and colleagues (Petersen, Fox, Posner, Mintun, & Raichle, 1989) in which a psychological processing model was used to establish paradigms that identified specific modes of processing via contrasts (Petersen et al., 1995). In Peterson's seminal PET study, a contrast was made between the simple task in which visual fixation was contrasted with passive word-reading, passive word-reading then was contrasted with repetition and finally repetition of a word was contrasted with a generation of verbs from a noun. Analysis of activation images from contrasts between these states identified key areas of language pathway in the left hemisphere. Subsequently, work has focused on understanding this in greater detail.

A current view can be briefly (and perhaps over-simplistically) summarised as follows. The posterior temporal gyrus is activated by both speech and non-speech sounds (Zatorre, Evans, Meyer, & Gjedde, 1992) in the auditory cortex. Adjacent areas appear to be multi-modal, critical to integration of information. For example, Calvert, Bullmore, Brammer, Campbell, Williams, Mcguire, Woodruff, Iversen and David (1997) showed that one adjacent area became active with lip-reading. Silent word reading contrasted with letter-string activation also activates a very similar area, lateralized to the left (Neville, Bavelier, Corina, Rauschecker, Karni, & Lalwani, Braun, Clark, Jezzard, & Turner, 1998). Inferior to this region in the middle and inferior temporal gyri are areas that appear to be more specifically activated with language-like sounds or meaningful language, as contrasted with meaningless noise. More inferior parts of the middle temporal gyrus may be relatively specific for word recognition as part of a lexical-semantic processing network. However, it is clear that semantic processing must involve a very wide area of the extra-Sylvian tissue language areas, particularly in the temporal lobe with activation of the fusiform gyrus (Brodmann area 17/20), temporal parietal cortex in the angular gyrus (Brodmann area 39), and the perisplenial area, including the precuneus (Binder, Frost, Hammeke, Cox, Rao, & Prieto, 1997). The prefrontal area is involved, although the activities of this area are quite complex.

The prefrontal cortex (including Broca's area) has long been recognized as a critical part of expressive language function. It clearly has a role in phonological tasks and perhaps in programming motor activation of the mouth for speech. However, there also is data that suggests that it may be very much involved in semantic transformation, as well (Buckner, Raichle, & Petersen, 1995). This emphasizes that meaning is not ascribed to language in a single area but is part of a very widely distributed retrieval network. Particularly with studies of patients with lesions in the left inferior and frontal area (Thulborn et al., 1999), it has become apparent that there may be involvement of homologous areas in the right hemisphere, although their precise function (whether identical or involved in some independent fashion, such as monitoring output) remains unclear.

However, functional imaging studies of language remain challenging for a number of reasons. First, development of paradigms with informative contrasts has demanded a firm psychological model — the best choice of which remains uncertain. Secondly, phenomena such as automatic processing have become apparent. This is a confound of paradigm design arising from the observation that single words may evoke cognitive processing even unconsciously. The concept is most directly seen in the phenomena of, for example, the Stroop effect, in which the reaction time for counting the number of words presented on a screen is greater if a number word is repeated on the screen, despite the fact that the subject is not been explicitly asked to read the words. More intriguingly, indirect evidence suggests that intrinsic brain processing may make use of parts of the same network used for semantic processing. Binder, Frost, Hammeke, Bellgowan, Rao, and Cox (1999) compared a 'resting state' in which there was no explicit cognitive activity with a tone perception task and found that it provided activation of the same left-lateralised semantic network previously identified with contrast switching for word meeting vs. simple perception. A practical consequence of these confounds has been that the design of paradigms to tease out specific aspects of language has become more complex as it has become apparent that allowance must be made for this implicit processing.

A particularly exciting area for investigation concerns the ways in which experience may modify the development of language in individual brains. A persuasive report by Kim, Relkin, Lee, and Hirsch (1997) demonstrated shifts in language activation in the inferior frontal cortex in subjects who had acquired a second language late in life relative to their native language. When languages were acquired very early, this shift was not seen. Interpretation of this result is not clear-cut, as it could reflect differences in the strategy used for production of the less familiar language. Alternatively, it may suggest that the network for later acquired language is distinct. The idea that there may be local functional plasticity in the representation of language is an exciting one for those interested in recovery after brain injury.

A second aspect of the developmental modulation of language representation concerns the effect of gender. Studies by the Yale group have suggested that brain activation associated with language tasks is different between men and women (Shaywitz, Shaywitz, Pugh, Constable, Skudlarski, & Fullbright, et al., 1995). Although this finding has not been easy to replicate, it raises a particularly interesting question for the understanding of orthographic languages such as Chinese, because gender differences in spatial processing also have been proposed. While this would not be expected to affect the primary language implementation pathway, it could have consequences for mediation networks linking concepts to language.

There are obviously many ways in which fMRI may be used for the exploration of language. The first lies in better mapping of the functional areas of the brain associated with language. This will involve particularly more precise paradigm design for isolation of processing functions with an appreciation for the need to precisely control or understand the baseline comparison states. The second area would be in using the paradigm time-course in order to distinguish processing functions on the basis of their temporal engagement. The application of 'single event' designs to this could be useful (Buckner, 1998; Burock, Buckner, Woldorff, Rosen, & Dale, 1998). Third, linking fMRI with lesion studies in-patients and with other mapping techniques (e.g., MEG) undoubtedly will prove powerful for language studies. Finally, the application of explicit strategies for modelling network behaviour in activation studies, such as an independent components analysis (ICA) may be useful in distinguishing distinct processing aspects of language (McKeown, Makeig, Brown, Jung, Kindermann, & Bell, et al., 1998).

Functional Magnetic Resonance Imaging Studies of Chinese Characters

Because Chinese has an orthographic representation, a popular hypotheses has been that reading Chinese characters might show a lower left hemispheric lateralization than do phonetic languages. An initial study (Kansaku, Shimoyama, Nakajima, Higuchi, Nakazaki, Kubota, et al., 1998) considered differences in activation in Japanese subjects presented with 'abstract' or 'concrete' objects represented by Chinese characters (kanji) in Japanese. In common with results from other language studies, there is bilateral activation in the occipital region. There appeared to be some stronger activation in the left occipital temporal regions with the concrete object words. This suggested a relative left lateralization as found with phonetic languages and is consistent with previous studies, which have suggested that kana (phonetic) and kanji are processed by similar neural pathways. However, a criticism that can be levelled at these studies is that Japanese assigns a phonetic representation to kanji characters in a similar way to kana.

Studies of Chinese character processing with native Chinese speakers have been performed more recently. Chee et al. demonstrated primary activations in the left hemisphere including in Brodmann areas 44/45 (Chee, Caplan, Soon, Sriram, Tan, Thiel, & Weekes, 1999; Chee, Tan, & Thiel, 1999). More posteriorly, activations were found bilaterally in the occipital and parietal regions (BA7). There was no indication that there was a right hemisphere predominance of activation with traditional Chinese characters.

A more complex problem was addressed by Tan, Spinks, Gao, Liu, Perfetti, Xiong, Pu, Liu, Stofer, and Fox (2000). They tested the hypothesis that the brain representations for single Chinese characters and for paired Chinese characters might be different. Because single Chinese characters have a number of structural units (strokes) organized to a square field, the unit is perceived in terms of the spatial relationships between the components. In contrast, a two character Chinese word may need to be analysed somewhat differently because of the necessity of binding together temporally distinctly processed units. This could be a special function of the left hemisphere. Classical psychophysical studies previously had have suggested that there may be a differential hemisphere lateralization for processing of one- and two-character words, for example.

More detailed analyses within the Tan et al. study highlighted the need to consider the relative lateralization of activation in specific cortical processing regions rather than in volumes as large as a hemisphere. They demonstrated a strong left lateralization for reading Chinese characters in both the frontal (BA9 and 47) and temporal (BA37) cortex. However, relative right lateralization was found for all forms of Chinese characters in the parietal and occipital cortex. It was clear that there was not a difference in lateralization in any of these areas between one- and two-character words.

These results are consistent with the hypothesis that relatively right hemispheric spatial processing is important in interpreting Chinese language, although it could not address directly the question of whether the right-sided activation was clearly significantly different from that with a phonetic language. The study clearly refutes the hypothesis that there is a distinct difference in lateralisation between the reading of single and double character words.

A Direct Comparison of Chinese Pinyin and Chinese Character Reading

In preliminary work, we have taken a somewhat different approach in testing whether there are unique areas involved in the reading of Chinese script. The purpose of our experiment was to investigate the brain areas that were involved in reading alphabetical and non-alphabetic scripts. Two kinds of scripts, Pinyin and Chinese characters, were used as stimuli in our study to represent alphabetic and non-alphabetic writing systems, respectively. As noted above, Chinese characters (morphograms) carry meaning, whereas Pinyin (syllabograms) have no semantic value and must be assembled on a syllable-by-syllable basis.

Each stimulus consisted of two characters or two Pinyins and was presented on the centre of the screen. The task for the native Mandarin-speaking Chinese who participated was to silently read the characters or Pinyins and judge whether they 'sound' like real words in Chinese by pressing corresponding keys with their right index ('yes') or middle finger ('no'). In Pinyin condition (PY), the subjects had to correctly sound out the phenomena represented by the Pinyins first.

Similarly, in character condition (CH), the subjects also had to correctly sound out the characters first, because the two characters in each stimulus were chosen not to make a real word in Chinese. Therefore, in both conditions, the subjects needed to access the phonology of stimuli first in order to perform the semantic task.

Fixation was used as a contrast stimulus in both Pinyin and character conditions to explore the activations involved in the reading of these two scripts. Direct contrast of these two scripts was also conducted. Therefore, three contrasts were scanned in present study: Pinyin vs. fixation, character vs. fixation, and Pinyin vs. character.

The data analysis was carried out using FEAT (FMRIB's[1] Easy Analysis Tool) within MEDx.[2] The following pre-statistical processing was applied: 3D motion correction, using AIR;[3] spatial smoothing using a Gaussian Kernel of FWHM 10 mm; global (volumetric) multipicative mean intensity renomalization; matched-Gaussian/Butterworth bandpass filtering. A Z-score statistic image was produced using Student's *t*-test and thresholded using clusters determined by Z 3.1 and a cluster significance threshold of P = 0.01. The resulting map of Z scores was transformed into the standard anatomical space of Talairach and Tournoux (1989).

An illustrative brain activation map for one subject is shown (Fig 2). Both the PY and CH activated bilateral brain areas likely important in concept formation, sensory mediation, and language. There was significant activation in the fusiform, lingual, cuneus/precuneus, and inferior occipital gyrus, prefrontal areas (inferior frontal gyrus, middle frontal gyrus) and parietal cortex (inferior parietal gyrus superior parietal lobule), motor, premotor and cerebellar areas (precentral gyrus, superior frontal/medial frontal gyrus, cerebellum), limbic areas (cingulate gyrus), and subcortical grey matter (thalamus/putamen). The areas that activated only in the left hemisphere included superior temporal gyrus and postcentral gyrus. Moreover, while the *CH-fixation* condition activated only the left insula, the *PY-fixation* condition activated both the left and right insula. Thus, although many regions are activated bilaterally, a relative left-lateralisation is very clear for the inferior frontal gyrus, middle frontal gyrus, postcentral gyrus, and inferior parietal gyrus.

The left inferior prefrontal cortex (LIPC) has been reported to be closely related to reading. Neuroimaging studies have provided evidence that the left frontal region is active during a wide range of language tasks, including those that do not involve overt production of speech (see Gabrieli, Poldrack & Desmond, 1998, for review). Recent neuroimaging studies provided some evidence that this classical Broca's area mediates storage of verbal information (Fiez & Petersen, 1998; Smith & Jonides, 1998). It seems that LIPC is involved in both semantic processing (e.g., Demb, Desmond, Wagner, Vaidya, Glover, & Gabriele, 1995) and phonological processing (e.g., Pugh, Shaywitz, Shaywitz, Constable, Skudlarski, Fulbright, Bronen, Shankweiler, Katz, Fletcher, & Gore,

1996). Poldrack, Wagner, Prull, Desmond, Glover, and Gabriele (1999) suggested that a distinct region in the left inferior frontal cortex (BA47) also is involved in semantic processing, whereas other regions in this area may subserve phonological processes engaged during both semantic and phonological tasks.

Consistent with this, we observed activations in left inferior frontal areas (both BA47 and BA44/45) for both Chinese character and Pinyin reading. In line with previous studies, we suggest that the BA44/45 activation may be related to the phonological processing of stimuli (e.g., subvocal rehearsal and phonological storage), whereas the BA47 activation may be related to the semantic decision processing.

Although the activations in inferior frontal gyrus were left dominant, there are right-sided activations in these regions in both Chinese character reading and Pinyin reading tasks. Where previous studies also have reported the right inferior frontal activations in semantic (e.g., Wagner et al., 1998) and phonological processing (e.g., Pugh et al., 1996), the right and left hemispheres may play distinct roles. Pugh, Shaywitz, Shaywitz, Shankweiler, Katz, Fletcher, Skudlarski, Fulbright, Constable, Bronen, Lacadie, and Gore (1997) suggested that the two hemispheres may differ in the 'grain size' of their processing. Poldrack et al. (1999) suggest that the grain size of phonological processing in the right hemisphere may be larger than a single phoneme, since significant right hemisphere activation was found during performance of a task that required attention to larger phonological features. Consistent with this, we found that the processing of both Chinese characters (whose pronunciation is based on the whole character and usually has 1–2 syllables in its pronunciation) and Pinyin gave significant right hemispheric activation, suggesting that the right hemisphere may process phonological units larger than a single phoneme.

Figure 1. Examples of stimuli that were used in the present study. The corresponding Chinese words and their meaning in English were also shown under the CH and PY that sounds like a word.

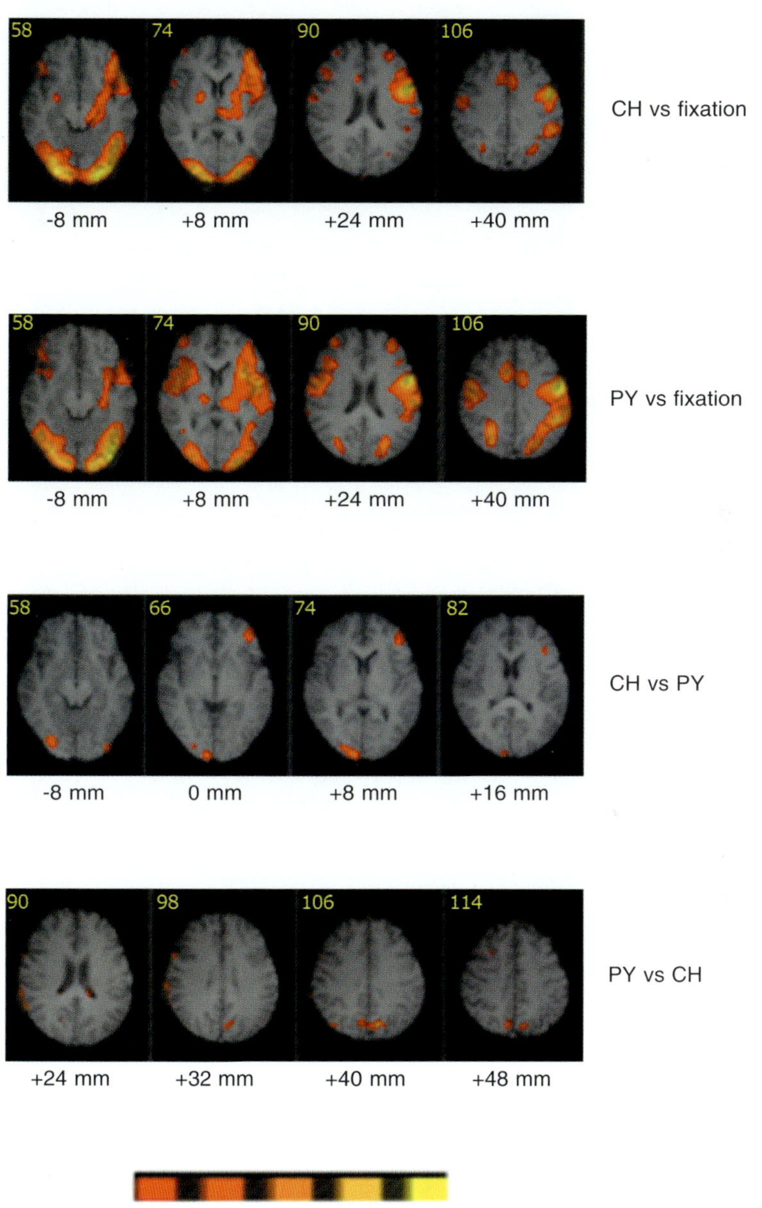

Figure 2. Brain activation maps that were obtained during CH vs. fixation, PY vs. fixation, CH vs. PY, and PY vs. CH. All of the maps are transformed into Talairach space and are overlaid on the Talairached structural image. The right sides of the slices represent the left sides of the brain.

Caplan (1989) proposed that right hemisphere processing is required when the task demands are high, as in our task (which had reaction times of as long as 3–4 seconds).

The anterior cingulate (ACC) previously has been associated with selective attention, attention-to-action, and executive functions (Pardo, Pardo, Janer, & Raichle, 1990; Posner & Petersen, 1990). In particular, this ACC region appears to be active in task situations where there is a need to override a prepotent response tendency, when responding is underdetermined, and when errors are made. Barch, Braver, Sabb, and Noll (2000) have hypothesized that the ACC serves to evaluate the demand or need for cognitive control by monitoring for the occurrence of conflict or crosstalk in information processing (Carter, Braver, Barch, Botvinick, Noll & Cohen, 1998). In our study, this ACC activation was observed in both Chinese character reading and Pinyin reading relative to fixation task, which can be accounted by greater demands on attentional resources for the high demanding semantic decision task (Posner, Petersen, Fox, & Raichle, 1988; Raichle, Fiez, Videen, MacLeod, Pardo, Fox, & Petersen, 1994). The present study provides no evidence for whether this ACC activation is specific to phonological processing or semantic processing, whether ACC is supplying or regulating the control function itself (e.g., Posner & Petersen, 1990), or whether ACC is monitoring or evaluating the cognitive control (e.g., Barch et al., 2000), however.

Both Chinese character and Pinyin reading activated bilateral fusiform, lingual and inferior occipital gyrus. Petersen, Fox, Snyder, & Raichle (1990) associated the visual word form system with the left medial extrastriate cortex. However, this medial occipital cortex activation can be accounted by string length, suggesting that it is not specific for word-like stimuli (Indefrey, Kleinschmidt, Merboldt, Kruger, Brown, Hagoort, & Frahm, 1997). Moreover, Tagamets et al. (2000) even suggested that there is no specific region for real words relative to pseudo-words. The present study shows that the activations in lingual gyrus and inferior occipital gyrus were stronger in the left hemisphere for both Chinese character reading and Pinyin reading relative to fixation task. Since the lingual gyrus and inferior occipital gyrus were activated in Pinyin reading and Pinyins themselves are not the real words in Chinese, we suggest that these areas are not the candidates for visual word form system of Chinese characters (note that although the two characters did not consist of a real word, they are real characters themselves). The activations in these areas may be generated by visual attention differences in reading relative to fixation condition and/or visual analysis differences. Further studies are needed in which the visual attributes (size, luminance, complexity, etc) are better controlled between the experimental condition (e.g., real words) and control (e.g., false fonts) in order to explore further the nature of orthographic processing of Chinese characters and Pinyin.

A PET study (Paulesu, Frith, & Frackowiak, 1993) identified area 44, the superior temporal gyri (BA 22/42), the supramarginal gyri (BA40) and the insula as forming the 'phonological, or articulatory, loop', which subserves the ability to repeat words in one's head. Left frontal and SMA (supplementary motor cortex) activity have been consistently activated in tasks thought to involve inner speech (Frith, Friston, Liddle, & Frackowiak, 1991; Wise, Chollet, Hadar, Friston, Hoffner, & Frackowiak, 1991; Demonet, Chollet, Ramsay, Cardebat, Nespoulous, Wise, Rascol, & Frackowiak, 1992; Paulesu et al., 1993). In our task, subjects had to 'sound out' silently first before they could decide whether the Chinese characters or Pinyins 'sound like' real words, since neither Chinese characters nor Pinyins 'look like' real Chinese words. Therefore, the decisions were based on the phonological characteristics of the stimulus rather than on the visual word forms. Similar to these studies, we observed left frontal and SMA/pre-SMA activations in both CH reading and PY reading relative to fixation task. We also observed left superior temporal and supramarginal gyrus activations in both Chinese character reading and Pinyin reading tasks, which confirms the important role of these two areas in phonological processing of reading.

Some brain areas were activated more during Chinese character reading than Pinyin reading. The contrast between CH and PY can provide us important hints on the brain areas differently involved in processing these two scripts. The results suggest that cerebellum is involved in processing both scripts with different parts preferentially processing with PY or CH. The cerebellum activation was strongly left dominant for CH reading relative to PY reading, suggesting the important role of left cerebellum in Chinese characters reading relative to Pinyin reading.

Different parts of inferior frontal gyrus were activated in processing CH and PY. The left inferior frontal areas that are activated more during CH reading are near BA9 and BA46, whereas the areas that activated more during PY reading are at right hemisphere near BA9.

The processing of CH also activated the right fusiform gyrus, right cuneus, and bilateral inferior occipital gyrus, which are often related to orthographic processing of the stimuli. This suggests that the orthographic processing of Chinese character involves stronger right visual and visual association area activations than the orthographic processing of Pinyin.

Some right parietal areas, including right inferior parietal gyrus, right superior parietal lobule, were activated more during PY reading than during CH reading. The activation in the right inferior parietal gyrus is corresponding to BA40, which is probably related to the letter by letter processing of Pinyin. The supramarginal gyrus activation has been reported by some phonological processing studies. The superior parietal lobule has been reported to be very important for Japanese kana (syllabogram) mirror-reading as compared with normal reading (Dong, Fukuyama, Honda, Okada, Hanakawa, Nakamura, Nagahama, Nagamine, Konishi, & Shibasaki, 2000), since visuospatial transformations might be required to recognize the mirror-reversed kana. In the present study, however, we observed right superior parietal lobule activations for Pinyin reading relative to Chinese character reading, without the needs of doing visuospatial transformations as that involved in mirror reading. One possibility is that this activation could be associated with greater eye movements in the Pinyin reading task, since they need to do letter-by-letter spelling to Pinyin, whereas they can access the phonology of Chinese character on the whole character level. This explanation seems unlikely, however, because the execution and suppression of eye movements involve bilateral frontal eye fields and superior parietal lobules, whereas there are only superior parietal lobule and near frontal eye field activations in the right hemisphere.

Conclusion

FMRI is a promising tool for the analysis of the functional organisation of language in the brain. Applications to the study of the Chinese language already have provided information suggesting that the surface form of the written language appears to make remarkably small differences in the pattern of brain activation. This suggests that lexical, semantic, and phonological processing dominate language processing. In searching for unique, language form-specific aspects of processing, primary attention therefore perhaps should be focused on 'mediation' or sensory pathways.

References

Barch, D. M., Braver, T. S., Sabb, F. W., & Noll, D. C. (2000). Anterior cingulate and the monitoring of response conflict: Evidence from an fMRI study of overt verb generation. *Journal of Cognitive Neuroscience, 12,* 298–309.

Binder, J. R., Frost, J. A., Hammeke, T. A., Bellgowan, P. S., Rao, S. M., & Cox, R. W. (1999) Conceptual processing during the conscious resting state. A functional MRI study. *Journal of Cognitive Neuroscience, 11,* 80–95.

Binder, J. R., Frost, J. A., Hammeke, T. A., Cox, R. W., Rao, S. M., & Prieto, T. (1997) Human brain language areas identified by functional magnetic resonance imaging. *Journal of Neuroscience, 17,* 353–362.

Buckner, R. L. (1998) Event-related fMRI and the hemodynamic response. *Human Brain Mapping, 6,* 373–377.

Buckner, R. L., Raichle, M. E., & Petersen, S. E. (1995) Dissociation of human prefrontal cortical areas across different speech production tasks and gender groups. *Journal of Neurophysiology, 74,* 2163–2173.

Burock, M. A., Buckner, R. L., Woldorff, M. G., Rosen, B. R., & Dale, A. M. (1998) Randomized event-related experimental designs allow for extremely rapid presentation rates using functional MRI. *Neuroreport, 9,* 3735–3739.

Calvert, G. A., Bullmore, E. T., Brammer, M. J., Campbell, R, Williams, S. C., Mcguire, P. K., Woodruff, P. W. R., Iversen, S. D., & David, A. S. (1997) Activation of auditory cortex during silent lipreading. *Science, 276,* 593–596.

Caplan, D. (1989). *Neurolinguistics and linguistic aphasiology: An introduction.* New York: Cambridge University Press.

Carter, C. S., Braver, T. S., Barch, D. M., Botvinick, M. M., Noll, D., & Cohen, J. D. (1998). Anterior cingulate cortex, error detection, and the online monitoring of performance. *Science, 280,* 747–749.

Chee, M. W, L., Caplan, D., Soon, C. S., Sriram, N., Tan, E. W., Thiel, T., & Weekes, B. (1999) Processing of visually presented sentences in Mandarin and English studied with fMRI. *Neuron, 23,* 127–137.

Chee, M. W. L., Tan, E., & Thiel, T. (1999). Mandarin and English single word processing studied with functional magnetic resonance imaging. *Journal of Neuroscience, 19,* 3050–3056.

Damasio, A. R., & Damasio, H. (1992). Brain and language. *Scientic American, 267,* 88–95.

Demb, J. B., Desmond, J. E., Wagner, A. D., Vaidya, C. T., Glover, G. H., & Gabriele, J. D. E. (1995). Semantic encoding and retrieval in the left inferior prefrontal cortex: a functional MRI study of task difficulty and process specificity. *Journal of Neuroscience, 15,* 5870–5878.

Demonet, J. F., Chollet, F., Ramsay, S., Cardebat, D., Nespoulous, J. N., Wise, R., Rascol, A., & Frackowiak, R. (1992). The anatomy of phonological and semantic processing in normal subjects. *Brain, 115,* 1753–1768.

Dong, Y., Fukuyama, H., Honda, M., Okada, T., Hanakawa, T., Nakamura, K., Nagahama, Y., Nagamine, T., Konishi, J., & Shibasaki, H. (2000). Essential role of the right superior parietal cortex in Japanese kana mirror reading: An fMRI study. *Brain, 123,* 790–799.

Fiez, J. A., & Petersen, S. E. (1998). Neuroimaging studies of word reading. *Proceedings of National Academic Sciences, USA, 95,* 914–921.

Frith, C. D., Friston, K., Liddle, P. F., & Frackowiak, R. S. J. (1991). Willed action and the prefrontal cortex in man: A study with PET. *Proceedings of the Royal Society of London, 244,* 241–246.

Gabrieli, J. D. E., Poldrack, R. A., & Desmond, J. E. (1998). The role of left prefrontal cortex in language and memory. *Proceedings of the National Academy of Sciences, USA, 95,* 906–913.

Indefrey, P., Kleinschmidt, A., Merboldt, K. D., Kruger, G., Brown, C., Hagoort, P., & Frahm, J. (1997). Equivalent responses to lexical and nonlexical visual stimuli in occipital cortex: A functional magnetic resonance imaging study. *Neuroimage, 5,* 78–81.

Kansaku, K., Shimoyama, I., Nakajima, Y., Higuchi, Y., Nakazaki, S., Kubota, M. et al. (1998). Functional magnetic resonance imaging during recognition of written words: Chinese characters for concrete objects versus abstract concepts. Republished, with corrections, *Neurosciences Research 30,* 361–364. First published in *Neurosciences Research, 30*(1), 83–86.

Kim, D. S., Duong, T. Q., & Kim, S. G. (2000) High-resolution mapping of iso-orientation columns by fMRI [see comments]. *Nature Neuroscience, 3,* 164–169.

Kim, K. H., Relkin, N. R., Lee, K. M., & Hirsch, J. (1997). Distinct cortical areas associated with native and second languages. *Nature, 388,* 171–174.

Matthews, P. M., Clare, S., & Adcock, J. (1999). Functional magnetic resonance imaging: clinical applications and potential. *Journal of Inherited Metabolic Disease, 22,* 337–352.

McKeown, M. J., Makeig, S., Brown, G. G., Jung, T. P., Kindermann, S. S., & Bell, A. J., et al. (1998). Analysis of fMRI data by blind separation into independent spatial components. *Human Brain Mapping, 6,* 160–188.

Neville, H. J., Bavelier, D., Corina, D., Rauschecker, J., Karni, A., Lalwani, A., Braun, A., Clark, V., Jezzard, P., & Turner, R. (1998) Cerebral organization for language in deaf and hearing subjects: Biological constraints and effects of experience. *Proceedings of the National Academy of Sciences, USA, 95,* 922–929.

Ogawa, S., Lee, T. M., Kay, A. R., & Tank, D. W. (1990) Brain magnetic resonance imaging with contrast dependent on blood oxygenation. *Proceedings of the National Academy of Sciences, USA, 87*(24), 9868–9872.

Pardo, J. V., Pardo, P. J., Janer, K. W., & Raichle, M. E. (1990). The anterior cingulate cortex mediates processing selection in the stroop attentional conflict paradigm. *Proceedings of the National Academy of Sciences, USA,* *87,* 256–259.

Paulesu, E., Frith, C. D., & Frackowiak, R. S. J. (1993). The neural correlates of the verbal component of working memory. *Nature, 362,* 342–345.

Petersen, S. E., Fox, P. T., Posner, M. I., Mintun, M. A., & Raichle, M. E. (1989). Positron emission tomographic studies of the processing of single words. *Journal of Cognitive Neuroscience, 1,* 153–170.

Petersen, S. E., Fox, P. T., Posner, M. I., Mintun, M. A., & Raichle, M. E. (1995) Positron emission tomography studies of the cortical anatomy of single-word processing. *Nature, 331,* 585–589.

Petersen, S. E., Fox, P. T., Synder, A. Z., & Raichle, M. E. (1990). Activation of extrastriate and frontal cortical areas by words and word-like stimuli. *Science, 249,* 1041–1044.

Poldrack, R. A., Wagner, A. D., Prull, M. W., Desmond, J. E., Glover, G. H., & Gabrieli, J. D. E. (1999). Functional specialization for semantic and phonological processing in the left inferior prefrontal cortex. *NeuroImage, 10,* 15–35.

Posner, M. I., & Petersen, S. E. (1990). The attention system of the human brain. *Annual Review of Neurosciences, 13,* 25–42.

Posner, M. I., Petersen, S. E., Fox, P. T., & Raichle, M. E. (1988). Localization of cognitive operations in the human brain. *Science, 240,* 1627–1631.

Pugh, K. R., Shaywitz, B. A., Shaywitz, S. E., Constable, R. T., Skudlarski, P., Fulbright, R. A., Bronen, Shankweiler, D., P., Katz, L., Fletcher, J. M., & Gore, J. C. (1996). Cerebral organization of component processes in reading. *Brain, 119,* 1221–1238.

Pugh, K. R., Shaywitz, B. A., Shaywitz, S. E., Shankweiler, D. P., Katz, L., Fletcher, J. M., Skudlarski, P., Fulbright, R. K., Constable, R. T., Bronen, R. A., Lacadie, C., & Gore, J. C. (1997) Predicting reading performance from neuroimaging profiles: the cerebral basis of phonological effects in printed word identification. *Journal of Experimental Psychology: Human Perception and Performance, 23,* 299–318.

Raichle, M. E., Fiez, J. A., Videen, T. O., MacLeod, A. M. K., Pardo, J. V., Fox, P. T., & Petersen, S. E. (1994). Practice-related changes in human brain functional anatomy during nonmotor learning. *Cerebral Cortex, 4,* 8–26.

Shaywitz, B. A., Shaywitz, S. E., Pugh, K. R., Constable, R. T., Skudlarski, P., & Fulbright, R. K., et al. (1995) Sex differences in the functional organization of the brain for language [see comments]. *Nature, 373,* 607–9.

Smith, E. E., & Jonides, J. (1998). Neuroimaging analyses of human working memory. *Proceedings of the National Academy of Sciences, USA, 95,* 12061–12068.

Tagamets, M.-A., Novick, J. M., Chalmers, M. I., & Friedman, R. B. (2000). A parametric approach to orthographic processing in the brain: An fMRI study. *Journal of Cognitive Neuroscience, 12,* 281–297.

Talairach, J., & Tournoux, P. (1988). *Co-planar stereotactic atlas of the human brain.* Translated by Mark Rayport. New York: Thieme Medical.

Tan, L. H., Spinks, J. A., Gao, J. H., Liu, H. L., Perfetti, C. A., Xiong, J., Pu, Y., Liu, Y., Stofer, K. A., & Fox, P. T. (2000). Brain activation in the processing of Chinese characters and words: a functional MRI study. *Human Brain Mapping, 10,* 27–39.

Thulborn, K. R., Carpenter, P. A., & Just, M. A. (1999). Plasticity of language-related brain function during recovery from stroke. *Stroke, 30,* 749–754.

Thulborn, K. R., Waterton, J. C., Matthews, P. M., & Radda, G. K. (1982). Oxygenation dependence of the transverse relaxation time of water protons in whole blood at high field. *Biochimica et Biophysica Acta, 714,* 265–270.

Villringer, A., & Dirnagl, U. (1995). Coupling of brain activity and cerebral blood flow: basis of functional neuroimaging. *Cerebrovascular Brain Metabolism Review, 7,* 240–276.

Wagner, A. D., Desmond, J. E., Glover, G., & Gabrieli, J. D. E. (1998). Prefrontal cortex and recognition memory: fMRI evidence for context-dependent retrieval processes. *Brain, 121,* 1985–2002.

Wise, R., Chollet, F., Hadar, U., Friston, K., Hoffner, E., & Frackowiak, R. (1991). Distribution of cortical neural networks involved in word comprehension and word retrieval. *Brain, 114,* 1803–1817.

Zatorre, R. J., Evans, A. C., Meyer, E., & Gjedde, A. (1992) Lateralization of phonetic and pitch discrimination in speech processing. *Science, 256,* 846–849.

Author Note

The authors thank the BBSRC (UK) and the MRC (UK) for generous support of their studies of the Chinese language using fMRI.

Endnotes

1. FMRIB: Oxford Centre for the Functional Magnetic Resonance Imaging of the Brain.
2. MEDx: multi-modality image processing and analysis software for medical imaging research (Sensor Systems, USA).
3. AIR: Automated Image Registration.

Emergent Semantic Structure and Language Acquisition: A Dynamic Perspective

Ping Li

The representation of language has been traditionally considered as a construction out of basic structural building blocks in the form of symbols and rules. This approach tends to look at linguistic representations statically. A contrasting approach, in the spirit of recent developments in connectionist networks and statistical learning, attempts to capture linguistic representations dynamically. It considers linguistic representations as emergent properties that evolve out of a continuously developing and adapting system. An easy way to understand this latter approach is to consider how a hexagonal shape emerges from the honeycomb: every honeybee packs a small amount of honey to the honeycomb from multiple angles, but no honeybee has a grand plan (or a genetically determined rule) for making the hexagonal structure (Bates, 1984).

This chapter will provide a dynamic perspective from connectionist and statistical approaches to examine language acquisition, in particular, the acquisition of semantic structure. I will first discuss empirical problems, and then theoretical perspectives.

The Acquisition of Tense-Aspect Morphology

The last twenty years have witnessed a large amount of research on the acquisition of tense-aspect morphology in connection with the acquisition of semantic categories (Slobin, 1985, 1992). These studies have investigated children learning Chinese (Erbaugh, 1978; Li, 1990, 1993a), English (Bloom, Lifter, & Hafitz, 1980; Brown, 1973; Harner, 1981), French (Bronckart & Sinclair, 1973), German (Behrens, 1993), Italian (Antinucci & Miller, 1976), Japanese (Shirai, 1993), Turkish (Aksu, 1978), among other languages.

One robust finding from these studies is that young children seem to associate tense-aspect markers initially with a set of verbs that encode particular lexical aspect properties. This is typically characterized by children's early use of past tense (e.g., the English *-ed*) or perfective aspect (e.g., the Chinese *-le*) to comment on an immediately completed event that results in a visible change of state (Brown, 1973; Slobin, 1985). For example, in English, Bloom et al. (1980) found that the distribution of children's use of tense and aspect markers is correlated with different semantic categories. In particular, between the ages of 1 year and 10 months, and 2 years and 4 months, *-ed* and irregular past tense forms occur overwhelmingly with verbs that name non-durative, completive events, i.e., events 'with a relatively clear result' such as *find*, *fall*, and *break*. In contrast to the past or perfective markers, progressive markers (e.g., *-ing*) occur in children's utterances almost exclusively with 'process-oriented' action verbs that name durative, non-completive events such as *play*, *ride*, and *write*. In Chinese, Li (1990, 1993a) conducted three experiments to test the significance of this 'result-process' distinction in children's acquisition of aspect markers between ages 3 and 6. The comprehension experiment reveals that children understand the perfective marker *-le* better with resultative verbs and the imperfective marker *zai* better with process verbs. The production experiment shows that there is a strong association between perfective aspect and resultative verbs and between imperfective aspect and process verbs in children's productive speech. The imitation experiment indicates that children repeat sentences with the perfective marker *-le* significantly better than those with the imperfective marker *zai* when the verb is resultative.

How do researchers interpret robust cross-linguistic findings of this type? These results, along with results from other languages, suggest that children initially focus on particular semantic properties of the lexical aspect (i.e., the inherent meanings of verbs), and associate these properties with the use of particular grammatical tense-aspect morphology. Slobin (1985), on the basis of some of these findings, proposed that *result*, together with its complementary notion *process*, constitute two basic temporal perspectives of the Basic Child Grammar (BCG). According to the BCG, children come to the language acquisition task with a pre-structured 'semantic space' containing a universal, uniform set of semantic notions that are at first neutral with respect to language-specific categories. These semantic notions are 'privileged' to be mapped onto grammatical forms of individual languages in the process of language acquisition. That is, prior to children's experience with specific properties of the grammar, these notions strongly attract grammatical forms of the input language in the form-meaning mapping processes. The temporal perspectives such as *result* and *process* would thus function early to define a semantic contrast in children's learning of tense and aspect systems.

In contrast to the BCG hypothesis, more recently, Li and Shirai (2000) have argued that the child's early associations between lexical meanings of verbs and grammatical morphology do not indicate pre-linguistic specifications of semantic categories. They systematically compared the acquisition of aspect and verb semantics in three languages: Chinese, English, and Japanese, and proposed that these associations reflect the learner's sensitivity to (and recognition of) the statistical properties of the input speech, which in turn reflect inherent constraints on language communication and event characteristics. Along this argument, in this chapter I will provide a feature-based, connectionist account of the cross-linguistic data, in contrast to the BCG hypothesis. Unlike proposals that place strong emphasis on innate specifications, our account provides a dynamic, emergentist explanation of the empirical patterns with particular reference to learning mechanisms.

High-dimensional semantic space and lexical semantic representation

To what extent can the learner extract word meanings from the input speech? Theories that emphasize the innate role of semantic categories such as the BCG or the semantic bootstrapping hypothesis (Pinker, 1987) would consider input information neither necessary nor sufficient for the establishment of semantic categories. However, a number of recent computational studies have examined the emergence of lexical representations in connectionist networks or similar statistical systems, suggesting that word meaning can be learned by the computation of statistical regularities inherent in the input data. In particular, Elman (1990, 1998) showed that categories of nouns and verbs, and subcategories of animates versus inanimates (within nouns) and transitives versus intransitives (within verbs), can emerge from the network's computing of lexical co-occurrence properties in a task of predicting what word will occur next in a sentence. Redington, Chater, and Finch (1998) also demonstrated that the use of distributional properties in large-scale speech corpus allows a statistical system to acquire basic syntactic categories. These studies are in many ways consistent with the empirical approach of distributional analysis of the linguistic input, as advocated by Maratsos and Chalkley (1980), among many others. They have revealed the power of distributional information in the input, and revived the interest in how the child uses linguistic input to derive accurate representations of the syntax and semantics of words.

One particularly relevant model in this context is the Hyperspace Analogue to Language (HAL) model (Burgess & Lund, 1997, 1999). According to HAL, the meaning and function of a given word is determined by lexical co-occurrence constraints in a high-dimensional space, that is, by what items may precede a word and what may follow it, and how often they do so. HAL focuses on global rather than local lexical co-occurrences: A word is anchored with reference not only to other words immediately preceding or following it, but also to words that are further away from it in a variable co-occurrence window, with each slot (occurrence of a word) in the window acting as a constraint dimension to define the meaning and function of the target word. Global lexical co-occurrence is a measure of a word's *total experience* in the context of other words. Word meanings, in this perspective, emerge from multiple constraints in a high-dimensional space of language use.

The original HAL model makes no specific claim about how word meanings are acquired in the learning process. Recently, however, Li, Burgess, and Lund (2000) have examined the role of global lexical co-occurrence constraints in the child's induction of word meanings. Our results are consistent with the syntactic bootstrapping hypothesis (Gleitman, 1990), according to which young children can explore the grammatical context in which a word occurs in the initial mapping of word meanings. The basic assumption of Gleitman's hypothesis is that certain classes of words typically occur in certain syntactic frames and grammatical structures, and the information of these frames and structures provides a useful initial guide to the child as to what the word could mean.

There is a debate, however, in the extent to which syntactic bootstrapping is sufficient for the child in learning word meanings. Pinker (1994) argued that syntactic bootstrapping suffers from the problem of allowing the learner to identify only kinds of meaning (*frame meaning*) and not semantic contents (*root meaning*). This is because syntactically similar words like *tear* and *break* occur in more or less the same syntactic frames but their semantic contents are different. Thus, if the child uses only syntactic bootstrapping, he or she would not be able to distinguish the meanings of words like *tear* and *break*. Indeed, this could be a problem for the learner, if the learner is concerned with the grammatical or contextual constraints only in the immediate environment of the target word: for example, direct objects, complement clauses, and prepositional phrases as the syntactic bootstrapping hypothesis stipulates for verbs. In the global lexical co-occurrence perspective of HAL, as outlined above, the learner would not have this problem: *tear* tends to co-occur with words like *paper*, *apart*, and *shreds* in a sentence, while *break* tends to co-occur with words like *cup*, *glass*, *pieces*, *window* and *toy*. Global lexical co-occurrence provides the contextual history that effectively defines the meaning and functions of words. Young children may very well explore this type of contextual history at early stages of semantic acquisition. Later in this chapter, I will present a connectionist model that incorporates global lexical co-occurrences in the acquisition of word meanings and show that such a model can indeed arrive at accurate semantic representations.

Emergent Semantic Structure and Language Acquisition

A connectionist perspective on the acquisition of tense-aspect categories

In this section, I return to the problem of the acquisition of tense-aspect morphology, as introduced earlier. In particular, I will discuss how a connectionist network can acquire semantic structures along with morphology, and display patterns of acquisition as children do. Such a network would suggest mechanisms of learning that are responsible for the empirical data observed. Connectionist models rely on the use of massively connected micro-processing units (neurons) that activate in parallel and adjust weights of connection through learning and processing. In contrast to discrete symbols and crispy learning rules, connectionist networks represent knowledge as distributed patterns of activation, and use non-linear probabilistic learning rules. The simple idea behind these networks is that individual processing units take care of micro-features of a concept or an action, while the joint forces of these units handle the grand scheme, provided that the units in the network are connected with appropriate weights in a non-linear fashion. Through detecting regularities in the input-output mapping processes, these networks demonstrate capabilities in inducing structures inherent in the learning data.

Connectionist principles of distributed representation, weight adjustment, and non-linear learning provide a mechanistic account of how syntactic and semantic structures emerge out of learning. Li (1993b) and Li and MacWhinney (1996) discussed more explicitly how a connectionist network develops internal representations of semantic structures (see also Li, in press-a for a summary of this approach). Using the acquisition of the English reversative prefix *un-* as an example, we examined the role of cryptotypes (covert, subtle semantic categories) in governing overgeneralization patterns in morphological acquisition. We proposed that semantic categories such as the *un-* cryptotype — the verb classes associated with the use of the English reversative prefix *un-* (Whorf, 1956; Bowerman, 1982), emerge out of the network's learning of multiple semantic features. In the acquisition of a semantic category, the feature-to-category relationship can vary in (a) how many features are relevant to category membership, (b) how strongly each feature is activated in the representation of the category, and (c) how features overlap with each other across category members. Traditional symbolic analyses are much less effective if not impossible to deal with these kinds of complex relationships. In a connectionist system, multiple features connected in a network support the formation of a semantic category. This idea is illustrated in Figure 1. The simulations showed that structured semantic representations develop from connectionist learning: the network forms internal representations of semantic categories that correspond to the *un-* cryptotype, on the basis of learning limited semantic features of verbs and morphological classes. In addition, the network produces overgeneralization errors similar to those observed in empirical data, indicating that emergent semantic structures underlie patterns of productivity in language acquisition (Bowerman, 1982, 1988; Clark, Carpenter, & Deutsch, 1995).

In Li (in press-b) and Li and Bowerman (1998), we applied this perspective to examine the acquisition of lexical and grammatical aspect in Chinese. We analysed how patterns of verb meaning and aspect

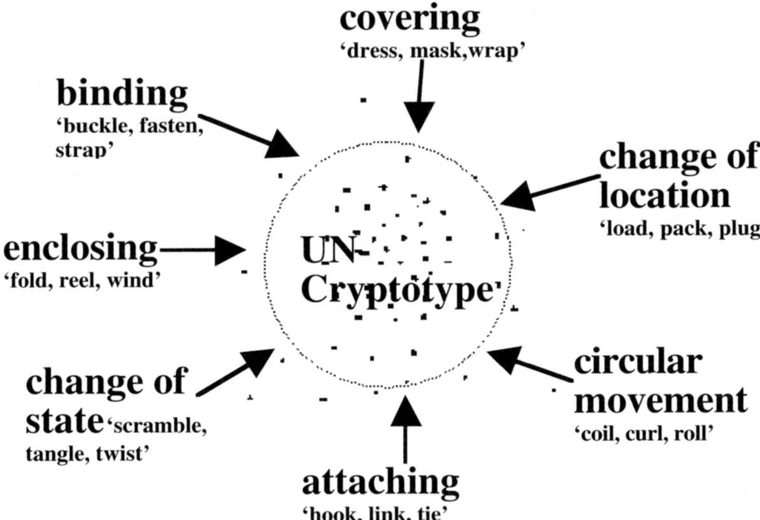

Figure 1. Multiple features support the formation of the *un-* cryptotype. Arrows represent the feature-to-category connection; the weights or strengths of connection are not shown here. Dots in the center of the circle represent words that fit the core of the cryptotype, while dots near the border of the circle represent borderline cases.

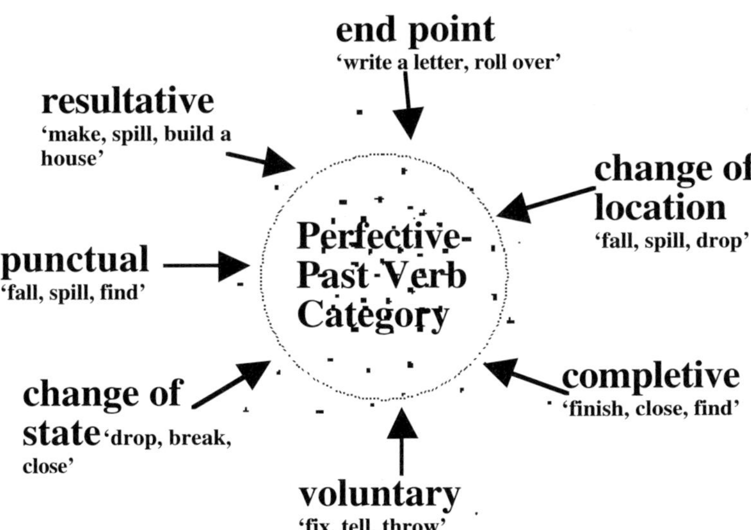

Figure 2. Multiple features support the formation of a lexical aspect category, which licenses the use of the past-perfective forms.

associations could arise from the learner's sensitivity to the linguistic input. We proposed that semantic features such as 'endpoint', 'result', and 'punctual' can interact collaboratively, in much the same way as in the case of cryptotypes, through summed activation to support the formation of a past/perfective aspectual category that licenses the use of past or perfective forms (e.g., English *-ed* or Chinese *-le*). This idea is illustrated in Figure 2. These features collaborate in the sense that a given verb can be represented with multiple features, and the features themselves often co-occur in the situations to which the verb applies. For example, *spill* may be viewed as indicating both a punctual and a resultative meaning; *close* may involve both a change of state and a completive meaning; and *build a house* implies both an end point and an end result. A feature may also vary in the strength with which it is represented in different verbs. For example, the feature 'punctual' may be represented more strongly in *jump* than in *fall*: in a natural setting a single jump occurs instantaneously, whereas falling needs not (e.g., we could still say that a leaf fell from a tree even if it drifted down slowly). With varying degrees of connections from semantic features to verb forms, verbs can form clusters or categories that differ overall in lexical semantic aspect. A distributed network representation of these features is necessary to accommodate the complex relationships inherent in the semantics of verb aspect, just as in the case of the *un-* cryptotype discussed earlier. In short, it is the relationships between the features that give rise to the category.

For the child, then, the learning of the past-perfective forms such as *-ed* in English or *-le* in Chinese is not simply the learning of a rule such as adding *-ed* or *-le* to a given set of verbs, but the accumulation of the connection strengths that hold between *-ed* or *-le* and a complex set of semantic features distributed across verbs. Within this scenario, the learning process is best described as a statistical process in which the learner implicitly tallies and registers the frequency of co-occurrences of a tense-aspect morpheme such as *-ed* or *-le* with a particular set of verbs that have particular features. Because the past-perfective category is supported by a composite set of features from many verbs that take *-ed* or *-le* in the input (see Brown, 1973), children will establish a prototype of the category and build strong connection between the prototype and the *-ed* or *-le* form. The result of this process is that they will initially use the *-ed* or *-le* form only with verbs that fall typically within the category. This explains the strong association that we found in Chinese, English, and many other languages as described in the beginning of this chapter.

More recently, we developed a self-organizing connectionist network to model the acquisition of tense and aspect (see Li, 1999 for a discussion of this model; Li, 2000 and Li & Shirai, 2000, for detailed application of the model to tense-aspect acquisition). Self-organizing networks are psychologically more plausible as models of language acquisition because they use unsupervised learning – in the natural setting, language acquisition (especially organization and reorganization of the lexicon) is largely a self-organizing process that proceeds without explicit teaching. In contrast to the classical connectionist models (i.e., back-propagation networks), self-organizing networks do not require the presence of a supervisor or an explicit teacher; learning is achieved entirely by the system's self-organization in response to the input. Self-organization in these networks typically occurs in a two-dimensional map (a self-organizing map, or SOM; Kohonen, 1982, 1989), where each processing unit in the network is a location on the map that can uniquely represent one or several input patterns. At the beginning of learning, an input pattern randomly activates one of the many units on the map. Once a unit becomes active in response to a given input, the weights to the unit and its neighboring units are adjusted such that they become more similar to the input and will therefore respond to the same or similar inputs more strongly the next time. This process continues until all the inputs can elicit specific response patterns in the network. As a result of this self-organizing process, the network gradually develops concentrated areas of units on the map (the so-called activity bubbles) that capture input similarities, and the statistical structures implicit in the high-dimensional space of the input are preserved on a two-dimensional space in the map.

We used a self-organizing model as illustrated in Figure 3 in our simulation. This model is similar to the one implemented by Miikkulainen (1997), who combined multiple (phonological, orthographic, and semantic) maps in a single network. In our model there is currently no orthographic map, because we are modeling lexical semantic development in young children who are pre-literate. As shown in Figure 3, the model consists of a lexical (phonological) map that processes phonological information of words (SOM1), and a semantic map that processes semantic information (SOM2). The two maps are connected via Hebbian learning (Hebb, 1949), according to which the associative strength between two units is increased if the units are both active at the same time. Upon training of the network, a phonological representation of the verb is presented to the network, and simultaneously, the semantic representation of the same verb is also presented to the network. By way of self-organization, the network forms an activity on the phonological

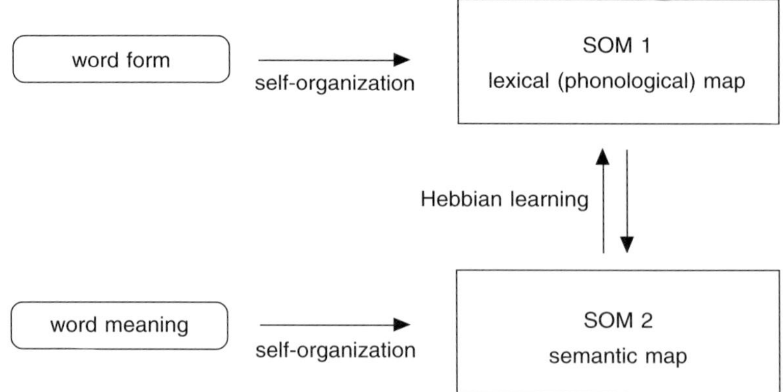

Figure 3.   A self-organizing feature-map model of the acquisition of the lexicon

map in response to the phonological input, and an activity on the semantic map in response to the semantic input. At the same time, through Hebbian learning the network forms associations between the two maps for all the active units that respond to the input.

In applying this model to the simulation of tense-aspect acquisition, we used the parental input speech in the CHILDES (Child Language Data Exchange System) database (MacWhinney, 2000) to determine the co-occurrence frequency of each verb with the three morphological markers: *-ed*, *-ing*, or *-s* that indicate perfective, progressive, and habitual aspect, respectively. An important finding from our simulation is that the morphological uses of *-ing* and *-ed* are constrained by the semantic structure that the network develops (i.e., using *-ing* with atelic verbs only and *-ed* with telic verbs only, consistent with empirical observations in child language). The semantic structure emerges in the SOM map as a result of the networks' continuous organization on the structural similarities inherent in the lexicon. After learning, the telic vs. atelic verbs are clearly separated by the network (see Li, 2000 for simulation details). The results match up nicely with our previous work on semantic cryptotypes and the overgeneralization of prefixes, whereby the network identifies the cryptotype that covers many *un-* verbs (*unclench*, *unlock*, *untie*), and generalizes the use of *un-* to other instances on the basis of semantic similarity (e.g., **unsqueeze*). Thus, the semantic categories developed by SOM 'dictate' which morphological marker a verb is to take (and in the case of new verbs, which direction the generalization is to go), due to strong associative links established between form and meaning. These results show that self-organizing neural networks can be used successfully to model and to provide insights into the acquisition of lexical and grammatical aspect, with respect to issues of the role of linguistic input, the representation of semantic structure of verbs, and the development of associations between lexical and grammatical aspect.

To summarize, in this section I have shown how semantic structures of the lexicon can emerge from learning in connectionist networks, and how the emergence of such structures underlies the acquisition of tense-aspect morphology. The results serve to illustrate that it is important for us to consider mechanisms of learning before we appeal to innate specifications for the existence of semantic structures. Given that the emergence of semantics in our network depends crucially on the statistical properties of the linguistic input to children, in the next section, I take a closer look at how our connectionist model can incorporate statistical regularities (e.g., lexical co-occurrences) to derive accurate lexical semantic representations.

A self-organizing connectionist model of the acquisition of semantics

In this section, I return to the problem of how semantic representations could be derived from statistical patterns in the input, as introduced earlier in this chapter. The role of linguistic input in deriving semantic representations would appear dubious to some researchers who stress the importance of innate structures, as discussed earlier. In particular, Pinker (1994) has argued that contextual information such as that postulated by the syntactic bootstrapping hypothesis is insufficient for the learner to derive accurate semantic representations of words.

In Li, Burgess, and Lund (2000), we showed that, in contrast to Pinker's claim, contextual information, if postulated as global lexical co-occurrences, can help the learner significantly in acquiring accurate word representations. We extracted from the CHILDES database all the utterances of the parents and caregivers, forming the parental corpus that consists of about 3.8 million words (tokens). We then applied the HAL method to analyse the lexical co-occurrence statistics for each word, and found that the context vectors derived from this method can give rise to meaningful word clusters in terms of both grammatical and semantic functions. The method not only groups together words that are similar in meaning, but also is able to distinguish between similar words, in contrast to an inability that Pinker assumed to be with syntactic bootstrapping (see p. 83). The implication of this study is that young children can acquire word meanings if they exploit the considerable amount of contextual information in the linguistic input, in this case, the adult speech as recorded in the CHILDES database.

However, Li et al.'s (2000) study does not qualify as a true developmental study, in that no real learning is involved in arriving at the semantic representations — only statistical analyses of the data are involved, and the parameters of window size, corpus size, and number of lexical constraints are all manipulated by the researchers. The lack of a learning component is due to the fact that HAL is largely a representation model and not a processing model, as Burgess and Lund (1999) pointed out.

To overcome this problem, Farkas and Li (2001) built a self-organizing model that incorporates the learning of lexical co-occurrences from input. The basic idea of the model is similar to HAL, but it has two major distinctive features: (1) it is based on unsupervised neural networks that learn on line, and (2) it incorporates a mechanism that leads to accurate word representations even when the training data are sparse. Figure 4 shows a sketch of the model.

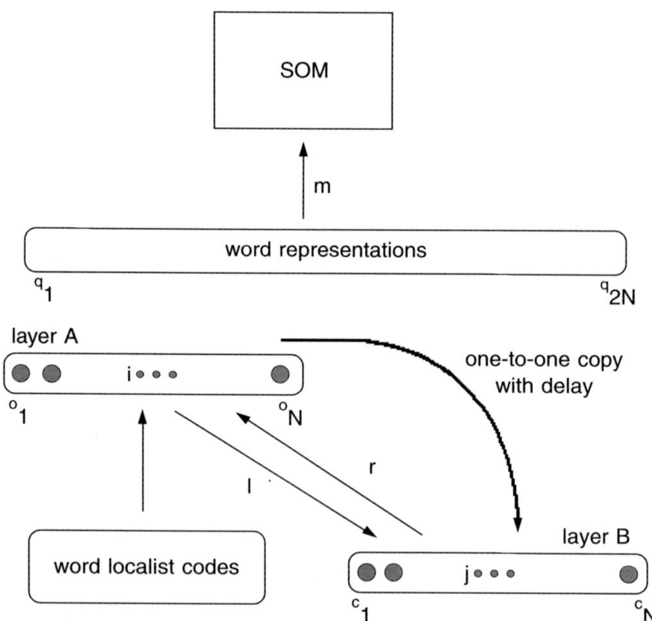

Figure 4. A self-organizing connectionist model of the acquisition of word meanings.

On the lower panel of Figure 4 is the WCD (word co-occurrence detector) network, a special recurrent neural network that learns the lexical co-occurrence constraints. The WCD reads through a stream of input sentences (from CHILDES parental speech), and given a lexicon sized N, it adapts the connections (l and r links) between layers A and B to approximate the transitional probabilities between successive words, and as such, they are trained by Hebbian learning with weight decay so that they become normalized. Specifically, l_{ij} (left context) is updated to capture the probability that word i precedes word j, and r_{ji} (right context) is updated to capture the probability that i follows j. A given word is then characterized by a concatenation of vectors $l_i = [l_{i1}, l_{i2}..., l_{iN}]$, and $r_i = [r_{1i}, r_{2i}..., r_{Ni}]$. The concatenated vectors, $q_i = [l_i, r_i]$, then serve as word meaning representations to the SOM, the self-organizing map shown on the upper panel (see Farkas & Li, 2001, for details).

Applying this model to the learning of several natural speech corpora, we found that it can provide accurate semantic representations for Chinese, English, and Chinese-English bilingual lexicons (see Farkas & Li, 2001; Li & Farkas, in press). Figure 5 presents a snapshot of our model on the *Corpus for Modern Chinese Research* (CMCR corpus; Beijing Language Institute, 1995). This corpus contains about 1.5 million word tokens, recorded from various contemporary written sources (e.g., newspapers). We extracted the 300 most frequent words from this corpus, and applied the model to the analysis of these 300 words (which covers 39% of the whole corpus). The resulting map of the network shows clear grammatical structures: nouns and verbs are separated on the map, and so are prepositions, adverbs, pronouns, particles, numerals, and classifiers. Each shaded area contains a number of words that share the category membership (it is not possible to show the details of the original figure here because the map contains 300 words spread on a 40 × 40 grid of 1,600 units). This result reminds us of the cluster trees in Elman (1990), with which he showed that a simple recurrent network can capture the grammatical classes of words in a next-word prediction task (in Elman's study, however, the network handled a vocabulary of only 29 words, whereas our network handled 300 words).

More important, our network also displays meaningful clusters with respect to the semantic similarity of words. For example, within the verb cluster, motion verbs are grouped together (e.g., *lai* 'come', *qu* 'go', *qi-lai* 'get up', *chu-lai* 'come out', *shang* 'ascend', and *xia* 'descend'), and so are verbs of cognitive activities (e.g., *ting* 'hear', *kan* 'look', *shuo* 'speak', and *xiang* 'think'); within nouns, words referring to people are grouped

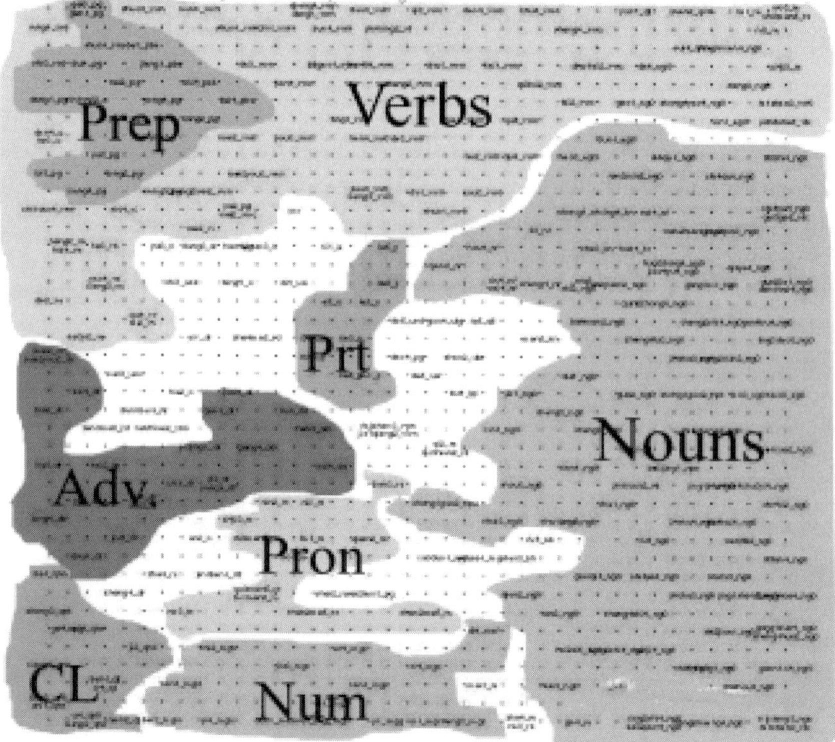

Figure 5. Emergence of lexical categories in a self-organizing connectionist model

together (e.g., *ganbu* 'cadre', *lingdao* 'leader', *jizhe* 'journalist', and *gongmin* 'citizen'), as well as words referring to abstract entities (e.g., *xingshi* 'state', *tiaojian* 'condition', and *qingkuang* 'situation'). Another very interesting finding here is that ambiguous meanings of a homograph are separated by the network into different regions, depending on the function of the word in different contexts (e.g., *xia* as a verb vs. a locative noun).

In Li and Farkas (in press), we presented a self-organizing connectionist model of bilingual processing, the SOMBIP, which is an extension of the model shown in Figure 4. We applied SOMBIP to the Hong Kong Bilingual Corpus (Yip & Matthews, 2000), which contains transcripts of conversations between a child and his native English-speaking father and native Cantonese-speaking mother. We extracted the parental speech from this corpus, which consists of about 185,279 words (tokens). We then applied our model to the 400 most frequent words (types) in the corpus. These 400 most frequent words happened to contain 184 Chinese words, and 216 English words, which effectively covers 56% of the entire data. Figure 6 presents a snapshot of the lexical representation of the two lexicons after our model has been trained on the 400 words.

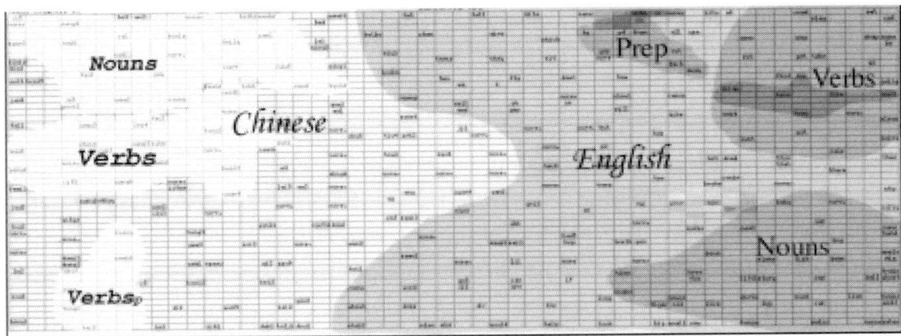

Figure 6.   Emergence of lexical categories in SOMBIP from Chinese-English bilingual data.

In Figure 6, we can see that the network separates the Chinese lexicon from the English lexicon, implicating that the model develops distinct lexical representations for the two languages (see Li & Farkas, in press, for detailed discussion). Moreover, the network treats nouns and verbs distinctly, in both Chinese and English, and also groups other words together as clusters that share the same grammatical categories (e.g., English prepositions occurred in the same neighbourhood). Within each of the categories (assuming there are enough instances), semantically similar words also occur together. For example, in English, the state verbs (e.g., *know, like, have, want*) are grouped together (see the darkest shaded area under the label 'Verbs'), in contrast to other activity verbs; in Chinese, words that are related to cooking/eating (within the verb category) are grouped together (e.g., *sik* 'eat', *jam* 'drink', *cit* 'cut', *gaau* 'gnaw'), as well as verbs indicating cognitive and perceptual activities (marked as 'Verbs-p', including *teng* 'listen', *tai* 'look', *gin* 'see', *seong* 'think'). These results match up closely with the monolingual results from Figure 5. The groupings displayed in the network also match up nicely with our intuitions about the semantic similarities of words.

To summarize, our self-organizing connectionist model, when incorporating lexical co-occurrence information in the input, can yield clearly structured semantic representations in the form of lexical categories and subcategories. When applied to natural speech corpora, the network identifies and displays lexical and semantic categories, in both the Chinese and the bilingual Chinese-English contexts. Our self-organizing model thus demonstrates the ability to learn word meanings as well as grammatical categories on the basis of linguistic input.

Conclusion

In this chapter I have attempted to provide a dynamic, computational perspective on a developmental issue. I started with two empirically related problems, the acquisition of tense-aspect morphology and the acquisition of lexical semantic representations. I then presented a connectionist approach to solve the problems. First, I discussed a connectionist model of the acquisition of semantic categories with tense-aspect morphology, to show how the mechanisms of learning in such a model helps us to understand the emergence of semantic structure, the role of input, and the association patterns in Chinese and English. Second, I discussed how a self-organizing connectionist model that incorporates statistical information can help us to understand the acquisition of lexical semantic representations through analysing lexical co-occurrences in the linguistic input. By looking at the connectionist model presented here, we can return to the issue of whether it is necessary to label semantic categories as 'pre-linguistic' or innate, or whether it is better to first consider mechanisms of learning and the learning environment as potential sources of solution. Thus, our model has significant implications for theories of language acquisition in general: It shows that the linguistic input contains very rich distributional information that the child can exploit in the acquisition of the lexicon, and that modular lexical categories (often considered innate) may emerge from the learning of statistical properties in a high-dimensional space of language use, as displayed in our network.

In short, we can start to understand some of the most difficult problems in the acquisition of lexical meanings and semantic structures, if we use the dynamic and computational perspectives of the kind described here. Structured semantic representations evolve naturally from statistical computations of the various constraints among lexical items, semantic features, and morphological markers, and the evolution and development of semantic representations as seen in child language are due to basic probabilistic, statistical procedures of the sort embodied in connectionist networks in the learning of form-to-form and form-to-meaning mappings. Such abilities of statistical analyses seem to be readily available to the child at a very early age, as recent studies of statistical learning in infants have revealed (Saffran, Aslin, & Newport, 1996; Saffran, Newport, Aslin, Tunick, & Barrueco, 1997). Of course, this is not to deny that the child needs other sources of information grounded in the learning environment to acquire lexical semantics. What I hope to demonstrate here is that children can amazingly acquire a rather accurate semantic representation if they can use statistical mechanisms of the sort in our connectionist model. When coupled with external cues such as visual and perceptual information in the actual learning environment, we can only expect that our model will yield more accurate and faithful representations of lexical semantics.

References

Aksu, A. (1978). *Aspect and modality in the child's acquisition of the Turkish past tense.* Ph.D. dissertation, University of California, Berkeley.

Antinucci, F., & Miller, R. (1976). How children talk about what happened. *Journal of Child Language, 3,* 169–189.

Bates, E. (1984). Bioprograms and the innateness hypothesis. *Behavioral and Brain Sciences, 7,* 188–190.

Behrens, H. (1993). *Temporal reference in German child language: Form and function of early verb use.* Ph.D. Dissertation, University of Amsterdam, the Netherlands.

Beijing Language Institute. (1995). *Corpus for Modern Chinese Research.* Beijing Language Institute Press.

Bloom, L., Lifter, K., & Hafitz, J. (1980). Semantics of verbs and the development of verb inflection in child language. *Language, 56,* 386–412.

Bowerman, M. (1982). Reorganizational processes in lexical and syntactic development. In E. Wanner & L. Gleitman (Eds.), *Language acquisition: The state of the art.* Cambridge University Press.

Bowerman, M. (1988). The 'no negative evidence' problem: How do children avoid constructing an overly general grammar? In J. Hawkins (Ed.), *Explaining language universals.* New York: Basil Blackwell.

Bronckart, J. P., & Sinclair, H. (1973). Time, tense and aspect. *Cognition, 2,* 107–130.

Brown, R. (1973). *A first language.* Cambridge, MA: Harvard University Press.

Burgess, C., & Lund, K. (1997). Modelling parsing constraints with high-dimensional context space. *Language and Cognitive Processes, 12,* 1–34.

Burgess, C., & Lund, K. (1999). The dynamics of meaning in memory. In E. Dietrich & A. Markman, (Eds.), *Cognitive dynamics: Conceptual and representational change in humans and machines* (pp. 17–56). Mahwah, NJ: Lawrence Erlbaum.

Clark, E., Carpenter, K., & Deutsch, W. (1995). Reference states and reversals: Undoing actions with verbs. *Journal of Child Language, 22,* 633–662.

Elman, J. (1990). Finding structure in time. *Cognitive Science, 14,* 179–211.

Elman, J. (1998). Generalization, simple recurrent networks, and the emergence of structure. In M. Gernsbacher and S. Derry (Eds.), *Proceedings of the Twentieth Annual Conference of the Cognitive Science Society.* Mahwah, NJ: Lawrence Erlbaum.

Erbaugh, M. (1978). Acquisition of temporal and aspectual distinctions in Mandarin. In *Papers and Reports on Child Language Development, 15,* 30–37. Department of Linguistics, Stanford University.

Farkas, I., & Li, P. (2001). A self-organizing neural network model of the acquisition of word meaning. In E. M. Altmann, A. Cleeremans, C. D. Schunn, & W. D. Gray (Eds.), *Proceedings of the Fourth International Conference on Cognitive Modeling* (pp. 67–72). Mahwah, NJ: Lawrence Erlbaum.

Gleitman, L. (1990). The structural sources of word meanings. *Language Acquisition, 1,* 3–55.

Harner, L. (1981). Children talk about the time and aspect of actions. *Child Development, 52,* 498–506.

Hebb, D. (1949). *The organization of behavior: A neuropsychological theory.* New York: Wiley.

Kohonen, T. (1982). Self-organized formation of topologically correct feature maps. *Biological Cybernetics, 43,* 59–69.

Kohonen, T. (1989). *Self-organization and associative memory.* Heidelberg: Springer-Verlag.

Li, P. (1990). *Aspect and aktionsart in child Mandarin.* Ph.D. dissertation, Leiden University, the Netherlands.

Li, P. (1993a). The acquisition of the *zai* and *ba* constructions in Mandarin Chinese. In J. C. P. Liang and R. P. E. Sybesma (Eds.), *From classical 'Fú' to 'Three inches high': Studies on Chinese in honor of Erik Zürcher* (pp. 103–120). Leuven/Apeldoorn: Garant Publishers.

Li, P. (1993b). Cryptotypes, form-meaning mappings, and overgeneralizations. In E. V. Clark (Ed.), *Proceedings of the 24th Child Language Research Forum* (pp. 162–178). Center for the Study of Language and Information, Stanford University.

Li, P. (1999). Generalization, representation, and recovery in a self-organizing feature-map model of language acquisition. In M. Hahn & S. C. Stoness (Eds.), *Proceedings of the Twenty-First Annual Conference of the Cognitive Science Society* (pp. 308–313). Mahwah, NJ: Lawrence Erlbaum.

Li, P. (2000). The acquisition of lexical and grammatical aspect in a self-organizing feature-map model. In L. Gleitman & Aravind K. Joshi (Eds.), *Proceedings of the Twenty-Second Annual Conference of the Cognitive Science Society* (pp. 304–309). Mahwah, NJ: Lawrence Erlbaum.

Li, P. (in press-a). Language acquisition in a self-organizing neural network model. In P. Quinlan (Ed.), *Connectionism and developmental theory.* Philadelphia & Brighton: Psychology Press.

Li, P. (in press-b). Aspect and cryptotype: A new approach to an old problem. In T. H.-T. Lee, G. Tang, & V. Yip (Eds.), *CUHK Papers in Linguistics* No. 5. (Special Issue on Language Acquisition: East Asian Perspectives).

Li, P., & Bowerman, M. (1998). The acquisition of lexical and grammatical aspect in Chinese. *First Language, 18,* 311–350.

Li, P., Burgess, C., & Lund, K. (2000). The acquisition of word meaning through global lexical co-occurrences. In E. Clark (Ed.), *Proceedings of the Thirtieth Stanford Child Language Research Forum.* Cambridge, MA: Cambridge University Press.

Li, P., & Farkas, I. (in press). A self-organizing connectionist model of bilingual processing. In R. Heredia & J. Altarriba (Eds.), *Bilingual sentence processing.* North-Holland: Elsevier.

Li, P., & MacWhinney, B. (1996). Cryptotype, overgeneralization, and competition: A connectionist model of the learning of English reversive prefixes. *Connection Science, 8,* 1–28.

Li, P., & Shirai, Y. (2000). *The acquisition of lexical and grammatical aspect.* Berlin and New York: Mouton de Gruyter.

MacWhinney, B. (2000). *The CHILDES project: Tools for analysing talk.* Hillsdale, NJ: Lawrence Erlbaum.

Maratsos, M., & Chalkley, M. (1980). The internal language of children's syntax: The ontogenesis and representation of syntactic categories. In K. Nelson (Ed.), *Children's language.* Vol.2. New York: Gardner Press.

Miikkulainen, R. (1997). Dyslexic and category-specific aphasic impairments in a self-organizing feature map model of the lexicon. *Brain and Language, 59,* 334–366.

Pinker, S. (1987). The bootstrapping problem in language acquisition. In B. MacWhinney (Ed.), *Mechanisms of language acquisition.* Hillsdale, NJ: Lawrence Erlbaum.

Pinker, S. (1994). How could a child use verb syntax to learn verb semantics? *Lingua, 92,* 377–410.

Redington, M., Chater, N., & Finch, S. (1998). Distributional information: A powerful cue for acquiring syntactic categories. *Cognitive Science, 22,* 425–470.

Saffran, J., Aslin, R., & Newport, E. (1996). Statistical learning by 8-month-old infants. *Science, 274,* 1926–1928.

Saffran, J., Newport, E., Aslin, R., Tunick, R., & Barrueco, S. (1997). Incidental language learning: Listening (and learning) out of the corner of your ear.

Psychological Science, 8, 101–105.

Shirai, Y. (1993). Inherent aspect and the acquisition of tense/aspect morphology in Japanese. In H. Nakajima & Y. Otsu (Eds.), *Argument structure: Its syntax and acquisition* (pp. 185–211). Tokyo: Kaitakusha.

Slobin, D. (Ed.). (1985). Crosslinguistic evidence for the Language-Making Capacity. In *The crosslinguistic study of language acquisition.* Vol. 2. Hillsdale, NJ: Lawrence Erlbaum.

Slobin, D. (Ed.). (1992). *The crosslinguistic study of language acquisition.* Vol. 3. Hillsdale, NJ: Lawrence Erlbaum.

Whorf, B. (1956). Thinking in primitive communities. In J. B. Carroll (Ed.), *Language, thought, and reality.* MIT Press.

Yip, V. & Matthews, S. (2000). Syntactic transfer in a Cantonese-English bilingual child. *Bilingualism, 3,* 193–208.

Author Note

Preparation of this article was supported by a Faculty Research Grant from the University of Richmond, and a grant from the National Science Foundation (#BCS-9975249). Part of this research was presented at the International Symposium on Cognitive Processes of the Chinese Language, the University of Hong Kong. I would like to thank the conference organizers and editors for bringing this important volume to the field. I also thank Igor Farkas, Brian MacWhinney, Risto Miikkulainen, and Hongbing Xing for their comments, contributions, and discussions on various parts of the research.

5

Picture-Word Interference Effects on Naming in Chinese

Brendan Weekes, Robert Davies and May Jane Chen

The presence of a semantic relationship between the name of a target picture and a distractor word (e.g., CAT-<u>dog</u>) hampers picture naming in a picture-word interference task, whereas a graphemic-phonological relationship between a distractor word and the name of a target picture (e.g., CAT-<u>cap</u>) facilitates word naming. One issue to emerge from this research is the relative contribution of graphemic and phonological information to the facilitation effect. In alphabetic languages, orthography and phonology are unavoidably confounded, making it difficult to establish the loci of graphemic and phonological facilitation effects. However, in non-alphabetic languages such as Chinese it is possible to examine independently the relative contribution of graphemic and phonological information to the facilitation effect. We report two experiments investigating semantic interference effects and graphemic-phonological facilitation effects on picture naming in Chinese. Results show three independent effects on picture naming latency: a semantic interference effect that is due to shared category membership between the target picture and a distractor word; a graphemic facilitation effect that is due to shared orthography between target and distractor words; and a phonological facilitation effect that is due to homophony between target and distractor names. We argue that semantic interference and graphemic facilitation effects can be accounted for by activation at the lemma level whereas phonological facilitation results from activation at the name retrieval stage.

Picture-Word Interference Paradigm

The picture-word interference task requires participants to name a target picture while ignoring an accompanying word distractor. Rather as in the Stroop task (Stroop, 1935; MacLeod, 1991), the presentation of a dual stimulus (Kantowitz, 1974) allows the experimenter to examine the effect of context (the distractor stimulus) on the processes supporting production of a response to the target stimulus. The picture-word method has great utility because the relation between target and distractor can fruitfully be manipulated in various ways. Different interference effects, elicited by distractor stimuli, have been accounted as indicative of different aspects of the information retrieved preparatory to speech. Two interference effects of particular interest have been observed over a wide range of different experimental studies: a *semantic inhibition* effect and a *graphemic-phonological facilitation* effect. In this study, we will examine whether these effects occur in picture naming in Chinese.

Picture-word interference effects are most often reported in terms of the difference between the naming latency or accuracy of participants' performance under related or unrelated lexical distractor conditions (e.g. Schriefers, Meyer & Levelt, 1990). The semantic inhibition effect is characterized by the finding that the naming latency to the target picture is slower when the target has been presented with a semantically related distractor in comparison to when it has been presented with an unrelated distractor (Glaser & Dungelhoff, 1984; Klein, 1964; Rosinski, 1977; Rosinski, Golinkoff, & Kukish, 1975; La Heij, 1988; Lupker, 1979; Schriefers et al., 1990; Starreveld & La Heij, 1995, 1996a).[1] For example, initiating a naming response to a picture of a PIG takes longer on average when the distractor is semantically related e.g. the co-ordinate word <u>sheep</u>, compared to when it is unrelated, e.g. the word <u>pen</u>.[2]

The semantic inhibition effect is obtained within a relatively restricted range of stimulus onset asynchronies (SOA).[3] Published observations span the interval from -300 ms to +150 ms SOAs (Damian & Martin, 1999; Glaser & Dungelhoff, 1984; La Heij, Dirkx & Kramer, 1990; Schriefers et al., 1990; Starreveld & La Heij, 1996a; Starreveld, 2000). In some studies, the particular SOAs at which the inhibition effect was observed have been found to vary in relation to the modality in which the distractor stimulus was presented. Damian and Martin (1999) compared the effect of stimulus modality on observed semantic interference by presenting auditory or visual distractors together with the target pictures. They found that semantic inhibition could be observed with visually presented distractors at 0 ms and +100 ms SOAs, but with auditory distractors at SOAs ranging from –200 ms to 0 ms SOAs. The reasons for this modality related difference in the time course of interference do not concern us, it is sufficient to note that the semantic inhibition effect is commonly observed at 0 ms SOA. An SOA of 0 ms was employed in the present investigation.

Most models of picture naming (e.g., Ellis & Young, 1988; Glaser & Glaser, 1989; Humphreys, Riddoch & Quinlan, 1988) assume that the processes of picture naming and word recognition share (at a minimum) two levels of representation: a semantic level and a lexical (name or word form) level. Glaser and Glaser (1989) proposed a model of picture naming encompassing two representational and processing stages. They postulated a semantic level where concepts known to a speaker are represented as non-decomposed nodes (after Collins & Loftus, 1975; but see e.g. Dell (1986) for a different view). It is assumed that a semantic node for example representing the concept *father (x,y)* is used to retrieve the word *father* and that the full sense of the concept meaning is retrieved through the activation of links to related concepts e.g. *male(x)* and *parent(x,y)*. Presentation of an object stimulus like a picture leads to activation of a corresponding concept node via a semantic executive system that is responsible for the parsing of physical objects or pictures. In addition, Glaser and Glaser (1989) proposed a lexical level at which all the words a speaker knows are represented. The linguistic properties of a word are represented in this model by the set of links between a word node and the nodes of similar words, or the nodes representing orthographic or phonological properties. In this account, the lexicon has no semantic properties. A lexical executive system furnishes input and output processes that support the perception of or production of lexical items. In picture naming, the parsing of the picture stimulus activates the corresponding concept. Semantic activation spreads to other related nodes and to all corresponding nodes in the lexicon, presenting a number of candidate words. Glaser and Glaser (1989) do not specify how the speech production system then decides on the right word to say from amongst the field of activated candidates, but Wheeldon and Monsell (1994) point out that the semantic inhibition effect indicates the speech system must compare rival candidates, deciding on one either through lateral inhibition or by means of some choice ratio mechanism (Luce, 1986). In common with Starreveld and La Heij's (1996a; see also Roelofs, 1992) account of lexical retrieval we might assume that in a system including only semantic and lexical name representations, the target word is selected for production if its activation exceeds the activation of all other candidates activated by the target picture, by some criterial amount.

In addition to the semantic and lexical levels mentioned, some theories of speech production assume that a level of processing, termed the *lemma level*, occurs between the semantic level and what we may now call the word name or lexeme level (Dell, 1986; Kempen & Huijbers, 1983; Levelt, 1989). The lemma level allows a distinction between two different kinds of organization of representations in the lexicon: one based on the form properties of words and one according to the meaning and syntactic properties of words. The distinction is motivated by a range of evidence.

Dell, Schwartz, Martin, Saffran and Gagnon (1997) claim that since the syntactic structure of a sentence is different to its conceptual or phonological structure, the speech production system must have the capacity to operate on purely syntactic terms. This claim motivates the separate representation in lemmas of the syntactic specifications for a word. Also, speech production errors appear to support the postulate of a lemma level. Word exchange errors often occur between words of the same syntactic category though the exchanged words may be entirely dissimilar in sound (Garrett, 1988). Word substitution errors are argued by Schriefers et al. (1990) to belong to one of two classes. Errors may involve either words that are semantically but are not phonologically related or words that are phonologically but not semantically related, usually called malapropisms (Fay & Cutler, 1977). In addition, lemma representations seem to be entailed by observations that people suffering from short-term failures to retrieve words (the tip-of-the-tongue state), or from a long-term impairment of retrieval (anomia), present preserved semantic or syntactic knowledge but partial phonological knowledge (Badecker, Miozzo, & Zanuttini, 1995; Brown & McNeill, 1966; Goodglass, Kaplan, Weintraub, & Ackerman, 1976; Vigliocco, Antonini, & Garrett, 1997). In theories of speech production that include a lemma level, lemma representations are activated as a result of activation spreading from the semantic level. Activation of the lemmas then results in the activation of the syntactic information necessary to build a surface structure for an utterance. The surface structure that is developed is then encoded phonologically.[4]

There is considerable debate in the literature regarding the location of the cause of the semantic inhibition effect. There are at least three different views (see reviews in Glaser & Dungelhoff, 1984; Lupker & Katz, 1981). Firstly, the *semantic decision account* assumes that the interference effect arises at the semantic level (Lupker & Katz, 1981;

Seymour, 1977). The semantic decision account supposes that when a picture activates its concept node at the semantic level, activation also spreads to all related concept nodes. This then lengthens response latencies because more time is required to decide between all activated concepts to select the concept that will be articulated. The second account, called the *name retrieval view* (Glaser & Glaser, 1989; Starreveld & La Heij, 1995, 1996a, 1996b) assumes that the semantic inhibition effect is caused at the lexical level, where lexical representations are word form representations absent of semantic content. The name retrieval view also supposes that activation of the picture concept node triggers the activation of a cohort of semantically related concept nodes. In contrast to the semantic decision theory, however, the name retrieval theory assumes that response selection occurs at the lexical level. If a picture is presented together with a distractor that is semantically related to the picture's name, the word nodes corresponding to both the target and the distractor are activated so that a response conflict arises. The semantic inhibition observed under related distractor conditions therefore reflects the time needed to select the correct word node for articulation from a field of candidates. The third account of the locus of semantic inhibition is the *lemma selection account* (Roelofs, 1992; Schriefers et al. 1990). In this view, presentation of the picture-word stimulus activates, as in the other accounts, a cohort of related concepts at the semantic level of representation. The key difference stems from the assumption in this account that the decision about which of the activated concepts may be output is made by a selection mechanism choosing between lemma rather than semantic or word form representations.

The location of the causes of the semantic inhibition effect has yet to be resolved in picture-word interference research. A number of studies have investigated the locus of the effect. We will discuss, firstly, studies which have tested whether the semantic inhibition effect is semantic or lexical. Lupker and Katz (1981) conducted a study in which they varied the modality of subjects' responses. They asked their experiment participants to indicate (by key-press or by verbal yes/no responses) whether or not a target picture was a picture of a dog. It was found that when the picture was accompanied by a distractor word if that word was semantically related to the target name then the identification response was delayed. The fact that such inhibition was observed in the absence of verbal responses indicated by Lupker and Katz's argument that the effect arose at the pre-lexical semantic level. This account has been criticized by La Heij (1988), however, because the targets chosen by

Lupker and Katz for this study form part of a semantic category (four-footed animals) with high visual similarity between category co-ordinates. After Neumann and Kautz (1982), La Heij (1988) argued that the inhibition Lupker and Katz observed in the study might therefore have been due to the problems induced by the distractor stimulus in the perceptual identification of the target. That is to say, Lupker and Katz may have observed a perceptual rather than a semantic interference effect. La Heij was able to demonstrate a semantic inhibition effect whilst controlling for visual similarity between and within semantic categories. Lupker and Katz's results from the 1981 study do not therefore seem relevant to discussion of the locus of the semantic inhibition effect. Further, other experimental investigations have shown that if participants are asked to respond non-verbally to picture-word stimuli (categorizing or sorting targets, producing key-press rather than vocalic responses) the semantic inhibition effect disappears (Damian, Bowers & Katz, 1997; Schriefers et al., 1990). It is difficult to interpret these null semantic interference results because one must be assured that the non-naming task was sufficient to tax semantic processing to the extent that semantic interference could be observed (Damian et al., 1997). The data may therefore be said to suggest a lexical rather than a semantic locus for the effect, though one must acknowledge the need for further experimentation.

Whether the effect is then located at a lemma or at a word form level is the subject of further controversy. Debate on the question has been bound up with the general question of whether one needs to postulate a lemma level of representation in the speech production system. In particular, two phenomena bear upon the discussion. The first is the observation by Schriefers et al. (1990; also, Damian & Martin, 1999) of a dissociation over time of semantic and phonological interference effects (the latter are considered below). In their study, semantic inhibition was recorded at –150 ms SOA but the facilitatory effect of phonological distractors was recorded at 0 ms and +150 ms SOAs. The dissociation was argued by Schriefers et al. (1990) to reflect the successive stages of lexical retrieval with phonological encoding following only after lemma selection has taken place. Recently, however, Starreveld (2000) has criticized this interpretation, arguing that the precedence of the semantic inhibition effect may simply be due to the fact that in the Schriefers et al. (1990) study, since distractors were presented auditorily, the whole distractor word had to be heard before its semantic content could be retrieved so that the semantic inhibition effect could only be observed at SOAs allowing pre-exposure of the distractor word. Further experimental work is needed in order to elucidate the interaction of both perceptual and production processes over time.

The second phenomenon germane to the present discussion is the recording of significant interactions between semantic and graphemic (or orthographic) interference effects (the latter are discussed in more detail, below) in picture-word studies that have factorially manipulated the different kinds of relatedness (Rayner & Springer, 1986; Starreveld & La Heij, 1995, 1996a). The interaction is important because it has been interpreted under the assumptions of the additive factors method (Sternberg, 1969) to indicate the co-location of the causes of both semantic and form relatedness interference effects at the word form level of representation (Starreveld & La Heij, 1995, 1996a, 1996b). The additive factors method allows that if two experimental factors have additive effects on response performance, they are likely to have their selective effects at separate processing stages; but if the factors interact statistically, they are likely to have their effect at the same stage.

In experiments reported by Starreveld and La Heij (1995, 1996a, 1996b) and by Rayner and Springer (1986), it has been found that when a distractor is semantically related alone, it causes semantic inhibition of naming performance; when it is graphemically related alone, it causes facilitation; but when it is both semantically and graphemically related, it has an effect which does not equal the graphemic facilitation effect plus the semantic inhibition effect, but rather is non-additive, in other words, an interaction effect.[5] Starreveld and La Heij (1995, 1996a, 1996b) have argued that the observation of an interaction supports the idea that the semantic inhibition effect is caused by difficulties experienced in response selection at the word form not the lemma level. This account has been contended by Roelofs, Meyer and Levelt (1996; see also Levelt et al., 1999) who point out that the interpretation of the additivity of experimental effects depends upon the assumptions employed.

Roelofs et al. (1996) claim that there is evidence for the existence of lemmas independent of the observation of an interaction between semantic and graphemic relatedness effects, for example, the speech error data described above. They argued that the facilitatory effect of graphemic relatedness can be caused by its influence on word name retrieval or, in restricted circumstances, by its influence on lemma selection. Thus, if one is investigating the loci of two effects but one effect may exert an influence at more than one location (as here, it is argued that graphemic relatedness can affect both lemma selection and word name retrieval) then the observation of an interaction need not warrant the supposition that both semantic and graphemic interference effects are to be located at the word name level. Rather, both effects might plausibly be ascribed to the influence of the different kinds of relatedness on the lemma level. The controversy surrounding the interpretation of the semantic-graphemic interaction awaits resolution. Therefore, both in the case of interference time course evidence and in the case of the interaction of semantic and graphemic interference effects, at present, the available data do not allow us to decide firmly on one location over others for the cause of semantic inhibition. The present study does not address the location of semantic inhibition. It does, however, address the location of the cause of graphemic interference effects.

As mentioned, the facilitatory effect of form relatedness is an important phenomenon in picture-word interference research. Picture naming performance is enhanced by the presentation of a distractor word that is graphemically similar to a target picture's name, compared to when the distractor word and picture name are unrelated. For example, naming a picture of a CAT is faster when a word with similar orthography e.g., <u>cap</u> is superimposed upon the picture, compared to when an unrelated word e.g., <u>pen</u> is superimposed upon the picture (Briggs & Underwood, 1982; Lupker, 1982; Posnansky & Rayner, 1977; Rayner & Posnansky, 1978; Rayner & Springer, 1986; Starreveld & La Heij, 1995, 1996a; Underwood & Briggs, 1984).

As with research into the locus of the semantic inhibition effect, the locus of the graphemic facilitation effect has been much debated. In the name retrieval account, the cause of the effect is located at the lexical (phonological word form) level (Levelt et al., 1999; Roelofs et al., 1996; Lupker, 1982; Starreveld & La Heij, 1995, 1996a, 1996b). In this view, presentation of the graphemically related distractor activates corresponding phonological feature representations at the lexical level via a mapping between graphemic and phonological representations (Coltheart, Curtis, Atkins & Haller, 1993). As a result of the overlap between the orthography of the distractor and target words, the presentation of the related distractor increases the activation of the target's phonological features, so that they are more readily selected for use. This speeds up the phonological encoding of the target name, so shortening the time needed for production of a response.

It has been suggested that graphemic relatedness may affect the retrieval of lemma as well as word form level representations (Levelt et al., 1999; Roelofs, Meyer & Levelt, 1996).[6] Roelofs et al. (1996), as mentioned, argued that the interaction between semantic and graphemic relatedness effects can be explained without resort to the assumption that both kinds of relatedness influence the word form level of representation if it is granted that graphemically related distractors can affect both lemma and phonological processing. Roelofs et al. (1996) reported evidence that semantic inhibition effects can be observed even when the distractors consist of word-initial fragments. That is, seeing or hearing <u>ta</u> (the initial for <u>table</u>) inhibited naming a DESK in comparison to the effect of seeing or hearing an initial of an unrelated word. This finding indicates that word form similarity may be one aspect of the organization of lemma representations, since perception of a mere word fragment was sufficient to activate the semantic content of form related words. Roelofs et al. (1996; Levelt et al., 1999) insist, however, that the facilitatory effect of form relatedness only affects lemma retrieval when that retrieval has already been delayed by a semantic relation. They argue that this may happen 'when lemma retrieval has non-linear aspects (e.g., a non-linear activation dynamics, which holds for Roelofs' 1992, 1993, model) . . .' (Roelofs et al., 1996, p. 249). Roelofs et al. demonstrate that a computational model including lemmas alone can simulate the interaction of semantic and form relatedness effects. They do not, however, provide any evidence that form relatedness can affect lemma retrieval only in the case of semantically as well as graphemically related words. In addition, Starreveld and La Heij (1996b) argue that the empirical basis of the simulation reported by Roelofs et al. (1996) is flawed. Whereas Roelofs et al. assume that observed decrease in semantic inhibition is dependent upon observed increase in shared orthography, Starreveld and La Heij point out that an item-wise analysis for their own stimulus set found that the percentage decrease in semantic inhibition was independent of the percentage of shared orthography for each related target-distractor stimulus. Thus, it remains an open question whether the graphemic relatedness may influence processing of lemma or of word form representations.

In alphabetic languages such as English and Dutch, the effect of a graphemic relation between a distractor word and a target picture is often assumed to be localized at the phonological encoding of the target's name. However, some evidence suggests that the locus of the graphemic effect may be quite distinct from phonological level representations. For instance, Underwood and Briggs (1984) found a facilitation effect in picture naming in the presence of graphemically related distractor words, but not in the presence of phonologically related distractor words. So for example, a picture of a LEAF was named faster when accompanied by the word <u>deaf</u>

than when the picture was accompanied by the word <u>dirt</u>, whereas there was no facilitation effect when the picture of a LEAF was accompanied by a phonologically related distractor word such as <u>thief</u> (see also Lupker, 1982, which reports a phonological facilitation effect that is very small in comparison to a robust graphemic facilitation effect).

Most of the research reporting graphemic facilitation effects have used alphabetic stimuli (specifically Dutch and English words) as distractors. In alphabetic languages, the facilitatory effects of orthography and phonology are unavoidably confounded because orthographic patterns that are alike also share phonological features (e.g., CAT-<u>cap</u>). This makes it difficult to evaluate the relative contribution of graphemic and phonological information to the facilitation effects observed in those languages. In contrast, in non-alphabetic scripts such as Chinese there are large numbers of visually dissimilar words that sound the same (Leck, Weekes & Chen, 1995), there are also visually similar words that sound dissimilar, so that it is straightforward to investigate separately the influence of graphemic and phonological facilitation on picture naming. The use of Chinese materials and subjects therefore provides a special opportunity to examine the interdependence of graphemic and phonological interference effects. Furthermore, a Chinese picture-word interference experiment allows one to address the question whether graphemic similarity may influence lemma retrieval or phonological encoding in speech.

So far as we are aware there are no published reports of Chinese picture-word interference experiments. Previous Chinese Stroop experiments reported by Biederman and Tsao (1979) and by Chen and Ho (1986) cannot be compared to picture-word studies of the kind reported by Schriefers et al. (1990). Biederman and Tsao (1979) as well as Chen and Ho (1986) compare naming of incongruent colour-word stimuli, e.g. the word <u>red</u> printed in BLUE ink with naming of colour patches. This is a comparison of performance under a condition equivalent to the related picture-word condition with performance under a condition entirely lacking a distractor component to the stimulus. Conventionally, however, picture-word interference studies are designed to serve an analysis of the effect of semantically related compared to unrelated lexical distractors on picture naming. The difference in performance, if any is observed, can be interpreted to signify the perturbation of a semantic stage of lexical retrieval by the semantically related distractor. The interference reported in the cited Chinese Stroop studies may simply reflect the negative effect on subjects' performance of having incongruent lexical distractors in comparison to having no distractors at all. That is to say, observed interference may be due just as much to the greater attentional demands of having a distractor rather than none, or it may be due to the effect of the semantic relatedness of the colour and colour name components of the incongruent Stroop stimulus. The present study compares the effect of semantically related or unrelated Chinese distractor words on picture naming in Chinese to allow the first observation of the effect of semantic relatedness in that language.

The aim of this study was to investigate interference effects in a Chinese picture naming study. The investigation exploits the characteristics of Chinese script to explore the relative effects of graphemic and phonological relatedness on picture naming in Chinese. In addition, the experiments to be reported present the first published examination of semantic inhibition in Chinese picture naming.

EXPERIMENT 1

In Experiment 1, we investigated whether there can be semantic inhibition of picture naming latency in Chinese. We also investigated whether there are form relatedness effects on picture naming in Chinese using two types of distractor words. *Graphemically related distractors* were defined as words that are visually similar but have a dissimilar sound compared with the target name. *Phonologically related distractors* were defined as words that have the same sound but are visually dissimilar to the target name. Naming latencies in these conditions were compared to a baseline condition where the distractor word was not related semantically, graphemically or phonologically to the target picture name.

METHOD

Participants   Twenty Mandarin speaking tertiary students studying in Beijing participated for a token reward. All participants had normal or corrected to normal vision.

Design   The experiment had a within-participants design with one independent variable: distractor type (identity; graphemically related; phonologically related; categorically related; and unrelated). The dependent variables consisted of the recorded picture naming latencies and naming errors.

Materials   Twelve picture stimuli taken from Snodgrass and Vanderwart (1980) matched for name familiarity, image agreement and visual complexity using norms published by Shu, Zhang, Li, Wang, and Chu (1992). All word stimuli were digitized images taken from the Mishu-Wuhan software package (version 1.1.X) measuring approximately 10mm by 10mm. Example stimuli in each of the five experimental conditions (identity; graphemically related; phonologically related; categorically related; and unrelated) are shown in Table 1. All target and distractor words were monosyllabic. Distractor words in each condition were matched for written word frequency based on normative information reported by the Beijing Institute of Language (1986). Pair-wise comparisons revealed that the mean frequencies of words in each condition were not significantly different from each other (all probability values greater than .05). Participants were tested individually in a single session. They were firstly trained to criterion on the picture naming task (specified elicitation) in order to reduce variability in the names used to refer to the pictures (cf. Schriefers et al., 1990; Starreveld and La Heij, 1995, 1996a). Participants were presented with each of the twelve target pictures, paired with the correct name of the picture, and were asked to name the picture aloud. This ensured that all participants knew the correct name of each picture before commencing the experiment. In the experimental task, participants were instructed to name each picture as quickly and accurately as possible and to ignore the distractor word that was *simultaneously* presented in the centre of the picture. Each participant received one block of 48 stimuli in the picture naming task presented in random order (12 stimuli repeated in four conditions). Each picture was presented for a maximum of 1500 milliseconds and remained on screen until a response was recorded. The inter-trial interval was set at 5 seconds.

Apparatus   Picture stimuli were presented online using a Macintosh computer which also recorded response latency. Error data were recorded by hand. Each target picture was presented simultaneously with a distractor word in black font in the centre of a pale screen. Response timing began with stimulus onset and was terminated by a voice-activated switch. The switch was triggered via a microphone positioned in front of the participant's mouth without obscuring participant's screen view.

RESULTS AND DISCUSSION

Analyses of variance were conducted on error corrected naming latencies. The mean naming latencies and errors in each condition are shown in Table 1.

Table 1
Mean Picture-naming Latencies in ms and Percentage of Errors With Standard Errors in Each Distractor Condition in Experiment 1

Condition	Example Stimulus	Mean Latencies	Standard error	Mean Errors	Standard error
Identity	蛇 she[2] snake	723.1	25.2	1.00	0.70
Graphemic	陀 tuo[2] top	730.1	30.7	8.00	1.80
Phonological	舌 she[2] tongue	729.3	28.1	7.80	1.90
Categorical	龟 gui[1] turtle	811.1	29.0	9.90	2.10
Unrelated	花 hua[1] flower	764.9	29.9	7.70	1.70

Data for each distractor type were analysed in a one way ANOVA with repeated measures on the factor termed distractor type. In the following, we report analyses conducted on both by-participants (F1) and by-items (F2) mean latencies or error rates. For naming latencies, there was a main effect of distractor type $F1[4,19] = 7.10$, $p < .01$; $F2[4,11] = 9.11$, $p < .01$. Dunnett t-tests ($p < .05$) showed that naming latencies were significantly longer to stimuli in the categorically related condition than in the unrelated condition. In addition, naming latencies to stimuli in the identity, graphemically related and phonologically related conditions were found to be significantly faster than naming latencies in the unrelated condition. Naming latencies in the graphemically related condition were no different to naming latencies in the phonologically related condition ($t < 1$). For errors, there was a main effect of distractor type $F1[4, 19] = 5.11, p < .05; F2[4, 11] = 3.22, p < .05$. Dunnett t-tests ($p < .05$) found that compared to the unrelated condition, participants made more errors in the categorically related condition and fewer errors in the identity condition.

In summary, we observed the inhibition of picture naming in Chinese due to semantic relatedness and the facilitation of naming due to graphemic as well as to phonological relatedness. These findings are consistent with the results of picture naming in English (Briggs & Underwood, 1982; Lupker, 1982; Posnansky & Rayner, 1977; Rayner & Posnansky, 1978; Rayner & Springer, 1986; Underwood & Briggs, 1984) and Dutch (Starreveld & La Heij, 1995, 1996a, 1996b). We also found that there was no significant difference between the amount of graphemic and phonological facilitation on picture naming in Chinese. None of these observations have previously been reported in the published research literature.

The observation of a graphemic facilitation effect is of special interest because it has been made using materials from a non-alphabetic language. These materials consist of pairs of target names and distractor words that are graphemically similar but phonologically dissimilar. We would claim that because the graphemically related distractors do not share phonological features with the target names it is unlikely that, in this instance, the locus of the influence of graphemic relatedness is at the phonological level of lexical retrieval in speech. Rather, we suggest that the presentation of the graphemic distractor activates the lemma representation of the target name, as a result of their shared graphemic features, causing the target lemma to be selected more quickly and so shortening response latencies in the test.

It could be the case, however, that presentation of the graphemic distractor may prime the mapping between representations of the target name's orthography and of its phonological word form, the mapping employed in oral reading. Weekes, Chen and Yin (1997) proposed a model of picture naming and word recognition in which proficient oral reading in Chinese can proceed either by a semantic pathway or by a direct pathway that maps orthographic representations directly onto phonological output. The activation of the target name's graphemic representations by the graphemically related distractor could be sufficient to lead to activation of the target's phonology, via the direct mapping route from orthography to phonology. In effect, therefore, despite the graphemic distractor's phonological dissimilarity to the target name, the graphemic interference effect may yet be localized at the phonological level. In the second experiment we further investigated the locus of the graphemic and phonological interference effects in Chinese. We sought to test the interpretation that graphemic relatedness affects lemma selection by manipulating factorially graphemic and phonological relatedness in another picture-word interference experiment.

EXPERIMENT 2

The results of Experiment 1 have established that graphemic and phonological similarity between target names and distractor words facilitates picture naming in Chinese. According to additive factors logic (Sternberg, 1969), if there is an interaction between graphemic and phonological similarity then the two factors are likely to influence the same level of processing. However, if there is an additive effect between graphemic and phonological similarity then the two factors are more likely to be localized at different processing levels.

We may recall at this point the debate surrounding the differing uses of additive factors logic presented by Roelofs et al. (1996) and by Starreveld and La Heij (1995, 1996a, 1996b). Roelofs et al. (1996) suggested that though semantic and graphemic relatedness effects may interact that interaction does not warrant the conclusion, proposed by Starreveld and La Heij (1995, 1996a, 1996b), that both factors affect word form retrieval because there is evidence that graphemic relatedness influences lemma retrieval as well as phonological encoding. Indeed, Roelofs et al.'s (1996) discovery that semantic inhibition could be elicited by visually or auditorily presented word fragments implies that lemma retrieval may be influenced by graphemic or phonological word similarity. In the present study, we may adopt Roelofs et al.'s assumption that graphemic relatedness can influence lemma retrieval but it is not certain that we need assume, as they do, that graphemic relatedness can only affect lemma retrieval if the distractor is semantically as well as graphemically related. The observation of an interaction between graphemic and phonological relatedness effects need not signify that both factors have their influence at the level of phonological encoding. Rather, the interaction between these factors could equally be carried by the joint effect of both types of form relatedness on lemma retrieval. It does seem reasonable to assume, however, that since spoken and not written responses are required in the present test, any effect of graphemic relatedness bearing an additive relation to the effect of phonological relatedness might confidently be ascribed to the effect of the target-distractor relation on the retrieval of the target's lemma, rather than its phonological representation.

In Experiment 2, we investigated whether there are interactive or additive effects of graphemic and phonological similarity between target and distractor words by including *graphemically and phonologically related* distractors as well as distractors that were only *graphemically* or *phonologically* related. If there is an interaction between graphemic and phonological similarity effects on picture naming in Chinese this would be consistent with the view that there is a common locus for graphemic and phonological facilitation effects. However, if there is no interaction between graphemic and phonological similarity on target naming, if the facilitatory effects are additive, this result would be consistent with the view that the graphemic and phonological facilitation effects observed in Experiment 1 have separate loci.

METHOD

Participants   Twenty Mandarin speaking tertiary students studying in Beijing participated for a token reward. All participants had normal or corrected to normal vision.

Design   A within-participants design with one independent variable distractor type (identity; graphemically related; phonologically related; graphemically and phonologically related; and unrelated). The dependent variables were picture naming latency and errors.

Materials   Sixteen picture stimuli were taken from Snodgrass and Vanderwart (1980) matched for name familiarity, image agreement and stimulus complexity using norms published by Shu et al. (1992). All word stimuli were digitized images taken from the Wuhan software package measuring approximately 10mm by 10mm. Example stimuli in each of the five experimental conditions are shown in Table 2. All target and distractor words were monosyllabic. Distractor words in each condition were matched for written word frequency based on normative information reported by the Beijing Institute of Language (1986). Pair-wise comparisons revealed the mean frequencies of words in each condition were not significantly different from each other (all p values greater than .05).

Procedure and apparatus   The same as reported for Experiment 1.

RESULTS AND DISCUSSION

Analyses of variance were conducted on error corrected naming latencies. The mean naming latencies in each distractor condition are presented in Table 2.

Table 2
Mean Picture-naming Latencies in ms and Percentage of Errors With Standard Errors in Each Distractor Condition in Experiment 2

Condition	Example Stimulus	Mean Latencies	Standard error	Mean Errors	Standard error
Identity	狐 hu[4] fox	720.6	15.2	0.80	0.90
Graphemic	呱 gua[1] croak	721.7	18.9	4.90	1.60
Phonological	湖 hu[4] lake	725.9	16.8	4.50	1.20
Graphemic and Phonological	弧 hu[4] arc	702.1	14.3	4.10	1.90
Unrelated	愣 leng[2] distracted	760.1	19.1	5.90	1.30

Data for each distractor type were analysed in a one way ANOVA with repeated measures on the factor distractor type. As before, both by-participants (F1) and by-items (F2) analyses are reported. For naming latencies, there was a main effect of distractor type $F1[4, 19] = 3.79$, $p < .05$; $F2[4, 15] = 4.86$, $p < .05$. Dunnett t-tests ($p < .05$) showed that naming latencies were significantly faster to stimuli in the identity, graphemically related; phonologically related; and graphemic and phonologically related conditions compared to naming latencies in the unrelated condition. Naming latencies to distractors in the graphemic-phonological condition were also significantly faster than those in both the graphemic and the phonological conditions. For errors, there was a main effect of distractor type $F1[4, 19] = 3.01$, $p < .05$; $F2 < 1$. Dunnett t-tests ($p < .05$) found that participants made fewer errors in the identity condition compared to the unrelated condition. The additive effects of graphemic and phonological similarity were tested by comparing each factor in a two-way factorial ANOVA. Results are shown in Figure 1.

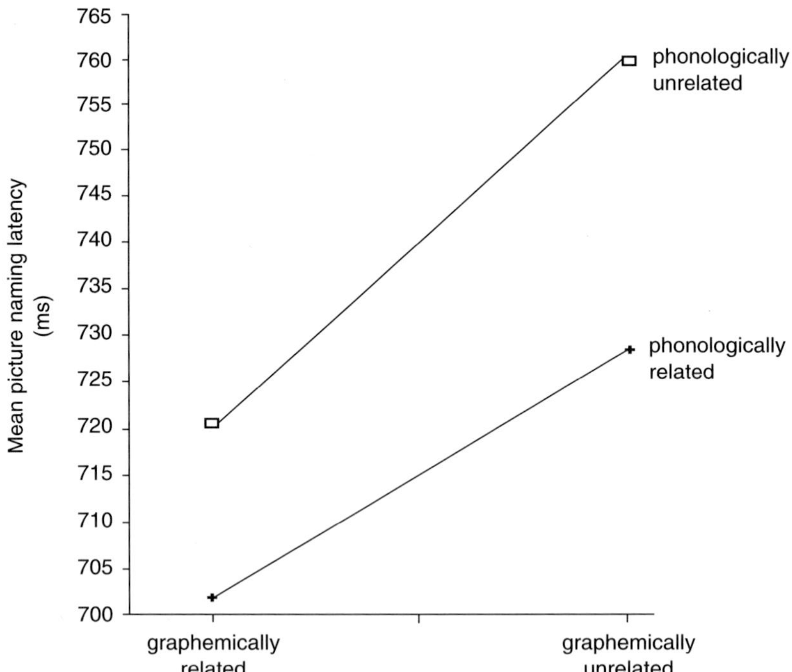

Figure 1.   Mean picture-naming latencies for graphemically and phonologically related and unrelated distractors.

There were significant effects of graphemic similarity $F(1, 19)$ = 3.78, $p < .05$ and phonological similarity $F(1, 19)$ = 4.09, $p < .05$ but there was no interaction between graphemic and phonological similarity $F < 1$ on picture naming latency.

In summary, we replicated the results of Experiment 1, showing graphemic and phonological facilitation effects on picture naming in Chinese. We also found that there was no interaction between graphemic and phonological facilitation effects on picture naming. This finding is unique in the study of picture-word interference effects.

We interpret the graphemic facilitation effect as strong evidence for the idea that graphemic relatedness influences lemma selection during picture naming in Chinese. In the languages commonly employed in picture-word interference studies, Dutch or English, the use of alphabetic scripts ensures the confounding of graphemic and phonological similarity. In contrast, the logographic nature of Chinese script meant that we were able to select words for our graphemically related condition that had no phonological similarity with the target picture name. It allowed us, also, to examine the effects of graphemic and phonological relatedness in a factorial experimental design that served the additive factors method of interpreting experimental effects. As noted, the additivity of effects of graphemic and phonological relatedness directs us to the conclusion that these effects have separate loci and moreover that the effect of graphemic relatedness is likely to have its cause at the level of lemma retrieval.

GENERAL DISCUSSION

In the present study we found three different interference effects in picture naming in Chinese: a semantic inhibition effect that is due to shared category membership of target and distractor words; a graphemic facilitation effect that is due to shared orthography between target and distractor; and a phonological facilitation effect that is due to the homophony of target and distractor names. These effects were shown to be reliable across participants as well as items. Our results also showed that the facilitatory effects of graphemic and phonological relatedness are additive, suggesting that graphemic and phonological distractor effects in Chinese picture naming influence different stages in Chinese speech production.

The categorical interference effect on picture naming latency in Chinese can be accounted for by the semantic decision account (Lupker

& Katz, 1981; Seymour, 1977), by the lemma selection view (Roelofs, 1992; Schriefers et al, 1990), or by the name retrieval account (Glaser & Glaser, 1989; Starreveld & La Heij, 1995, 1996a, 1996b). We are not able to arbitrate between the semantic decision account and the lemma selection view using the present data. Further work on picture naming is clearly needed to resolve these issues but a fruitful means of localizing the semantic inhibition effect, at least in Chinese, is suggested below.

We believe the graphemic facilitation effect can only be accounted for by supposing that graphemic relatedness between target and distractor words enhances the selection of the target name lemma (see Levelt, 1989; Levelt et al., 1999; Roelofs et al., 1996, for related views; see also, Starreveld & La Heij, 1995, 1996a, 1996b). The presentation of a written distractor word is assumed to affect directly the activation of both lemma level and phonological word form representations in the speech production system. This assumption is supported by the elicitation of semantic inhibition by word fragment distractors, reported by Roelofs et al. (1996), together with the observation of a phonological facilitation effect noted in the present study (see also Perfetti & Zhang, 1995). The fact that the graphemic distractors were unrelated in sound to the target names indicates however that the facilitation effect these distractors evoked was unlikely to be due to the influence of graphemic similarity at the phonological level. This conclusion is supported by the observation in the second experiment that the graphemic and phonological facilitation effects did not interact.

We may now return to the question of where in the speech system the observed semantic inhibition effect may be localized. Granted that the graphemic relatedness of a distractor influences target lemma selection we propose that a factorial manipulation of graphemic and semantic target-distractor relatedness would allow one to locate the semantic inhibition effect by means of additive factors logic. As discussed in the foregoing, it is difficult at present to arbitrate between lemma level and phonological level loci of the causes of the semantic inhibition effect. The graphemic relatedness effects observed in Dutch or English picture-word experiments might equally be localized at the lemma or at the phonological levels because of the confound between graphemic and phonological relatedness in those languages. Therefore, the interaction between semantic and graphemic relatedness observed in a number of studies (Rayner & Springer, 1986; Starreveld & La Heij, 1995, 1996a, 1996b) signifies a location for the causes of the semantic inhibition effect either at the lemma or at the phonological levels. In the case of a language such as Chinese, as shown, we are more confidently able to pinpoint the locus of the graphemic interference effect as being at the lemma level. A study manipulating graphemic and semantic relatedness in Chinese would consequently permit a firm conclusion on the location of the causes of the semantic inhibition effect. Whether that conclusion can be generalized to encompass other languages is another question, though it is one that faces, equally, theories that are based on data gathered in Dutch or English language experiments.

We can explain the observed phonological facilitation effect in terms of a name retrieval account. Just as the additivity of the graphemic and phonological interference effects implies that these effects are localized at different processing levels, we can also argue that the graphemic interference effect can be localized at the lemma level, so we can claim that the phonological facilitation effect is likely to be due to the influence of phonological relatedness at the lemma level. The presentation of the phonologically related distractor activates corresponding phonological feature representations at the lexical level via the mapping between graphemic and phonological representations which serves oral reading (Coltheart et al., 1993). As a result of the overlap between the phonological word form of the distractor and target words, the related distractor primes the activation of the target's phonological features so that they are more readily selected for use. This speeds up the phonological encoding of the target name and decreases response latencies.

We have assumed implicitly that there is a lemma level of representation in Chinese in common with the assumption in many accounts of a lemma level of representation in English or Dutch (Dell, 1986; Kempen & Huijbers, 1983; Levelt, 1989). What are the grounds for our assumption? Most certainly, we can suppose (after Dell et al., 1997, and others) that in Chinese as in other languages, the syntactic structure of a sentence is not the same as its conceptual or phonological structure. 'Sentence production requires the manipulation of words as syntactic entities according to purely syntactic considerations' (Dell et al., 1997, p. 804). The assumption of a lemma level of representation would therefore seem warranted on the grounds of syntactic processing requirements, at the least.

If our claim that there is a lemma level of representation for Chinese speakers is correct, then there are implications for current models of picture naming and word recognition in Chinese. Weekes et al. (1997) proposed a model of picture naming and word recognition in which proficient oral reading in Chinese can proceed via one of two pathways:

a *semantic* pathway that maps orthography to phonological output via semantic representations; and a *direct* reading pathway that maps representations of orthographic directly onto phonological output, by-passing semantic representations. An additional assumption of the Weekes et al. model is that picture naming and oral reading share the mappings that link semantic representations with phonological output. However, the model does not incorporate a lemma level of representation between semantic representations and phonological output.

The Weekes et al. (1997) model can account for the significant categorical interference effects found in Experiment 1 as the possible result of competition between conceptual representations at the semantic level. In the picture-word interference paradigm, these representations are activated by simultaneously presented pictorial and orthographic stimuli that come from the same semantic category. The model can also account for phonological facilitation effects on picture naming as the result of a lowered threshold for phonological activation of target names due to the direct mappings from orthography to phonological output. However, the model is unable to account for orthographic facilitation effects on picture naming in Chinese from orthographically but not phonologically related distractor words. Thus, some modification to the Weekes et al. model to include an additional lemma level of representation between semantic representations and phonological output may be required.

In conclusion, we have observed for the first time three different interference effects in a Chinese picture-word interference experiment. We observed an effect of semantic inhibition, that picture naming is slowed by the presentation of a lexical distractor categorically related to the target name. We also recorded two effects of form relatedness. Picture naming was facilitated by distractors that were graphemically *or* phonologically related to the target name as well as by distractors that were graphemically *and* phonologically related to the target name. Upon further examination we discovered that the graphemic and phonological effects are quite independent. We were able to observe a facilitatory effect of graphemic relatedness though the graphemic distractors were phonologically dissimilar to the target names. In addition, we found that the graphemic and phonological distractor effects did not interact in an experiment in which both factors were factorially manipulated. The latter observations support the theory that the effect of graphemic relatedness can be localized at the lemma level rather than at the phonological level of representation in the speech system.

References

Badecker, W., Miozzo, M., & Zanuttini, R. (1995). The two-stage model of lexical retrieval: Evidence from a case of anomia with selective preservation of grammatical gender. *Cognition, 57,* 193–216.

Beijing Institute of Language (1986). *Modern Chinese frequency dictionary.* Beijing Institute of Language Press.

Biederman, I., & Tsao, Y. C. (1979). On processing Chinese ideographs and English words: Some implications from Stroop-Test results. *Cognitive Psychology, 11,* 125–132.

Briggs, P., & Underwood, G. (1982). Phonological coding in good and poor readers. *Journal of Experimental Child Psychology, 34,* 93–112.

Brown, R., & McNeill, D. (1966). The 'tip of the tongue' phenomenon. *Journal of Verbal Learning and Verbal Behaviour, 5,* 325–337.

Chen, H.-C., & Ho, C. (1986). Development of Stroop interference in Chinese-English bilinguals. *Journal of Experimental Psychology, 15,* 316–325.

Collins, A. M., & Loftus, E. (1975). A spreading-activation theory of semantic processing. *Psychological Review, 82,* 407–428.

Coltheart, M., Curtis, B., Atkins, P., & Haller, M. (1993). Models of reading aloud: Dual-route and parallel-distributed-processing approaches. *Psychological Review, 100,* 589–608.

Damian, M. F., Bowers, J. S., & Katz, M. A. (1997). Are semantic effects in the picture-word interference procedure lexical or conceptual? Unpublished manuscript.

Damian, M. F., & Martin, R. C. (1999). Semantic and phonological codes interact in single word production. *Journal of Experimental Psychology: Learning, Memory and Cognition, 25,* 345–361.

Dell, G. S. (1986). A spreading activation theory of retrieval in sentence production. *Psychological Review 27,* 124–142.

Dell, G. S., Schwartz, M. F., Martin, N., Saffran, E. M., & Gagnon, D. A. (1997). Lexical access in aphasic and nonaphasic speakers. *Psychological Review, 104,* 801–838.

Ellis, A., & Young, A.W. (1988). *Human cognitive neuropsychology.* London: Lawrence Erlbaum Associates.

Fay, D., & Cutler, A., (1977). Malapropisms and the structure of the mental lexicon. *Linguistic Inquiry, 8,* 505–520.

Garrett, M. F. (1988). Processes in language production. In F. J. Newmeyer (Ed.), *Linguistics: The Cambridge Survey. Vol. III. Psychological and biological aspects* (pp. 69–96). Cambridge, MA: Harvard University Press.

Glaser, W. R., & Dungelhoff, F.-J., (1984). The time course of picture-word interference. *Journal of Experimental Psychology: Human Perception and Performance, 10,* 640–654.

Glaser, W. R., & Glaser, M. O. (1989). Context effects on Stroop-like word and picture processing. *Journal of Experimental Psychology: General, 118,* 13–42.

Goodglass, H., Kaplan, E., Weintraub, S., & Ackerman, N. (1976). The 'tip of the tongue' phenomenon in aphasia. *Cortex, 12,* 145–153.

Humphreys, G. W., Riddoch, M. J., & Quinlan, P. T. (1988). Cascade processes in picture identification. *Cognitive Neuropsychology, 5*(1):67–104.

Kantowitz, B. H. (1974). Double stimulation. In B.H. Kantowitz (Ed.), *Human information processing: Tutorials in performance and cognition.* Hillsdale, NJ: Erlbaum.

Kempen, G., & Huijbers, P. (1983). The lexicalisation process in sentence production and naming: Indirect election of words. *Cognition, 14,* 41–104.

Klein, G. S. (1964). Semantic power measured through the interference of words with color-naming. *American Journal of Psychology, 77,* 576–588.

La Heij, W. (1988). Components of Stroop-like interference in picture naming. *Memory and Cognition, 16,* 400–410.

La Heij, W., Dirkx, J., & Kramer, P. (1990). Categorical interference and associative priming in picture naming. *British Journal of Psychology, 81,* 511–525.

Leck, K. J., Weekes, B. S., & Chen, M. J. (1995). Visual and phonological pathways to the lexicon: Evidence from Chinese readers. *Memory and Cognition, 23,* 468–476.

Levelt, W. J. M. (1989). *Speaking: From Intention to Articulation.* Cambridge, MA: MIT Press.

Levelt, W. J. M., Roelofs, A., & Meyer, A. S. (1999). A theory of lexical access in speech production. *Behavioural and Brain Sciences, 22,* 1–38.

Luce, R. D., (1986). *Response times and their role in inferring elementary mental organization.* New York: Oxford University Press.

Lupker, S. J. (1979). The semantic nature of response competition in the picture-word interference task. *Memory and Cognition, 7,* 485–495.

Lupker, S. J. (1982). The role of phonetic and orthographic similarity in picture-word interference. *Canadian Journal of Psychology, 36,* 349–367.

Lupker, S. J., & Katz, A. N. (1981). Input, decision, and response factors in picture-word interference task. *Journal of Experimental Psychology: Human Learning and Memory, 7,* 269–282.

MacLeod, C. M. (1991). Half a century of research on the Stroop effect: An integrative view. *Psychological Bulletin, 109,* 163–203.

Mishu-Wuhan Version 1.1.X. Xanatech, Cambridge, MA.

Neumann, O., & Kautz, L. (1982). *Semantische Forderung und semantische Interferenz im Benennungsexperiment* (Semantic facilitation and semantic interference in a naming experiment). Bericht Nr. 23/1982. Bochum, Federal Republic of Germany: University of Bochum.

Perfetti, C. A. & Zhang, S. L. (1995). Very early phonological activation in Chinese reading. *Journal of Experimental Psychology: Learning, Memory and Cognition, 21*(1), 24–33.

Posnansky, C. J., & Rayner, K. (1977). Visual-feature and response components in a picture-word interference task with beginning and skilled readers. *Journal of Experimental Child Psychology, 24,* 440–460.

Rayner, K., & Posnansky, C. J. (1978). Stages of processing in word identification. *Journal of Experimental Psychology: General, 107,* 64–80.

Rayner, K., & Springer, C. J. (1986). Graphemic and semantic similarity effects in the picture-word interference task. *British Journal of Psychology, 77,* 207–222.

Roelofs, A. (1992). A spreading-activation theory of lemma retrieval in speaking. *Cognition, 42,* 107–142.

Roelofs, A. (1993). Testing a non-decompositional theory of lemma retrieval in speaking: Retrieval of verbs. *Cognition, 47,* 59–87.

Roelofs, A., Meyer, A. S., & Levelt, W. J. M. (1996). Interaction between semantic and orthographic factors in conceptually driven naming: Comment on Starreveld and La Heij (1995). *Journal of Experimental Psychology: Learning, Memory and Cognition, 22,* 246–251.

Rosinski, R. R. (1977). Picture-word interference is semantically based. *Child Development, 48,* 643–647.

Rosinski, R. R., Golinkoff, R. M., & Kukish, K. S. (1975). Automatic semantic processing in a picture-word interference task. *Child Development, 46,* 247–253.

Schriefers, H., Meyer, A. S., & Levelt, W. J. (1990). Exploring the time course of lexical access in language production: Picture-word interference studies. *Journal of Memory and Language, 29,* 86–102.

Seymour, P. H. K. (1977). Conceptual encoding and the locus of the Stroop effect. *Quarterly Journal of Experimental Psychology, 29,* 245–265.

Shu, H., Zhang, H., Li, W., Wang, A., & Chu, Q. (1992). A new technique for cognitive experiments: Chinese norms for a set of pictures and a computer program for experiments. *Acta Psychologica Sinica, 4,* 386–392 (in Chinese).

Snodgrass, J. G. & Vanderwart, M. (1980). A standardized set of 260 pictures: Picture-word interference studies. *Journal of Memory and Language, 29,* 86–102.

Starreveld, P. A. (2000). On the interpretation of onsets of auditory context effects in word production. *Journal of Memory and Language, 42,* 497–525.

Starreveld, P. A., & La Heij, W. (1995). Semantic interference, orthographic facilitation, and their interaction in naming tasks. *Journal of Experimental Psychology: Learning, Memory and Cognition, 21,* 686–698.

Starreveld, P. A., & La Heij, W. (1996a). Time course analysis of semantic and orthographic context effects in picture naming. *Journal of Experimental Psychology: Learning, Memory and Cognition, 22,* 896–918.

Starreveld, P. A., & La Heij, W. (1996b). The locus of orthographic and phonological facilitation: Reply to Roelofs, Meyer, and Levelt (1996).

*Journal of Experimental Psychology: Learning, Memory and Cognition,
22*, 252–255.
Sternberg, S. (1969). The discovery of processing stages: Extensions of Donders'
method. *Acta Psychologia, 30*, 276–315.
Stroop, J. R. (1935). Studies of interference in serial verbal reactions. *Journal
of Experimental Psychology, 18*, 643–662.
Underwood, G., & Briggs, P. (1984). The development of word recognition
processes. *British Journal of Psychology, 75*, 243–255.
Vigliocco, G., Antonini, T., & Garrett, M. F. (1997). Grammatical gender is
on the tip of Italian tongues. *Psychological Science, 8*, 314–317.
Weekes, B. S., Chen, M.-J., & Yin W.-G. (1997). Anomia without dyslexia in
Chinese. *Neurocase, 3*, 51–60.
Wheeldon, L. R., & Monsell, S. (1994). Inhibition of spoken word production
by priming a semantic competitor. *Journal of Memory and Language, 33*,
332–356.

Author Note

This research was carried out while the first author was a visiting scientist
at the Chinese Academy of Science supported by a grant from the Royal
Society (652033.Q601).

Endnotes

1. In this chapter, the use of the terms 'inhibition' and 'facilitation' is purely
    descriptive. An effect is inhibitory if task performance under the related
    condition is slower or less accurate than performance under the unrelated
    condition. An effect is facilitatory if related performance is faster or more
    accurate than that under the unrelated condition.
2. Target picture names are in capitals whereas distractor names are shown
    underlined.
3. In the picture-word interference research literature, conventionally, when
    the distractor onset is prior to target onset, the SOA is negative, and when
    distractor onset follows target onset, the SOA is positive.
4. It should be noted in passing that in Levelt's (1989; Levelt, Roelofs &
    Meyer, 1999) theory of speech production, which does propose a lemma
    level, the selection of target utterances occurs at the lemma level (Roelofs,
    1992) rather than at the word form level.
5. In most languages graphemic relatedness is confounded with phonological

relatedness, so that commonly one may refer interchangeably to graphemic or phonological interference effects. As will be discussed, in Chinese this graphemic-phonological confound is not the case hence it is reasonable to focus, as here, on observations of form relatedness effects in studies employing visual distractor presentation, as a prelude to discussing the investigation of the separate effects of graphemic and phonological relatedness. Examples of studies reporting phonological interference effects using auditorily presented distractors include: Damian & Martin (1999); Meyer & Schriefers, 1991; Schriefers et al. (1990).

6. A phonological relation could in principle affect later stages of production after name retrieval has taken place. However, Lupker and Williams (1989) concluded that a combined orthographic and phonological facilitation effect is most likely not a production effect. This is because orthographically and phonologically related primes produced facilitation effects of about the same magnitude on target naming as they did on target categorizing. As participants did not have to produce the target name in the categorization task, it seems unlikely that a phonological relation influenced the stages involved in the articulation.

6

Speed of Getting at the Phonology and Meaning of Chinese Words

Rumjahn Hoosain

In psycholinguistic studies of the Chinese language we have witnessed two myths. An earlier one was that processing of the ideographic symbols is lateralized in the right hemisphere. Its empirical support came from: (a) the finding of greater Stroop effect for Chinese, with Biederman and Tsao (1979) suggesting that both the processing of colours and Chinese colour names were lateralized in the right hemisphere and thus producing greater interference compared with colour names printed in English, (b) reports of crossed aphasia in Chinese aphasic patients (e.g., April & Tse, 1977), with right hemisphere damage resulting in language impairment, and (c) the contrast in findings of left visual field (right hemisphere) advantage for single Chinese characters and right visual field (left hemisphere) advantage for two-character Chinese words. It was thought that single characters were visual wholes while two-character words involved sequential or analytic processing, and the right and left hemispheres respectively specialized in holistic and analytic processing.

Eventually, when we obtained a better picture, the incidence of crossed-aphasia for Chinese did not appear higher than for English (cf. April & Han, 1980). It was also realized that the difference between single characters and two-character words in tachistoscopic perception was due to the degradation of the visual signal related to exposure time and other stimulus factors, and not any particular orthographic characteristic of Chinese (Hasuike, Tzeng & Hung, 1986; Ho & Hoosain, 1989).

The other myth is that getting at the meaning of Chinese words is more direct than English. The origin of this myth could be traced to observations by distinguished linguists such as Yuen Ren Chao and William Wang. Chao (1968) thought that when reading Chinese text the characters stared the reader in the face. Although referring only to pictographs which make up a small percentage of Chinese characters, Wang (1973) thought that when looking at the character for horse, we could almost see the animal galloping in front of us. In the tradition of psycholinguistics going after the psychological reality of linguistic notions (notably of transformational grammar in the sixties), investigators of Chinese psycholinguistics have been working on the question of directness of access to meaning of characters for the past two decades. My view is that, in contrast to the earlier myth of cerebral lateralization, this one of more direct access to Chinese meaning is 'one of truest myths in Chinese mythology' (in the words of Chao, 1968, referring to another — the monosyllabic myth). I shall briefly discuss the evidence for this position in the rest of this paper.

As with any other orthography, processing the meaning of Chinese words has to take place in some temporal relationship with processing of phonology. Of course, we are not just interested in the question of which process takes place sooner or can be completed faster, but also the implications that could be drawn. For example, if it could be established that getting at the meaning of a word can be faster that getting at the pronunciation, then it is possible to argue that the former can be done without the latter. In other words, phonological recoding is not necessary for accessing meaning of words. And in doing so, we get some understanding of the reading process.

The comparison of the speed of accessing phonology versus meaning, in the context of possible orthographic difference between Chinese and English, can be expressed in the form of a four-fold table indicated in Figure 1. The speed of access can be looked at both within a given language and between different languages. This provides some converging evidence for the question at hand. What is indicated in Figure 1 represents a good set of working hypotheses that is viable in the context of available evidence so far.

The underlying reason for three of the four notations in Figure 1 (except for the faster times for accessing phonology compared with accessing meaning of English) is the nature of script-sound-meaning relations in Chinese. One crucial aspect of Chinese orthography is that while almost all characters are each a morphemic unit, pronunciation of

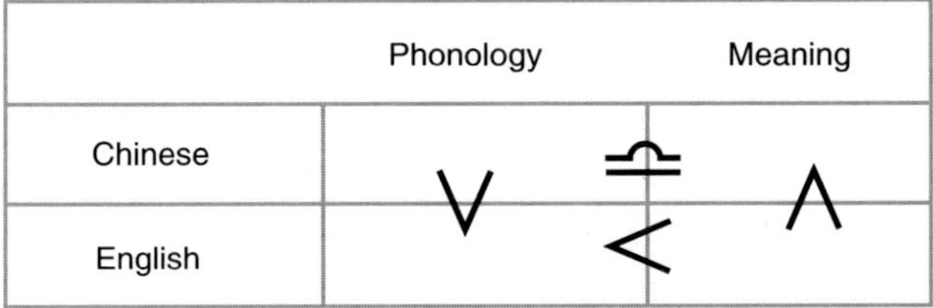

Figure 1.   Speed of getting at the phonology and meaning of Chinese and English words.

a character is not spelled out, but has to be memorized individually. In other words, phonology has to be addressed and not assembled. Even if the phonetic radicals within some Chinese characters have similar pronunciation as the characters in which they are embedded, which are the ones that do and which do not are not rule governed and have to be learned individually. The pronunciation of the phonetic radicals themselves (which are often individual characters on their own, and there are about 800 of them) after all has to be memorized individually. If the primary function of elements of the orthography is not to assemble phonology (as is the case with letters of the alphabet) the script-sound-meaning relation raises the possibility that the reading process is different.

Accessing Meaning of Chinese Words is Faster than Accessing Meaning of English Words

Indications that accessing meaning of Chinese characters is faster than accessing meaning of English come from both direct and indirect comparisons. Indirect evidence is from what I have called evidence that meaning of Chinese words is more manifest (Hoosain, 1991), that access to their meaning is more direct, and therefore could produce greater interference if word meaning is inconsistent with physical features of the word. An earlier example is the finding by Biederman and Tsao (1979) that the Stroop effect is greater for Chinese than for English. This means that access to meaning of Chinese colour names is more direct or unavoidable, so that there is greater interference of the meaning of the colour names with the task of naming the colour in which the words are printed. This way of looking at the cross-language Stroop effect dispenses with the need to refer to the possibility of same hemisphere processing of physical colour and Chinese colour names (Biederman & Tsao, 1979).

A similar phenomenon was also found using number names, which showed the size incongruity effect. With pairs of Chinese number names printed in different sizes, response to number names printed in incongruous size (e.g., if a number name with bigger numerical value was printed in smaller size) took more time. However, no such effect was found for English number names (Tzeng & Wang, 1983). But the effect was found with Arabic numerals, which are also ideographic symbols (Besner & Coltheart, 1979). The similarity of the results with Chinese number names and Arabic numerals on the one hand, and the difference between both types of items and English on the other hand, indicate that accessing meaning of ideographic symbols is different from accessing meaning of alphabetic symbols. The pattern lends weight to the view that accessing meaning of Chinese characters is more direct than English.

In another line of evidence, Chinese participants perceived the affective meaning of Chinese words and decided if they were positive (e.g., *heaven*) or negative (*hell*) faster than English speaking participants responding to comparable English words (Hoosain & Osgood, 1983). This is the only direct comparison of Chinese and English in the literature, although the speed of accessing affective meaning only was involved.

Accessing Phonology of English Words is Faster than Accessing Meaning of English Words

Since we are mainly interested in Chinese, the evidence for the faster access to phonology compared with the meaning of English words will not be reviewed in detail here. But the comparison of access to phonology and meaning of English words completes the picture in Figure 1. The universal phonological principle of Perfetti and his colleagues (Perfetti & Zhang, 1995; Perfetti, Zhang & Berent, 1992) as well as the strong phonological theory of Frost (1998), would be in line with the position that access to the phonology of English words is faster than access to their meaning. Such positions could include the view that phonological processing is mandatory and perhaps automatic, that the prelexical phonological computation is very fast although it could be at different levels of specification, and that the core lexical representation is phonological. The activation of multiple levels of phonology is an interesting concept. I shall refer to the corresponding activation of multiple levels of meaning later in the paper. However, it should be noted that there is some evidence inconsistent with fast, mandatory, or automatic activation of phonology. For example, Taft and van Graan (1998) found that it was possible to read a word for meaning without phonological mediation. In a semantic categorization task involving target words that had definable meanings (e.g., *pint*) or were given names (*Pam*), there was no difference between regular definable words (*plank*) and irregular definable words (*pint*), even though there was a difference in naming such words.

Accessing Phonology of Chinese Words is Slower than Accessing Phonology of English Words

In the comparison of access to phonology it would seem inappropriate to make direct comparisons of, say, naming latencies since the syllabic length and articulatory characteristics of Chinese and English words could be different. However, there are a couple of indirect comparisons that provide interesting information. Chen and Tsoi (1990) compared the naming times for *plus, minus, multiply* and *divide* with those of their Chinese translation equivalents as well as the corresponding arithmetic symbols, the former being alphabetic and the latter two types of items being ideographic symbols. The naming times for the arithmetic symbols (pronounced in Chinese) and their respective names in Chinese characters were comparable. But the naming times for the symbol names spelt out in English (*plus, minus,* etc.) were faster than times for the symbols themselves (+, −, etc.) named in English, both for native English speakers and for Chinese-English bilinguals. The naming of the arithmetic symbols in the respective native languages provided a basis for comparison of latencies for pronouncing the names of the symbols in Chinese and English. Within the Chinese language, naming times for the two types of ideographic symbols were about the same. Within English, naming times for the arithmetic (ideographic) symbols were longer than for the alphabetic names. Thus, we have indication that naming times for alphabetical symbols are faster than for comparable ideographic symbols. Also, this difference was obtained when the same pronunciations were involved, eliminating the possibility of differences due to articulation time for different languages.

Another line of evidence comes from the contrast that for English, naming latencies for words tend to be faster than lexical decision times and the word frequency effect is smaller for naming than for lexical decision (e.g., Foster & Chambers, 1973; Waters & Seidenberg, 1985). But for Chinese, naming is slower than lexical decision and the frequency effect is greater for naming single character words than for lexical decision (Liu, 1998; Wu, Chou & Liu, 1994). The account of the data for English, by Balota and Chumbley (1984, 1985), was based on breaking up the components of the naming and lexical decision tasks. The use of the technique of delayed naming indicated that the effect of frequency was largely localized in the production stage in the naming task rather than lexical access. On the other hand, in lexical decision, the decision task (discriminating word targets from non-word distractors) after lexical access was an unfamiliar task and more affected by familiarity of the stimulus.

The syllabic length of individual Chinese characters in these naming tasks tended to be shorter than that of English words in corresponding studies. For example, Foster and Chambers (1973) used one-third monosyllabic and two-thirds bisyllabic English words, and obtained faster naming latencies than lexical decision times. Yet Wu et al. (1994) found the longer naming times than lexical decision times with single Chinese characters. Given that naming latencies are longer for items with greater syllabic length (Eriksen, Pollack & Montague, 1970), the accessing of phonology of Chinese characters must be slower than that of English words to produce the longer naming latencies for Chinese, compared with lexical decision times. Addressed phonology is the only route for Chinese, while both addressed and assembled phonology are possible for English. Particularly for multisyllabic English words, it is possible to prepare the motor programme for articulation of the beginning syllable(s) while assembling subsequent syllables, resulting in faster naming latencies (which are determined by the onset of the beginning pronunciation).

For Chinese characters the phonology as a whole has to be addressed before the activation of the motor programme for articulation. Particularly with lower familiarity characters, the access to their phonology would be delayed. Wu and Liu (1997) found that naming embedded phonetics took longer time than naming the embedding character, and that character frequency but not the frequency of the phonetic radical had an effect on naming latencies for characters. In general, phonetic radicals tend to be familiar items, even those embedded in low frequency characters. But with alphabetic words, the assembling of the phonology is less subject to the familiarity of each word as a whole. We can even proceed to assemble the phonology of entirely unfamiliar words in English. Thus, the lexical decision task provides a basis to compare Chinese and English, with the respective relative latencies for naming in the two languages yielding the contrast to indicate that access to Chinese phonology is slower than access to English phonology.

Accessing Phonology and Meaning of Chinese Words Can Have Different Relative Speeds Depending on the Situation

The approximately equal sign in Figure 1, for comparison between getting at the sound and getting at the meaning of Chinese words, indicates that accessing phonology can sometimes be faster but accessing meaning can in turn be faster in other situations. A determining factor is what aspect of meaning is involved, whether one has to process meaning in an open-ended manner or whether the purpose is to get at a specific aspect of meaning. An assumption is that phonological access is not always needed for getting at the meaning of ideographic Chinese words.

We should note that in phonological processing or phonological recoding, there is only one target, namely the phonology of a character. There can be only one pronunciation for each character (for most of the time, except for the few characters with different pronunciations in different contexts). On the other hand there can be many different aspects of word meanings. Furthermore, in typical experiments comparing speed of activation of a word's phonology versus meaning, word pairs with identical pronunciation and other word pairs with only related meaning are compared. In the recent literature, the strongest evidence that activation of phonology is faster than that of meaning comes from the work of Perfetti, Tan, and their colleagues (e.g., Perfetti & Tan, 1998). Procedures used included priming and backward masking. This line of work has enabled the authors to suggest that the time course of activation of graphic, phonological, and semantic information of a Chinese word was in the order of graphic information within 43 ms, then phonological information within 57 ms and finally semantic information within 85 ms. However, in this line of research, to assess the phonological effect the target and prime/mask had identical pronunciation, but to assess semantic effect they only had similar or related meaning. The manner in which semantic relatedness was embodied in different pairs of items could vary a lot, sometimes in the same block of trials.

The following are some examples of different types of semantic similarity/relatedness found in word pairs used in this line of research:

(1) 媽 母: These two are synonymous, (which incidentally is not often the case with items used in these studies), both meaning 'mother'.

(2) 松 林: These two mean 'pine' and 'wood/forest' respectively and form a two-character word together (which is sometimes referred to as having associative semantic relation), meaning 'pine forest'.

(3) 節 假: The first character when combined with words like 'Christmas' means 'festival', although it also can mean 'segment'. The second character, when combined with other words can mean 'vacation', although it also means 'false' by itself. Thus when respectively combined with appropriate words they can mean 'vacation' and 'festival' and have semantic relatedness, but such relatedness is not necessary when the respective characters are considered on their own.

(4) 究 查: The first character is a bound morpheme and does not stand on its own. But when combined with different characters, it can mean 'research' or 'verify'. The second character means 'inspect', and the two can also be combined together, in reverse order, to mean 'investigate'.

Thus, character pairs used to embody semantic relatedness sometimes are genuinely synonymous, but sometimes not. Sometimes they form a word together and sometimes they do not. Particularly when different manners of semantic relatedness are involved within the same block of trials, and when only the first of a pair of items is presented, it is difficult for the participant to know beforehand what aspect or level of meaning is going to be related to the following item. This dilutes the semantic relatedness/similarity effect. And this is to be compared with the effect of homophone pairs followed by homophone pairs in the contrasting block of trials. To be fair, the corresponding situation for phonological similarity or relatedness would be to have item pairs that sometimes have similar onset, or similar rhyme, etc. Otherwise, the faster or greater homophone effect compared with semantic relatedness/similarity effect found in such studies is not really valid evidence for faster phonological activation. It is also not reliable. Chen (1998), for example, reported finding the opposite effect using such a procedure.

Another line of work also showed ambivalent results as to whether phonological activation or semantic activation is faster. The reasoning behind this approach is that if phonological activation is faster, then it would be possible to obtain homophone interference effect in some semantic tasks. A variety of semantic tasks have been used. Treiman, Baron, and Luk (1981) found a smaller homophone interference effect for Chinese compared with English, in a sentence verification task. But Chen, Flores d'Arcais, and Cheung (1995) found no difference between homophone foils and non-homophone words in semantic categorisation tasks for Chinese. More recently, Chua (1999) found homophone interference effect in a semantic task involving judgment of whether a target word fitted a definition.

One point that should be noted is that the occurrence of the homophone interference effect in a semantic task does not necessarily mean that phonological activation is faster than semantic activation, or that phonological recoding is necessary for semantic access. It would be so only if there is no reciprocal semantic interference effect in phonological tasks. Otherwise, it is possible that inconsistent phonological and semantic activation interferes with each other, no matter if the task at hand is semantic or phonological. In the strong phonological theory of Frost (1998), it is considered that although the initial phase of phonological recoding is very fast, its product could be an impoverished phonological representation and subsequent cycles would produce a final form of the phonology. A similar situation could obtain with semantic activation, with different levels or aspects of meaning activated at different speeds. Affective meaning, for example, is accessed very quickly (cf. Zajonc, 1980).

With the possibility of multi-levels of specification of meaning, one approach to a fair comparison of activation of phonology and activation of meaning would be to specify the level or aspect of meaning to be activated, just as the form of phonology to be activated is specified. For example, Chen, Yung, and Ng (1988) presented a character as a graphemic, phonemic, or semantic cue, followed by a few characters one of which could be different from the others along the feature specified by the cue character. The exception item could have a missing component radical (for graphemic search), did not rhyme with the cue (for phonemic search), or was not synonymous (for semantic search). Thus the form of both the phonological search and semantic search was specified and stable throughout the experiment. They found no significant difference between graphemic and semantic search, and both were faster than phonemic search.

In another comparison, with specified level of phonological and semantic access, I have also found faster times for getting at the meaning of characters compared with the sound. Participants were asked to scan through a few rows of unrelated characters, either to look for a character with a specific pronunciation (illustrated with a homophone character) or to look for a character that belonged to a specific semantic category (such as 'musical instrument'). Table 1 shows a set of preliminary data for this study. It is clear that, for both high frequency characters and mixed frequency characters, scanning for meaning is faster than scanning for pronunciation.

Table 1
Scanning for Pronunciation and Meaning: Processing Times (ms) and Miss Rates.

	Pronunciation	Meaning
Mixed Frequency	340 (21.4%)	263 (9.6%)
High Frequency	351 (12.5%)	281 (6.3%)

It appears that in direct comparison of the speed of phonological activation and semantic activation, the former is faster in situations where the level of phonological specification is clear but level of semantic specification is not. Where both are specified, semantic access is faster. The reason for the latter would appear to be related to the possibility of more direct access to meaning of Chinese words. It should be noted that the possibility of more direct access to meaning of Chinese words does not necessarily mean that reading of Chinese text (with the ultimate purpose of getting at the meaning of the text) is faster than reading English. A number of other considerations render the eventual reading speed for the two languages comparable.

Reading Text

Reports from eye-movement studies indicate that fixation time and frequency of regressions when reading Chinese and English texts are comparable (cf. Peng, Orchard & Stern, 1983; Sun, Morita & Stark, 1985). Forward saccadic span is also comparable, but only in terms of number of words, about 1.7 to 1.9 for both languages. Given that Chinese is usually written or printed more densely, so that the same content in Chinese takes up less length of text to be covered by the eyes (cf. Hoosain, 1991), the comparable saccadic span in terms of number of words also means a smaller saccadic span for Chinese in respect of physical distance. The question becomes why forward saccadic spans are physically shorter when reading Chinese. A couple of factors may be relevant.

Visually, individual Chinese characters occupy a more or less square space, one after another either horizontally or vertically in a text. Written or printed Chinese usually has higher spatial frequency (greater density of lines within the same space) compared with English. High spatial frequency input in parafoveal vision actually results in low discrimination. Also, in English there is variation in word length, and other aspects of the envelope of individual words indicated by such features as *l* and *h* sticking above the line of text, and *p*, *q*, or *g* reaching below, providing useful visual information. Thus, the usefulness of sensory information beyond the fixation point could be lower for Chinese characters in ordinary text.

There is no word boundary in written or printed Chinese. While there is regular character boundary, and words can be one or two characters long (and sometimes longer) there is no word boundary over and above character boundary. Liu, Yeh, Wang, and Chang (1974) tried to provide word boundaries over and above character boundaries in Chinese text, but found that it did not facilitate reading. Obviously, the lack of familiarity with this novel format could limit its usefulness. But what might be more crucial is that the notion of the word in Chinese does not have much psychological reality. There is a lot of variation in what people think constitutes a word. When asked to mark word boundaries in ordinary Chinese sentences, there is a lot of discrepancies (Hoosain, 1992). This would mean that the word boundaries provided in the experiment of Liu et al. could be inconsistent with the notion of where some participants thought the boundaries should be, and thus could be less than helpful.

Parsing is an integral part of language comprehension. In reading Chinese, the morphology needs to be sorted out first from the continuous parade of separate characters. This is complicated by some factors. Most educated readers are familiar with classical Chinese. In classical Chinese, as contrasted with modern Chinese, each character usually functions as a linguistic word. Also, numerous characters are capable of forming multi-character words in modern Chinese, sometimes as the first component character of certain words and the second (and sometimes third, and so on) component character for other words (cf. Hoosain, 1991). So, where the beginning of a word is and where the end is, in the continuous parade of individual characters, needs to be determined in the early stage of parsing.

The combination of the above factors means that it is more necessary to attend to individual characters in eye movement when reading Chinese text. This leads to comparable reading speed for texts of Chinese and English, even though the possibility of more direct access to meaning of individually presented words (whether single-character or two-character) would lead us to expect otherwise.

References

April, R. S. & Han, M. (1980). Crossed aphasia in a right-handed bilingual Chinese man: A second case. *Archives of Neurology, 37,* 342–346.

April, R. S. & Tse, P. C. (1977). Crossed aphasia in a Chinese bilingual dextral. *Archives of Neurology, 34,* 766–770.

Balota, D. A. & Chumbley, J. I. (1984). Are lexical decisions a good measure of lexical access? The role of word frequency in the neglected decision stage. *Journal of Experimental Psychology: Human Perception and Performance, 10,* 340–357.

Balota, D. A. & Chumbley, J. I. (1985). The locus of word-frequency effects in the pronunciation task: Lexical access and/or production? *Journal of Memory and Language, 24,* 89–106.

Besner, D. & Coltheart, M. (1979). Ideographic and alphabetic processing in skilled reading of English. *Neuropsychologia, 17,* 467–472.

Biederman, I. & Tsao, I. C. (1979). On processing Chinese ideographs and English words: Some implications from Stroop-test results. *Cognitive Psychology, 11,* 125–132.

Chao, R. Y. (1968). *Language and symbolic systems.* New York: Cambridge University Press.

Chen, H. C. (1998). *Semantics without phonology: Evidence from replications of Perfetti and Tan (1998).* Paper presented at the 39th Annual Meeting of the Psychonomic Society, Dallas, Texas.

Chen, H. C., Flores d'Arcais, F. & Cheung, S. L. (1995). Orthographic and phonological activation in recognising Chinese characters. *Psychological Research* 58:144–153.

Chen, H. C. & Tsoi, K. C. (1990). Symbol-word interference in Chinese and English. *Acta Psychologica, 75,* 123–138.

Chen, H. C., Yung, Y. F. & Ng, T. W. (1988). The effect of context on perception of Chinese characters. In I. M. Liu, H. C. Chen & M. J. Chen (Eds.), *Cognitive aspects of the Chinese language* (pp. 27–40). Hong Kong: Asian Research Service.

Chua, F. K. (1999). Phonological recoding in Chinese logograph recognition. *Journal of Experimental Psychology: Learning, Memory, and Cognition, 25,* 876–891.

Eriksen, C. W., Pollack, M. D. & Montague, W. E. (1970). Implicit speech: Mechanism in perceptual encoding? *Journal of Experimental Psychology, 84,* 502–507.

Foster, K. I. & Chambers, S. M. (1973). Lexical access and naming time. *Journal of Verbal Learning and Verbal Behavior, 12,* 627–635.

Frost, R. (1998). Toward a strong phonological theory of visual word recognition: True issues and false trails. *Psychological Bulletin, 123,* 71–99.

Hasuike, R., Tzeng, O. J. L. & Hung, D. L. (1986). Script effects and cerebral lateralization: The case of Chinese characters. In J. Vaid (Ed.), *Language processing in bilinguals: Psycholinguistic and neuropsychological perspectives* (pp. 275–288). Hillsdale, NJ: Erlbaum.

Ho, S. K. & Hoosain, R. (1989). Right hemisphere advantage in lexical decision with two-character Chinese words. *Brain and Language, 37,* 606–615.

Hoosain, R. (1991). *Psycholinguistic implications for linguistic relativity: A case study of Chinese.* Hillsdale, NJ: Erlbaum.

Hoosain, R. (1992). Psychological reality of the word in Chinese. In H. C. Chen & O. J. L. Tzeng (Eds.), *Language processing in Chinese* (pp. 111–130). Amsterdam: Elsevier.

Hoosain, R. & Osgood, C. E. (1983). Information processing times for English and Chinese words. *Perception and Psychophysics, 34,* 573–577.

Liu, I. M., Yeh, J. S., Wang, L. H. & Chang, Y. K. (1974). Effects of arranging Chinese words as units on reading efficiency. *Acta Psychologica Taiwanica, 16,* 25–32.

Liu, Y. (1998, November). *The semantic consistency of Chinese two-character words.* Paper presented at the Advanced Study Institute on Advances in Theoretical Issues and Cognitive Neuroscience Research of the Chinese Language, the University of Hong Kong, Hong Kong.

Peng, D. L., Orchard, L. N. & Stern, J. A. (1983). Evaluation of eye movement variables of Chinese and American readers. *Pavlovian Journal of Biological Sciences, 18,* 94–102.

Perfetti, C. A. & Tan, L. H. (1998). The time course of graphemic, phonological, and semantic activation in visual Chinese character identification. *Journal of Experimental Psychology: Learning, Memory, and Cognition, 24,* 101–118.

Perfetti, C. A. & Zhang, S. (1995). The universal word identification reflex. In D. L. Medin (Ed.), *The psychology of learning and motivation.* Vol. 33

(pp. 159–189). San Diego: Academic Press.

Perfetti, C. A., Zhang, S. & Berent, I. (1992). Reading in English and Chinese: Evidence for a 'universal' phonological principle. In R. Frost & L. Katz (Eds.), *Orthography, phonology, morphology, and meaning* (pp. 227–248). Amsterdam: North-Holland.

Sun, F. C., Morita, M. & Stark, L. W. (1985). Comparative patterns of reading eye movement in Chinese and English. *Perception and Psychophysics, 37,* 502–506.

Taft, M. & van Graan, F. (1998). Lack of phonological mediation in a semantic categorisation task. *Journal of Memory and Language, 38,* 203–224.

Treiman, R. A., Baron, J. & Luk, K. (1981). Speech recoding in silent reading: A comparison of Chinese and English. *Journal of Chinese Linguistics, 9,* 116–125.

Tzeng, O. J. L., Hung, D. L. & Wang, W. S.-Y. (1977). Speech recoding in reading Chinese characters. *Journal of Experimental Psychology: Human Memory and Learning, 3,* 621–630.

Tzeng, O. J. L. & Wang, W. S.-Y. (1983). The first two R's. *American Scientist, 71,* 238–243.

Wang, W. S.-Y. (1973). The Chinese language. *Scientific American, 228,* 51–60.

Waters, G. S. & Seidenberg, M. S. (1985). A distributed, developmental model of word recognition and naming. *Memory and Cognition, 13,* 557–572.

Wu, J.-T., Chou, T. L. & Liu, I. M. (1994). The locus of the character/word frequency effect. In H. W. Chang, J. T. Huang, C. W. Hue & O. J. L. Tzeng (Eds.), *Advances in the study of Chinese language processing* (pp. 31–58). Taipei: Department of Psychology, National Taiwan University (in Chinese).

Wu, J.-T. & Liu, I.M. (1997). Phonological activation in pronouncing characters. In H.-C. Chen (Ed.), *Cognitive processing of Chinese and related Asian languages* (pp. 47–64). Hong Kong: Chinese University Press.

Zajonc, R. B. (1980). Feeling and thinking. *American Psychologist, 35,* 151–175.

Reading Efficiency and Reading Strategies

Yi-Ping Chen

Current word recognition models consider that single word reading may involve the activation of the orthographic, phonological and semantic codes of written words in parallel (Seidenberg & McClelland, 1989). However, even if all information sources of written words are activated and become available, readers may not necessarily use them all at the same time. They may select different kinds of information (such as visual, semantic and phonological) for reading. The use of different information sources of written words is sometimes called *reading strategies* or *skill* (Barron, 1978, 1981). The association between reading skill and reading strategies has been extensively studied (especially some developmental studies) in English (Baron, 1973; Barron, 1978, 1981). The present study is primarily concerned with the ways in which different visual, phonological and semantic decoding strategies are related to the efficiency of reading Chinese *two-character Ci*, the most frequently used lexical items in modern Chinese language.

Paradigm and Rationale

The experimental paradigm is the computerised lexical decision with two-character Ci in Chinese. Two-character Ci plays an important lexical role in Chinese. Multi-character Ci, especially the two-character Ci, are the most frequently used lexical items in both spoken and written Chinese since 1920s. The two-character Ci is, to some extent, analogous to the English compound word, containing two free morphemes (cart horse, armchair, toothbrush, headache). They both consist of independent characters and are used as more or less as fixed expressions in the language. The lexical decision task for two-character Ci requires the subject to judge whether or not the two characters together form a Ci in Chinese. Unlike some specific tasks such as naming and semantic categorization tasks, the lexical decision task does not specify the nature of the information on which the judgements are made. It is in a way similar to reading in real life in that subjects can use any information from the prints available to them during the reading processing. However, it should be pointed out that lexical decision with two-character Ci is different from the conventional lexical decision task in English (i.e., whether or not a written symbol is a word) in at least two ways. First, lexical decision with two-character Ci involves two characters written separately in Chinese. Apart from recognition of the individual characters, the task demands the recognition of a specific lexical association between the two characters. Second, for 'No' responses, 'non-Ci' or 'pseudo-Ci' consists of two legitimate Chinese characters, but in a meaningless combination. It is the combination, not the individual elements that must be judged. In the present study, lexical decision with two-character Ci involves not only character recognition but also recognition of the lexical association between characters, which thus more closely approximates real reading.

The present study is concerned with the utilization of different information resources in reading two-character Ci. This was approached by means of calculating a number of processing indices. Each process was inferred from a specific experimental effect, assumed to be associated with it. The processing index was further adjusted by the general speed of the same subjects in judging all stimuli on those judgments.

First, the extent to which orthographic-lexical processing is the limiting factor in subjects' performance may be inferred from frequency effects on word recognition (Besner & McCann, 1987). The frequencies of two-character Ci were derived from the *Frequency Dictionary of Modern Chinese* (Beijing Language Institute, 1986). In this experiment, the effects of Ci frequency on lexical decisions of real Ci were examined. Second, a two-character Ci may be classified as concrete (e.g., 电话 'telephone') or abstract (e.g., 懊悔 'regret'). A concreteness effect may thus reflect semantic processing. Third, phonological processing was investigated by constructing Ci-homophones, in which two legitimate characters together 店化 *dian*[4] *hua*[4] sounds exactly the same (including tones indicated by the number) as the meaningful two-character Ci 电话 *dian*[4] *hua*[4] 'telephone', but are meaningless in combination 'shop turn'. Unlike many homophones in English, the Ci-homophones used in the present study share no orthographic similarity with their base Ci (i.e., 电话 vs. 店化). Finally, lexical decomposition was examined, based on manipulations of the semantic components (SC) and the phonetic components (PC) of the individual characters. This was addressed by constructing the so-called SC-conjunct-Ci and PC-conjunct-Ci. SC-conjunct-Ci consists of two characters, which together neither sounds like nor looks like a meaningful two-character Ci (e.g., 晤报 'meeting paper'). Nevertheless, the SC of one character (e.g., 日 in 晤) combines with the other characters as a whole (i.e., 报) would form a meaningful two-character Ci, i.e., 日报 'newspaper'. PC-conjunct-Ci was formed in the same way except that the conjunct component was PC. It has been demonstrated that skilled native readers of Chinese attended to SC and PC respectively in semantic and phonological comparison tasks of single character words (Chen & Allport, 1995; Chen, Allport and Marshall, 1996). Also, Chinese children learning to read Chinese were able read pseudo-characters made up by one semantic component and one phonetic component (Ho, 1994). Suppose subjects also attend to the component (SC or PC) of characters rather than individual characters as whole in reading two-character Ci in the present study, they would have longer reaction times and/or more false alarm errors on the SC- or PC-conjunct Ci than they would on the control. The difference in reaction time (RT) or error rate between SC-conjunct-Ci or PC-conjunct-Ci condition and the control may therefore reflect the degree of subjects attending to the component of individual characters, i.e., the degree of using decompositional strategies. Moreover, we want to know if the decompositional strategy based on SC and PC is associated with semantic and phonological strategy respectively (e.g., Perfetti & Zhang, 1991; Tzeng, Hung, & Wang, 1977).

METHOD

Participants   Sixteen native readers and speakers of Chinese (8 males and 8 females), aged 25 to 35, were paid to participate. All subjects had graduated from universities in mainland China and were D.Phil. students at the University of Oxford. They all speak Mandarin. For nine of them, Mandarin is their native dialect; the other three use Mandarin regularly for communication on formal occasions.

Stimuli and design   A total of 360 stimulus-pairs consisted of equal number of real Ci and non-Ci. The 180 real Ci was divided into two groups of high and low frequency and in each group they were further divided into high, medium and low concrete conditions. The other 180 non-Ci were divided into Ci-homophone, pseudo-Ci including SC-conjunct- and PC-conjunct-Ci, and the control. All stimuli consisted of two legitimate characters in the simplified version. The total of 360 pairs of characters were presented in randomized order with the constraint that no more than three consecutive trials occurred with the same response ('yes' or 'no'). The randomization was determined by a computer programme and was different for individual subjects. The stimuli in each condition are described as follows:

Two-character real Ci

A total of 180 two-character real Ci was selected from three frequency bands of high, medium and low. The high-frequency band ranged from 152 to 1120 per million. The medium-frequency band ranged from 15 to 150 per million and the low-frequency one 3 to 13 per million. Ci frequency was based on the frequency of the occurrences of two-character Ci in print according to the *Frequency Dictionary of Modern Chinese* (Beijing Language Institute, 1986). Two-character Ci in each frequency group were further classified into high-, medium- and low- concrete Ci. High-concrete Ci are names of objects. By contrast, Ci that refer to internal feelings or mental states or processes, such as *love, regret, hope,* were classified as low-concrete Ci. Ci that could not easily be classified into these two categories but which were also of low imageability, e.g., *origin, success, again,* are treated as a third, medium category.

Pseudo-Ci

Complete homophones: Two characters, which together cannot be a meaningful two-character Ci, but nonetheless sound like a real two-character Ci (including tone). For instance, 店化 *dian*[4] *hua*[4], in which the individual characters mean 'shop' and 'turn', sounds exactly the same (including tone) as the real two-character Ci: 电话 *dian*[4] *hua*[4], meaning 'telephone'.

SC-conjunct-Ci: 晤报 'meet paper' is not a meaningful two-character Ci in Chinese. However, 日, the SC of 晤, in conjunction with the other whole character 报 forms a potential Ci: 日报 'daily newspaper'.

PC-conjunct-Ci: 刑刀 'punishment knife' is meaningless both visually and phonologically. However, 开, the PC of 刑 together with 刀 i.e., 开刀 mean 'surgery'.

The position of the conjunct component, i.e., SC or PC was either on the left (e.g., SC left: 晤报; PC left: 刑刀) or on the right (e.g., SC right: 旧常; PC right: 盼布) and it was balanced across component-conjunct stimuli in the experiment.

Control

Control stimuli were those in which neither the two single characters together nor any component of them in conjunction with other whole character would look like or sound like a two-character Ci. For example, 肘炉 'elbow-oven' *zhou*[3] *lu*[2].

Apparatus   The experiment was carried out on a Packard Bell IBM PC-AT286 monograph computer, which was programmed to control stimulus presentation, record reaction times (RT) and calculate the means. The programme connected with a Chinese word processing package ET to retrieve Chinese characters. Two characters were presented simultaneously side by side in white on a black background. Each character was 1 cm × 1 cm and the two characters were spaced 1.5 cm centre to centre. Each pair of stimuli covered a visual angle of about 4.5° horizontally by 2° vertically from a viewing distance of 30 cm or so.

Procedure   The task was to judge whether or not the two characters together formed a meaningful attested two-character Ci. The Z and / keys, located in the left and right corner of the keyboard, were used for responding. They were labelled 是 'yes' and 否 'no' in Chinese. Subjects were asked to respond as accurately and quickly as possible, using the index finger of each hand. All subjects used the left hand for 'yes' responses and the right hand for 'no' responses.

Each trial began with a fixation cross, '+', of size 0.2 cm × 0.2 cm. This cross appeared for 0.5 seconds in the centre of the screen and then disappeared. After a further 0.5-second interval, two characters appeared immediately on the left and right side of the fixation point. They remained on the screen until a response key was pressed. Once a response key was pressed, the stimuli would immediately disappear from the screen. After a 0.5 second interval, the fixation cross '+' would appear to start the next trial.

Written instructions on the screen as well as oral explanations by the experimenter were given before the experiment. There were 30 pairs of warm-up trials. At the end of this practice session, the mean reaction time and error rate were shown on the screen. If the mean error rate of the practice trials was equal to or larger than 20%, more practice with different stimuli was given until an accuracy of at least 85% was reached.

After every 120 trials, there was a break of 2 minutes, accompanied by a piece of quiet electronic music.

Data analyses
Reading strategy indices
1) Orthographic-lexical strategy was inferred from the difference in RT (or error rates) between low-frequency and high-frequency Ci, divided by the mean RT (or error rate) for all 180 Ci.
2) Semantic strategy was inferred from each individual subject by the difference between low-concrete Ci and high-concrete Ci in mean RT (or error rates), divided by the mean RT (or error rate) of total Ci.
3) Phonological strategy was inferred from the difference in RT (or error rate) between the Ci-homophone condition and control condition, divided by the mean RT (or error rate) of the control.
4) Lexical decomposition strategy was inferred from both the SC- and PC-conjunction indices, based on responses to the SC- and PC-pseudo-Ci.
   (a) SC conjunction was inferred from the difference between SC-conjunct condition and the control, divided by the control, on RT and error rates.
   (b) PC conjunction was inferred from the difference between PC-conjunct condition and the control, divided by the control, on RT and error rates.

Reading efficiency
This was inferred from the subject's overall mean RT (and error rate) in responding to all the Ci. First of all, it was established that there was no significant speed-accuracy trade-off between lexical decision RT and accuracy on the 180 real Ci ($r^2 = 0.00$, $P = 0.99$). Reading speed (RT) and accuracy were hence treated as two independent variables, and were examined separately.

RESULTS

Association between reading speed and indices of the reading strategies   The results of the correlation analyses between the reading speed and accuracy and each of the processing index are summarized in Table 1 with RT and error rate data summarized in Table 1a and 1b, respectively. As indicated in Table 1a, individual subject's reading speed was significantly associated with each of the different decoding strategy indices, except with the orthographic-lexical-frequency-dependence index. The latter inferred from the susceptibility of each subject to Ci frequency effects marginally affected the speed of decision for the low-frequency Ci. However, the corresponding frequency-dependence index based on

Table 1a
Association Between Each Reading Strategy Index and Lexical Decision Times for 180 Real Ci in Experiment 1

| | Ortho-lex. *(Ci-FQ)* | | Semantic *(Concreteness)* | | Phonological *(Ci-homophone)* | | Lexical Decomposition | | | |
| | | | | | | | SC-Conjunction | | PC-Conjunction | |
Ci	r^2	*P*	r^2	*P*	r^2	*P*	r^2	*P*	r^2	*P*
Total (180)	0.10	0.23	0.24	0.05	0.37	0.01	0.27	0.04	0.37	0.01
HFQ (90)	0.00	0.79	0.21	0.07	0.34	0.02	0.18	0.10	0.34	0.01
LFQ (90)	0.23	0.06	0.25	0.05	0.35	0.01	0.34	0.02	0.36	0.01

Table 1b
Associations Between Each Reading Strategy Index and Accuracy (%) of Lexical Decisions for 180 Real Ci in Experiment 1

| | Ortho-lex. *(Ci-FQ)* | | Semantic *(Concreteness)* | | Phonological *(Ci-homophone)* | | Lexical Decomposition | | | |
| | | | | | | | SC-Conjunction | | PC-Conjunction | |
Ci	r^2	*P*	r^2	*P*	r^2	*P*	r^2	*P*	r^2	*P*
Total (180)	0.01	0.67	0.16	0.12	0.15	0.31	0.57	0.02	0.00	0.81
HFQ (90)	0.03	0.49	0.01	0.69	0.07	0.49	0.21	0.21	0.00	0.82
LFQ (90)	0.76	0.00	0.17	0.11	0.13	0.35	0.51	0.03	0.01	0.84

Note. Ortho-lex. = Orthographic-lexical; Ci-FQ = Ci-frequency; HFQ = High-frequency; LFQ = Low-frequency. Correlations of Ci and non-Ci: RT: $r^2 = 0.4$, $P = 0.0086$; Error rates: $r^2 = 0.085$, $P = 0.2722$. Correlations of RT & Error rates for Ci: $r^2 = 2.314E-6$, $P = 0.99$ and non-Ci: $r^2 = 0.038$, $P = 0.47$

accuracy data was highly predictive of lexical decision accuracy, but again for the low-frequency Ci only ($r^2 = 0.76$, $P < 0.001$; see Table 1b). Indeed, it was the only one of these indices to show such an association. The reading speed (i.e., lexical decision time) for two-character Ci was also significantly associated with both the semantic and phonological processing indices. As illustrated in Figure 1, faster reading was associated

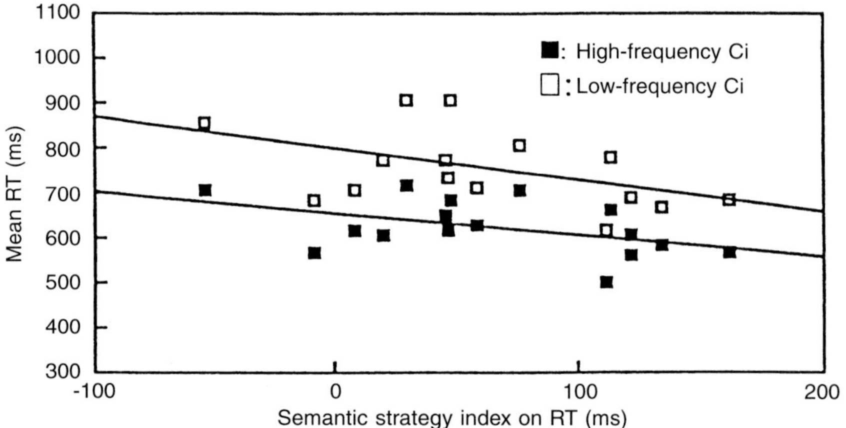

Figure 1. The correlation between RT of high- or low-frequency Ci and semantic strategy index, over 16 subjects.

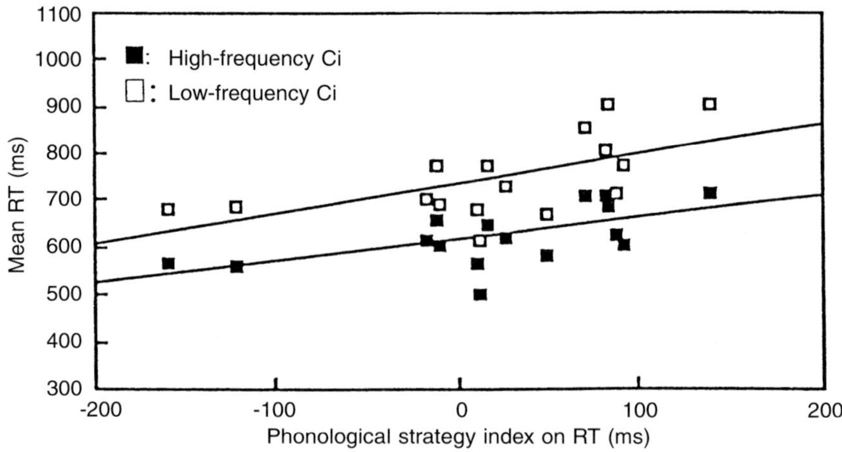

Figure 2. The correlation between RT of high- or low-frequency Ci and phonological strategy index, over 16 subjects.

with a higher semantic decoding strategy index. By contrast, slow reading was associated with a high phonological decoding strategy index and this was especially evident in responding to the low-frequency Ci (Figure 2). In other words, the greater the subject's dependence on semantic strategy (i.e., large Ci-concreteness effect), the faster his/her overall lexical decision times. Whereas the greater the subject's dependence on phonological decoding (i.e., larger the Ci-homophone interference effect), the slower his/her overall lexical decision times. Finally, as indicated in Figure 3, both slower and less accurate lexical decision was significantly associated with higher indices of lexical decomposition especially the SC-conjunction index. This was particularly evident in responding to low-frequency Ci.

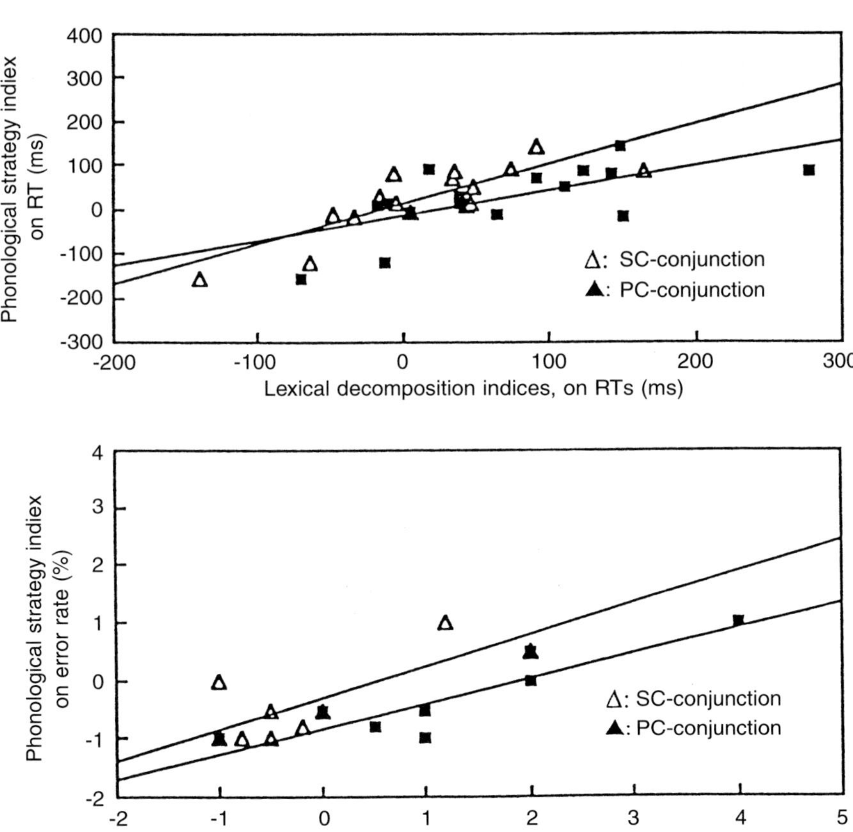

Figure 3. The correlation between phonological recoding index and two types of lexical decompostion indices on RT and error rates, over 16 subjects.

Correlation among different reading strategies   Table 2a presents the results of the correlation and regression analyses between the various processing indices. Table 2a shows the regression analyses based on the RT data; 2b shows the equivalent analyses based on error rates. There was a significant inverse association between semantic and phonological processing in the lexical decision speed with two-character Ci ($r^2 = 0.31$, $P < 0.05$). As illustrated in Figure 3, the phonological decoding index was

Table 2a
Association Among Various Reading Strategies, Based on RTs, in Experiment 1, with Regression Analyses

| | Semantic (*Concreteness*) | | Phonological (*Ci-homophone*) | | Lexical Decomposition | | | |
| | | | | | SC-conjunction | | PC-conjunction | |
	r^2	P	r^2	P	r^2	P	r^2	P
Orthographic-Lexical	0.05	0.38	0.03	0.50	0.23	0.06	0.03	0.50
Semantic (*Concreteness*)			0.31	0.02	0.26	0.04	0.09	0.26
Phonological (*Ci-homophone*)					0.68	0.00	0.42	0.01
Lexical Decomposition (*Radical*)							0.38	0.01

Table 2b
Association Among Various Reading Strategies, Inferred From Different Processing Indices in Experiment 1, With Regression Analyses on Error Rates

| | Semantic (*Concreteness*) | | Phonological (*Ci-homophone*) | | Lexical Decomposition | | | |
| | | | | | SC-conjunction | | PC-conjunction | |
	r^2	P	r^2	P	r^2	P	r^2	P
Orthographic-Lexical	0.02	0.59	0.01	0.78	0.00	0.99	0.00	0.98
Semantic (*Concreteness*)			0.06	0.52	0.00	0.88	0.00	0.87
Phonological (*Ci-homophone*)					0.60	0.01	0.72	0.00
Lexical Decomposition (*SC-conjunction*)							0.29	0.13

also highly significantly associated with both the SC- and PC-conjunction indices, in both RT and error rates (Table 2a,b). The indices of SC- and PC-conjunction were also positively correlated with each other (Table 2a).

DISCUSSION

The present study mainly concerned the relationship among different reading strategies and their implication for reading efficiency. Indices of four different reading strategies were obtained, based on each individual's performance. Unlike many studies of the relationships between reading strategy and reading skill in English, which have used good and poorer readers, as assessed by standard reading scores (e.g., Barron, 1981), this experiment used only skilled native readers, who all had a university degree in Chinese. The association between different reading strategies and reading efficiency may be understood in the light of the strategies themselves, rather than as constant for any one individual. Reading strategies can, of course, vary consistently from one individual to another. However, for the same individual, they may also vary over time and in different contexts. Unless some disturbance precludes the use of a certain strategy (such as patients with word-meaning blindness may not be able to use the semantic strategy), a reading strategy is not necessarily constant for an individual. First, the semantic decoding index varied inversely with RT. That is, a 'semantic' strategy was correlated with faster performance. By contrast, the phonological decoding index (indicating a 'phonological' strategy) was associated with slower performance. This suggests that at least for lexical decision with two-character Ci, a phonological strategy is less efficient.

The phonological and semantic strategies were themselves inversely related, suggesting that some features of processes involved in phonological decoding conflicts with efficient semantic decoding (or possibly vice versa). It will be argued, below, that this conflicting feature is lexical decomposition.

With regard to lexical decomposition, the SC-conjunction and PC-conjunction indices were strongly positively associated with the phonological decoding index. It seem that lexical decomposition is clearly associated with a phonological decoding strategy. The two lexical decomposition indices are themselves significantly correlated (though only on RT). This can be attributed to the fact that PC, i.e., the phonetic component, is by name non-specific and identifying the PC has to be based on identifying the specific form and position of its counterpart, SC. Less clearly is that SC-conjunction index was not associated with the semantic processing index inferred from the concreteness effect. It seems that lexical decomposition of this kind is less likely to occur in the semantic processing than in the phonological processing. Alternatively, this may be attributed to the fact that semantic processing index inferred from the concreteness effect may depend more upon the imageability of the characters while the function of SC is to indicate the semantic category of characters. Thus SC effect may be more likely to be evident in a semantic categorisation task. Both of these lexical decomposition indices were also correlated with slower lexical decision performance with the two-character Ci. The PC-migration index has the slightly stronger relationship with overall speed of performance, accuracy is better predicted by the SC-conjunction index. It suggests that lexical decomposition tends to associate with slow reading.

As one final note of caution, it should be addressed that any attempt to generalize from these results with skilled adult reading to children learning to read is full of risks. The direct strategies of children learning to read in Chinese can be seen in recent work on how children learn to read Chinese (Chan, 1997; Ho, 1994).

Conclusion

In the light of these findings from the present study, several conclusions may be drawn. First of all, in accord with the general view of reading Chinese, efficient lexical decision does seem to be mainly based on orthographic processing and its interface with the semantic domain, i.e., the lexical route, at least for skilled adult readers. A phonological strategy is shown to be less efficient. These two strategies themselves have an inverse relationship. As an optional strategy, lexical decomposition, involving segmenting the non-radical component (i.e., the stem of the individual characters), is clearly associated with a phonological decoding strategy. This suggests that orthographic knowledge, such as knowledge of the form and position of the lexical radicals in Chinese orthography (e.g., Hung & Tzeng, 1981), may play an important role in word recognition, only in so far as phonological decoding is involved.

References

Baron, J. (1973). Phonemic stage not necessary for reading. *Quarterly Journal of Experimental Psychology 25*, 241–246.

Barron, R. W. (1978). Access to the meaning of printed words: Some implications for reading and learning to read. In F. B. Murray (Ed.), *The recognition of words* (pp. 34–56). Newark, DE: International Reading Association.

Barron, R. W. C. (1981). Reading skill and reading strategies. In A. M. Lesgold and C. A. Perfetti (Eds.), *Interactive processes in reading.* (pp. 299–327). Hillsdale, NJ: Lawrence Erlbaum.

Beijing Language Institute (1986). *Frequency dictionary of modern Chinese.* Beijing Language Institute Press (in Chinese).

Besner, D. & McCann, R. S. (1987). Word frequency and pattern distortion in word identification and production: An examination of four classes of models. In M. Coltheart (Ed.), *Attention and Performance XII: The psychology of reading* (pp. 201–219). Hillsdale, NJ: Lawrence Erlbaum.

Chan, L. (1995). *Children learn to read and write Chinese analytically.* Doctoral dissertation, University of London.

Chen, Y. P. & Allport D. A. (1995). Attention and lexical decomposition in Chinese word recognition: Conjunctions of form and position guide selective attention. *Visual Cognition 2*, 235–268.

Chen, Y. P., Allport D. A. & Marshall, J. C. (1996). What are the functional orthographic units in Chinese word recognition: The stroke or the stroke-pattern? *Quarterly Journal of Experimental Psychology 49A*, 1024–1043.

Ho, C. (1994). *A cross-cultural study of the precursors of reading.* D. Phil dissertation, University of Oxford.

Hung, D. L. & Tzeng, O. J. L. (1981). Orthographic variations and visual information processing. *Psychological Bulletin 90*, 377–414.

Perfetti, C. A. & Zhang, S. (1991). Phonological processes in reading Chinese characters. *Journal of Experimental Psychology: Learning, Memory and Cognition 17*, 633–643.

Seidenberg, M. S. & McClelland, J. L. (1989). Distributed, Developmental Model of word recognition and naming. *Psychological Review 96*, 523–568.

Tzeng, O. J. L., Hung, D. L. & Wang, S. Y. (1977). Speech recoding in reading Chinese characters. *Journal of Experimental Psychology: Human Learning and Memory 3*, 621–630.

Early Phonological Activation in Reading Kanji: An Eye-Tracking Study

Sachiko Matsunaga

Many researchers agree that regardless of the script type, phonology plays a crucial role in holding information in working memory during reading (e.g., Dewey, 1996; Hayes, 1988; Kleiman, 1975; Treiman, Baron & Luk, 1981; Tzeng & Hung, 1980; Tzeng, Hung & Wang, 1977; Zhang & Perfetti, 1993). However, the timing of phonological activation (i.e., whether prelexical or lexical phonology is possible) during reading remains a controversial issue, especially in non-alphabetic languages like Chinese and Japanese that employ kanji (Chinese characters; see Leong & Tamaoka, 1998; also see Wang, Inhoff & Chen, 1999).

In both Chinese and Japanese, there are studies in support of early phonology (e.g., Cheng, 1992; Mizuno, 1997; Perfetti & Zhang, 1991, 1995; Tan, Hoosain & Peng, 1995; Tan, Hoosain & Siok, 1996; Wydell, Patterson & Humphreys, 1993), as well as those against it (e.g., Chen, Flores d'Arcais & Cheung, 1995; Zhou & Marslen-Wilson, 1996). The results from these studies vary, perhaps because the type of the tasks (e.g., naming and lexical decision at the word level or semantic decision at the sentence level) used in these studies is not only different but also unnatural. Natural reading involves reading texts for comprehension (Rayner & Pollatsek, 1989). Thus, despite their valuable contribution, it is difficult to make a generalization about the timing of phonology in reading kanji based on these data alone; what is needed is an on-line measure, such as eye tracking.

There are a few eye-tracking studies that specifically investigated the timing of phonology in natural reading. In English, for example, Daneman and Reingold (1993), Daneman et al. (1995) and Inhoff and Topolski (1994) measured first fixation duration and consecutive fixation durations on target words (homophonic or non-homophonic to the contextually correct words) in passages. The assumption was that if early phonology is possible, then homophone effects should be observed in the first fixation duration (i.e., the duration of the first fixation placed on the error) as well as in the gaze duration (i.e., the total fixation time spent on the error before the eye moves off) on the target words. Under this assumption, longer first fixation duration and gaze duration would be observed on the non-homophonic errors than on the homophonic errors, reflecting homophone interference effects (i.e., difficulty with noticing the homophone errors). If, on the other hand, only postsemantic phonology is possible, then homophone effects should be observed only on the total fixation duration (i.e., the sum of durations of fixations on the error, including later fixations that are the result of regressions). Presumably, shorter total fixation duration would be observed on the homophone errors than on the non-homophonic errors, reflecting homophone facilitation effects (i.e., ease with recovering the correct meanings from the homophone errors).

The results from these studies, however, are not compatible. The data from Inhoff and Topolski's study (Experiment 1) showed homophone interference effects on the first fixation duration in addition to the gaze duration, and thus the researchers argued for presemantic phonology. By contrast, Daneman and Reingold and Daneman et al. reported significant differences between homophonic and non-homophonic errors on neither the first fixation duration nor on the gaze duration, but significant homophone facilitation effects on the total fixation duration. Thus, Daneman and Reingold and Daneman et al. argued against presemantic or lexical phonology but for postsemantic phonology.

One reason for the difference in results between these studies could be that Daneman and Reingold and Daneman et al. used real but contextually inappropriate words (e.g., *hare* or *hire* for *hair*) as their stimuli, whereas Inhoff and Topolski used pseudo-words (e.g., *proon* or *ploon* for *prune*) as well as contextually inappropriate real words (e.g., *price*). When the stimuli are real words which can lexically stand alone, the meanings of the stimuli could be accessed without being noticed as errors; as a result, no difference could be observed between the homophonic and non-homophonic errors on such measures as the first fixation duration and gaze duration. That is, in the studies by Daneman and Reingold and Daneman et al., it is possible that their participants noticed neither type of errors until the meanings of the stimuli were accessed, and thus their first fixation duration and gaze duration were the same for both types of errors. If this interpretation is correct, then it would not be surprising that their data on these variables did not reveal homophone interference effects.

By contrast, in the Inhoff and Topolski study, the data on the unnoticed errors were excluded from the analyses, and thus the analysed data revealed how the meaningless errors (i.e., pseudo-words) were noticed. The data on their participants' first fixation duration and gaze duration showed that it is through phonology that the readers noticed the errors.

As for non-alphabetic languages, Wong and Chen (1999) argued against presemantic phonology in reading kanji in Chinese, by reporting results that were compatible with those of Daneman and Reingold's study and Daneman et al.'s study. However, the stimuli used in the Wong and Chen study were meaningless two-character words with the first character being contextually erroneous. Therefore, unlike Daneman and Reingold's study and Daneman et al.'s study, the meanings of their stimuli could not be accessed at the word level.

Wong and Chen analysed the first and consecutive fixation durations at the position of the errors (at N), at the position of the erroneous words (at Nw), and at the positions of the next two characters (at N + 1 and N + 2), using sound similarity and visual similarity as independent variables. Their results showed homophone effects to be: (a) none on the first fixation duration and gaze duration at N; (b) none on the first fixation duration and weak on the gaze duration at Nw and N + 1; (c) weak on the first fixation duration and strong on the gaze duration at N + 2; (d) strong on the total fixation duration at all three positions. By contrast, visual similarity effects were evidenced on the total fixation duration as well as on the other two measures at Nw, N + 1, and N + 2. Based on these findings, Wong and Chen concluded that it is orthography, not phonology, which is processed early.

Interestingly, however, Wong and Chen's data indicated that there were neither visual similarity effects nor homophone effects on the errors early in the process (i.e., no effects on the first fixation duration or gaze duration at N). Does this mean that the errors were processed without being noticed as errors, or was their erroneous status noticed regardless of the error type? The answer is not clear, because in Wong and Chen's study there was no control group who read the correct versions of the stimuli. One could argue that these errors were not noticed until the next character was viewed or fixated, and were detected visually at Nw or N + 1. However, finding errors that were visually dissimilar to the correct versions might have affected the way in which the participants read the passages; once finding visually obvious errors, they might have paid more attention to the visual features of individual characters than they normally do. It seems necessary, therefore, to further investigate the involvement or lack of involvement of phonology at N (i.e., erroneous kanji) in a task that approximates natural reading to a greater extent.

The present study attempted to satisfy this need by utilizing materials (i.e., newspaper articles) in two different versions, which were read by two groups of native Japanese readers for comprehension. One of the two versions was error free, read by the control group; the other version contained homophonic or non-homophonic kanji errors, both of which were visually similar to the contextually correct ones, read by the experimental group. In this study, visually dissimilar characters were not included as errors in order to avoid errors that were too obvious, and thus to minimize the possibility of the task becoming an error search. The errors replaced one character (first, second or last character) in the kanji compounds that appeared in the articles, making the compounds meaningless. The investigator observed what Japanese readers would do upon encountering the errors while monitoring their eye movements. It was hypothesized that if phonology is activated early, then homophone interference effects should be observed on the first fixation duration as well as the gaze duration on the errors, as in the case of the Inhoff and Topolski study. If, on the other hand, only postsemantic phonology is possible, then only homophone facilitation effects should be observed on the total fixation duration on the errors, as in the cases of the Daneman and Reingold study, Daneman et al. study, and Wong and Chen study.

METHOD

Participants The participants were 65 Japanese native speakers, who had completed at least high school education in Japan, and who were tourists, business people and university students, residing in Hawaii at the time of the experiment. Of the 65 participants, 29 were male and 36 were female, aged 18 to 62. They were randomly assigned to two groups: 35 in the experimental group, the other 30 in the control group. In terms of the background of the participants (sex, age, level of education in Japan, and the length of residence in the United States), the two groups did not differ significantly ($p > .05$).

Apparatus   The participants were tested individually in the University of Hawaii at Manoa Educational Psychology Department's laboratory. The laboratory was equipped with a 19-inch computer monitor, a Macintosh computer, and an eye-movement monitor called *Eye View Monitor System*, Applied Science Laboratory's (ASL) corneal reflection system model 1998. The 19-inch computer monitor, located 30 inches away from the participant, displayed the reading materials. The Macintosh computer was operated by the investigator to control the experiment, while running the software written at the University of Hawaii at Manoa. The ASL eye-movement monitor was operated by an assistant.

Materials   The reading materials were seven newspaper articles (one for the practice session; six for the experimental session) taken from *Asahi shinbun*, a Japanese daily newspaper. The kanji contained in these articles were commonly used and taught by the ninth grade in Japan. The average number of symbols per passage was 123.33, and the average percentage of kanji per passage was 47.25 (the rest of the texts were written in Japanese syllabic scripts and a few alpha-numerals). The topics of the articles were: 'Travel Consultation Survey', 'School Lunch Incident', 'Opinion Poll', 'Trip of Secretary of Defence', 'Rocket Engine Experiment', and 'Japanese Tourists Abroad'.

For the control group, the six passages contained no errors; for the experimental group, four of the six passages contained two types of erroneous characters, and two of them contained no errors. There were two reasons for including two error-free passages for the experimental group. One was to minimize the possibility that they start looking for errors. According to Just and Carpenter (1987) and Rayner and Pollatsek (1989), proofreading or error search is not the same as true reading. The interest of this study was to investigate true reading behaviours. The other reason was to make sure that there is no significant difference between the two groups in terms of their eye movement patterns in normal reading. This was done by comparing the two groups' data on the error-free passages in terms of the total reading time, the total number of fixations per passage, the percentage of the number of fixated kanji, and the average number of fixations and fixation duration per fixated kanji. No significant difference was found between the groups in any of these measures ($p > .05$)

Among the four erroneous passages read by the experimental group, two of them contained five homophonic errors each, and the other two contained five non-homophonic errors each. Therefore, the experimental group saw 10 homophonic errors in two passages, 10 non-homophonic errors in two other passages, and no errors in the other two passages. The errors were commonly used kanji, and were randomly dispersed throughout the test materials.

Both homophonic and non-homophonic errors were similar (+) in forms and dissimilar (-) in meanings to the correct versions; the only difference between the two types of errors was the similarity or dissimilarity in sounds to the correct ones. The three elements of sound, form and meaning were thus 'S+F+M-' for the homophonic errors (e.g., 粉失 *funshitsu* for 紛失 *funshitsu* 'loss'), and 'S-F+M-' for non-homophonic errors (e.g., 被片 *hihen* for 破片 *hahen* 'fragment'). All of the errors were inserted into the Sino-Japanese words (nouns or nominals) in the texts. In terms of the position of the erroneous character within the word, there was no significant difference between the two types of errors ($p > .1$). All of these Sino-Japanese words are commonly used, and appeared on the list made by Kokuritsu Kokugo Kenkyûjo (The National Language Research Institute) in *Gendai shinbun no kanji* (A Study of Uses of Chinese Characters in Modern Newspapers; 1976, pp. 127–435).

The selection of the kanji errors was done by asking three native speakers of Japanese who did not participate in the experiment to decide whether pairs of correct characters and their erroneous counterparts were similar or dissimilar in forms and in meanings. The errors used in this experiment were taken from those pairs on which two of the three or all of the three native speakers agreed in terms of the similarity or dissimilarity of their features. Statistically, there was no significant difference between the two types of erroneous kanji ($p > .1$) or between their correct versions ($p > .1$) in their frequency rank made by Kokuritsu Kokugo Kenkyûjo (1976).

In addition to the passages and the errors, five comprehension questions were prepared for each passage. These were true or false questions, and were designed to test overall understanding of the content of each passage. The participants were expected to answer no less than three out of the five questions correctly if they were reading the passage for comprehension. Thus, the data from those who failed to answer three or more questions correctly were dropped from the analyses.

Procedure   First, the participant was seated in front of the computer monitor, and asked to position his or her head against the headrest, and to rest his or her chin on the chin rest. When the participant's head and chin were stabilized, his or her eyes were calibrated. Calibration required the participant to look at nine points in a 3 by 3 grid corresponding to the area of the visual field containing the stimuli. Then, the experimental procedure was explained in Japanese. In the explanation, the participant was asked to read each of the six passages for comprehension, and was informed that he or she would be asked true or false questions after reading each one. The participant was also told that there was no need to be able to answer all the comprehension questions correctly, and therefore was also encouraged to read as naturally as possible.

A tape-recorder was set to record the participant's answers during the experiment, so as to allow the investigator to check them. During a practice session, the participant silently read an error-free passage on the screen, then orally answered five comprehension questions. None of the participants was informed about the possibility of seeing erroneous characters. Thus, the experimental group and the control group experienced exactly the same preparation: Both read the passages for comprehension without expecting to see errors.

After the participant understood the experimental procedure, the experimental session began. With his or her head and chin stabilized, the participant read each of the six passages for comprehension with another calibration at the end of the session. The order of the passage presentation was counter-balanced across participants in order to avoid a possible order effect on their performance. After the experiment, the participant was asked to fill out the questionnaire, and paid for his or her participation.

RESULTS

First, the data from those participants who failed to answer three or more comprehension questions correctly and the inaccurate data were eliminated. The remaining data (24 in the experimental group; 20 in the control group) were then analysed in terms of three eye-fixation duration measures: (a) the average first fixation duration per target character, (b) the average gaze duration per target character, (c) the average total fixation duration per target character. First fixation duration is the duration of the first fixation placed on the target character. Gaze duration is the total fixation time spent on the target character before the eye moves off. The total fixation duration includes the durations of later fixations on the target character that are the result of regressions. The calculation on all measures was based on the fixated target characters (see Table 1 for the skipping rates of the target characters). The interest of the study was to see whether longer fixation durations were placed by the experimental group on the non-homophonic errors than the homophonic errors in all three measures, and whether their fixations were longer than those placed by the control group on the correct versions of the errors. The results from the analysis in each category will be presented in turn.

Table 1
Skipping Rates: Average Percentage of Target Characters Without First Fixation or Later Fixation

		Error type	
Group		Homophonic	Non-homophonic
		No first fixation	
Experimental[a]			
	M (SD)	25.833 (16.396)	21.042 (13.830)
Control[b]			
	M (SD)	33.268 (18.860)	40.262 (16.448)
		No later fixation	
Experimental[a]			
	M (SD)	21.667 (15.788)	18.125 (11.870)
Control[b]			
	M (SD)	28.268 (15.409)	34.262 (15.361)

Note: [a]$n = 24$. [b]$n = 20$. The experimental group saw the errors, while the control group saw their correct versions.

First fixation duration   The mean values for the average first fixation duration per fixated target character for the experimental and control groups are presented in Table 2.

By employing two independent variables – group type (the between subjects factor) and error type (the within subjects factor) – a two-way Analysis of Variance (ANOVA) was performed. The main effect of error type was not significant ($p > .1$), but the main effect of group type was marginally significant, $F(1, 42) = 3.972$, $p = .0528$; there was no significant interaction between the two variables ($p > .1$). According to the item analysis, there was no significant main effect of error type ($p > .1$) or

Table 2

Average First Fixation Duration, Gaze Duration, and Total Fixation Duration Per Fixated Target Character (in s)

	Error type	
Group	Homophonic	Non-homophonic
	Average first fixation duration	
Experimental[a]		
M (SD)	0.207 (0.029)	0.225 (0.051)
Control[b]		
M (SD)	0.194 (0.044)	0.193 (0.049)
	Average gaze duration	
Experimental[a]		
M (SD)	0.236 (0.067)	0.296 (0.103)
Control[b]		
M (SD)	0.209 (0.043)	0.223 (0.069)
	Average total fixation duration	
Experimental[a]		
M (SD)	0.321 (0.101)	0.462 (0.207)
Control[b]		
M (SD)	0.261 (0.089)	0.295 (0.114)

Note: [a]$n = 24$. [b]$n = 20$. The experimental group saw the errors, while the control group saw their correct versions.

interaction ($p > .1$); however, the main effect of group type was significant, $F(1, 18) = 6.180$, $p < .05$.

The ANOVA for simple effects further indicated that the experimental group placed significantly longer first fixation on non-homophonic errors than the control group did on their correct versions, $F(1, 42) = 4.427$, $p < .05$, while the group effect on homophonic errors was not significant ($p > .1$). Moreover, the experimental group placed marginally longer first fixation on non-homophonic errors than on homophonic errors, $F(1, 24) = 3.667$, $p = .0680$. The item analysis also indicated that the group effect was significant only on the non-homophonic errors, $F(1, 9) = 6.365$, $p < .05$; no other effects were significant ($p > .1$).

Gaze duration   The mean values for the average gaze duration per fixated target character for the experimental and control groups can be found in Table 2.

A two-way ANOVA showed that there were significant main effects of group type, $F(1, 42) = 6.138$, $p < .005$, and of error type, $F(1, 42) = 14.641$, $p < .001$; there was also a significant interaction between the two variables, $F(1, 42) = 84.914$, $p < .05$. According to the item analysis, the main effect of error type was significant, $F(1, 18) = 20.185$, $p < .001$, and that of group type was marginally significant, $F(1, 18) = 3.819$, $p = .0664$; the interaction between the two variables was also marginally significant, $F(1, 18) = 3.363$, $p = .0833$.

The ANOVA for simple effects further indicated that the experimental group placed significantly longer gaze duration on non-homophonic errors than the control group did on their correct versions, $F(1, 42) = 7.280$, $p < .01$. Moreover, the experimental group placed significantly longer gaze duration on the non-homophonic errors than on the homophonic errors, $F(1, 23) = 18.170$, $p < .001$, while there were no other significant differences ($p > .1$).

According to the item analysis, the group effect was significant on the non-homophonic errors, $F(1, 9) = 16.102$, $p < .005$, and was marginally significant on the homophonic errors, $F(1, 9) = 4.669$, $p = .0590$. The effect of the error type was significant for the experimental group, $F(1, 18) = 6.103$, $p < .05$. There was no significant difference between the correct versions of the two types of errors seen by the control group ($p > .1$).

Total fixation duration   The mean values for the average total fixation duration per fixated target character for the experimental and control groups are shown in Table 2.

A two-way ANOVA showed that there were significant main effects of group type, $F(1, 42) = 11.775$, $p < .005$, and of error type, $F(1, 42) = 12.710$, $p < .001$; there was also a significant interaction between the two variables, $F(1, 42) = 4.285$, $p < .05$. The item analysis indicated that there were significant main effects of group type, $F(1, 18) = 15.580$, $p < .001$, and of error type, $F(1, 18) = 5.083$, $p < .05$; the interaction between the two variables was marginally significant, $F(1, 18) = 3.158$, $p = .0924$.

The ANOVA for simple effects further indicated that the experimental group placed significantly longer total fixation duration on non-homophonic errors than the control group did on their correct versions, $F(1, 42) = 10.396$, $p < .005$. The difference between the two groups on the average total fixation duration per homophonic error was also significant, $F(1, 42) = 4.272$, $p < .05$. Moreover, the experimental group placed significantly shorter total fixation duration on the homophonic errors than on the non-homophonic errors, $F(1, 23) = 10.461$, $p < .005$; the average total fixation durations on the correct versions of the two types of errors did not differ significantly for the control group ($p > .1$).

According to the item analysis, the group effect was significant on the non-homophonic errors, $F(1, 9) = 9.215$, $p < .05$, and on the homophonic errors, $F(1, 9) = 10.503$, $p < .05$. The effect of the error type was significant for the experimental group, $F(1, 18) = 5.251$, $p < .05$. The difference between the correct versions of the two types of errors was not significant for the control group ($p > .1$).

DISCUSSION

The present study investigated whether early phonology is possible in reading kanji in Japanese texts, by employing an eye-tracking methodology. It was hypothesized that if phonology is activated early, then homophone interference effects should be observed on the first fixation duration and gaze duration on the errors, as in the case of the Inhoff and Topolski (1994) study (Experiment 1). If, on the other hand, only postsemantic phonology is possible, then only homophone facilitation effects should be observed on the total fixation duration on the errors, as in the cases of the Daneman and Reingold (1993) study, Daneman et al. (1995) study, and Wong and Chen (1999) study.

The results from this study were compatible to a large extent with those in the Inhoff and Topolski study. The present data on the first fixation duration showed a significant group difference only on the non-homophonic errors and a marginally significant homophone interference effect. On the gaze duration, furthermore, a significant homophone interference effect was evident, and a significant group difference was again found only on the non-homophonic errors (the group difference was marginally significant on the homophonic errors only by item). These results seem to indicate the experimental group's difficulty with noticing the homophonic errors. In addition, the data on the total fixation duration showed strong group effects on both types of errors and a strong homophone facilitation effect. A longer total fixation duration found on the non-homophonic errors than on the homophonic errors seems to indicate the difficulty with recovering from the non-homophonic errors.

As pointed out earlier, one reason for the difference between the results from the present study and the Inhoff and Topolski study, on one hand, and those from the studies by Daneman and Reingold and Daneman et al., on the other hand, could be the difference in the type of stimuli. The former two studies used meaningless words as stimuli, and the latter two studies used real words whose meanings were contextually erroneous.

In other words, the meanings of the stimuli used in the studies by Daneman and Reingold, and Daneman et al. might have been accessed before noticing errors regardless of their type; hence, their data revealed no homophone interference effects on the first fixation duration and gaze duration.

By contrast, in the present study, the experimental group could access the meanings of the correct versions of the stimuli either by not noticing the errors (i.e., reading them as the correct words due to the visual similarities), or by noticing and recovering from the errors. The results showed that: (a) the experimental group noticed the errors (as evidenced in the consistent group effects found especially on the non-homophonic errors); (b) the sounds mattered for them to notice the errors (as evidenced in the homophone interference effects found weakly on the first fixation duration and strongly on the gaze duration), and also to recover from the errors (as evidenced in the homophone facilitation effect found on the total fixation duration). These results seem possible only if phonology is activated early; they differ from those in the Wong and Cheng study, perhaps because in the present study all errors were visually similar to the contextually correct characters, which may have minimized the possibility of the task becoming unnatural reading.

Another interesting result obtained in this study is that the group effect was significant on the homophonic errors only on the total fixation duration (the group difference on the gaze duration was marginally significant only by item), whereas the same effect was significant on the non-homophonic errors on all three measures. This result seems to suggest that the non-homophonic errors were noticed as early as at the first fixation through phonological processing, and that the homophonic errors were noticed only at later fixations through semantic processing and/or visual check (Van Orden, 1987). Thus, these data appear to serve as additional support for the early involvement of phonology.

In conclusion, it seems reasonable to argue, based on the eye-movement data from the present study and the Inhoff and Topolski study, that the timing of phonological activation in natural reading could be earlier than postsemantic in both English and Japanese. More specifically, the present data suggested that even when reading non-alphabetic scripts like kanji, sounds could begin to be processed as early as the first fixation, and be fully processed before the eyes move off. Unfortunately, however, it is not possible to assert from the present study that the evidenced involvement of phonology is presemantic. To fully investigate the possibility of presemantic phonology, it is necessary to examine the existence or absence of phonology before the first fixation (i.e., parafoveally). With its presence being demonstrated in English (e.g., Henderson, Dixon, Petersen, Twilley & Ferreira, 1995; Pollatsek, Lesch, Morris & Rayner, 1992) and in Chinese (e.g., Pollatsek, Tan & Rayner, 2000), such studies in Japanese would provide valuable information on whether presemantic phonology is universally possible in natural reading, and would enhance our understanding of reading processes in general.

References

Chen, H.-C., Flores d'Arcais, G. B., & Cheung, S. L. (1995). Orthographic and phonological activation in recognizing Chinese characters. *Psychological Research, 58*, 144–153.

Cheng, C.-M. (1992). Lexical access in Chinese: Evidence from automatic activation of phonological information. In H. C. Chen & O. J. L. Tzeng (Eds.), *Language processing in Chinese, Advances in Psychology, 90* (pp. 67–91). Amsterdam: Elsevier Science Publishers B. V.

Daneman, M., & Reingold, E. M. (1993). What eye fixations tell us about phonological recoding during reading. *Canadian Journal of Experimental Psychology, 47*, 153–178.

Daneman, M., Reingold, E. M., & Davidson, M. (1995). Time course of phonological activation during reading: Evidence from eye fixations. *Journal of Experimental Psychology: Learning, Memory, and Cognition, 21*, 884–898.

Dewey, D. P. (1996). Strategies used in encoding kanji in short-term memory. In S. T. Hayes & E. Takahashi (Eds.), *Proceedings of the eighth annual conference of the Lake Erie Teachers of Japanese* (pp. 58–81). Pittsburgh, PA: The Lake Erie Teachers of Japanese.

Hayes, E. B. (1988). Encoding strategies used by native and non-native readers of Chinese Mandarin. *The Modern Language Journal, 72*, 188–195.

Henderson, J. M., Dixon, P., Petersen, A., Twilley, L. C., & Ferreira, F. (1995). Evidence for the use of phonological representations during transsaccadic word recognition. *Journal of Experimental Psychology: Human Perception and Performance, 21*, 82–97.

Inhoff, A. W., & Topolski, R. (1994). Use of phonological codes during eye fixations in reading and in on-line and delayed naming tasks. *Journal of Memory and Language, 33*, 689–713.

Just, M. A., & Carpenter, P. A. (1987). *The psychology of reading and language comprehension*. Boston: Allyn & Bacon.

Kleiman, G. M. (1975). Speech recoding in reading. *Journal of Verbal Learning and Verbal Behavior, 14,* 323–329.

Kokuritsu Kokugo Kenkyûjo. (1976). *Gendai shinbun no kanji* [A study of uses of Chinese characters in modern newspapers]. Tokyo: Shûei-sha.

Leong, C. K., & Tamaoka, K. (Eds.). (1998). Cognitive processing of the Chinese and the Japanese languages. *Reading and Writing: An Interdisciplinary Journal, 10,* 155–316.

Mizuno, R. (1997). *Kanji hyôkigo no oninshori jidôka kasetsu no kenshô* (A test of a hypothesis of automatic phonological processing of Kanji words). *The Japanese Journal of Psychology, 68,* 1–8.

Perfetti, C. A., & Zhang, S. (1991). Phonological processes in reading Chinese characters. *Journal of Experimental Psychology: Learning, Memory and Cognition, 17,* 633–643.

Perfetti, C. A., & Zhang, S. (1995). Very early phonological activation in Chinese reading. *Journal of Experimental Psychology: Learning, Memory and Cognition, 21,* 24–33.

Pollatsek, A., Lesch, M., Morris, O. K., & Rayner, K. (1992). Phonological codes are used in integrating information across saccades in word identification and reading. *Journal of Experimental Psychology: Human Perception and Performance, 18,* 148–162.

Pollatsek, A., Tan, L. H., & Rayner, K. (2000). The role of phonological codes in integrating information across saccadic eye movements in Chinese character identification. *Journal of Experimental Psychology: Human Perception and Performance, 26,* 607–633.

Rayner, K., & Pollatsek, A. (1989). *The psychology of reading.* Englewood Cliffs, NJ: Prentice Hall.

Tan, L. H., Hoosain, R., & Siok, W. T. (1996). Activation of phonological codes before access to character meaning in written Chinese. *Journal of Experimental Psychology: Learning, Memory, and Cognition, 22,* 865–882.

Tan, L. H., Hoosain, R., & Peng, D.-L. (1995). Role of early presemantic phonological code in Chinese character identification. *Journal of Experimental Psychology: Learning, Memory, and Cognition, 21,* 43–54.

Treiman, R. A., Baron, J., & Luk, K. (1981). Phonological coding in silent reading: A comparison of Chinese and English. *Journal of Chinese Linguistics, 9,* 116–124.

Tzeng, O. J. L., & Hung, D. (1980). Reading in a non-alphabetic writing system. In J. F. Kavanagh & R. L. Venezky (Eds.), *Orthography, reading, and dyslexia* (pp. 221–226). Baltimore: University Park Press.

Tzeng, O. J. L., Hung, D. C., & Wang, W. S.-Y. (1977). Phonological coding in reading Chinese characters. *Journal of Experimental Psychology: Human Learning and Memory, 3,* 621–630.

Van Orden, G. C. (1987). A ROWS is a ROSE: Spelling, sound, and reading. *Memory & Cognition, 15,* 181–198.

Wang, J., Inhoff, A. W., & Chen, H.-C. (Eds.). (1999). *Reading Chinese script: A cognitive analysis*. Mahwah, NJ: Lawrence Erlbaum Associates.

Wong. E. K., & Chen, H.-C. (1999). Orthographic and phonological processing in reading Chinese text: Evidence from eye fixations. *Language & Cognitive Processes Special Issue: Processing East Asian Languages, 14*, 461–480.

Wydell, T. N., Patterson, K. E., & Humphreys, G. W. (1993). Phonologically mediated access to meaning for kanji: Is a *Rows* still a *Rose* in Japanese kanji? *Journal of Experimental Psychology: Learning, Memory, and Cognition, 19*, 491–514.

Zhang, S., & Perfetti, C. A. (1993). The tongue-twister effect in reading Chinese. *Journal of Experimental Psychology: Learning, Memory, and Cognition, 19*, 1082–1093.

Zhou, X., & Marslen-Wilson, W. (1996). Direct visual access is the only way to access the Chinese mental lexicon. In G. Cottrell (Ed.), *Proceedings of the Eighteenth Annual Conference of the Cognitive Science Society* (pp. 714–719). Hillsdale, NJ: Lawrence Erlbaum Associates.

Author Note

This study is a complete reanalysis of the data reported in the author's unpublished doctoral dissertation submitted to the University of Hawaii at Manoa (1994).

Part 3

Structural Relationship of Components of Chinese Characters

Visual-Spatial Properties and Orthographic Processing of Chinese Characters

Xuefeng Chen and Henry S. R. Kao

The term *orthography* is used by some authors for spelling patterns and for correct or standard spelling rules of scripts (Richards, Platt, & Weber, 1985). From writing system to writing system, orthographic information differs. Mason (1975) identified orthographic information as a form of redundancy that can be used to augment visual feature information. She initially isolated four possible sources of information in word recognition. The first two are the direct visual information about the distinctive features of individual letters within a word and the direct visual information about the spatial position of letters in a letter string. Mason's definition implies a strong visual factor in the nature of orthographic information.

For most alphabetic scripts, the word is composed of left-to-right letters. Word reading follows a unidirectional or one-dimensional scanning path. However, for Chinese, each character occupies an imaginary space of identical size. The shapes of the characters reflect a two-thousand-year history of brushwork calligraphy, in which one of the most important features is equi-dimensionality (Martin, 1972). This feature comes from the imaginary space inherent in each character, a square. Chinese characters should be treated as contained in a rigid square of uniform size, occupying 2-dimensional space both in height and width. The characters have been called *Fang*[1]*kuai*[4] *Zi*[4] (square script) since the development of clerical script. Related descriptions can be seen from the more popular literature on the Chinese language (e.g. Hu, 1992; Huang

& Hu, 1990; Liu, 1999; Lu, 1987) or from psychological research (e.g., Chen, 1997; Huang & Wang, 1992; Jackson, Lu, & Ju, 1994; Taft & Zhu, 1997a).

According to the most general principle of Gestalt psychology, the law of *Pragnanz*, people tend to organize forms in the simplest way possible. A square, among other 2-D geometric patterns, is the simplest pattern (Koffka, 1935). It incorporates all the visual properties most strongly suggested by Gestalt principles: symmetry (in four axes, i.e., horizontal, vertical and two diagonals), closure, continuity and balance, which contribute to the matter of simplicity. Therefore, it is obviously easier to be alerted by vision than any other patterns. A square, however, is much more than these. It contains some other regular visual properties as well, such as collinearity, connectivity and parallelism. With an implied correspondence between the shape of the square and the character, characters may vary in terms of the extent to which they possess the geometric properties of the square. Recently, Kao (2000) analysed the most primitive writing systems, including Egyptian writing, Sumerian script and Chinese oracle bone script. He found that there is an existence of several common visual properties in primitive writing systems: they tend to be pictographic, closed, parallel, and symmetric. Therefore, we may say that the primitive writing systems are the direct and natural projection of human's visual perception to the outside world. However, Chinese script is the only written language that inherits most of the distinctive visual features from its ancestral versions.

The visual effect of these properties has been investigated in many visual studies. Chen (1982) conducted three experiments on tachistoscopic perception of geometric figures. The results demonstrated that the visual system is sensitive to global topological properties and suggested that a primitive and general function of the visual system might be the perception of global topological properties. Connectivity and closure are typical topological properties invariant under continuous and one-to-one transformations. But collinearity, parallelism, symmetry, orientation, etc., are not. Further evidence indicated that the extraction of topological properties is a basic factor in perceptual organization. The visual systems are superior at perceiving topological properties before perceiving more detailed geometrical properties of stimuli (Todd, Chen, & Norman, 1998).

A more detailed theoretical and empirical description came from Biederman (1987). He developed a theoretical hierarchical model of perceptual recognition of single objects, called Recognition-by-Components (RBC). The highlight of our discussion is the detection of non-accidental properties, which is a stage involved in this model. Properties are defined as non-accidental in terms of the central organizational principle. Certain properties of edges in a two-dimensional image are taken by the visual system as strong evidence that the edges in the three-dimensional world contain those same properties. Therefore, such properties are quite stable and only slightly affected by accidental alignments of viewpoints and object features. Collinearity, curvilinearity, symmetry, parallelism, and cotermination are summarized as five salient non-accidental properties by this model. There is considerable evidence supporting the assumption that these non-accidental properties can serve as primary organizational constraints in human image interpretation (e.g., Ballesteros, Millar, & Reales, 1998; Kanade, 1981; Palmer, 1980).

So far we have got much of the evidence supporting the early facilitating effect of the non-accidental visual-spatial properties in visual perception from purely visual studies. Most of the studies used non-linguistic stimuli such as geometric figures, line drawings, and 2-D or 3-D objects. Moreover, most visual studies have used explicit visual property detection tasks, such as search tasks (i.e., searching a target with a distinctive property from distracters with the same property or with the opposite property, e.g., linear vs. non-linear; symmetry vs. asymmetry; closed vs. unclosed), which necessarily draw attention to the properties. However, these studies raised a very interesting question. As discussed above, Chinese characters are structurally 2-D, and non-accidental properties are found abundantly in the intersections among strokes and inflections of strokes. Does the primal access to the non-accidental properties exist at the early stage of the recognition of Chinese characters and further trigger the orthographic processing of Chinese characters?

It is fairly common in the literature on orthographic processing for researchers to refer to orthographic processing as 'visual processing' as though these two terms are essentially synonymous. However, from the definition of orthography, orthographic processing should be more accurately defined as 'visual processing specific to written words' (Berninger, 1994, p. xii). There is a paucity of research to probe the effect of visual-spatial properties on the processing of Chinese characters. In an early work, Ai (1948/1965) found that characters with linear strokes were recognized easier than those with non-linear strokes and characters with symmetric structures were recognized easier than those with asymmetric structures. More recently, Peng and Zhang (1984) also observed the facilitating effect of the symmetric structure in the recognition of characters. Yu, Zhang, and Pan (1997) first considered collinearity as the main variable in their study and confirmed the same effect of linear strokes as Ai reported. Chen and Huang (1999) first considered symmetry as the main variable in their study and also found the main effect of symmetry in character recognition. Another set of findings was from Kao (1998, 2000). Kao developed a psycho-geometric theory of Chinese handwriting that has its foundations upon the basic relationship between human perception and motion. This theory predicts that characters containing or conforming to the visual-spatial properties of a square, the outer structure of characters, will have a greater behavioural impact on the writer than those characters lacking such properties. The visual properties manipulated as variables in a series of experiments conducted by Kao included collinearity, closure, symmetry, and orientation. Significant cognitive changes associated with the geometric variations of the characters included clerical speed and accuracy, spatial ability, abstract reasoning, digit span, short-term memory, picture memory, and cognitive reaction time. Kao's findings seem encouraging. However, it is still questionable whether these findings can also be applicable to the recognition of Chinese characters.

This study aimed to investigate whether the visual-spatial properties inherent in the characters could be used quickly enough to provide a perceptual basis for the orthographic processing of Chinese characters. Do they further trigger the orthographic processing? Although there have been several related studies, they usually isolated one property as the independent variable regardless of the possible interactions of different properties that might be incorporated simultaneously in the same character. This is the first systematically designed study to report the effect of the visual properties on the orthographic processing of Chinese characters. Moreover, considerable evidence has been available to support the main effects of character complexity (stroke number) and character familiarity (frequency) on Chinese character processing (see Peng & Wang, 1997; Taft & Zhu, 1997a). What will be the relationships between the effect of those visual properties, if any, and the effects of these two factors?

EXPERIMENT 1

The hypothesis was that the visual-spatial properties inherent in the characters can be quickly used and facilitate the orthographic processing of Chinese characters. The visual-spatial properties under consideration were linearity, parallelism, closure, and symmetry. According to Fu (1985), there are five kinds of fundamental strokes in Chinese characters: 一, 丨, 丿, 乀, and 乛. We calculated '一' and '丨' as linear strokes and the others as non-linear strokes. Parallelism includes linear parallel (e.g., 二) and non-linear parallel (e.g., 彡). Closure could be linear, i.e., 口 with different sizes, or non-linear (e.g., 女). Symmetry could be any kind of symmetric structures of the whole character, such as symmetry through a horizontal axis (e.g., 巨), through a vertical axis (e.g., 且) or with repeated components (e.g., 朋). We did not separate these properties very clearly in this study. We defined the characters with more than 70% linear or parallel strokes of the whole stroke number (e.g., 刊), and/or with one or more linear closed hole (e.g., 味), and/or with symmetric structure (e.g., 杏) as 'characters with rich visual-spatial properties' or 'rich characters'. We further defined the asymmetric characters with less than 30% linear or parallel strokes of the whole stroke number (e.g., 令), as 'characters with poor visual-spatial properties' or 'poor characters'. The latter might have non-linear holes (e.g., 好). We also considered the variables of the complexity of characters (quantified by stroke number) and the familiarity of characters (whether learned by the subjects or not), both of which are known to have significant effects on the recognition of Chinese characters.

METHOD

Subjects   50 fourth-grade school children (12 girls, 38 boys) with normal intelligence and normal or corrected to normal vision from six primary schools located in Guangzhou city, China, participated in this research. All of the children were native Chinese, and spoke Putonghua, which is the language of instruction in school. They are all right-handed.

Design   A within-subjects design with three independent variables: two levels of character complexity (less than 9 stroke number vs. more than 10 stroke number), two levels of character familiarity (learned vs. unlearned), and three levels of visual-spatial properties of the pairs of stimuli (rich-rich, rich-poor, and poor-poor) was used. The dependent variables were visual judgement latency and errors.

Materials   There were a total number of 120 pairs of stimuli, with 10 pairs in each of the 12 experimental conditions. All the 240 characters were selected from textbooks used by all the primary schools in Guangzhou, of which the learned characters were selected from the new character lists of grade 1–4, whereas the unlearned characters were selected from the new character lists of grade 5–6. The stroke numbers of the stimuli were carefully matched. The mean stroke number was 6.4 for the first level, and 11.3 for the second level. The characters with rich properties had mean proportions of .86 and .87 for parallel strokes and linear strokes, ranging from .71 to 1. Characters with poor properties had a mean proportion of .17 for linear strokes and .06 for parallel strokes, ranging from 0 to .29. Eighty-three percent of the rich characters had linear closures, and 34% had symmetric structure. Whereas only 24% of the poor characters had non-linear closures, and none was symmetric.

All the stimuli were presented on the centre of a computer monitor in Song style (the most popularly used font in Chinese printed materials). The size of the character is 3 cm in height and 2.5 cm in width. The order of stimuli was randomized over all factors and conditions, so that each subject received a new order of stimuli. The responses for 'left' and 'right' were balanced. We also controlled the order of 'left' or 'right' responses so that the same response would happen consecutively no more than 5 times.

The apparatus was a PC computer with Pentium II processor and VGA display in a lab with natural light. Stimuli were presented white on black. The computer recorded the latency from the presentation of the stimuli to the subjects' response and the accuracy of the response as well. The programme used was developed in Visual Basic 6.0.

Procedures   The subjects were tested singly in the laboratory. They were seated directly in front of the screen, at a distance of about 50 cm. To start a trial, the subject pressed a key, which produced a cross in the centre of the monitor. The subjects were instructed to fixate this cue. The fixation cue was replaced after 200 ms by a target character, which was exposed for 500 ms, after which comparison stimuli (one of which was the target just presented) appeared in the same position until the response was made. A new trial started with a cross after 2 seconds. The task was to judge which one of the stimuli was identical with the target. Two response keys 'left' and 'right' were marked on letter 'S' and 'L' on the keyboard of the computer, and the subjects assigned their corresponding hand on each key. The index finger of the hand was used to indicate responses. The subjects were asked to work as quickly and accurately as possible. No feedback was given to the subjects until all conditions had been completed. All subjects received 10 practice trials prior to the real test.

RESULTS AND DISCUSSION

The overall percentage of errors was 6.4. The mean judging latencies excluded the latencies of error responses. The latencies over 2 standard deviations from the mean were regarded as outliers and were not included in the analysis. Mean judging latencies and errors in each experimental condition are given in Table 1.

Table 1
Mean Latencies (in ms) and Percentage of Errors With Standard Errors in Each Condition in Experiment 1

Target complexity	Target familiarity	Visual property	Character examples	Mean latencies (Standard error)	Mean errors (Standard error)
Stroke number <=9	Learned	Rich-rich	刊 刑	670.8 (23.4)	6.7 (1.7)
		Poor-poor	设 没	687.1 (26.3)	3.1 (0.8)
		Rich-poor	星 念	565.4 (15.8)	2.5 (1.1)
	Unlearned	Rich-rich	吨 肫	698.3 (27.2)	7.2 (1.5)
		Poor-poor	沈 沉	718.7 (22.8)	13.9 (1.7)
		Rich-poor	灯 叨	589.2 (17.8)	1.4 (0.8)
Stroke number >9	Learned	Rich-rich	挂 桂	735.6 (23.4)	7.9 (1.4)
		Poor-poor	谈 淡	763.5 (27.5)	7.8 (1.6)
		Rich-poor	蛙 淤	605.0 (17.5)	1.9 (1.4)
	Unlearned	Rich-rich	喧 暄	745.6 (26.7)	7.8 (1.4)
		Poor-poor	梁 粱	791.6 (28.1)	12.9 (1.6)
		Rich-poor	滚 肆	606.4 (18.7)	3.7 (0.9)

Latencies   A 2(target complexity) × 2(target familiarity) × 3(visual property) ANOVA with repeated measures showed significant main effects for all of the three variables. It was easy to know that the judging latencies were significantly faster for simple characters with less stroke number than for complex characters with more stroke number ($F(1, 48) = 66.7$, $p < .001$). It should also be clear that the judging latencies were significantly faster for learned characters than for unlearned characters ($F(1, 48) = 12.0$, $p < .01$). In general, the latencies were significantly descending from poor-poor character pairs to rich-rich ones and then to rich-poor ones ($F(2, 96) = 93.1$, $p < .001$). However, the interaction effect of target complexity × visual property was also significant ($F(2, 96) = 6.1$, $p < .01$). Bonferroni tests of simple main effects ($p < .05$) revealed that the pair-wise significant differences in latencies between the three kinds of character pairs only happened to the complex characters. But for the simple characters, the differences between rich-poor and the other two levels were significant, whereas the difference between rich-rich and poor-poor was not significant, although the same tendency still existed.

Errors   A 2(target complexity) × 2(target familiarity) × 3(visual property) ANOVA with repeated measures showed significant main effects for target familiarity ($F(1, 48) = 22.9$, $p < .001$) and visual property ($F(2, 96) = 35.1$, $p < .001$), but not for target complexity ($F(1, 48) = 3.4$, $p > .05$). Judgment of learned characters was more accurate than was for those of unlearned characters. In general, the errors were significantly descending from poor-poor character pairs to rich-rich ones and then to rich-poor ones. Regarding the interactions, the target familiarity × visual property interaction effect was significant ($F(2, 96) = 19.9$, $p < .001$). The three-way interaction effect was also significant ($F(2, 96) = 4.2$, $p < .05$). Bonferroni tests of simple main effects ($p < .05$) revealed that for simple learned characters, only the difference between the errors of rich-rich and rich-poor was significant. For complex learned characters, there were significant differences between the errors of rich-poor and the other two kinds of stimuli, but there was no difference between rich-rich and poor-poor. However, for unlearned characters, the judgement of rich-poor characters was significantly more accurate than that of rich-rich ones, which in turn were judged significantly more accurately than those of poor-poor ones. Moreover, the main effect of target familiarity only appeared on poor-poor character pairs, whereas there were no differences between the judging accuracy of learned and unlearned rich-poor characters and rich-rich characters.

Both the results from latencies and errors showed that characters with a set of visual properties could be more easily detected from characters with different visual properties (rich-poor) than from characters with similar visual properties (rich-rich or poor-poor), even though the task did not direct attention to those visual properties explicitly. This finding is consistent with previous visual studies using geometric patterns, line drawings, or English letters (e.g., Ballesteros, et al, 1998; Biederman, 1987; Kanade, 1981; Palmer, 1980), strongly suggesting that the visual-spatial properties are used quickly enough to provide a perceptual basis for the orthographic processing of Chinese characters. Furthermore, the results also showed that there were quicker responses and fewer errors in judging pair of characters with rich visual properties (rich-rich) than for those with poor visual properties (poor-poor). This is consistent with the assumption of the facilitating effect of non-accidental properties on the orthographic processing of Chinese characters.

The results from latencies showed significant effects of character complexity and familiarity on Chinese character recognition, which have been well accepted by psycholinguistic researchers. The interaction showed no facilitating effect of non-accidental visual properties for simple characters, which could be attributed to the dominant facilitating effect of less stroke number. However, the significant main effect of character complexity only showed in the latencies, though the same trend was evident in errors also. An interesting finding from the errors was that the facilitating effect of non-accidental visual properties only showed in unfamiliar characters, but not for familiar ones. On the other hand, the effect of character familiarity disappeared in rich-rich and rich-poor character judgement, and the effect only showed in poor-poor characters. These findings further confirmed the obvious facilitating effect of the visual properties inherent in characters on the orthographic processing of Chinese characters.

EXPERIMENT 2

In Experiment 1, we did not analyse the different visual-spatial properties individually. The visual-spatial properties under consideration in Experiment 2 also included linearity, parallelism, closure, and symmetry. This experiment was run in order to test whether all of the four properties inherent in the characters can be quickly used and facilitate the orthographic processing of Chinese characters. Moreover, on the assumption that these visual properties provided redundancy to orthographic information of Chinese script, it was expected that the characters with more visual properties would have a stronger facilitating effect on the orthographic processing than would those with less visual properties. We also considered the variables of the complexity of characters (quantified by stroke number) and the familiarity of characters (quantified by character frequency reported by Shanghai Communication University, 1988).

METHOD

Subjects   The same 50 fourth-grade students as in Experiment 1 also took part in this experiment.

Design   A within-subjects design with three independent variables: two levels of character complexity (less than 9 stroke numbers vs. more than 10 stroke numbers), two levels of frequency ($> = .0800$ vs. $< .0800$), and four levels of visual-spatial properties (parallel and linear (PL); parallel, linear, and closed (PLC); parallel, linear, closed, and symmetric (PLCS); and none (None, i.e., non-parallel, non-linear, unclosed, and non-symmetric). The dependent variables were visual matching latency and errors.

Materials   There were a total number of 160 pairs of stimuli, with 10 pairs in each of the 16 experimental conditions. Every pair of stimuli was composed of two physically identical characters. All the 160 characters were selected from textbooks used by all the primary schools in Guangzhou. The mean stroke number was 6.6 for the first level, and 11.3 for the second level. The mean frequency was .7496 for the first level, and .0318 for the second level. The parallel and linear characters (PL) had a mean proportion of .81 for linear strokes as well as for parallel strokes, ranging from .7 to 1. Whereas the none characters (None) only had a mean proportion of .15 for linear strokes, ranging from 0 to .29, and of .05 for parallel strokes, ranging from 0 to .27. The closed characters (PLC) contained one or more linear holes, and had a mean proportion of .92 for both linear and parallel strokes, ranging from .8 to 1. The symmetric characters (PLCS) had all of their strokes symmetric either from the right-left axis or top-down axis, and had the same mean proportion of linear and parallel strokes within the same range as did the closed characters.

All the stimuli were presented on the centre of a computer monitor in Song style. The size of the character is 3 cm in height and 2.5 cm in width. In order to balance the 'yes' or 'no' response, we added 320 characters to form 160 pairs of fillers. The order of stimuli was randomized over all factors and conditions, so that each subject received a new order of stimuli. We also controlled the order of 'yes' or 'no' responses so that the same response would happen consecutively no more than 5 times.

The same apparatus as in Experiment 1 was used.

Procedures   Similar with the procedures in Experiment 1, the subjects were also instructed to fixate a cross, which was replaced after 200 ms by a pair of stimuli in the same position. The stimuli remained on the screen until the subject made a response. The task was to judge whether the two characters were physically identical. Two response keys 'yes' and 'no' were marked on the letter 'L' and 'S' on the keyboard of the computer. The subjects received 10 practice trials and had a rest for about 5 minutes after 120 trials.

RESULTS AND DISCUSSION

The overall percentage of errors was 5.8. The mean visual matching latencies excluded the latencies of error responses. The latencies beyond 2 standard deviations from the mean were regarded as outliers and were excluded from the analysis. Mean latencies and errors in each experimental condition are given in Table 2.

Latencies   A 2(character complexity) × 2(character familiarity) × 4(visual property) ANOVA with repeated measures showed significant main effects for character complexity ($F(1, 49) = 31.0, p < .001$) and visual property ($F(3, 147) = 34.9, p < .001$), but not for character frequency ($F(1, 49) = 2.89, p > .05$). Again, the matching latencies of simple characters were significantly quicker than were those of complex characters. In general, the matching latencies were significantly descending from characters with least visual properties (None) to characters with most visual properties (PLCS). However, the interaction effect of character frequency × visual property was also significant ($F(3, 147) = 3.0, p < .05$). Bonferroni tests of simple main effects ($p < .05$) revealed that the pair-wise significant differences in latencies between the four kinds of characters only happened in low-frequency level. But for the high-

Table 2

Mean Latencies (in ms) and Percentage of Errors With Standard Errors in Each Condition in Experiment 2

Character complexity	Character frequency	Visual property	Character examples	Mean latencies (Standard error)	Mean errors (Standard error)
Stroke number <=9	Frequency >=.0800	PL	正	848.4 (34.5)	5.9 (1.4)
		PLC	叶	829.0 (37.3)	3.5 (0.8)
		PLCS	曲	782.9 (32.3)	3.9 (1.1)
		None	必	871.3 (47.2)	6.5 (1.2)
	Frequency <.0800	PL	仙	858.4 (42.3)	5.9 (1.2)
		PLC	吐	780.3 (34.2)	5.3 (1.4)
		PLCS	朋	749.4 (30.1)	4.3 (1.0)
		None	戈	914.5 (57.7)	5.3 (1.1)
Stroke number >9	Frequency >=.0800	PL	排	886.7 (32.7)	7.8 (1.6)
		PLC	副	886.3 (41.8)	5.1 (1.1)
		PLCS	罪	821.1 (37.4)	6.5 (1.5)
		None	深	892.6 (39.4)	4.5 (1.2)
	Frequency <.0800	PL	崖	915.5 (32.3)	8.4 (1.5)
		PLC	暑	893.3 (37.0)	5.5 (1.1)
		PLCS	曹	851.4 (36.7)	5.1 (1.2)
		None	愁	950.7 (35.2)	9.0 (1.5)

frequency characters, the differences between PLCS and the other three kinds of characters were significant, whereas the pair-wise differences between None, PL, and PLC were not significant, although the descending tendency still existed. Moreover, considering how the four levels of visual property influenced the effect of character frequency, an interesting finding was that the effect of character frequency only happened in the characters with least visual properties (None), but not for the others (PL, PLC, PLCS).

Errors   A 2(character complexity) × 2(character familiarity) × 4(visual property) ANOVA with repeated measures showed the significant main effect for character complexity ($F(1, 49) = 4.9$, $p < .05$) and visual property ($F(3, 147) = 3.8$, $p < .05$), but not for character frequency ($F(1, 49) = 1.3$, $p > .05$). Simple characters were matched with fewer errors than were complex characters. Bonferroni test ($p < .05$) revealed that only the accuracy in PL and PLC were different from each other, but they were not different from PLCS and None. No significant interaction effects were found.

The results from latencies showed a significant facilitating effect of visual properties on the recognition of Chinese characters, which is consistent with the results in Experiment 1. Furthermore, with the increasing of the visual properties inherent in characters, the latencies were significantly descending, which is consistent with previous visual studies using simple or complex objects (Biederman, 1987). The latency advantage enjoyed by the characters with more visual properties is an effect that would be expected if their additional visual properties were affording a redundancy gain from more possible diagnostic matches to their representations in memory. Moreover, the successively decreasing effect of latencies from characters with least visual properties to those with most properties revealed that the visual properties probed here, i.e., linearity, parallelism, closure, and symmetry, were all used, and produced significant facilitating effects in the orthographic processing of Chinese characters. These findings provided stronger evidence supporting the previous studies using Chinese characters (Ai, 1948/1965; Chen & Huang, 1999; Kao, 1998, 2000; Peng, & Zhang, 1984; Yu et al, 1997).

Both the results from latencies and errors showed a significant main effect of character complexity, which is consistent with Experiment 1 as well as previous psycholinguistic studies. However, the main effect of character frequency, which was expected also, showed neither in latencies nor in errors. The possible interpretation might be that the counting of the frequencies came from the readings of adults, which might not apply to children very well. But a more interesting interpretation might come from the interaction effect between character frequency and visual property, which showed a unique effect of character frequency on characters with least visual properties (None). This finding further confirmed the strong facilitating effects of visual properties in character recognition, since they had covered the frequency effect.

GENERAL DISCUSSION

Biederman (1987) summarized five non-accidental properties in object recognition: collinearity, curvilinearity, parallelism, symmetry, and cotermination. Cotermination refers to coincidence of edges of an object. It is an important determinant as to whether a given component is volumetric or planar, because planar components lack such a property. Chinese characters, however, are planar structures. Therefore, we excluded this property from the non-accidental properties of Chinese characters considered in this study.

Collinearity and curvilinearity actually stand in the two ends of one property. We refer to it as linearity here, since Yu et al (1997) found that characters with more than 88% linear strokes were recognized significantly quicker than those with no more than 14% linear strokes. According to Tseng, Chang, and Chen (1965), using frequency of linear strokes counted from 30,000 characters is about 60%, which makes linearity a very distinctive visual property of Chinese characters. Parallelism was regarded as coexisting with linearity in Chinese characters in this study. The proportion of parallel strokes and linear strokes among the whole stroke number of the same Chinese character seldom differ significantly in terms of quantitative analysis. In other words, very few characters stand linear but non-parallel, or vice versa. Symmetry, summarized by Biederman as a well-known visual facilitating property, is also very common in Chinese characters. However, a more common visual property of Chinese characters, closure, was not mentioned there, but emphasized as a visual facilitating property by both topological research (Chen, 1982) and Gestalt psychology (Koffka, 1935). Therefore, we defined linearity, parallelism, closure, and symmetry as four non-accidental visual properties of Chinese characters in this study.

Experiment 1 found that the visual-spatial properties inherent in Chinese characters could be used quickly enough to provide a perceptual basis for the orthographic processing. Moreover, there was a facilitating effect of these visual properties. Experiment 2 consistently supported this facilitating effect. It further demonstrated that more visual properties produced more facilitating effect on the orthographic processing of Chinese characters. Thus, stronger evidence is now available for us to define linearity, parallelism, closure, and symmetry as 'non-accidental' properties of Chinese characters.

Biederman explained in his Recognition-by-Components or RBC model the effects of non-accidental properties on recognition of objects from the central organizational principle, which governs the relationship between two-dimensional images and the three-dimensional real world. For example, if there is a straight line in the image (collinearity), the visual system infers that the edge producing that line in the 3-D world is also straight. The visual system ignores the possibility that the property in the image might be a result of an accidental alignment of eye and curved edge. The detection of these properties is generally invariant over viewing position and image quality. Chinese characters, however, are 2-D entities and basically have no 3-D correspondences themselves. Therefore, Biederman's explanation should not be applicable to the facilitating effect of non-accidental properties on Chinese character recognition.

The topological perspective could not be used to account for all the findings here as well. Among the visual properties involved in this study, only closure is the topological property. However, the facilitating effect not only appeared in the recognition of characters with closures but also appeared in that of characters with linear as well as parallel properties but without closures.

The visual facilitating effect of every single property on the orthographic processing of Chinese characters could be well interpreted by the Gestalt's principles. Let us take the principles of proximity, similarity, and simplicity into account. When composing a character, the linear strokes stand either horizontal or vertical, showing a strong organizational regularity. They generate a proximal and similar effect which makes the character look compact and holistic and thus easily to be caught by vision. So do the parallel strokes, which stand in the same direction all the time and usually in linear styles. Nonetheless, the non-linear and non-parallel strokes, such as ㇐, ㇀, 丿, ㇄, ㇏, etc., usually shown in diverse directions and shapes, generate a loose and disordered effect on the characters (e.g., 必) and thus require more time and attention to perceive. A closure, according to Gestalt's perspective, is a *Pragnanz* (translated from German as 'good form'), which is easily to be organized by vision. It conforms to the principles of continuity and connectedness as well. The strokes within a closure are more likely to be perceived as a whole other than separate shapes and thus could be quickly recognized. However, that is not the case for the unclosed strokes. As to symmetry, it is a direct outcome of the law of Pragnanz. A symmetric visual organization should be the simplest one amongst the other possible patterns, because its components are no more than similar but completely duplicated patterns and stand in perfect balance. Thus it is easier to find and interpret the facilitating effect of symmetric structures on the orthographic processing of Chinese characters.

Although Gestalt psychologists never made it an explicit assertion, we can still assume that the visual patterns conforming to more Gestalt's principles should be more easily caught by vision. The cumulating effects of the visual properties inherent in the characters, i.e., the characters with more non-accidental properties could be recognized more quickly, can be interpreted easily with this assumption. The redundancy of Chinese characters could be those non-accidental visual properties that can be used to augment orthographic information in the identification of characters.

The characters with more of such properties, which conform to more Gestalt's principles, could provide more redundancy. The advantage of such characters is due to the reduction of information in orthographic processing from redundant features.

As to the basic perceptual unit involved in reading Chinese characters, Peng and Wang (1997) asserted that the strokes should be the first level of units of Chinese lexicon by the findings that the main effect of the stroke number existed universally disregarding the involvement of other factors. Our study also supported their findings. From this point of view, we can say that the linear, parallel, closed and symmetric characters can be identified quicker than those with less such properties. This is because: (a) these properties conform to Gestalt's principles and thus facilitate an initial encoding stage of orthographic processing, and (b) the linear, parallel, closed and symmetric strokes are mainly duplicated in composing such characters whereas the processing time for the whole character would be remarkably reduced by encoding strokes of same shapes (here we could borrow the term *repetition priming effect* from Taft and Zhu (1997b)).

A top-down model of reading could hardly interpret the effect of stroke number as well as the effect of non-accidental properties found in this study. However, a bottom-up model of reading also suffers from the difficulty to interpret the effect of word familiarity showing in this study. Therefore, an interactive activation framework should be adopted here to interpret all the findings of this study. Taft and Zhu (1995) have proposed a multilevel interactive activation model in which there are sets of units that can become activated when a word is visually presented. These units exist at different levels of representation with activation passing up (and back down) the different levels. The links by which the activation passes have different connection strengths, depending on the frequency with which the particular link is used. They further demonstrated that the lowest level of lexicon processing in Chinese might be features and strokes; then are the radicals; above the radicals in the hierarchy come the characters (Taft & Zhu, 1997a, 1997b).

Although Taft and Zhu suggested visual features, together with the strokes, as a level of Chinese lexicon, they did not pay much attention to the features and give no detailed descriptions to them as well. Huang and Wang (1992) proposed a stage model for Chinese character recognition modified from Biederman's RBC model. In this model, non-accidental properties like collinearity, curvilinearity, parallelism, symmetry, and cotermination are first searched within the character, and the character regions are parsed. Then they serve as precursors to trigger the activation of character components and their relations. Activation of the character model is followed by character identification after completion of a chain of interactive processes. The main ideas behind Taft and Zhu's and Huang and Wang's models are not conflicting, but they can complement each other. However, even in Huang and Wang's model, we still cannot find clear definitions for the non-accidental properties in Chinese characters corresponding to those in 2-D or 3-D objects described by Biederman. The present study makes this much less ambiguous than the previous works.

In terms of the interactive activation perspective, lexical access passes through the activation of stroke level, in which the non-accidental visual properties and stroke number should have impacts on the activation strength. Moreover, the activation of the character level passes back down to the lower levels in an interactive way. As expected, the more non-accidental properties or the fewer strokes the character contains, the quicker and easier is the identification of the character. As well, there exists a significant interaction between character familiarity and the visual properties. For familiar characters, they are more than compositions of individual strokes but have been grouped into a holistic image because of sufficient exposure. Therefore, the activation at the character level is quite strong, even for those characters with little non-accidental properties, which produces a significant holistic effect. The strong holistic effect covers the effects of visual properties to some extent. On the other hand, the effect of character familiarity only appears in the detection of characters with poor visual properties ('poor-poor' in Experiment 1 and 'none' in Experiment 2). These findings reveal that the holistic effect could also be covered by the effects of visual properties, if they could provide enough redundancy.

Consideration of the featural basis for the structural descriptions for each character also suggests that a similarity measure can be defined on the basis of the common versus distinctive visual properties for any pair of characters. The studies using Chinese characters usually have to control for the similarity of the shapes of the characters. However, previous judgement of similarity was mostly intuitive and subjective. For examples, those characters with the same radicals would be seen as similar to each other, or the degree of similarity between the characters would be defined in terms of subjects' evaluation. These aspects of judgement were untested and non-quantitative. Yeh, Li, and Chen (1997) conducted a similarity analysis in terms of visual features of characters (e.g., linearity, symmetry, closure, and connectivity). Unfortunately, they demonstrated that such a feature analysis was far from good enough to be a similarity measure. However, their study was inconclusive since it was not a very rigorous study. Firstly, they did not give an operational definition to the features, and thus did not manipulate the features quantitatively (e.g., the proportion of specific strokes, and the number of holes). Secondly, in terms of the multilevel interactive activation model, the stroke, the radical and the whole character are all involved in the processing of Chinese characters. Therefore, while measuring the similarity of the characters on the basis of non-accidental visual properties, the stroke number and the structure of the characters (top-down, left-right, and so on) should be taken into account at the same time.

In summary, the present study showed that linearity, parallelism, closure, and symmetry are non-accidental visual-spatial properties inherent in Chinese characters. They could be used quickly enough to provide a perceptual basis for the orthographic processing of Chinese characters. Significant facilitating effects of these properties were also found, which were further confirmed to be cumulating effects with the increasing of these visual properties possessed by the characters. The cumulating effects implied a quantitative similarity measure for Chinese characters. Gestalt's principles could be used to account for the effects of all the four non-accidental properties. Moreover, significant main effect of character complexity and interaction effect of character familiarity × visual properties were also found in this study. All these effects fit in well with interactive activation models of Chinese character recognition. The study enriched the content of the models as well by systematically probing the effects of non-accidental visual properties on the orthographic processing of Chinese characters, to which the reading models and previous studies of Chinese language paid little attention.

References

Ai, W. (1965). *The psychology of reading: problems with Chinese characters.* Taipei: National Bian Yi Guan (in Chinese). (Original work published in 1948).

Ballesteros, S., Millar, S., & Reales, J. M. (1998). Symmetry in haptic and in visual shape perception. *Perception & Psychophysics, 60,* 389–404.

Berninger, V. W. (Ed.). (1994). Preface. In *The varieties of orthographic knowledge I: Theoretical and developmental issues* (pp. xi–xvi). Dordrecht: Kluwer Academic Publishers.

Biederman, I. (1987). Recognition-by-components: A theory of human image understanding. *Psychological Review, 94,* 115–147.

Chen, C. F., & Huang, X. T. (1999). Research on characteristics of visual recognition to symmetrical structural Chinese characters. *Acta Psychologica Sinica, 31,* 154–161 (in Chinese).

Chen, H. C. (1997). Cognitive processing of Chinese reading. In D. L. Peng (Ed.), *Cognitive research on Chinese language* (pp. 65–82). Jinan: Shandong Educational Press (in Chinese).

Chen, L. (1982). Topological structure in visual perception. *Science, 218,* 699–700.

Fu, Y. H. (1985). Analysis and statistics of the structures and components of Chinese characters. *Chinese Language, 4,* 261–272 (in Chinese).

Hu, Y. S. (Ed.). (1992). *Modern Chinese language.* Hong Kong: San Lian Press (in Chinese).

Huang, J. T., & Wang, M. Y. (1992). From unit to Gestalt: Perceptual dynamics in recognizing Chinese characters. In H. C. Chen & O. J. L. Tzeng (Eds.), *Language processing in Chinese* (pp. 3–35). Amsterdam: North-Holland.

Huang, J. Z., & Hu, P. J. (1990). *Han Zi Xue Tong Lun* (General introduction to Chinese characters). Wuhan: Hua Zhong Normal University Press.

Jackson, N. E., Lu, W. H., & Ju, S. (1994). Reading Chinese and reading English: Similarities, differences, and second language reading. In V. W. Berninger (Ed.), *The varieties of orthographic knowledge I: Theoretical and developmental issues* (pp. 73–109). Dordrecht: Kluwer Academic Publishers.

Kanade, T. (1981). Recovery of the three dimensional shape of an object from a single view. *Artificial Intelligence, 17,* 409–460.

Kao, H. S. R. (1998, November). *Visual spatial aspects of Chinese character writing.* Paper presented at the Advanced Study Institute on Advances in Theoretical Issues and Cognitive Neuroscience Research of the Chinese Language, University of Hong Kong, Hong Kong.

Kao, H. S. R. (2000). The visual-spatial properties of Chinese characters and psycho-geometric theory of Chinese character writing. In H. S. R. Kao (Ed.), *Chinese calligraphy therapy* (pp. 3–41). Hong Kong: Hong Kong University Press (in Chinese).

Koffka, K. (1935). *Principles of Gestalt psychology.* New York: Harcourt, Brace & World.

Liu, Z. J. (1999). *Han Zi Ti Tai Lun* (Morphology of Chinese characters). Nanning: Guangxi Educational Press.

Lu, S. X. (1987). *Scientific research of Chinese characters.* Beijing: Guangming Daily Press (in Chinese).

Martin, S. E. (1972). Nonalphabetic writing systems: Some observations. In

J. F. Kavanagh & I. G. Mattingly (Eds.), *Language by ear and by eye: The relationships between speech and reading* (pp. 81–109). Cambridge, MA: MIT Press.

Mason, M. (1975). Reading ability and letter search time: Effects of orthographic structure defined by single letter positional frequency. *Journal of Experimental Psychology: General, 104,* 146–166.

Palmer, S. E. (1980). What makes triangles point: Local and global effects in configurations of ambiguous triangles. *Cognitive Psychology, 12,* 285–305.

Peng, D. L., & Wang, C. M. (1997). Basic processing units of Chinese character recognition: Evidence from stroke number effect and radical number effect. *Acta Psychologica Sinica, 29,* 8–17 (in Chinese).

Peng, R. X., & Zhang, W. T. (1984). Some characteristics in tachistoscopic recognition of Chinese characters. *Acta Psychologica Sinica, 1,* 49–54 (in Chinese).

Richards, J., Platt, J., & Weber, H. (1985). *Longman dictionary of applied linguistics.* London: Longman.

Shanghai Communication University (1988). *A dictionary of Chinese character information.* Beijing: Science Press.

Taft, M., & Zhu, X. (1995). The representation of bound Morphemes in lexicon: A Chinese study. In L. Feldman (Ed.). *Morphological aspect of language processing* (pp. 293–316). Hillsdale, NJ: Lawrence Erlbaum.

Taft, M., & Zhu, X. (1997a). Sub-morphemic processing in reading Chinese. *Journal of Experimental Psychology: Learning, Memory & Cognition, 23,* 761–775.

Taft, M., & Zhu, X. (1997b). Model of lexicon processing: Orthography, phonology, and morpheme. In D.L. Peng (Ed.), *Cognitive research on Chinese language* (pp. 65–82). Jinan: Shandong Educational Press (in Chinese).

Todd, J. T., Chen, L., & Norman, J. F. (1998). On the relative salience of Euclidean, affine, and topological structure for 2-D form discrimination. *Perception, 27,* 273–282.

Tseng, H. C., Chang, L. H., & Chen, C. K. (1965). The relative frequencies of the various stroke-types of the Chinese ideograms. *Acta Psychologica Sinica, 3,* 213–214 (in Chinese).

Yeh, S. L., Li, J. L., & Chen, I. P. (1997). The perceptual dimensions underlying the classification of the shapes of Chinese characters. *Chinese Journal of Psychology, 39,* 75–92 (in Chinese).

Yu, B. L., Zhang, S. L., & Pan, Y. J. (1997). Effects of stroke type on identification of upright and tilted Chinese characters. *Acta Psychologica Sinica, 29,* 23–28 (in Chinese).

10

Psycho-Geometric Analysis of Commonly Used Chinese Characters

Ding-Guo Gao and Henry S. R. Kao

Although there are almost one hundred thousand Chinese characters, which have been used across different historical periods (see Wan & Hsia, 1957; Zhou, 1999), there are only around 5,000 characters, which are in active usage in modern Chinese language (e.g., Ann, 1986; Suen, 1986; Wang & Chang, 1986). According to Ann, 3,500 most frequently used characters in Hong Kong cover 99.80% of the common usage of Chinese characters. Generally, a person would on the average be able to read 99. 80% of all the characters contained in selected texts in a 1,000-character article if she or he masters these 3,500 characters. Wang and Chang (1986) found similar results for the characters used in the Chinese mainland. They showed that 3,500 characters occupy 99.87% of usage and with a skewed distribution of frequency of usage as summarized in Table 1.

As a result, it is important to analyse the perceptual or orthographic features of these commonly used Chinese characters in order to help people learn Chinese. Ai (1948/1965) argued in his book *Issues in Chinese Characters* that characters with symmetric, closed, and/or linear (horizontal and/or vertical lines) features or with less than ten strokes are recognized more easily than those with other configurations. Kao (2000) has developed a psycho-geometrical theory of reading and writing Chinese characters, in which characters with balance, closure and holes, linearity, centre of gravity, orientation, connectivity, symmetry, and parallelism should be recognized and learned faster and/or easier.

Table 1
The Skewed Distribution of the Frequency of Usage of Chinese Characters (in Descending Order of Frequency)

Characters	Cumulative frequency (%)	Characters	Cumulative frequency (%)
First		First	
10	15.85	1619	96.60
20	23.10	2000	98.07
50	35.08	3000	99.63
100	47.70	3156	99.73
116	50.24	3500	99.87
500	79.76	4000	99.96
1000	91.37	4574	100

(Source: Wang & Chang, 1986)

A conceptual framework is advanced to highlight the above observations within a systematic analysis of the components in each Chinese character. The main points in the psycho-geometric approach to Chinese character reading are presented below.

At the body-character interface, some visual-spatial patterns are more salient or important than others. They are those closely reflecting or conforming to basic topological properties of visual perception. Fundamentally, a Chinese character should be seen to portray an imaginary or visible rigid square, although modern forms may be written within a rectangular shape. A square is the perfect geometric pattern as it incorporates hole, linearity, symmetry, parallelism, connectivity and/or orientation. With an implied correspondence between the shape of the square and the symbol, characters may vary in terms of the extent to which they possess the geometric properties of the square.

Cognitive changes associated with the geometric variations of the characters include clerical speed and accuracy, spatial ability, abstract reasoning, digit span, short-term memory, picture memory, and cognitive reaction time and accuracy.

Stylistic variations of Chinese characters reflect individualized forms of strokes organization in the character. The patterns of geometricity in the character may include: Shape, e.g., △ (triangle), □ (square), □ (rectangle); size; balance (e.g., 朋 'friend'); closure and holes (singular or plural) (e.g., 口 'mouth', 目 'eye'); linearity (e.g., 正 'right'); centre of gravity (e.g., 回 'return'); orientation (e.g., 山 'mountain'); connectivity (e.g., 弓 'bow'); symmetry (e.g., 卒 'soldier', 門 'door'); parallelism (e.g., 二 'two', 三 'three'); inside-outside relationships (e.g., 困 'trap' vs. 呆 'retard'), and global and detailed figures.

The present paper aims to establish a database and analyse the most commonly used Chinese characters in modern Chinese through a psycho-geometric approach developed by Kao (2000).

METHOD

Source of the selected Chinese characters   A set of 4,574 most frequently used Chinese characters was extracted from Wang and Chang's book, *A Frequency Dictionary in Modern Chinese* (1986), which has been a widely cited handbook in Chinese language research. These characters represented a total of 1,808,114 characters selected from: a) articles in politics, economy, philosophy, history, military, etc. in popular newspapers, magazines and periodicals, b) scientific articles which focus on the issues of daily life, c) spoken materials from drama, libretto and scenario, commentaries, and songs, d) novels, essays and tales, and e) articles from elementary and secondary school textbooks.

Data Collection and Analysis   All the data of the selected characters were compiled by Foxpro and processed by SPSS 7.0. In the present investigation, only the structure, stroke, hole, connectivity, linearity, symmetry and balance of a Chinese character were analysed.

RESULTS

Structure of Chinese characters   According to Fu (1993), Chinese characters are basically classified into ten kinds in structure, which are showed as follows: a) left-right (和 'and'), b) top-down (字 'word'), c) fully closed (回 'return'), d) partially surrounded with roof and left flank (壓 'press'), e) partly surrounded with floor and left flank (達 'arrival'), f) partly surrounded with roof and right flank (句 'sentence'), g) surrounded without floor (同 'same'), h) surrounded without right flank (巨 'great'), i) surrounded without roof (凶 'violent'), and j) independent (中 'centre'). Some researchers also roughly defined all the d, e, f, and g structures as the partially surrounded. We found all the selected characters can be categorized into the ten groups mentioned above (see Table 2).

Table 2
Distribution of Different Structures Among the Selected Chinese Characters

| | Characters | | |
Structure	First 100	First 500	Total (4574)
a) left-right	30	202	2823
b) top-down	18	129	1028
c) fully closed	1	5	23
d) partly surrounded with roof and left flank	6	22	192
e) partly surrounded with floor and left flank	6	18	117
f) partly surrounded with roof and right flank	1	5	45
g) surrounded without floor	1	3	33
h) surrounded without right flank	0	1	14
i) surrounded without roof	0	1	6
j) independent	37	114	293

The results reveal that over 60% of Chinese characters are of left-right structure, about 20% of top-down structure and the remaining (less than 20%) of other structures. Although the first two kinds of structures dominate the distribution, characters with independent structures (in which most are connected in strokes) are significant as well. Among the first 100 most frequently used Chinese characters (51% of usage), there are 37 characters with independent structures (37%), and among the first 500 most frequently used characters (almost 70% of usage), there are 114 such characters (22.8%).

Frequency of usage and number of strokes   Loo (1989) found the frequency of characters, whether they are simplified or traditional, is inversely proportional to the number of strokes. The more frequently the characters are used, the less strokes they will have. This implies the simplification trend of Chinese characters, although the psychological or cognitive effect with reference to this should be further investigated. In addition, simplified characters have around 22.50% lesser strokes than the traditional form, which may translate into cost savings in the printing industries and time saving in manual writing and facsimile transmission.

Table 3 shows the relationship of frequency and stroke number. Interestingly, for low-frequency characters, almost no correlation exists between frequency and stroke number, while the high- and medium-frequency parts do show some correlation (0.196 and 0.129 respectively and both reach significance level). Although at present it is hard to conclude whether simplified Chinese characters are easier or more difficult to learn, this finding and the fact that simplified Chinese characters are given official writing system status in mainland China and Singapore suggest that simplified characters will at least not be inferior to traditional Chinese characters currently used in Hong Kong, Macao and Taiwan. For high-frequency characters, they are about 2 strokes less than those with medium-frequency, and around 3 strokes less than those with low-frequency characters. These results are consistent with those in Loo's study (Loo, 1989).

Table 3
Correlation of Frequency and Stroke and Mean Strokes

Characters	n	Mean Strokes	SD	Pearson Correlation
High-frequency	1621	8.66	3.12	−0.196
Medium-frequency	1591	10.59	3.42	−0.129
Low-frequency	1362	11.45	3.69	−0.011
Total	4574	10.16	3.59	−0.183

Holes   A hole can be operationally defined as an entity consisting of a finite line (straight, cursive or mixed) without an end point. One of the most apparent features of a hole is closure which is seen as one of three fundamental properties of topological geometry (the other two are connectivity and inside and outside relations, see Chen, 1989). According to Chen (1982, 1985) and Todd, Chen and Norman (1998), a primitive and general function of the visual system is the perception of global topological properties and the relative perceptual salience of object properties may be systematically related to their structural stability under change, in a manner that is similar to the Klein hierarchy of geometries. Piaget (1953) even found topological ideas, which include proximity, separation, order, enclosure, and continuity, developed earlier in children than the Euclidean. In fact, one of the methods to construct a character is topological transformation under which two characters are topologically equivalent (see Liu, 1993). That is, the processing of topological feature is earlier than those of Euclidean, affine and projective geometries features.

A hole can centralize people's vision in a frame and thus receives the most attention (Kao, 2000). On the above studies, it is assumed that there will be superiority in perceiving, recognizing and learning a Chinese character with hole(s).

Table 4 presents the holes in the total 4,574 characters. It can be seen that 65% of characters contain hole(s) ranging from 1 to 12, indicating most of commonly used Chinese characters consist of hole(s). Among those with hole(s), most consist of 1 or 2 holes. The distributions of holes across frequency are 959 characters of high frequency, 1,069 of medium frequency and 945 of low frequency.

Table 4
Distribution of Holes Among the Selected Chinese Characters

Holes	Characters			
	High-frequency	Medium-frequency	Low-frequency	Total
Without	662	522	417	1601
With	959	1069	945	2973
1	389	365	291	1045
2	265	278	281	824
3	139	191	141	471
4	110	146	118	374
5	36	47	65	148
6	14	28	21	63
7	4	8	17	29
8	1	5	5	11
9	1	1	2	4
10	0	0	2	2
11	0	0	1	1
12	0	0	1	1

n = 4574

Connectivity   Connectivity refers to an entity without separation. Objects connected with each other would be more probable to be perceived as a whole according to Chen (1989) and Koffka (1935). There are some Chinese characters with the property of connectivity, e.g. 十 'ten' and 面 'face'. The distribution of the connected characters was extremely skewed: Among the first 300 characters, around 30% of them were connected and 71% of the connected characters were of high frequency, while only 6% of the total selected characters held this feature, suggesting that the most frequently used Chinese characters are connected (see Table 5). As most of the connected characters are constructed independently, the results are in fact consistent with those for characters with independent structure in Table 2. The results from these two investigations provide evidence that the connected Chinese characters will be easier to learn because the most frequently used characters should are easiest to read, according to the principle of economy in learning. Again, further behavioural evidence is needed.

Table 5
Distribution of Connectivity in Selected Chinese Characters

Characters	Connected	Disconnected
In descending order of frequency		
First		
100	33	67
200	62	138
300	88	212
500	116	384
1000	167	833
Total	275	4299
Across levels of frequency		
High-frequency	196	1425
Medium-frequency	54	1537
Low-frequency	25	1337

n = 4574

Linearity   In line with Ai's research (1948/1965), we suggest that characters consisting of 75% of straight lines (horizontal or vertical such as 正 'correct' and 生 'birth') or with 75% of curves including dot and oblique line such as 多 'many' and 狡 'cunning' should be defined as those with high or low linearity, respectively. A character with high linearity is supposed to be recognized easily and conversely a character with low linearity is hard to be perceived. However, one should be cautious making any solid conclusion before further empirical evidence is given. Table 6 shows there are 260 characters with the former construction and 212 with the latter one among the 4574 selected characters. In addition, although there was no difference in linearity across the frequency of the usage of characters, it might not fit the case of traditional Chinese characters as the simplification of the Chinese characters may have changed the linearity.

Table 6
Distribution of Linearity in Selected Chinese Characters

| | Linearity | |
Characters	High	Low
High-frequency	115	103
Medium-frequency	76	65
Low-frequency	69	44
Total	260	212

n = 4574

Symmetry   Symmetry of an object is a transformation that leaves it apparently unchanged. The number and type of such transformations depend on the geometry of the object to which the transformations are applied. The meaning and variety of symmetry transformations may be illustrated by considering a square placed on a table. In all patterns there are four basic symmetry transformations or rigid motions: translation (rigid motion with repetition along a line), reflection (rigid motion with repetition across an axis), glide reflection (rigid motion with reflected repetition along a line), and rotation (rigid motion with repetition around a point). A circle would be said to have higher symmetry because, for instance, it could be rotated through an infinite number of angles (not just multiples of 90 degrees) to give an identical circle.

For Chinese characters, symmetry takes place through reflection and translation. Most of symmetric characters are of the bilateral symmetrical type, which is produced if there exists some reflection of object invariance — that is, unchanged in appearance. Some characters are bilaterally symmetric through a vertical axis, e.g., 辛 'hot' and 再 'again' and some through a horizontal one (the case can also be named as vertical symmetry although it is a variation of bilateral symmetry), e.g., 凹 'narrow' and 巨 'large'. However, symmetry in Chinese characters also appears through translation, e.g., 林 'forest' and 朋 'friend'. Everyday experiences and much empirical evidence have indicated that symmetry is an important visual primitive and facilitates processing in vision. Research, for example, has showed that the presence of symmetry in a pattern or visual composition can be detected more quickly than its absence, and some types of symmetry, such as bilateral, are more readily verifiable than others (see Ballesteros, Millar & Reales, 1998; Baylis & Driver, 1994; Biederman, 1987; Bruce & Morgan, 1975; Koffka, 1935; Locher & Nodine, 1989; Marr, 1982; Wenderoth, 1997). In the present paper, the authors analysed a character through the classification of symmetry, including near symmetry, as it was hard to determine strictly mathematically symmetry in Chinese characters. As an example, 用 'use' shows partial symmetry, meaning one or more components in a character are symmetric but the whole is asymmetric, e.g., 匝 'bundle', and asymmetry, e.g., 丐 'beggar'.

The results from Table 7 show that 39% of characters are fully or partially symmetric and most of the fully symmetric characters are of high frequency. In addition, partially symmetric or asymmetric characters are approximately equally distributed across the frequency of usage. There exist some characters with both bilateral and vertical symmetries. They are shown as follows: 一 'one', 工 'work', 中 'centre', 十 'ten', 三 'three', 回 'return', 口 'mouth', 日 'sun', 目 'eye', 田 'field', 王 'king', 川 'river', 丰 'many', 申 'state', 曰 'say', 卅 'thirty', 噩 'bad' and 非 'false'. In fact, there are other cases that a character contains more than one symmetry such as bilateral plus repeated (through translation), e.g., 晶 'light', 品 'quality', 矗 'stand', and 雙 'double'.

Table 7
Distribution of Symmetry in Selected Chinese Characters

	Symmetry			Asymmetry
	Bilateral	Vertical	Partial	
High-frequency	172	5	505	939
Mid-frequency	81	5	518	987
Low-frequency	53	3	450	856
Total	306	13	1473	2782

Note. The data of some characters with both bilateral and vertical symmetries are only regarded as bilateral symmetry, such as 日 'sun'.

Balance   Ai (1948/1965) argued that if a character with left-right structure has 13 or more strokes and the stroke difference between the two sides are over 10, the character should be difficult to read. We define this feature as the *balance of a character*. A character meeting Ai's definition would be named as *weak balance*. There are in total 86 characters of this kind, with 9 of high frequency, 31 of mid-frequency and 46 of low frequency.

Summary

Over 60% of frequently used Chinese characters are of left-right structure, around 20% of top-down structure and the remaining less than 20% of other structures. The frequency of characters is inversely proportional to the number of strokes, i.e., the more frequently the characters are used, the fewer strokes they will have. Specifically, for low-frequency characters, almost no correlation exists between frequency and stroke number. For high-frequency characters, they are about two strokes less than those with medium frequency and around three strokes less than those with low frequency.

Most of the frequently used Chinese characters consist of hole(s) (65% in total), and among which most contain 1 or 2 holes. No apparent difference is revealed in the distributions of hole(s) across frequency (959 characters for high frequency, 1,069 for medium frequency and 945 for low frequency).

Only 6% of the total selected characters are connected in construction but the distribution of connectivity is extremely skewed. Among the first 300 characters, around 30 percent of them are connected and 71 percent of the connected characters are of high-frequency usage, suggesting that the most frequently used Chinese characters are connected.

There are 260 characters with high linearity and 212 with low linearity but the result may not fit the traditional Chinese case. Thirty-nine percent of the characters are fully or partially symmetric and most of the fully symmetric characters are of high frequency. Partially symmetric or asymmetric characters are approximately equally distributed across the frequency of usage. There are also some characters with two or more symmetries. Moreover, there are 86 characters in total with weak balance, that is, 9 of high frequency, 31 of mid-frequency and 46 of low frequency.

References

Ai, W. (1965). *Some issues in Chinese characters*. Taipei: National Publishing House (in Chinese). (Original work published in 1948.)

Ann, T. K. (1986). *Cracking the Chinese puzzles* (Vol. 5). Hong Kong: Stockflow.

Ballesteros, S., Millar, S., & Reales, J. M. (1998). Symmetry in haptic and in visual shape perception. *Perception and Psychophysics, 60,* 389–404.

Baylis, G. C., & Driver, J. (1994). Parallel computation of symmetry but not repetition within single visual shapes. *Visual Cognition, 1,* 377–400.

Biederman, I. (1987). Recognition-by-components: A theory of human image understandings. *Psychological Review, 94,* 115–147.

Bruce, H. B., & Morgan, M. J. (1975). Violations of symmetry and repetition in visual patterns. *Perception, 4,* 239–249.

Chen, L. (1982). Topological structure in visual perception. *Science, 218,* 699–700.

Chen, L. (1985). Topological structure in the perception of apparent motion. *Perception, 14,* 197–208.

Chen, L. (1989). Topological perception: A challenge to computational approaches to vision. In A. Pfeifer, Z. Schreter, F. Fogelman-Soulië & L. Steels (Eds.), *Connectionism in perspective* (pp. 317–329). Amsterdam: Elsevier.

Fu, Y.-H. (1993). The Structure and construction of Chinese characters. In Y. Chen (Ed.), *Computational analysis of modern Chinese characters* (pp. 108–169). Shanghai: Shanghai Educational Press (in Chinese).

Kao, H. S. R. (Ed.). (2000). The visual-spatial features of Chinese characters and a psychogeometric theory of Chinese character writing. In *Chinese calligraphy therapy* (pp. 3–41). Hong Kong: Hong Kong University Press (in Chinese).

Koffka, K. (1935). *Principles of Gestalt psychology.* New York: Harcourt, Brace & World.

Liu, L.-Y. (1993). Topological structure of Chinese characters. In Y. Chen (Ed.), *Computational analysis of modern Chinese characters* (pp. 15–32). Shanghai: Shanghai Educational Press (in Chinese).

Locher, P., & Nodine, C. (1989). The perceptual value of symmetry. *Computers and Mathematics with Applications, 17,* 475–484.

Loo, S. C. (1989, September). *Some characteristics of commonly used Chinese characters and words: A statistical viewpoint.* Paper presented at the Inter-Faculty Seminar on Application of Statistics, National University of Singapore, Singapore.

Marr, D. (1982). *Vision.* San Francisco, CA: Freeman.

Piaget, J. (1953). How children form mathematical concepts. *Scientific American, 189,* 74–79.

Suen, C. Y. (1986). *Computational studies of the most frequent Chinese words and sounds*. Philadelphia, PA: World Scientific.

Todd, J. T., Chen, L., & Norman, J. F. (1998). On the relative salience of Euclidean, affine, and topological structure for 3-D form discrimination. *Perception, 27*, 273–282.

Wan, G., & Hsia, T.-T. (1957). *Most commonly used Chinese characters and how to find them in dictionaries without using radicals*. New Haven, CT: Far Eastern Publications, Yale University.

Wang, H., & Chang, B.-Y. (1986). *A frequency dictionary in modern Chinese*. Beijing: Beijing Language Institute Press (in Chinese).

Wenderoth, P. (1997). The effects on bilateral-symmetry detection of multiple symmetry, near symmetry, and axis orientation. *Perception, 26*, 891–904.

Zhou, W.-B. (29 November 1999). A new Chinese character database by 'Guo'an Informatics'. *The Guangming Daily* (in Chinese).

Author Note

Preparation of this paper was supported in part by Research Grant-01BYY003 to the first author from the National Social Sciences Foundation of China. We thank Lin Chen, Che Kan Leong, Li Hai Tan, Chen Xuefeng, and Stephanie Lee for their comments on the preparation and revision of this article, and He Ling-Hui of Sun Yat-Sen University Library for her assistance of programming the Foxpro data files.

11

Frequency and Position Effects of Component Combination in Chinese Character Recognition

Buxin Han

The morphological constituent of Chinese character has been named as 'radical' or 'component'. A radical is the structural unit of character used for sorting or retrieving related characters, as used in dictionaries (e.g., 木, 氵, 灬); whereas a component is the structural constituents of a character (e.g., 广, 刂, 厶, 又). Therefore, all radicals are included in a component set, but a component is not necessarily a radical (Wang, Cui, & Chai, 1997). A component has been shown to be a functional unit (Han, 1994a; Peng & Wang, 1997; Yu, Cao, Feng, & Li, 1990; Zhang & Feng, 1992). Another structural unit, the component combination, has been ignored for a long time. A component combination consists of two serial neighbouring components in one character, such as 立/口 in character 部. As a structural unit interval between a component and a character, it can be shared by a group of characters. For example, 立/口 is shared by the characters 部, 剖, 陪, 菩 etc., and holds some cognitive property as a common feature among these characters. As a possible functional unit of Chinese character, a component combination can be used to group characters and investigate the effect on the character recognition process (Han, 1995).

As an orthographic structural unit between the whole character and stroke, a component is more suitable to the principle of cognitive simplicity. Over 80% of characters contain components (radicals) which more or less indicate the pronunciation of the whole character. In one word, a component means more than a stroke, as both morphological and phonological constituents of the character. However, the frequency effect of components in the visual recognition of Chinese characters has been a rare topic in earlier studies on cognitive processing of Chinese, partly because of the complexity of its position in characters and the lack of possible manipulating index.

The Frequency Database of Chinese Character Components and Component Combination (Han, 1994b) was developed to provide a statistical basis for future studies. The database includes both token and type frequency of 567 components and 7,583 component combinations, which reflected the statistical features (e.g., stroke number, frequency, phonological and morphological component, etc.) of 6,763 simplified Chinese characters included in GB2312–80 (Han, 1993). The databases are useful for further study on linguistic computing of Chinese (Lai & Huang, 1997), Chinese information processing by computers (Han, 1998; Han & Chen, 1993; Han & Ren, 1996), in addition to its application on the study of Chinese cognition.

There are three kinds of component frequencies. *Type frequency* is the number of characters containing a component. For example, type frequency of 吏 is two because it was used in two characters, i.e., 使 and 吏. *Token frequency* is the summary occurrence of those characters containing a component in the Chinese media. For example, token frequency of 吏 is 1.9952‰ summed from 1.9734‰ (使) and 0.0218‰ (吏). It means that there were 1.9952 occurrence of 吏 in every 1000 characters in published media. *Position frequency* (which can be type or token as defined above) is the component frequency with respect to its position in characters. For example, five characters use the component 本. They are 本 (2.2720‰), 苯 (0.0446‰), 笨 (0.0126‰), 体 (1.9142‰), 钵 (0.0111‰) with their token frequency shown in brackets. The type and token position frequency of 本 at bottom position is 2 and .0572‰ respectively (Han, 1994b). Similarly, a component combination also has type, token, and position frequency.

Han (1994a) found the frequency effect and position effect of components in visual recognition of characters. A left component had a facilitating effect, i.e., characters with high component frequency can be recognized faster. This effect was significant only in low-frequency characters. When two components were presented separately, the right component inhibited the recognition latency for the whole character. The component in a left-right character was easier to recognize than that in a top-down character. A left component was more difficult to recognize than a right component. The second (right) component facilitated the recognition of the first (left) component. A component is a functional unit in character recognition, as a special kind of stroke pattern (such as component 氵, Chen, Allport, & Marshall, 1996).

Components of Chinese characters may correspond to letters of English words (Han & Lin, 1995), in light of the structural correspondence between stoke-letter-word and stoke-component-character. This correspondence has been used for developing and evaluating computer keyboard input system (Zhuang, Liu, & Zhang, 1998). Cognitive studies on alphabetic languages indicated that letter cluster is one of the basic perceptual units in word recognition. Recognition possibility of letter clusters is the monotonic progressive increasing function of their token frequency (Morton, 1969). Mason (1975) found that the position frequency of letter clusters is a sufficient condition of word superiority effect. According to Feigenbaum and Simon's (1986) Model of Primary Perception and Memory, a familiar unit is the strongest stimulus component. Frequency is a good index for familiarity. Given the correspondence between components in Chinese and letters in alphabetic languages, component combinations could be the correspondent structure of letter clusters.

Three experiments investigated whether component combinations have similar frequency effects as components on character recognition, or as letter clusters in word recognition. With respect to their two dimensional orthographic structure and the more transparent global and local relationship to phonological and semantic features, component combinations should have stronger effects than letter clusters in character/word recognition. Since component combinations lie between components and characters and many of them also have orthographic, phonetic, and semantic functions within the whole character, we also expected similar frequency and position effects of component combinations as components.

EXPERIMENT 1

In two components compound characters, such as 棵, the frequency of a component combination is actually the character frequency if its type frequency is one. For example, the components 血 and 半 combine only in the character 衅, thereby the token frequency of components combination 血/半 is equal to the frequency of 衅 (0.0074‰). Combination frequency in characters with two components can be regarded as a global feature. However, if the type frequency of components combination is more than two, the familiarity with the combination will be formed from the familiarity with the characters (as shown by token frequency of related characters) and the familiarity with the group (as shown by the type frequency). For example, the combinations 日/一 form the character 旦 and are embedded in over forty characters (e.g., 查, 量, 坦, etc.). Experiment 1 explored the combination frequency effects on the recognition of characters with two components.

METHOD

Participants   Eighteen third-year university students, 9 male and 9 female, aged 19–22, took part in the experiment. All participants were paid for participating, and were tested separately through all the characters.

Materials   Seventy-two compound characters with two components were used in Experiment 1, as shown in Table 1. All 2,373 characters with two components in GB2312–80 were divided into four groups according to their frequency of component combinations (about 3.33, 1.03, 0.26, and 0.10‰, respectively). Eighteen characters were sampled from each group. Frequencies of the two components in each character were controlled at high levels (at average 34.06 and 26.13‰, respectively). All components could be named or were characters. There were equal ratios of high- and low-frequency characters, top-bottom and left-right characters at each level of component combination frequency. All characters had less than ten strokes.

Table 1
Characters Used in Experiment 1

| | Low-frequency characters | | High-frequency characters | |
Combination	Top-bottom	Left-right	Top-bottom	Left-right
3.33	加如叶	叭叮扣吐泪	古另台穴只	呆旦杏杳杲
1.03	计利放	柏肚斩付呐	呈皇孟苗虽	胃吊寺旨娄
0.26	池打伏	伐仿灿垃肋	否李旱岩香	帛杰男芍秃
0.10	祖找状	钞炊冯劫砍	泵导亩怎突	宝甫胄劣辛

Procedure   Stimulus presentation and timing were controlled by a computer connected to a voice switch and a microphone. Discrimination of the colour monitor was 640 × 350. Distance between subject and monitor screen was 60 cm. White characters, sized 1.8 cm × 1.2 cm and formed at about 1.72 × 1.15° visual angle, were presented one at a time at random order in the centre of black background on the computer screen for 25 ms. Individual participants were asked to name the characters as rapidly and correctly as possible. Instructions were presented on the screen in the same size and font to check if the participants could read them clearly. Participants practised twelve times to learn the proper reaction. Only those participants with average reaction times (RTs) less than 1000ms were included in the data analysis.

RESULTS

Reaction time (RT) and error rate (ER) of recognizing characters with two components are shown in Table 2. Repeated measures MANOVA RTs of recognizing high and low frequency character were 555 ms and 602 ms respectively, $F(1, 17) = 43.91$, $p < .001$. RTs at four levels of combination frequency (0.10, .26, 1.03, 3.33‰) were 609, 586, 548, and 571 ms respectively, $F(3, 51) = 13.75$, $p < .01$. A posteriori Tukey Honestly Significant Difference (HSD) test showed that 609 and 571, 609 and 548, 548 and 586 were significantly different from each other. There was a significant interaction between character frequency and combination frequency, $F(3, 51) = 4.70$, $p < .01$. Combination frequency showed a significant effect when recognizing high-frequency characters (RTs were 600, 566, 511, and 542 ms respectively at four levels of combination

Table 2
Reaction Time (ms) and Error Rate (%) of Recognition of Characters With Two Components

Frequency of component combination (‰)	Low-frequency characters		High-frequency characters	
	Top-bottom	Left-right	Top-bottom	Left-right
0.10	603±67(20)	633±72(7)	604±52(9)	596±94(4)
0.26	609±47(13)	604±76(18)	596±88(2)	537±27(4)
1.03	577±35(2)	593±53(0)	512±47(2)	510±26(4)
3.33	626±72(22)	572±61(16)	541±51(4)	544±32(0)

Note. Reaction time is presented as: RT±SD. Error rate is in brackets.

frequency); but not when recognizing low-frequency characters (RT were 618, 606, 584, and 599 ms respectively).

Repeated measures MANOVA showed that error rates (ERs) of recognizing high- and low-frequency character were 3.6% and 12.2% respectively ($F(1, 17) = 44.69$, $p < .001$). Combination frequency also had a significant effect ($F(3, 68) = 5.39$, $p < .01$). There was a significant interaction of combination frequency and character frequency ($F(3, 68) = 11.93$, $p < .01$). ERs (13.3, 15.6, 1.1, 18.9% respectively) at four levels of combination frequencies differed significantly when recognizing low-frequency characters, but not when recognizing high-frequency characters. Structural types did not have an effect on both RT and ER.

DISCUSSION

Component combination frequency facilitated the recognition of high frequency compound characters with two components. Combination frequency as a global characteristic showed similar effects as the character frequency. The combination activated a list of related characters. The length of the list increased along with the increasing of combination frequency. High frequency characters were more easily recognized from the list and therefore the RT would not be slower by too much. The low frequency characters were not so salient in the list, so the facilitating effect of combinations would be offset by the slowing effect of a long list. In general, combination frequency effect was significant when recognizing high frequency character.

Combination frequency also revealed the inseparability between the two components. High combination frequency indicated that two components were presented together frequently, and therefore produced an inseparable connection as a unit of information processing. Experiment two tested this probability.

EXPERIMENT 2

The intensive connection between two components and the global characteristics of component combination may be decomposed by presenting two components separately. The integrated recognition in this experiment should test this notion. If separation decreases the combination frequency effect (i.e., the variation of RT along with the changing of combination frequency), the connection should be the precondition of recognition. If the combination frequency effect is increased, the integration is not the precondition but a better expression of combination frequency.

METHOD

Participants   Sixteen fourth-year university students, 4 females and 12 males, aged 20–24, took part in Experiment 2.

Materials   The same materials as in Experiment 1 were used.

Procedure   Each component was presented for 25 ms at 120 ms intervals. Components were presented in the same form and position as in the original characters. RT was the time lapse between presentation of the component (i.e., the left one or top one) and recognition of the character. The characters were presented in two halves: One half starting with the first component and the other half starting with the second component.

RESULTS

RTs and ERs of integrated recognition of characters with two components are shown in Table 3. Repeated measures MANOVA showed that RT of recognizing high- and low-frequency characters were 572 and 673 ms respectively ($F(1, 15) = 13.61$, $p < .01$). High-frequency characters were integrated faster for recognition than low frequency characters. RTs at four levels of combination frequencies (0.10, 0.26, 1.03, 3.33‰) were 701, 576, 569, and 624 ms respectively ($F(3, 45) = 5.46$, $p < .01$). A posteriori HSD test showed that there was a significant difference between 701 ms and other three RTs. RTs for top-bottom and left-right characters were 670 and 574 ms respectively ($F(1, 15) = 50.32$, $p < .001$). Left-right type characters were faster to be integrated for recognizing than top-bottom characters were. There was a significant interaction between structural type and character frequency ($F(1, 15) = 4.59$, $p < .05$).

Table 3
Reaction Time (ms) and Error Rate (%) of Integrated Recognition of Characters With Two Components

Frequency of component combination (‰)	Low-frequency characters		High-frequency characters	
	Top-bottom	Left-right	Top-bottom	Left-right
0.10	909±284(43)	627±222(28)	627±140(38)	640±112(29)
0.26	664±96 (33)	601±136(38)	608±100(43)	512±160(21)
1.03	663±200(43)	566±177(28)	537±140(40)	508±168(42)
3.33	753±282(40)	598±260(38)	604±180(35)	540±194(13)

Note. Reaction time is presented as: RT±SD. Error rate is in brackets.

Repeated measures MANOVA showed that the ERs for recognizing top-bottom and left-right characters were 39.4% and 29.3% respectively, ($F(1, 15) = 16.16$, $p < .001$). Left-right type characters were easier to be integrated and recognized than top-bottom characters. There was a significant interaction between character frequency and combination frequency ($F(3, 45) = 10.47$, $p < .001$). ERs for integrated recognizing high frequency characters were 33.3, 32.6, 41, and 23.8% at four levels of component frequency (0.10, 0.26, 1.03, and 3.33‰ respectively, $F(3, 124) = 4.78$, $p < .01$). ERs for integrated recognizing low frequency characters were not significantly different.

DISCUSSION

The separate presentation of two components increased RT, but did not break the facilitating effect as found in Experiment 1. This revealed that the global characteristic of combination frequency was decreased by separation, but it still had an effect on the integrated recognition process. Both RT and ER data showed that left-right type characters were easier to be integrated and recognized than top-bottom characters. This confirmed that the connection between components in top-bottom character is more intensive than left-right characters (Yu, Cao, Feng, & Li, 1990). This was not revealed in the normal recognition task in Experiment 1.

EXPERIMENT 3

Experiments 1 and 2 showed similar frequency effect of component combination, compared with component frequency effect with the integrated recognition paradigm (Han, 1994a). However, it did not reveal the difference between the integrated processing of component and component combination since combination is a global feature in characters with two components. The frequency effect of combination is related to but different from the frequency effect of the whole character. There are 40% three components character, such as 拐, in GB2312–80 character set (2,702 of 6,763 characters). This is the highest percentage compared with characters consisting of one component (4.6%), two components (35%), four components (15%), and five or more components (4.4%) (Han, 1993). This means that component combination can be embedded in most characters. Experiment 3 explored the combination frequency effect in characters with three components, where combination was the local feature and located in specific positions of characters.

METHOD

Participants   Thirty third-year university students, 20 males and 10 females, aged 18–22, took part in Experiment 3.

Materials   Ninety left-right type characters with three components were sampled from 2,702 characters in GB2312–80, as shown in Table 4. Components in each character were characters or can be named. Half of

Table 4
Characters Used in Experiment 3

Frequency of component combination (‰)	Low-frequency characters			High-frequency characters		
	⊟	⊞	⫼	⊟	⊞	⫼
High	涂略轻 联况	敏劲胡 数部	侧例倒 雌树	峭舵袒 晦拐	魂勋敛 毓郡	靴讹咖 挪咧
Medium	旋湿腔 拖将	鼓创散 剥教	渐概谢 脚倾	禅呛肮 捏蝎	雏鹃剔 鹊剐	鸿坳卿 绑渺
Low	摆临挖 伤摇	凯叔款 飘荆	柳傲掀 辩御	琐谍淹 聘吮	颏颖甄 鸹剃	湃粥狱 撇嗽

the characters were of high frequency, the other half were of low frequency. Combination frequency of the target combination with two components was divided into three levels (3.33, 0.58, and 0.08‰ respectively). Components were combined in three ways, as shown by '⊟ (one component on the left, other two components on the right)', '⊟ (two components on the left, one component on the right)', and '⦀ (three components in parallel from left to right)'.

Procedure   The same procedure as in Experiment 1 was followed.

RESULTS

Recognition RT and ER of characters with three components are shown in Table 5. Repeated measures MANOVA showed that RT for high- and low-frequency characters were 632 and 743 ms respectively ($F(1, 29) = 365.26, p < .0001$). RTs for characters under three levels of combination frequencies (3.33, 0.58, 0.08‰) were 676, 703, 683 ms respectively ($F(2, 58) = 8.77, p < .001$). A posteriori HSD test showed that 703 was significantly different from 676 and 683. The lowest RT is related to the medium-frequency component combination. RT for recognizing ⊟, ⊟, and ⦀ types of character were 661, 705, and 696 ms respectively ($F(2, 58) = 38.4, p < .0001$). There was a significant interaction between character frequency and combination frequency ($F(2, 58) = 3.64, p < .05$). RTs for recognizing high-frequency characters at three levels of combination frequency differed significantly, but not for recognizing low-frequency characters. There was also a significant interaction between character frequency and character type ($F(2, 58) = 15.8, p < .001$). For high-frequency characters, RTs were 600, 637, and 658 ms for ⊟, ⊟, and ⦀ types of character respectively. For low-frequency characters, RTs were 723, 774, and 734 ms for ⊟, ⊟, and ⦀ types of character respectively. There was also a significant interaction between character type and combination frequency. Under the three levels of combination frequencies (3.33, 0.58, 0.08‰), RTs were 659, 692, and 634 ms for recognizing ⊟ type characters (634 differed significantly from 692); RTs were 673, 730, and 712 ms for recognizing ⊟ type characters (673 differed from 730); RTs did not differ significantly from each other for recognizing ⦀ type characters.

Repeated measures MANOVA showed that ERs for recognizing high- and low-frequency characters were 4.3 and 18.4% respectively ($F(1, 29)$

Table 5
Reaction Time (ms) and Error Rate (%) of Recognition of Characters With Three Components

Frequency of component combination (‰)	Low-frequency characters			High-frequency characters		
	田	目	川	田	目	川
Low	694±91 (7)	770±105 (36)	746±73 (13)	574±57 (2)	654±56 (3)	662±75 (9)
Medium	754±74 (16)	794±90 (21)	714±68 (11)	629±75 (2)	667±80 (7)	660±68 (3)
High	722±80 (17)	757±86 (17)	741±93 (26)	596±53 (0)	590±73 (1)	653±81 (12)

Note. Reaction time is presented as: RT±SD. Error rate is in brackets.

= 75.43, $p < .0001$). ERs for recognizing 田 , 目 , and 川 type characters were 7.3, 14.3, and 12.3% respectively ($F(2, 58) = 18.1$, $p < .001$). There was a significant interaction between character frequency and combination frequency ($F(2, 58) = 9.74$, $p < .01$). For high frequency characters, ERs were 1.3, 3.8, and 7.8% for 田 , 目 , and 川 type characters respectively; but for low frequency characters, ERs were 13.3, 24.9, and 16.9% respectively. There was also significant interaction between combination frequency and character type ($F(4, 116) = 10.68$, $p < .001$). Under the three levels of combination frequencies (3.33, 0.58, 0.08‰), ERs were 11, 7, 19.7% respectively for recognizing 川 type characters; ERs were 19.7, 14, and 9.3% respectively for recognizing 目 type characters; ERs were not differed significantly with each other for recognizing 田 type characters.

DISCUSSION

Both RT and ER showed a consistent pattern of combination frequency effect. 田 was recognized with lowest RT and ER, 目 type was recognized with highest RT and ER, and 川 type was in between. A single component was easier than combination to activate the list of related characters, because of the higher complexity of component combination and the requirement of further segmentation and processing. This was confirmed by the fact that the combination type of component showed different effect with respect to character frequency. For high-frequency characters, the increasing order of RT and ER is ⿱, ⿰, and ⿲. For low-frequency characters, the increasing order of RT and ER is ⿱, ⿲, and ⿰. Studies have shown that high-frequency characters tend to be processed automatically, while low-frequency characters tend to be processed serially (feature analysis, Zheng, 1981).

Three components in ⿲ type characters were connected loosely with each other, as shown by the fact that there was no difference of RTs between three levels of combination frequency. For example, compared with the combination 另 in 拐 the connection within the combination 卯 in 柳 is rather loose.

When naming the left-right type characters combining with 3 components, the components combination on the left position of the whole character showed a facilitating effect, while the combination on the right position showed an inhibitory effect.

GENERAL DISCUSSION

Frequency effect and position effect of component combination

Three experiments showed a consistent character frequency effect with respect to both RTs and ERs, in normal and integrated recognition of compound characters with two or three components. Character frequency revealed significant superiority over the frequency of single components or component combination. As a global feature, character frequency is the most important factor affecting recognition performance.

Frequency effects of component combination on recognition interacted with character frequency and position of combination. Our studies on frequency effect and position effect showed that either component or component combination as local feature has facilitasting effects on the left position or inhibitory effects on the right position (Han, 1994a, 1996).

Two recently published studies (Feldman & Siok, 1997; Taft & Zhu, 1997) showed a different pattern of frequency effect and position effect of components. Taft and Zhu (1997) found that the frequency of the right-hand radical (i.e., component) affected responses to 2-radical characters. The impact of radical frequency was shown to be sensitive to radical position. For 3-radical characters, it appeared that the frequency of a compound radical had no effect on responses, whereas the frequency of the sub-radicals did. They concluded that simple but not compound radicals are independently activated in the process of character recognition, with position effect. However, Feldman and Siok (1997) found that when component function was considered, character decision latencies varied with component frequency but not reliably with position.

Although the frequency effect of components was confirmed in all studies, the direction of the facilitating or inhibitory effect was different, with respect to the position of component. Possible reasons might be the different visual recognition tasks (naming vs. character decision) and frequencies (type vs. token) adopted in the studies. It is argued here that token frequency represented familiarity with component/combination better than type frequency, especially in recognition tasks where RT was the independent variable. Further studies are needed to verify this notion, especially for component combination. In addition, whether and how the position (left/right, top/down, and inside/outside) of component and/or combination affect recognition need further study.

Frequency effects of components and component combinations interacted with structural type of characters, and were found mainly from left-right structure compound characters. Given that 60% of the characters are of the left-right type and over 21.5% character are of the top-bottom type, the structural feature of character and its effect on cognitive processing of Chinese information should be explored further in future studies.

Comparability between studies Statistical research on modern Chinese developed several databases about many indices, such as frequency of orthographic units (word, character, component, stroke, etc.; Bei & Zhang, 1988; Beijing Language Institute, 1986; Beijing Library, 1988; Fu, 1990; Han, 1994b; Li & Liu, 1988). Given that these databases provide a firm framework for cognitive study on Chinese, it is still a problem whether frequencies provided by different sources are comparable. If the answer is no, it will be questionable to compare the results of studies on Chinese character recognition using different frequencies.

Statistical linguistics oriented studies often bias towards either orthographic or phonetic information (Tan & Perfetti, 1998). Some studies controlled one variable while studying another, some studies simply ignored other variables. Studies on the effect of component on character recognition should be put in a broader theoretical framework. Ideally, morphological, phonological and semantic features of components should be treated simultaneously.

Useful standards of Chinese information exchange for cognitive study on Chinese   The database technique assists both psychologists and linguists in designing their studies more strictly. The latest result based on the International Standard Character Set (20,902 characters) of Chinese Information Exchange (ISO/CEO10646 or GB13000–1) is *The International Standard Chinese Character Dictionary* (CD-ROM version; Fu, 1999). However, some new indices, such as phonetic regularity of component/combination with the whole character, should be developed for future linguistic and psychological studies.

The importance of standard dissemination is apparent for both linguistic studies (e.g., number of component/combination in given character sets) and cognitive studies (e.g., psychological reality of the structural units in characters based on standard segmentation). More importantly, the psychological reality of the standard segmentation will be strengthened along with the application of GF3001–97 in computer keyboard input system design and primary educational system. *Chinese Character Component Standard of GB 13000.1 Character Set for Information Processing* (GF 3001–97; Wang, Cui, & Chai, 1997) defines standard segments of character structure. For example, the character 疸 can be segmented in three ways with increasing depth of segmentation, either 疒 > (日/一), or (疒// 冫) > (日/一), or ((丶/厂) // 冫) > (日/一). Each of these segments seems reasonable but only the first one is acceptable according to GF3001–97.

Conclusion

In visual recognition of Chinese characters, component combinations showed a facilitating effect on the left position of the character, or an inhibitory effect on the right position of the character. These effects interacted with the frequency, structure, and presenting procedure of the whole character. The frequency and position effects have been partially supported by recent studies. Similar with components, component combination can also be a functional unit in visual recognition of Chinese characters.

References

Bei, G., & Zhang, X. (1988). 汉字频率统计 (Statistics on frequency of Chinese character). Beijing: Electronic Industry Press.

Beijing Language Institute. (1986). 现代汉语频率词典 (Frequency dictionary of modern Chinese). Beijing: Beijing Language Institute Press.

Beijing Library. (1988). 汉字属性字典 (Dictionary of Chinese features). Beijing: Shumu Wenxian Press.

Chen, Y. P., Allport, D. A., & Marshall, J. C. (1996). What are the functional orthographic units in Chinese word recognition: The stroke or the stroke pattern? *Quarterly Journal of Experimental Psychology, 49A,* 1024–1043.

Feldman, L. B., & Siok, W. W. (1997). The role of component function in visual recognition of Chinese characters. *Journal of Experimental Psychology: Learning, Memory, and Cognition, 23,* 776–781.

Feigenbaum, E. A., & Simon, H. A. (1986). EPAM-like models of recognition and learning. *Cognitive Science, 8,* 305–336.

Fu, Y. (1990). 汉字属性字典 (Dictionary of Chinese features). Beijing: Chinese Language Press.

Fu, Y. (1999). 国际标准汉字大字典多媒体版 (International standard Chinese character dictionary) (CD-ROM version). Beijing: Beijing University Press.

Han, B. (1993). Application of the feature Information database of Chinese characters in the research of Chinese character recognition. *Journal of Developments in Psychology, 1*(4), 29–35 (in Chinese).

Han, B. (1994a). Frequency effect of constituents in Chinese character recognition. In Q. Jing, H. Zhang, & D. Peng (Eds.), *Information processing of Chinese language* (pp. 87–98). Beijing: Beijing Normal University Press.

Han, B. (1994b). Development of database of Chinese constituents information — Statistical analysis of the frequency of the constituents and their combinations. *Acta Psychologica Sinica, 26,* 147–152 (in Chinese).

Han, B. (1995). Components combination — A latent Chinese character structure level. *Journal of Chinese Information Processing, 9*(3), 27–32 (in Chinese).

Han, B. (1996). Frequency effect of components combination in Chinese character recognition. *Acta Psychologica Sinica, 28,* 9–13 (in Chinese).

Han, B. (1998) Evaluating Chinese character inputting coding methods — Compatibility between component sets. In W. Karwowski & R. Goonetilleke (Eds.), *Manufacturing agility and hybrid automation-II* (pp. 188–191). Santa Monica, CA: IEA Press.

Han, B., & Chen, Y. (1993). The effects of the spatial position of Chinese character and its implication to computer recognition of Chinese characters. *Journal of Chinese Information Processing, 7*(4), 60–66 (in Chinese).

Han, B., & Lin, Z. (1995). On the cognitive correspondence between components of Chinese characters and letters of English words. *Psychological Science, 18,* 334–336 (in Chinese).

Han, B., & Ren, X. (1996). The equitable arrangement of brevity coding words for Chinese input. *Journal of Chinese Information Processing, 9*(4), 41–45 (in Chinese).

Lai. C., & Huang, J-T. (1997, August 29 – September 2). *A comparative study concerning the frequency counts of Chinese character constituents.* Paper presented at the International Symposium on Cognitive Processes of the Chinese Language, University of Hong Kong, Hong Kong.

Li, G., & Liu, R. (Eds.). (1988). 汉字信息字典 (Dictionary of Chinese character information). Beijing: Science Press.

Mason, M. (1975). Reading ability and letter search time: Effects of orthographic structure defined by single-letter positional frequency. *Journal of Experimental Psychology: General, 104,* 146–166.

Morton, J. (1969). The interaction of information in word recognition. *Psychological Review, 76,* 165–178.

Peng, D., & Wang, C. (1997). Basic processing unit of Chinese character recognition: Evidence from stroke number effect and radical number effect. *Acta Psychologica Sinica, 29,* 8–17 (in Chinese).

Taft, M., & Zhu, X. (1997). Sub-morphemic processing in reading Chinese. *Journal of Experimental Psychology: Learning, Memory, and Cognition, 23,* 761–775.

Tan, L. & Perfetti, C. (1998). Phonological codes as early sources of constraint in Chinese word identification: A review of current discoveries and theoretical accounts. *Reading and Writing: An Interdisciplinary Journal, 10,* 165–200.

Wang, N., Cui, Y., & Chai, H. (1997). 信息处理用 GB13000.1 字符集汉字部件规范 (Chinese character component standard) of GB 13000.l character set for information processing (GF 3001–1997). Beijing: China State Language Commission.

Yu, B., Cao, H., Feng, L., & Li, W. (1990). Effect of morphological and phonological processing of Chinese characters on the perception of components. *Acta Psychologica Sinica, 22,* 232–239 (in Chinese).

Yu, B., Feng, L., Cao, H., & Li, W. (1990). Visual perception of Chinese characters: Effect of perception task and Chinese character attributes. *Acta Psychologica Sinica, 22,* 141–148 (in Chinese).

Zhang, W., & Feng, L. (1992). A study on the unit of processing in recognition of Chinese characters. *Acta Psychologica Sinica, 24,* 379–385 (in Chinese).

Zheng, Z. (1981). Cognitive process of Chinese character. *Chinese Journal of Psychology, 23,* 137–153 (in Chinese).

Zhuang, J., Liu, Y., & Zhang, K. (1998). A mathematical model of compatibility between Chinese parts and English letters. *Acta Psychologica Sinica, 30,* 143–148 (in Chinese).

Author Note

The financial support of the China Natural Science Foundation (39670255) is gratefully acknowledged. I am very grateful to Dr Che Kan Leong for his helpful comments on the earlier versions of this paper.

Part 4

Learning Chinese Characters and Words

12

Segmental Analysis and Reading in Chinese

Che-Kan Leong

In learning to read, children need to make contact from their developed ability of listening and speaking with what the graphic symbols in different writing systems or orthographies represent. Emergent readers need to be aware of, or sensitive to, the mapping between speech sounds and the basic graphic units in order to access print. While there are certain universal phonological principles governing the translation from speech sounds to orthographic representation, the phonological involvement is constrained by variations in language or orthography systems (Frost & Katz, 1992; Leong, 1997; Leong & Joshi, 1997). The English orthography, for example, is morphophonemic and is represented by phonemes, syllables with their onsets and rimes and other sublexical units. Sensitivity to these units is important in emergent literacy. For the more consistent German orthography, phonological knowledge is still important in emergent literacy and is reinforced by orthographic knowledge in an interactive manner (Landerl, Frith, & Wimmer, 1996). In the biscriptal Japanese syllabary with its kanji and kana scripts, each Japanese kana symbol represents a speech unit known as *mora*, which is more of a subsyllabic and a timing unit on which the rhythm of the Japanese language is based (Leong & Tamaoka, 1995, 1998; Otake, Hatano, Cutler, & Mehler, 1993). Thus, if phonological awareness is a precursor to learning to read Japanese (at least for hiragana and katakana script), then the sensitivity to morae as units of segments of speech in both speech perception and production becomes important (Leong, 1995).

The aim of this chapter is to explore the nature of what is usually termed metalinguistic awareness (Leong, 1991) or sensitivity to speech-sounds and its relation to learning to read Chinese. The interplay with orthographic form, which, in the English literature, is usually defined in terms of the 'systematic relationships to phonological properties of the word' (Ehri, 1980, p. 313), is discussed. Chinese language learning principles and classroom practices in emergent literacy all emphasize the integration of orthographic or spelling patterns (shape), speech sounds and meaning at the word level. The psychological principles of redundancy and precision are important in enhancing early reading and spelling.

Manipulating Speech Sounds by Chinese Subjects

Since the prototypic study by Read, Zhang, Nie and Ding (1986) of speech sounds manipulation by Chinese adults has spurred on subsequent research, the work will be briefly revisited as the starting point of our discussion. Related studies by Holm and Dodd (1996), Huang and Hanley (1995), Hanley and Huang (1997), Ho and Bryant (1997a, 1997b) and Cheung (1999) will also be outlined.

Studies by Read et al. (1986) and Holm and Dodd (1996) with Chinese adults

In essence, Read et al. (1986) predicated their phonemic segmentation study on the logic of the Brussels group of Morais and Bertelson (Morais, Bertelson, Cary, & Alegria, 1986; Morais, Cary, Alegria, & Bertelson, 1979) and used similar tasks. The Read et al. finding of performance difference in a phoneme deletion or addition task of real and pseudo-English words by adult Chinese literates, exposed or not exposed to the Chinese Pinyin (alphabetic) transliteration system, generally replicated the results of the Brussels study with Portuguese illiterates and ex-literates.

This early work by Read et al., just as the research program by the Brussels group, is important in showing that segmental analysis of phoneme deletion and addition does not develop spontaneously and needs to be instilled in, if not taught explicitly to, learners. This is the puzzlement raised and partly answered by the authors in that their Chinese adult literates may have had many years of 'reading and writing non-alphabetically in a language rich in implicit examples like rhymes, minimal pairs, and phonetic radicals, not to mention Spoonerisms ...' (Read et al., 1986, p. 43); and yet the non-alphabetic group performed much below chance level.

With hindsight, readers may ponder the reasons for the almost ceiling performance of the Pinyin group of 12 adults as compared with the almost floor performance of the non-alphabetic group of 18 adults in adding or deleting phonemes (Figures 1 and 2 of Read et al., 1986). The rather distinct bimodal distributions may pertain to subject characteristics, to the actual tasks used, or to both variables.

On the stimulus materials of adding or deleting the phonemes of /d/, /s/, and /n/ in Read et al. (1986), it would appear that the extremely low performance by the 18 non-alphabetic adults may be explained in terms of the *sonority* principle. This principle relates to the alternating, rhythmic characteristics of succession of sounds and was first articulated by Jesperson (1904), Bloomfield (1933/1962), and further elaborated by such theoretical linguists as Goldsmith (1990) and psycholinguists such as Treiman (1989), among others. If it can be assumed that the sonority principle applies to the perception of initial consonants or consonant clusters (onsets), then /d/ as a voiced stop is extremely low in sonority, /s/ as an alveolar fricative and /n/ as a nasal stop also have medium to low 'rating' on the sonority continuum. The medium to low sonority rating of the phoneme items obviously did not encourage the performance of the non-alphabetic group.

Still, the sonority principle of speech perception does not explain why the alphabetic group performed almost at ceiling level despite the two groups being 'similar in education and experience' except for the reported alphabetic learning. Perhaps the non-alphabetic group was sensitive to phonological tasks other than the segmental analysis of phonemes. What needs to be emphasized is the effect of linguistic structure on performance in segmentation or related phonological processing tasks. The Read et al. study and related studies by the Brussels group provide evidence that there is generalized or global phonological ability, as shown in rhyming tasks, and this global phonological ability may differ from the more analytic segmental analysis. This distinction is also drawn in a recent study with preschool, kindergarten and grade-school Brazilian children (Cardoso-Martins, 1994).

More recently, Holm and Dodd (1996) examined first and second language literacy in a total of 40 college students from China, Hong Kong,

Vietnam and Australia. The results suggested that students from Hong Kong had limited phonemic awareness and this limitation might be due to their use of an *orthographic strategy* in transferring their first language (L1) knowledge of Chinese to learning their second language (L2) of English. Holm and Dodd asserted that development of phonemic awareness requires *alphabetic literacy*, and not just literacy in general. This notion needs to be further developed.

One possible reason for the lower performance in phonemic awareness of the Hong Kong students, compared with their mainland China counterparts, might be attributed to the *differential-frequency account* in processing Chinese and English words in that the Hong Kong students experience English more in print than in speech (Liu, Zhu, & Wu, 1992). If L1 for Hong Kong students interferes with their L2 learning, the effect could well be the other way round in what is known as *intercession* or *backward transfer* from L2 to L1, as discussed by Leong and Hsia (1996).

Studies of Chinese children's and adolescents' phoneme segmentation and phonological processing

There are other issues implicit in the Read et al. study. These are issues of the nature of access to the phonological structure by Chinese learners and the relationship to reading. Hanley and Huang (1997) and Huang and Hanley (1995) addressed some of these issues with well-designed tasks. These researchers examined the effect of phonological awareness (rhyming and alliteration) in spoken words (the same tone for the Chinese items), English and Chinese phoneme deletion tasks for the respective subjects, and visual skills (discrimination and paired associates) on the reading ability of 137 eight-year-old primary-school children in Taiwan, Hong Kong and England. It should be noted that children in Hong Kong use traditional Chinese orthography, while children in Taiwan use *Zhuyin Fuhao* (a set of phonetic symbols along the lines of IPA transcription) in learning to read.

There are several interesting findings in the Hanley and Huang and Huang and Hanley studies. One main result is that when general ability and vocabulary were partialled out, the performance of the Chinese children on the phonological tasks did not relate significantly to their reading. The other finding is that the Taiwanese children's performance on the Chinese phoneme deletion task was 'reminiscent' of the results of Read et al. (1986).

Another main finding is that the English subjects outperformed their Chinese age-peers in deleting the first sound from consonant-vowel-consonant-consonant (CVCC) words, whereas Hong Kong children did significantly better than their British peers in deleting first sounds from consonant-consonant-vowel-consonant (CCVC) words. The explanation given by the researchers is that the consonant clusters were treated by the British children as single units; whereas the Hong Kong children performed well on consonant clusters because 'there are no consonant blends whatsoever in Chinese syllables' (Huang & Hanley, 1995, p. 95). This is a strong statement as the aspirated affricate /ts/ in the consonantal onsets of some Chinese characters could be considered the closest to consonant clusters (Chao, 1968).

Moreover, from their studies of syllables containing clusters and those not containing clusters, Treiman and Zukowski (1991) stated that in terms of syllable structure on phonological awareness: '... the present results suggest that clusters are *not* always harder than single phonemes' (p. 76, original emphasis). It would thus be instructive to know the precise nature of the phoneme deletion tasks in both English and Chinese, as used by Hanley and Huang. In the last analysis, it is the linguistic status and structure that are critical in our understanding of access to linguistic structure.

In their studies of young Chinese children, Ho and Bryant (1997a) found that phonological processing based on information on speech sound in the phonetic radicals of Chinese characters was predictive of later reading of real and pseudo- characters. Ho and Bryant (1997b) further showed that this facilitation applied only to high-frequency and not low-frequency characters and more with single characters than with two-character words. Moreover, while their sample of 90 first- and second-graders do rely on phonological awareness and script-sound phonetic regularity of the radicals, sensitivity to sub-syllabic components such as rimes through analogic reasoning is also needed to enhance the reading of new characters and words.

In his study of phonological awareness of younger (aged 13) and older (aged 16) Cantonese-speaking Chinese adolescents, Cheung (1999) examined the effects of training of segmentation skills (phoneme blending and deletion and rime judement) on reading English words. Using a pre- and post-test design, Cheung found that the training improved sub-syllabic segmentation in the younger adolescents, but not the older ones, and for low-proficiency readers but not high-proficiency ones. The general finding was that training in segmentation skills enhances the Chinese readers' word reading in a later learned alphabetic English script.

Segmental and Syllabic Analysis by Chinese College Students

The recent study of Leong and Hsia (1996) on phonological and morphological processing of Chinese university students in Hong Kong within the framework of componential analysis of reading (Hsia, 1992; Leong, 1992) is relevant here. Of interest is that part of the overall study dealing with segmental and syllabic analysis of Chinese and English by 82 Cantonese-speaking Chinese subjects.

The hypothesis tested was that students in the Putonghua language (PL) subgroup (n = 24 students) receiving Putonghua segmental and syllabic training should perform better in phonological tasks than would their counterparts in the Cantonese language (CL) subgroup (n = 58 students) not receiving such training. These two subgroups were equated in their reading comprehension and memory span prior to the main study. Using the term *training* in the broad classroom sense, we put forward the very tentative suggestion that the learning of Putonghua and segmental training promote the learning of phonological and phonetic principles in English. This tentative suggestion still holds but needs to be refined from further, fine-grained analysis of the relevant data.

Deeper linguistic explanation of results

To examine the segmental and syllabic analysis of the Putonghua and Cantonese language subgroups, these tasks, among others, were given:
(1) Segmental analysis of English initial consonants or consonant clusters (EIC) and English final consonants (EFC). There were 16 English (C)CVC(C) pseudo-words (4 to 7 letters) such as PRINGS, SHEEKS and THAVES. The procedure for the EIC task was as follows: 'If I say -ANK (for the pseudo-word VANK), what is the *beginning sound* left out of the letter string?' The EFC task for the same 16 pseudo-words was: 'If I say VAN- (for VANK) what is the *end sound* left out of the letter string?' All the items were randomized and the subjects were required to supply the deleted initial consonant or consonant clusters or the deleted final consonants, as applicable.
(2) Segmental analysis of Cantonese initial consonants (CIC) in 25 Chinese characters/words across 3 Cantonese tones with Cantonese phonemes such as liquids /l/ and nasals /n/, the velar stop /k/, and the guttural /h/. The linguistic basis of the design of the 'written

Cantonese' and written Chinese items was motivated by Bauer's (1988) detailed analysis of registers of spoken Cantonese. Subjects were required to say the Cantonese equivalent of English words such as NYLON, [a] PEAR, where the initials /l/ and /n/ are critical for discrimination in Cantonese.

In general, statistical analyses comparing the performance of the subgroup of 24 students with training in Putonghua segmental analysis and the subgroup of 58 students without such training showed significant differences, task for task, with the exception of the English segmentation task for final consonants (EFC). The performance of the two subgroups on the three tasks is shown in Figure 1.

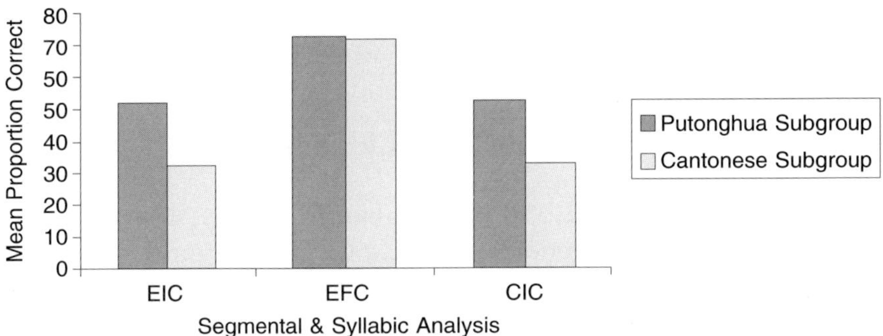

Figure 1.   Performance of two subgroups of Cantonese-speaking university students in Hong Kong on segmental analysis of English initial consonants or consonant clusters (EIC), English final consonants (EFC), and segmental analysis of Cantonese initial consonants (CIC).

On the surface, the above results as summarized in Leong and Hsia (1996) seem to support the findings of the prototypic Read et al. (1986) and the more recent Huang and Hanley (1995) and Hanley and Huang (1997) studies in suggesting that segmental analysis is promoted in Chinese students who learn the phonetic system of Putonghua or its variant Zhuyin Fuhao. Further analysis of the within-task data and the items themselves points to the critical role of linguistic variables that will add to the behavioural results.

Leong and Hsia (1996) explain the differential performance of the 82 Cantonese-speaking students in the Putonghua and non-Putonghua subgroups in terms of typological markedness invoked by Eckman (1981) to account for the difficulty of his Mandarin-speaking Chinese subjects in pronouncing English word final-voiced obstruents. Further evidence comes from Flege, McCutcheon, and Smith (1987) who show that Chinese adults find it difficult to distinguish voiceless /p/, /t/, and /k/ from voiced /b/, /d/, and /g/, and are not effective in implementing /b/, /d/, and /g/ sounds.

It should be noted that the performance of the Putonghua subgroup on both the English initial consonant (EIC) and the Chinese initial consonant (CIC) tasks was at about the chance level (mean proportion correct of 51.8% and 52.3% respectively), while the Cantonese subgroup did much worse (32.4 and 32.7% respectively). The English final consonant (EFC) task did not discriminate between the two subgroups (72.4% and 72%). It would appear that the sonority principle offers a viable explanation for the chance performance on the initial consonant segmentation tasks for both English and Chinese.

Sonority Contour Principle as Explanatory

In emphasizing Chinese as morphosyllabic (DeFrancis, 1989) the link between syllables and phonology is evident. The relationship between syllables and sonority contour was long emphasized by Jesperson (1904). In his classic book *Language*, Bloomfield (1933/1966) explains the sonority principle as follows:

> In any succession of sounds, some strike the ear more forcibly than others: differences of *sonority* play a great part in the transition effects of vowels and vowel-like sounds. Thus, other things (especially, the stress) being equal, a low vowel, such as [a], is more sonorous than a high vowel, such as [i]; any vowel is more sonorous than a consonant; a nasal, trill, or lateral more than a stop or spirant; a sibilant [s, z], with its concentration of the breath-stream into a narrow channel, more than another spirant; a spirant more than a stop; a voiced sound more than an unvoiced. In any succession of phonemes there will thus be an up-and-down of sonority. (Bloomfield, 1966, p. 120, original emphasis)

The sonority contour principle relating the internal structure of segments to the measurable peaks of sonority could provide an explanation for such tasks as segmental analysis of initial and final consonants. For the English initial consonant task, 11 of the 16 items contained consonant clusters. Could this be the possible reason for the performance at 52% and 32% correct for the Putonghua and the non-Putonghua subgroups? We should also note the caution by Treiman and Zukowski (1991) discussed earlier, that consonant clusters may not necessarily be more difficult to perceive. Still, what might be the reason for the much lower performance of the Cantonese subgroup in perceiving and producing the missing initial consonants? Similar questions could be asked about the accuracy rate of 52% compared with the 33% in the performance of the Cantonese initial consonants. Could the sonority principle also explain the low performance because of the considerable number of items requiring the discrimination and production of the Cantonese liquid /l/ and nasal /n/, both of medium range in sonority?

In contrast, the overall performance for the English final consonants was at 72% accuracy for both subgroups and there was no significant difference. Closer examination of the 16 items reveals that of the 8 final <s>, 4 are voiceless /s/ and 4 voiced /z/; and as alveolar fricatives, these end /s/ and /z/ have medium sonority (Goldsmith, 1990). There are 2 items each of the alveolar stop /d/ and the labial stop /p/, 2 velar stop /k/, and 1 each for labial fricative /v/ and interdental fricative /q/.

Results from psychological studies suggest superiority for fricatives and in isolating final consonants, at least under certain conditions (Treiman & Weatherston, 1992). Moreover, Treiman (1989) has shown for her adult subjects that rimes containing vowels followed by stops or fricatives are easier to divide into phonemes than rimes followed by liquids. Of the 16 items 8 items end in fricatives and 6 in stops, the overall performance of 72% accuracy seems to support the Treiman (1989) and Treiman and Weatherston (1992) findings.

I would agree with Treiman and Danis (1988, p. 100) that 'Sonority differences may need to be built into theories of syllabification as well as theories of the structure of individual syllables.' In a recent study with disyllabic and tri-syllabic stimulus materials, Treiman, Fowler, Gross, Berch, and Weatherston (1995) further show syllabic-based and word-based structures play a role in the processing of spoken English words. Similar sonority contour principle may explain such phonological processing tasks as segmental and syllabic analysis of Chinese.

However, the question as to why the Cantonese subgroup performed so much poorer than their Putonghua counterparts still remains. While Leong and Hsia (1996) are tentative in suggesting possible 'training' effect, I would now add that perhaps other aspects of phonological processing should be examined in our quest to understand the role of phonemic awareness and segmentation in Chinese learners. Should we even look for segmentation of phonemes in initial and final positions and its possible link to reading? By its very nature, Chinese syllables emphasize initials (onsets) and finals (rimes) subserved by peaks and codas. The phonological processing of what Chao (1968) terms *sociological words* may lie more in syllabification as shown with English children and adults by Treiman and her colleagues (Treiman, 1989; Treiman & Danis, 1988; Treiman & Zukowski, 1990, 1991). The autosegmental constituent of Chinese tones may merit attention. Furthermore, we should be examining the integral aspects of character complexes of configuration, speech sound and meaning in Chinese word reading. I want to outline other aspects relating to research into phonological processing as it may apply to learning to read/spell Chinese.

Importance of Onset-Rime Internal Structure

The utilization of Zhuyin Fuhao and the more versatile Pinyin alphabetic principle in early reading raises a number of issues for research. The pertinent questions include the more precise nature of the phonology involved, the role of the autosegmental tones, the mechanisms in processing and if sensitivity to phonology is the main means to acquiring literacy in Chinese.

Since Chinese is morphosyllabic, with initial (onset) and final (rime) and further decomposable into peak (nucleus) and coda along not dissimilar linguistic lines to English, more fruitful results may emerge from examination of the hierarchical structure of the Chinese syllable and the effect on reading. This aspect has been argued forcefully by Treiman (1989, p. 49) in the case of English. She raises the rhetorical question as to whether or not onset/rime is also a psychological universal in addition to 'speculations' of onset/rime being a linguistic universal. Furthermore, studies of intravocalic consonants such as the role of rhyme (*yun*) in Chinese in relation to the main vowel, medial glide and syllabic ending, from speech errors and word games (e.g., tongue-twisters as in '*xia da wu, kan bu qing lu*' [heavy fog, can't see the road clearly]), are all relevant and important.

Orthographic Aspects

What is the role of the orthographic aspect in addition to phonology in acquiring literacy in Chinese? Children's insight into the components or radicals of Chinese characters is also important. Some of the research questions relate to the morphological decomposition of characters into phonetic and semantic radicals with their constituent strokes. These questions include: What are the effective morphological and morphographic constituents for Chinese character recognition? Radicals? Strokes? Or both? What is the nature of 'partial character' superiority effect (Sue & Liu, 1996) among others?

Studies of processing of radicals and strokes by Chinese adults

These are the questions addressed in the studies by Chen, Allport and Marshall (1996) and Sue and Liu (1996). Working within the framework of selective visual attention of conjoint encoding of complex visual figures such as Chinese characters, Chen et al. report results that skilled native Chinese readers show a bias toward the phonetic radical in phonological tasks and a bias toward the semantic radical in semantic judgment tasks. Chen et al. suggest that 'stroke patterns', rather than the number of strokes, as salient higher-order Chinese orthographic units for recognition. Their argument for radicals as functional orthographic units is weakened somewhat by the use of the blocking (by item type) experimental design, as they readily acknowledge.

In some contrast to the Chen et al. (1996) results is the study by Sue and Liu (1996) on character and word (with two characters) superiority effects in Chinese. In several experiments Sue and Liu find a word-nonword effect and a character-noncharacter effect and also partial character superiority effect. This latter refers to the number of strokes and the interaction with positional effects. The partial character superiority effect is in keeping with Liu's (1995) *component-decidability* (CD) model in computing the pronunciation latencies of Chinese characters. The general notion of CD is that detectable pronunciation cues are extracted from smaller components and extend to include neighbouring components in a serial fashion until a unique pronunciation is obtained for a character. Thus characters are processed in terms of larger and larger spelling units, beginning with initials (onsets) and ending with finals (rimes). The component-decidability model of Liu (1995) makes use of Glushko's

(1979) analogy model, and offers the mathematical means to compute pronunciation latencies in terms of initials and finals.

Liu's (1995, p. 156) notion of part-character utilization in pronouncing Chinese characters is particularly important in that 'most Chinese characters are exception characters'. In a recent frequency count study by Y. Fan and myself on low-frequency characters using primers *Yuwen* published in Beijing (People's Education Press, 1994) and *Huayu* published in Hong Kong (1989–90) and their student workbooks, we found a preponderance of exception characters, thus corroborating Liu's statement. Within our context, exception characters are those with sounds and tones different from the constituent phonetic radicals. Regular consistent characters are those characters pronounced the same way as the phonetic radicals and with the same tones. Regular inconsistent characters are those pronounced with the same sound as the phonetic radicals but with different tones. The percentage count of the low-frequency characters in the grades 1 to 2 primers is shown in Figure 2. A similar pattern is also found with the grades 1 to 3 primers. Admittedly, the number of around 220 characters sampled randomly is small and verification is needed. Nevertheless, there being many more low-frequency exception Chinese characters than regular ones obliges Chinese readers to use both the constituent parts and the speech-sounds of characters in reading them.

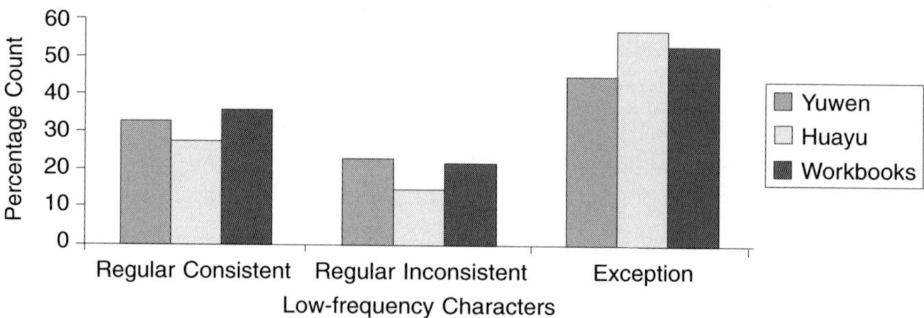

Figure 2. Percentage count of regular consistent, regular inconsistent and exception low-frequency Chinese characters from selected grades 1 and 2 primers and student workbooks.

Studies of orthographic awareness by Chinese children

If there are many more exception Chinese characters than regular ones in school textbooks, the issue of utilization of relevant orthographic parts to read these characters is important for both theoretical and practical reasons. There is evidence from Shu and Anderson (1997) that Chinese children are aware of the relationship between phonetic and the meaning radicals and that the better readers are those with greater radical awareness. Such awareness is necessary, but may not be sufficient, without well-developed knowledge of orthography-to-phonology correspondence (OPC).

This aspect is emphasized by Tzeng, Lin, Hung, and Lee (1995) in their study using regular, exception and *mixed* (according to the number of 'friendly' orthographic neighbours) Chinese characters with grades 3 to 6 good and poor readers. Tzeng et al. show that by third-grade Chinese children are sensitive to the roles of the radicals in reading and also utilize the much broader orthographic knowledge to pronounce novel Chinese characters. Recall the studies by Ho and Bryant (1997a, 1997b), in which they stress the role of sensitivity to subsyllabic segments of rimes through orthographic analogies in understanding the orthography-to-phonology correspondence. In agreement with Tzeng et al., Ho and Bryant suggest that from second grade onward readers should be helped to learn more about exceptions to OPC rules. This suggestion takes into account the large number of exception Chinese characters and the need to add to the development of OPC rules in reading Chinese.

Classroom Practices

In his insightful chapter in the Festchrift in honour of Paul Bertelson, Brian Byrne (1992) draws attention to the multitude of processes in reading and to the complexity of real-life classroom situations beyond experimental psychology. It is with the same spirit that I examine briefly principles and current practices of teaching beginning Chinese reading and spelling.

Emphasis on explicit, systematic teaching of word knowledge

In a recent symposium on curriculum changes and challenges for Chinese communities in Southeast Asia (China, Taiwan, Hong Kong and Singapore), the symposiasts on teaching and learning Chinese in elementary grades all emphasize the integration of the primary linguistic activities of listening, speaking; and the secondary linguistic activities of reading and composing, including spelling (Lam, Wong, & Fung, 1993). These curriculum specialists all stress explicit and systematic instruction of *sociological* and *syntactic* words (Chao, 1968), then proceeding to text materials in a proper linguistic environment. Emphasis on morphosyllabic processes of Chinese aims at enhancing both quantitative and qualitative aspects of word knowledge as necessary for reading comprehension. Figure 3 shows the foundational aspects of teaching and learning both sociological and syntactic Chinese words in meaningful linguistic and real-life contexts.

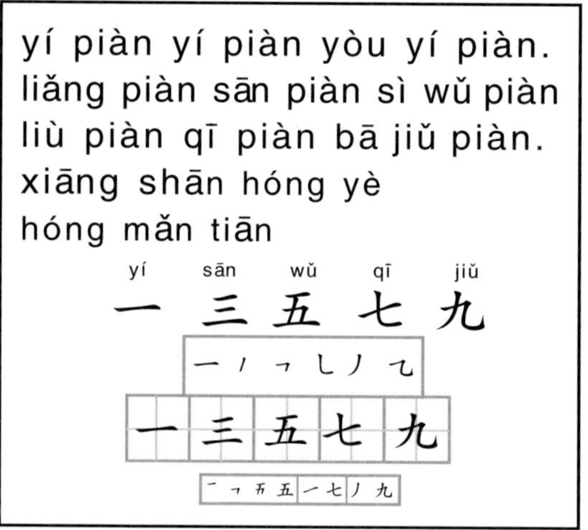

Figure 3.   Sample page from an early lesson in grade 1 Chinese primer.

The summary sample lesson deals with the early weeks of teaching and learning first-grade Chinese in China (People's Education Publishing, 1994). Several features should be noted. First, the characters taught are carefully controlled and sequenced in terms of iconicity (few strokes), and meaningfulness in real-life situations. Second, the children learn through pictures, songs and games the small number of characters, first from Pinyin with tone assignment. Third, the children are guided in their recognition of the characters and are taught to write them almost simultaneously with their word reading. In their writing (spelling) in their workbooks, they are given help in the correct sequence of strokes. This help in the form of writing the first, second, then third stroke and subsequent strokes in the correct sequence to the complete character is in accordance with the scaffolding principle.

Principle of redundancy and precision

The integrative approach in teaching and learning Chinese is supported by the redundancy principle articulated by Byrne (1992) and Perfetti (1992). Byrne (1992) considers reading and literacy acquisition as complex systems, which require backups and backups for backups to minimize breakdowns in a manner analogous to the complex systems in modern passenger aeroplanes. Perfetti (1992) suggests that redundancy is provided by the interplay of phonetic and orthographic strings and the 'bonding' of orthographic with phonological representations, while precision is concerned with fully specified representations as compared with partial or variable representations. The redundancy and precision principles enhance the quantity and quality of words that children know in their becoming proficient readers and spellers (Perfetti, 1992).

Thus from a different route, the integrative approach in emphasizing constituent parts, speech sound and meaning in accessing the linguistic structure of Chinese is in accord with current theories of reading psychology and psycholinguistics. Liberman and Shankweiler (1985, p. 10) emphasize the 'understanding of linguistic structure', 'metalinguistic awareness of the internal structure of words' and 'becoming aware of sublexical structure for the purpose of developing word recognition strategies'. Ehri (e.g., 1984, 1994) in her research program has argued forcefully that written language (spelling) provides a powerful visuospatial representation analogous to the temporal-sequential representation of speech, particularly at the phonetic and lexical levels. Her amalgamation theory of word reading is in accord with Perfetti's (1992) explication of lexical representation of words according to both the redundancy and precision principles. Classroom practices in teaching and learning reading and spelling in Chinese may be seen along similar dimensions.

Conclusion

One central question in learning to read in alphabetic and syllabic languages is the involvement of phonological and orthographic processes and their interplay. Chinese is morphosyllabic and has a phonological basis in analytic word reading. A paradigmatic analysis in emphasizing a network of linguistic connections is a potent approach to examine the access issue. The internal structures of the syllable with its onset (initial in Chinese syllables) and rime (final in Chinese syllables), further decomposable into peak (nucleus) and coda, are particularly relevant for analytic Chinese word reading and spelling. The sonority contour principle seems to play an important role in perceiving and analysing speech and lexical units of processing, which are necessary for emergent literacy in Chinese. Chinese children are sensitive to the orthographic constituents such as radicals and this sensitivity helps in pronouncing characters.

Current curriculum and classroom practices in teaching Chinese in primary schools are emphatic on explicit, systematic instruction to promote knowledge of sociological and syntactic words (Chao, 1968), beginning with Pinyin before progressing to text materials with scaffolding to guide learners. This integrative approach involving understanding of the sounds of words, their internal structure, their meaning in local and global contexts and the simultaneous teaching and learning of listening, speaking, reading and writing including spelling is in accord with the morphosyllabic characteristics of Chinese. Furthermore, the integrative classroom practices are supported by the psychological principles of redundancy and precision to achieve higher quality lexical representation.

References

Bauer, R. S. (1988). Written Cantonese of Hong Kong. *Cahiers de Linguistique Asie Orientale, 17,* 245–293.

Bloomfield, L. (1962). *Language.* London: George Allen & Unwin. (Original work published in 1933).

Byrne, B. (1992). Experimental psychology and real life: The case of literacy acquisition. In J. Alegria, D. Holender, J. J. de Morais, & M. Radeau (Eds.), *Analytic approaches to human cognition* (pp. 169–182). Amsterdam: North-Holland.

Cardoso-Martins, C. (1994). Rhyme perception: Global or analytical? *Journal of Experimental Child Psychology, 57,* 26–41.

Chao, Y. R. (1968). *A grammar of spoken Chinese.* Berkeley, CA: University of California Press.

Chen, Y. P., Allport, D. A., & Marshall, J. C. (1996). What are the functional orthographic units in Chinese word recognition: The stroke or the stroke pattern? *The Quarterly Journal of Experimental Psychology, 49A,* 1024–1043.

Cheung, H. (1999). Improving phonological awareness and word reading in a later learned alphabetic script. *Cognition, 70,* 1–26.

DeFrancis, J. (1989). *Visible speech: The diverse oneness of writing systems.* Honolulu: University of Hawaii Press.

Eckman, F. R. (1981). On the naturalness of interlanguage phonological rules. *Language Learning, 31,* 195–216.

Ehri, L. C. (1980). The development of orthographic images. In U. Frith (Ed.), *Cognitive processes in spelling* (pp. 311–338). London: Academic Press.

Ehri, L. C. (1984). How orthography alters spoken language competencies in children learning to read and spell. In J. Downing & R. Valtin (Eds.), *Language awareness and learning to read* (pp. 119–147). New York: Springer-Verlag.

Ehri, L. C. (1994). Development of the ability to read words: Update. In R. B. Ruddell, M. R. Ruddell, & H. Singer (Eds.), *Theoretical models and processes of reading* (4th ed., pp. 323–358). Newark, DE: International Reading Association.

Flege, J. E., McCutcheon, M. J., & Smith, S.C. (1987). The development of skill in productive word-final English stops. *Journal of the Acoustical Society of America, 82,* 433–447.

Frost, R., & Katz, L. (Ed.). (1992). *Orthography, phonology, morphology, and meaning.* Amsterdam: North-Holland.

Glushko, R. J. (1979). The organization and activation of orthographic knowledge in reading aloud. *Journal of Experimental Psychology: Human Perception and Performance, 5,* 674–691.

Goldsmith, J. A. (1990). *Autosegmental and metrical phonology.* Oxford: Basil Blackwell.

Hanley, J. R., & Huang, H. S. (1997). Phonological awareness and learning to read Chinese. In C. K. Leong, & R. M. Joshi (Eds.), *Cross-language studies of learning to read and spell: Phonologic and orthographic processing* (pp. 361–378). Dordrecht: Kluwer Academic Publishers.

Ho, C. S. H., & Bryant, P. (1997a). Phonological skills are important in learning to read Chinese. *Developmental Psychology, 33,* 946–951.

Ho, C. S. H., & Bryant, P. (1997b). Learning to read beyond the logographic phase. *Reading Research Quarterly, 32,* 276–289.

Holm, A., & Dodd, B. (1996). The effect of first written language on the acquisition of English literacy. *Cognition, 59,* 119–147.

Hsia, S. (1992). Developmental knowledge of inter- and intraword boundaries: Evidence from American and Mandarin Chinese speaking beginning readers. *Applied Psycholinguistics, 13,* 341–372.

Huang, H. S., & Hanley, J. R. (1995). Phonological awareness and visual skills in learning to read Chinese and English. *Cognition, 54,* 73–98.

Jesperson, O. (1904). *Lehrbuch der Phonetik* (Dictionary of phonetics). Leipzig & Berlin: B.G. Teubner.

Lam, C. C., Wong, H. W., & Fung, Y. W. (Eds.). (1993). *Curriculum changes for Chinese communities in Southeast Asia: Challenges of the 21st century.* Hong Kong: The Chinese University of Hong Kong Faculty of Education (in Chinese and English).

Landerl, K., Frith, U., & Wimmer, H. (1996). Intrusion of orthographic knowledge on phoneme awareness: Strong in normal readers, weak in dyslexic readers. *Applied Psycholinguistics, 17,* 1–14.

Leong, C. K. (1991). From phonemic awareness to phonological processing to language access in children developing reading proficiency. In D. J. Sawyer & B. J. Fox (Eds.), *Phonological awareness in reading: The evolution of current perspectives* (pp. 217–254). New York: Springer-Verlag.

Leong, C. K. (1992). Cognitive componential modelling of reading in ten- to twelve-year-old readers. *Reading and Writing: An Interdisciplinary Journal, 4,* 327–364.

Leong, C. K. (1995). Orthographic and psycholinguistic considerations in developing literacy in Chinese. In I. Taylor & D. R. Olson (Eds.), *Scripts and literacy: Reading, and learning to read alphabets, syllabaries and characters* (pp. 163–183). Dordrecht: Kluwer Academic Publishers.

Leong, C. K. (1997). Paradigmatic analysis of Chinese word reading: Research findings and classroom practices. In C.K. Leong, & R.M. Joshi (Eds.), *Cross-language studies of learning to read and spell: Phonologic and orthographic processing* (pp. 379–417). Dordrecht: Kluwer Academic Publishers.

Leong, C. K., & Hsia, S. (1996). Cross-linguistic constraints on Chinese students learning English. In M. H. Bond (Ed.), *The handbook of Chinese psychology* (pp. 63–78 + ref.). Oxford: Oxford University Press.

Leong, C. K., & Joshi, R. M. (Eds.). (1997). *Cross-language studies of learning to read and spell: Phonologic and orthographic processing.* Dordrecht: Kluwer Academic Publishers.

Leong, C. K., & Tamaoka, K. (1995). Use of phonological information in processing kanji and katakana by skilled and less skilled Japanese readers. *Reading and Writing: An interdisciplinary Journal, 7,* 377–393.

Leong, C. K., & Tamaoka, K. (Eds.). (1998). *Cognitive processing of the Chinese and the Japanese languages.* Dordrecht: Kluwer Academic Publishers.

Liberman, I. Y., & Shankweiler, D. P. (1985). Phonology and the problems of learning to read and write. *Remedial and Special Education, 6(6),* 8–17.

Liu, I.-M. (1995). Script factors that affect literacy: Alphabetic vs. logographic languages. In I. Taylor, & D. R. Olson (Eds.), *Scripts and literacy: Reading and learning to read alphabets, syllabaries and characters* (pp. 145–162). Dordrecht: Kluwer Academic Publishers.

Liu, I.-M., Zhu, Y., & Wu, J.-T. (1992). The long-term modality effect: In search of differences in processing logographs and alphabetic words. *Cognition, 43,* 31–66.

Morais, J., Bertelson, P., Cary, L., & Alegria, J. (1986). Literacy training and speech segmentation. *Cognition, 24,* 45–64.

Morais, J., Cary, L., Alegria, J., & Bertelson, P. (1979). Does awareness of speech as a sequence of phones arise spontaneously? *Cognition, 7,* 323–331.

Otake, T., Hatano, G., Cutler, A., & Mehler, J. (1993). Mora or syllable? Speech segmentation in Japanese. *Journal of Memory and Language, 32,* 258–278.

People Educational Publishing (1994). *Yuwen Vol. 1: Teachers' manual.* Beijing: Author (in Chinese).

Perfetti, C. A. (1992). The representation problem in reading acquisition. In P. B. Gough, L. C. Ehri, & R. Treiman (Eds.), *Reading acquisition* (pp. 145–174). Hillsdale, NJ: Lawrence Erlbaum.

Read, C., Zhang, Y.-F., Nie, H.-Y., & Ding, B.-Q. (1986). The ability to manipulate speech sounds depends on knowing alphabetic writing. *Cognition, 24,* 31–44.

Shu, H., & Anderson, R. C. (1997). Role of radical awareness in the character and word acquisition of Chinese children. *Reading Research Quarterly, 32,* 78–89.

Sue, I.-R., & Liu, I. M. (1996). Word and character superiority effects in Chinese. *Chinese Journal of Psychology, 38,* 11–30 (in Chinese).

Treiman, R. (1989). The internal structure of the syllable. In G. N. Carlson & M. K. Tanenhaus (Eds.), *Linguistic structure in language processing* (pp. 27–52). Dordrecht: Kluwer Academic Publishers.

Treiman, R., & Danis, C. (1988). Syllabification of intervocalic consonants. *Journal of Memory and Language, 27,* 87–104.

Treiman, R., Fowler, C. A., Gross, J., Berch, D., & Weatherston, S. (1995). Syllable structure or word structure? Evidence for onset and rime units with disyllabic and trisyllabic stimuli. *Journal of Memory and Language, 34,* 132–155.

Treiman, R., & Weatherston, S. (1992). Effects of linguistic structure on children's ability to isolate initial consonants. *Journal of Educational Psychology, 84,* 174–181.

Treiman, R., & Zukowski, A. (1990). Toward an understanding of English syllabification. *Journal of Memory and Language, 29,* 66–85.

Treiman, R., & Zukowski, A. (1991). Levels of phonological awareness. In S. A. Brady & D. P. Shankweiler (Eds.), *Phonological processes in literacy: A tribute to Isabelle Y. Liberman* (pp. 67–83). Hillsdale, NJ: Lawrence Erlbaum.

Tzeng, O. J. L., Lin, Z. H., Hung, D. L., & Lee, W. L. (1995). Learning to be a conspirator: A tale of becoming a good Chinese reader. In B. de Gelder, & J. Morais (Eds.), *Speech and reading: A comparative approach* (pp. 227–246). Hove, Sussex: Erlbaum (UK), Taylor & Francis.

Author Note

The preparation of this paper was assisted in part by research grant SSHRC 410–96–0186 from the Social Sciences and Humanities Research Council of Canada. I am grateful for the assistance. Over the years I have benefited from the work of H.-C. Chen, R. Hoosain, H. S. R. Kao, I.-M. Liu, and O. J. L. Tzeng on the cognitive processing of the Chinese language. I alone am responsible for any shortcomings in this paper.

Endnote

The tonal marks for the Chinese terms are shown in the Pinyin translation.

13

Biscriptal Reading in Chinese

Agnes S. L. Lam

The Chinese language offers unusual opportunities for exploring the psycholinguistic effects in reading two closely related linguistic systems because the same writing script can be read in different dialectal pronunciations. At the same time, two scripts can be read with a single pronunciation. Earlier work (Lam, Perfetti & Bell, 1991) has already obtained interesting effects concerning automatic phonetic transfer for bidialectal readers. Readers fluent in both Putonghua and Cantonese cannot suppress the pronunciation of their first dialect when asked to read only in their second dialect. The present study focuses on the effects of reading two scripts with one pronunciation. The two scripts are: the traditional script (complex characters, sometimes referred to as complicated characters) and the newer script (simplified characters). The investigation pertains to the ease or difficulty that Hong Kong learners may have in acquiring biscriptal ability or the ability to read two different scripts with one pronunciation (in their case, Cantonese). The difficulties that learners who are already familiar with the simplified script, such as those educated in Beijing, may have in reading the complex script are also given some consideration.

Two areas of research are especially relevant for this study: the work on the development and analysis of the Chinese script and the investigation into models of word recognition and text comprehension.

The Chinese Script

The Chinese script is estimated to have about 60,000 characters (Cheng, 1991, p. 26). However, the number of characters needed for reading general materials is estimated to be about 3,000 characters. More specialized needs require a larger vocabulary. For example, according to a character list published by the Beijing Scientific Standards Press in 1981, a total of 6,763 characters are in use, with 3,755 identified as Frequently Used Characters and 3,008 characters listed as Less Frequently Used Characters (Cheng, 1991, p. 30).

Character simplification

Estimated to be at least 3,000 years old (Norman, 1988, p. 58), the Chinese script has inevitably undergone much development. Character simplification into the forms in current use, however, took place from the mid-1950s to the mid-1980s and was part of a national initiative to promote literacy after the People's Republic of China was established. The First Character Simplification Scheme was publicized in 1956 and expanded on in 1964. The 1964 list was reprinted in 1986. The list of simplified characters in current use, a total of 2,236 characters (Cheng, 1991, p. 76) is based on the 1986 list. (Ramsey (1987, p. 146) notes a total of 2,238 characters while the Curriculum Development Council in Hong Kong (1996, p. 31) records the total as 2,235 characters, the difference in number owing to the repetition of a few characters.)

Several systems have been developed to categorize the processes in character simplification. The Curriculum Development Council in Hong Kong (1996, p. 33–36) provides an overview of six different systems developed from the 1920s to the 1980s. The types of simplification, ranging from 4 to 8 in each system, are largely based on a comparison of a simplified character with its complex counterpart in terms of their graphic, phonetic or semantic similarity (Curriculum Development Council, 1996, p. 33; see also Norman, 1988, p. 81–82.) For the purpose of this study, six types of simplification were identified (Table 1). They are:

1.   Simplification of a common radical
2.   Omission of a common radical
3.   Partial simplification of the character (not involving a common radical)

4. Partial omission of the character (not involving a common radical)
5. Substitution with a phonetically similar but graphically simpler form
6. Total substitution with no or little resemblance

Table 1

Types of Simplification in Character Lists

1. Simplification of common radical (List 1A)

Simplified form	红	们	记	饭	吗
Complex form	紅	們	記	飯	嗎
Putonghua pronunciation	hong2	men2	ji4	fan4	ma1
Cantonese pronunciation	hung4	moon4	gei3	faan6	ma3

2. Omission of common radical (List 7A)

Simplified form	采	电	虽	亲	开
Complex form	彩	電	雖	親	開
Putonghua pronunciation	cai3	dian4	sui1	qin1	kai1
Cantonese pronunciation	choi3	din6	sui1	chan1	hoi1

3. Partial simplification of character (not common radical) (List 5A)

Simplified form	伞	树	笔	桥	队
Complex form	傘	樹	筆	橋	隊
Putonghua pronunciation	san3	shu4	bi3	qiao2	dui4
Cantonese pronunciation	saan3	sue6	bat1	kiu4	dui6

4. Partial omission of character (not common radical) (List 9A)

Simplified form	气	乡	业	从	厂
Complex form	氣	鄉	業	從	廠
Putonghua pronunciation	qi4	xiang1	ye4	cong2	chang3
Cantonese pronunciation	hei3	heung1	yip6	chung4	chong2

5. Substitution with phonetically similar simpler form (List 3A)

Simplified form	园	机	担	态	粮
Complex form	園	機	擔	態	糧
Putonghua pronunciation	yuan2	ji1	dan4	tai4	liang2
Cantonese pronunciation	yuen4	gei1	daam3	taai3	leung4

6. Total substitution with no or little resemblance (List 11A)

Simplified form	叶	书	旧	脏	头
Complex form	葉	書	舊	髒	頭
Putonghua pronunciation	ye4	shu1	jiu4	zang1	tou2
Cantonese pronunciation	yip6	sue1	gau6	jong1	tau4

Simplified characters, complex characters and characters without dual forms

Since not all characters in common use can be written in both scripts, general reading texts only have a percentage of characters that are printable in both scripts. From an analysis of a sample of articles from a daily newspaper in Hong Kong, *Ming Pao*, the proportion of characters that have dual forms is only about 30.78%. A similar percentage (39.08%) is found in the recommended character list for Hong Kong primary schools (Table 2 based on Curriculum Development Commission, 1992, p. 69–76). Of a total of 2,600 characters to be learned by the end of Primary Six, only 1,009 characters have dual forms.

Table 2
Characters With Dual Forms in the Hong Kong Primary School Syllabus

Grade	No. of characters			No. of characters with dual forms			% of characters with dual forms		
	Act.	Pass.	Total	Act.	Pass.	Total	Act.	Pass.	Total
One	373	86	459	96	19	115	25.74	22.09	25.05
Two	368	133	501	123	44	167	33.42	33.08	33.33
Three	530	0	530	232	0	232	43.77	0	43.77
Four	590	0	590	270	0	270	45.76	0	45.76
Five	260	0	260	101	0	101	38.85	0	38.85
Six	260	0	260	124	0	124	47.69	0	47.69
M	397	37	433	158	11	168	39.21	9.20	39.08

Note. Based on Curriculum Development Council, 1992, p. 69–76.
Key.   Act. – Active use of characters (i. e., writing and reading ability)
Pass. – Passive use of characters (i. e., recognition only)
Total – Total number of characters (both Active and Passive use)

It is very important to bear in mind that though Chinese is said to have two scripts, the complex script and the simplified script, this is only true of about one-third of the Chinese characters in general use. The other two-thirds are characters *without* dual forms and, as such, should be familiar to a proficient reader of Chinese, regardless of whether that person was first taught to read Chinese in the simplified script or the complex script. To a person learning the simplified script first, these characters without dual forms may be thought of as characters in the simplified script while those learning the complex script first may think of these characters without dual forms as complex characters. In this study, I shall continue to refer to these characters as 'characters without dual forms', which by default will be characters in a familiar script to a Chinese learner whichever script he or she was first taught to use in reading or writing.

Use of the Two Scripts and Biscriptal Ability

Since the People's Republic of China adopted simplified characters in 1956, other countries such as Singapore from 1969, the United Nations from 1971 and Malaysia from 1983 (Curriculum Development Council, 1996, p. 37) have also used them. In Hong Kong and Taiwan, the complex script is still in common use.

With the return of Hong Kong to Chinese sovereignty, apart from interaction arising from geographical proximity, biscriptal ability or the ability to read the simplified script and the complex script has become useful. A teaching package was made available to Hong Kong schools in 1996 to teach the recognition of the simplified script in Forms 4 and 5, though it can also be used with Forms 3 and 6 students (Curriculum Development Council, 1996). Such a step has not been taken without due consideration as some people think that it is difficult to learn the simplified script in addition to the complex one. A study of biscriptal reading is therefore of immediate social and pedagogical relevance.

The psychology of biscriptal reading

One hypothesis in this study is that context effects can help the recognition of an unfamiliar script. Context effects in reading have been widely studied and confirmed (for example, McClelland & Rumelhart, 1985), though the timing of effects at different processing stages is still under investigation (Harley, 1995, p. 53). In this study, context is broadly defined as 'information available from the previous sensory input (the prior context) to higher knowledge sources (e.g. lexical, syntactic, semantic, and pragmatic information)' (Harley, 1995, p. 53). An example demonstrating context effects specific to reading Chinese is Chen's study (1992). Studies of word recognition have also shown various effects according to phonetic or semantic priming (e.g., Perfetti & Zhang, 1991). Although these experiments have been designed to illustrate, in particular, the nature of phonetic or semantic activation in reading, their results do not preclude the hypothesis that graphic information about a character, even if incomplete, can facilitate its recognition.

It is consistent with current models of interactivity from multiple sources of information in language perception (e.g., Dijkstra & De Smelt, 1996) to predict that while simplified characters read in isolation may pose some difficulty to Hong Kong learners, who are used to reading the complex script, such difficulty will diminish in the context of reading texts. Secondly, since simplified characters have various types of similarity to their complex counterparts, they offer different cues to a reader familiar with the complex script. Hence, there should be different degrees of difficulty for the Hong Kong learners according to the type of character simplification. Similar effects should be obtained for readers who normally read the simplified script, such as those educated in Beijing, if they are presented with the complex script. These effects, though similar, might not be identical because having more information in the character pattern may involve different processes of pattern recognition than having less information. In the case of the Hong Kong learners, reading some types of simplified characters may be akin to reading poor handwriting in everyday reading. For the Beijing readers, however, reading the complex characters may, in some instances, be more like reading new characters if they cannot identify a familiar simplified character embedded in some way within the unfamiliar pattern of its complex counterpart.

Hypotheses

The two hypotheses in this study were:
1. That while learners have difficulty identifying characters in an unfamiliar script out of context (such as character lists without a related domain to foster associations), such difficulty is greatly diminished when they are read in context (such as reading texts).
2. That unfamiliar characters (e.g., simplified characters to Hong Kong Chinese readers) read out of context pose different degrees of difficulty because they bear various types of similarity to a familiar script (e.g., complex characters to Hong Kong Chinese readers) which learners already know.

Two experiments were conducted. The main experiment was conducted in Hong Kong (Experiment 1) and a follow-up experiment was conducted in Beijing (Experiment 2).

EXPERIMENT 1 – HONG KONG

METHOD

Participants   The participants were 33 undergraduate students in the Department of Psychology at the University of Hong Kong. Their age ranged from 19 to 22 years old. Six were male and 27 were female.

Materials   The experimental materials consisted of 12 character lists and 8 reading texts. Each list had 20 characters. The selection of the 240 characters used in the materials was based on the Hong Kong primary school recommended character list (Curriculum Development Commission, 1992, p. 69–76) because this study was pedagogically motivated. Six lists (120 characters) were characters that could be written in the simplified script or the complex script. These Hong Kong participants in the study were shown these 6 lists of characters in the simplified script (an unfamiliar script to them). The other 6 lists (also 120 characters) were characters without dual forms, which were therefore characters in a familiar script to them. Likewise, in 4 of the reading texts, 30.74% of each text was in simplified script (unfamiliar to the participants) and 69.26% of each text was in characters without dual forms (familiar to the participants). In the other 4 reading texts, 30.74% of each text was in complex script (familiar to the participants), and 69.26% was in characters without dual forms (also familiar to participants). The reading texts were taken from a daily newspaper on topics of general interest. The average length of the reading texts was 251 words.

Design and procedure   Each subject was tested individually. Participants were given some practice examples before reading the experimental materials aloud. Two measures were used in the experiments, reading time per character (RT) and percentage of error (PE). RTs were obtained with a stop-watch controlled by the researcher. When the subject began reading a character list or a reading text aloud, the researcher started the time count. When the subject stopped reading, the time was stopped, recorded and reset before the next list or text was read. The reading time per character was then computed from the total reading time as an average over the total number of characters in the character list or the reading text. Errors in pronunciation were recorded by the researcher on the experimental form. Both measures were tested by t-tests at $\alpha = .05$.

RESULTS

Simplified characters, an unfamiliar script to Hong Kong Chinese participants, were significantly more difficult by both measures at $\alpha = .05$ (Table 3). RT per character when reading character lists in the simplified script (the unfamiliar script) was 0.830 s while that for reading characters without dual forms (the familiar script) was only 0.561 s. The difference in error rates was even more evident with simplified character lists scoring 21.035 per cent in errors but hardly any errors were recorded for reading characters without dual forms (0.858%). As predicted, these differences were greatly diminished when simplified characters were read in the context of reading texts. The RTs per character for reading texts were 0.321 s for passages with simplified characters and 0.259 s for passages with complex characters. Error rates were greatly reduced at 1.038 per cent and 0.167 per cent respectively. Although these differences

Table 3

Comparison of Reading Times and Error Rates for Character Lists and Texts (Hong Kong Experiment)

Reading condition	Reading time per character (seconds)	Error rates (%)
1. Simplified character lists (unfamiliar script)	0.830	21.035
2. Lists of characters without dual forms (familiar)	0.561	0.858
3. Texts with simplified characters (unfamiliar)	0.321	1.038
4. Texts with complex characters (familiar)	0.259	0.167
Mean	0.493	5.775

n = 33

Note. At $\alpha = .05$, Conditions 1 and 2 were significantly different and so were Conditions 3 and 4. The results at $\alpha = .01$ were the same.

for reading texts were still statistically different, the differences were less than those for character lists. Hence, the results supported the hypothesis that the difficulty with characters in the unfamiliar script (simplified characters) was greatly diminished when they were read in context. The results at α = .01 were the same.

The second prediction that different types of simplification would result in different degrees of difficulty was also largely supported by the results on reading character lists designed to represent different types of simplification (Table 4). The use of a simpler radical (Type 1) was significantly easier than all other types while most other types were significantly different from two or more types on both measures. Apparently, there was a range of difficulty posed by the variation in the type of simplification, with the use of a phonetically similar form (Type 5) and the creation of a form with little or no graphic resemblance (Type 6) being more difficult than the other types. RTs ranged from 0.661 s for the use of a simpler radical (Type 1) to 0.946 s for a form with no or little resemblance (Type 6). Error rates ranged from 4.242% (Type 1) to 32.273% (Type 6).

Table 4

Reading Times and Error Rates for Character Lists (Hong Kong Experiment)

Type of character simplification	Reading time per character		Error rates	
	seconds	At α = .05, different from	%	At α =. 05, different from
1. Simpler radical	0.661	All other types	4.242	All other types
2. Omitted radical	0.785	All except Type 3	13.182	All other types
3. Partial non-radical simplification	0.808	All except Types 2 & 4	23.030	All except Types 4 & 5
4. Partial non-radical omission	0.848	All except Type 3	25.606	All except Types 3 & 5
5. Phonetically similar form	0.930	All except Type 6	27.878	All except Types 4 & 6
6. No or little resemblance	0.946	All except Type 5	32.273	All except Type 5
M	0.829		21.035	

n = 33

Note. Results at α = .01 for reading times were the same. For error rates, the results were also the same at α = .01, except that Type 3 was not significantly different from Type 5 and Type 4 not from Type 6.

DISCUSSION

That the RT for reading texts containing simplified characters was not much longer than that for texts with complex characters (Table 3) could partially be attributed to the fact that only one third of the characters in the texts were simplified characters. This was so because only about a third of the characters in normal reading can have dual forms. Further experiments to define context more narrowly (e.g., in sentences) would be necessary to confirm these findings.

The use of a phonetically similar form (Type 5) was high on the difficulty scale. It might be that being able to pronounce a character is not in itself closure for lexical access. This is a reasonable explanation in view of the great number of homophones in the Chinese lexicon. Phonetic similarity might even cause interference thereby delaying semantic closure.

EXPERIMENT 2 – BEIJING

METHOD

Participants   Experiment 2 in Beijing involved 18 students studying at the Graduate School of the Chinese Academy of Sciences. They were mostly 21 to 24 years old, though two were 27 years old and one was 33 years old. Eight were male and 10 were female.

Materials   The materials from the Hong Kong experiment were altered so that the simplified script in 6 character lists were replaced by complex forms, because, to the Beijing learners, the complex form for characters with dual forms would be the unfamiliar script. Lists of characters without dual forms remained unchanged; these would appear as a familiar script to the Beijing participants. Another variation in the Beijing experiment was that instead of 8 reading passages, only 4 were used, 2 using the complex script for characters with dual forms and the other 2 using the simplified script for characters with dual forms.

Design and procedures   The procedures were the same as in Experiment 1 in Hong Kong.

RESULTS

The results for the Beijing experiment were similar to those for Experiment 1 in Hong Kong (Table 5).

Table 5
Comparison of Reading Times and Error Rates for Character Lists and Texts (Beijing Experiment)

Reading condition	Reading time per character (second)	Error rates (%)
1. Complex character lists (unfamiliar script)	0.799	9.213
2. Lists of characters without dual forms (familiar)	0.545	0.370
3. Texts with complex characters (unfamiliar)	0.335	0.559
4. Texts with simplified characters (familiar)	0.315	0.326
Mean	0.499	2.617

$n = 18$
Note. At $\alpha = .05$ and $\alpha = .01$, Conditions 1 and 2 were significantly different by both measures. But Conditions 3 and 4 were not significantly different by either measure.

The unfamiliar script (complex characters in this case) was found to be more difficult; character lists were read with an RT per character of 0.799 s and an error rate of 9.213%. The character lists in the familiar script were read with an RT of 0.545 s and an error rate of 0.370%. These differences ($\alpha = .05$) disappeared in the context of reading texts. Texts containing the unfamiliar script were not read at significantly slower speeds than texts in the familiar script ($\alpha = .01$). The respective RTs were 0.335 s and 0.315 s while the error rates were 0.559% and 0.326% respectively.

In terms of the degrees of difficulty posed by different types of simplification, as for the Hong Kong learners, there was also a range (Table 6). However, the rank order of the types in terms of difficulty was not exactly the same. (Compare the results in Table 6 with those in Table 4.) This supported the argument that the processing for additional information in a complex graphic image might not be like that for a simplified graphic image. Notably, Type 2 (the omission of a radical as a simplification method) ranked higher in difficulty for the Beijing learners than for the Hong Kong learners. This could be because for the Beijing learners, reading a complex character of this type would mean processing an additional radical (not an omitted radical as for the Hong Kong learners). The addition of radicals has been used in Chinese to create new characters. Thus, to the Beijing learners, reading these complex forms might be like reading new characters. In terms of RT results, simpler radical (Type 1), partial non-radical simplification (Type 3) and partial non-radical omission (Type 4) were significantly easier than omitted radical (Type 2) and phonetically similar form (Type 5) and no or little resemblance (Type 6).

Table 6

Reading Times and Error Rates for Character Lists (Beijing Experiment)

Type of character simplification	Reading time per character		Error rates	
	seconds	At α = .05, different from	%	At α =. 05, different from
1. Simpler radical	0.656	Types 2, 5 & 6	1.944	All except Type 4
2. Omitted radical	0.936	Types 1, 3 & 4	13.889	All except Types 5 & 6
3. Partial non-radical simplification	0.682	Types 2, 5 & 6	5.833	All except Type 4
4. Partial non-radical omission	0.686	Types 2, 5 & 6	4.722	All except Types 1 & 3
5. Phonetically similar form	0.951	Types 1, 3 & 4	18.333	All except Type 2
6. No or little resemblance	0.882	Types 1, 3 & 4	10.556	All except Type 2
M	0.799		9.213	

n = 18

Types 1, 3 and 4 were not significantly more or less difficult (α = .05) than each other. Neither were Types 2, 5 and 6 significantly different from each other. The RTs for the six types ranged from 0.656 s for the use of a simpler radical (Type 1) to 0.951 s for the use of a phonetically similar form (Type 5).

In terms of error rates, there was also a range from 1.944% for the use of a simpler radical (Type 1) to 18.333% for the use of a phonetically similar form (Type 5). In comparison with the rank order for RTs, there was some slight modification. Partial non-radical simplification (Type 3) attracted a higher error rate than partial non-radical omission (Type 4). The error rates also appeared to fall into two groups, with simpler radical (Type 1), partial non-radical simplification (Type 3) and partial non-radical omission (Type 4) having lower error rates and omitted radical (Type 2), phonetically similar form (Type 5) and no or little resemblance (Type 6) resulting in higher error rates.

DISCUSSION

That the types of simplification appeared to fall into two groups was especially interesting. The three types in the second group — an additional radical (Type 2), a phonetically similar form (Type 5) or a grapheme with little or no resemblance to the familiar character (Type 6) — all posed greater difficulty. They might be processed like new characters while the other three types (Types 1, 3 and 4) were still somewhat recognizable from their simplified counterparts.

One rather obvious difference between the results of the two experiments was that in the Beijing experiment, the difficulty with the unfamiliar script experienced in character lists was so greatly diminished in context that it disappeared entirely. One possible explanation was that the Beijing participants were more experienced readers of Chinese than the Hong Kong participants and therefore more able to make use of higher order context effects.

The two experiments taken together demonstrated that in Chinese character recognition, the processing of incomplete data (simplified script for Hong Kong learners) might not be the same as processing with additional graphic or phonetic noise (e.g., homophones used in character simplification). In the first case, the simplified form itself might function as an immediate context towards the recognition of the character (like identifying a word from a graphic prime just before seeing the target item). In the latter case, the additional information might lead the reader to consider the graphic image as a new and unknown character (like trying to find an English word within a longer string of letters).

Conclusion

Although further experiments under more controlled conditions would be needed to fine tune the general findings in this pedagogical study based on possible classroom tasks, the study largely supported the two hypotheses: first, that context would enhance the recognition of an unfamiliar script; and, secondly, that different types of character modification could result in different degrees of difficulty for the reader. This suggests that one educational strategy that should be encouraged is to provide wider exposure to the unfamiliar script in extensive reading together with the introduction of character types to be taught incrementally according to processing difficulty. In terms of the design of new orthographies, the addition or subtraction of graphic information has to be carefully considered, as they do not appear to have the same effects. These findings, while immediately relevant to the acquisition of biscriptal ability in Chinese, can be considered more generally with reference to the learning of a second language with orthographic similarity to one's first language.

References

Chen, H.-C. (1992). Reading comprehension in Chinese: Implications from character reading times. In H. C. Chen and O. J. L. Tzeng (Eds.), *Language processing in Chinese* (pp. 175–205). Amsterdam: North-Holland.

Cheng, C. F. (程祥徽). (1991). 繁簡由之 (Complex and simplified choices). Hong Kong: Joint Publishing (HK) Co. Ltd. (in Chinese).

Curriculum Development Council. (1992). *Primary School Curriculum Abstract*. Hong Kong: Education Department.

Curriculum Development Council. (1996). 簡化字學習套：教師手冊 (Package for learning simplified characters: Teachers' handbook). Hong Kong: Education Department (in Chinese).

Dijkstra, T., & De Smelt, K. (Eds.). (1996). *Computational psycholinguistics*. London: Taylor & Francis.

Harley, T. A. (1995). *The psychology of language: From data to theory*. East Sussex: Erlbaum (UK), Taylor & Francis.

Lam, A., Perfetti, C. A., & Bell, L. (1991). Automatic phonetic transfer in bidialectal reading. *Applied Psycholinguistics 12*, 299–311.

McClelland, J. L., & Rumelhart, D. E. (1985). An interactive activation model of context effects in letter perception. In H. Singer & R. B. Ruddell (Eds.), *Theoretical models and processes of reading* (3rd ed., pp. 276–322). Newark, DE: Lawrence Erlbaum.

Norman, J. (1988). *Chinese*. Cambridge, UK: Cambridge University Press.

Perfetti, C. A., & Zhang, S. (1991). Phonological processes in reading Chinese characters. *Journal of Experimental Psychology, 17,* 633–643.

Ramsey, S. R. (1987). *The languages of China*. Princeton, NJ: Princeton University Press.

Author Note

This research was funded by a grant from the University of Hong Kong. The participants in the study were recruited with the help of the Department of Psychology at the University of Hong Kong and the Department of Foreign Languages at the Graduate School, Academia Sinica. I am also most grateful for the support of my assistants, Ms. Ma Ka Lee and Ms. Yim Wai Kin, at different times.

Differences in Chinese Character Identification Between Skilled and Less Skilled Young Readers

Judy Huei-Yu Wang and John T. Guthrie

Achievement differences in reading English are related to the accurate and rapid identification of words (Cunningham & Stanovich, 1998; Daneman, 1991). Research shows that the phonological process is central to identify a word and plays a significant role in accounting the differences between good and poor readers (Guthrie & Tyler, 1976; Jorm & Share, 1983; Perfetti, Finger, & Hogaboam, 1978). This results from the fact that English is an alphabetic writing system, in which readers must first learn the spelling-to-sound rules and then the meaning unit of a word (see details in Ehri, 1994). Unlike English, Chinese is a logographic writing system that uses graphic symbols to represent mainly units of meaning or morphemes (Hoosain, 1991). The identification of Chinese characters seems to be dominated by graphic-morpheme correspondences. Recent research on Chinese reading has claimed that phonology plays an important role in the lexical processing of Chinese characters for adult readers (Perfetti & Tan, 1998; Perfetti & Zhang, 1995; Tan, Hoosain, & Siok, 1996).

However, whether the role of phonology plays in determining individual differences in Chinese character identification has not yet been investigated. This motivated the current study in investigating whether the variation between skilled and less-skilled young Chinese readers pertains to character identification and whether phonological process plays an influential role. We will first outline the lexical processing of Chinese characters as shown by previous studies, and then report the empirical results of three experiments in relation to our questions.

Graphic, phonological, and semantic information in a Chinese character is fundamental to its identification. Peng, Guo, and Zhang (1985) stated that graphic information of Chinese characters was the most efficient indicator in the judgment task for both the young child and the adult. The young child could perform more accurately and faster if the graphic information was not separated from the phonological information. Chen, Yung, and Ng (1988) used the visual search paradigm in two experiments to investigate the recognition of some features in Chinese characters and monosyllabic English words, and the differential effects of semantic and phonemic cueing in identifying Chinese characters and English words. They showed that graphemic and semantic cues were quickly identified and had a closer relationship to Chinese, whereas phonemic features dominated the perceptual process of English.

Current studies show that phonology is involved 'at lexicality' in identifying Chinese characters and words (Cheng, 1992; Cheng & Shih, 1988; Hue, 1992; Perfetti & Tan, 1998; Perfetti & Zhang, 1991, 1995; Tzeng & Hung, 1980; Tzeng, Hung, & Wang, 1977). The general finding is that phonological processing of Chinese characters is rapid and automatic and this process is different from the prelexical assembling of phonology in English word identification (Perfetti, Bell, & Delaney, 1988). As examples, Tan, Hoosain, and Siok (1996) showed that homophonic masks facilitated the identification of target characters relative to control masks, whereas semantic masks did not have such effects. Further, associatively related masks (the strength of association from target to mask, and vice versa) significantly facilitated the identification of targets with precise meaning rather than those with vague meaning. There was no significant difference in the facilitation between homophonic masks and associative masks with precise targets. These results suggest that phonology precedes semantic activation and is activated before the associative masks in the situation of targets with vague meaning. Perfetti and Tan (1998) further showed that phonological and semantic information of a character was automatically activated in its identification and phonological information preceded the activation of semantic information in naming a character. All these results support the notion that the graphic-phonological relationship is from form to form (from graphic to phonological), rather than from form to meaning directly.

○ Using Different Clues to Identify Chinese Characters

Cheng (1981) stated that Chinese character identification is related to the context in which a character is embedded, such as number and accuracy of words. Using a forced-choice procedure, Cheng (1981) inspected the word superiority effect on Chinese character identification and found that a character (察) in a two-character word (觀察) was easier to identify than in a two-character non-word (緉察).

As a forced-choice procedure in detecting the word superiority effect in Chinese characters seemed to be far from real reading situations, Chen (1986) applied the unitization model to test the word effect in Chinese by decoding the component of a character as radical. The results of this study showed that participants had inferior radical detection when characters were embedded in a large section, such as ten characters or a passage. A possible explanation was that, when a reader quickly identified a given character, he or she would then immediately proceed to the next character no matter what the components of the target word were. This identification showed that the components of a target character and the character were processed in parallel. Moreover, if a target character stood alone from other words around it, readers would split the character into its components after the character was identified. For radicals, the word superiority effect appeared in the single-character display and the word inferiority effect easily occurred in continuous character displays.

Hue (1989) used naming tasks to examine the word superiority and word inferiority effects in two-character Chinese words. The results showed that the naming latency of high-frequency words was shorter than that for low-frequency words, whereas naming low-frequency words was faster than non-words. The naming latency of four-character words was longer than that of two-character words. The experiment also found that a character embedded in a word context could be identified more readily, and a character embedded in a passage had an inferior effect because readers would not focus on the word information. Further, Hue (1992) used regular, irregular and unique characters with high or low frequency to test the naming latencies. Regular characters (e.g., 由, you2) serve as phonetic radicals and their pronunciation is consistent with their stems (油, you2) as phonetic-logographic compounds. Irregular characters (e. g., 抽, chou1) contain phonetic radicals (由), but they are not consistently pronounced as their phonetic radicals. Unique characters (e.g., 毛, mau2) are logographic compounds without phonetic clues. The experiment found that the type of characters produced a significant difference in low-frequency characters, but not in high-frequency characters. For low-frequency characters, the regular characters were named faster than unique characters. Participants made more errors in naming the irregular characters. This study showed that phonetic-logographic compounds influenced character naming.

These results as outlined above lend credence to the role of the phonological process in Chinese character identification. Reading Chinese characters involves identifying phonological information despite the absence of spelling-to-sound rules. The purpose of this study was to evaluate the learning differences between skilled readers and less-skilled readers. It examined whether or not skilled readers use different strategies from less-skilled readers in character identification. It was hypothesized that skilled readers can figure out an unknown character by means of context clues. The context clues include the meaning in the text, Pinyin cues, and the components of an unknown character, such as semantic and phonetic radicals. A skilled reader can coordinate all cues to identify an unknown character. Conversely, a less-skilled reader just coordinates a few cues, or even none, to identify an unknown character.

Two main questions were put forward in this study: 1) Are different strategies associated with higher or lower reading achievements? 2) Which cues do children choose most frequently in reading Chinese characters? Three experiments were conducted in this study.

EXPERIMENT 1

Experiment 1 used protocol analysis to inspect children's thoughts and actions while reading unknown characters. Protocol analysis is a verbal reporting method in which subjects have to report their thinking while doing a task (Pressley & Afflerbach, 1995). Participants in Experiment 1 were asked to read aloud a story that they had not yet read. Participants were separated to read the story individually. When the participants encountered some unknown characters, which were difficult to pronounce, we guided participants to report what they observed in the unknown characters and how they solved their problems to subsequently name the unknown characters in terms of identification strategies.

METHOD

Participants   Ten fifth-grade students in Taiwan participated in Experiment 1. All were native Chinese speakers and were divided into two groups: five skilled readers (three girls and two boys) and five less-skilled readers (three boys and two girls). The definition of skilled and less-skilled readers refers to achievement differences in reading characters and comprehension. Information about reading achievement was obtained from their homeroom teacher. The five skilled readers had reading grades in the top 5% of the class and the five less-skilled readers were in the bottom 5% of the class. Reading grades were used for this division, as there were no standardized test scores available in the elementary schools of Taiwan.

Materials   The verbal material used in this experiment was a story, 'Single Wild Goose' (孤雁), from volume one of a Chinese textbook that was issued to middle schools in Taiwan. To make this experiment more challenging for the participants, we edited the content of this story by putting some low-frequency characters to the text. Those low-frequency characters had not been taught to fifth-grade students and rarely appear in children's books, even in newspapers or magazines. The story was composed of a total of 496 characters. The protocol analysis of this study showed that the average number of unknown characters for the skilled readers was 16 (SD = 2.49) characters and 29 (SD = 3.27) characters for the less-skilled readers. These two mean scores were significantly different at .000 level. The unknown characters refer to low frequency characters whose pronunciations and meanings are unknown by readers.

Procedure   For this experiment, three questions were administered to each participant. First, the child was asked to read the story aloud: 'Could you read it aloud for me, please?' When he or she stopped reading and gazed at a character, the second question was asked: 'Could you tell me how you read this character?' When a period of time passed and the child could not self-report, the author reminded him or her to think about the unknown character. Three additional sub-questions were then asked. First, 'Do you know what the right (or upper) side of the character means?' Second, 'What does the left (or lower) side mean?' Third, 'How do you determine the sound of the character?' After the child finished reading a sentence where some characters were barely pronounced, the author asked him or her to go back to those initially unknown characters and to repeat aloud his or her strategy. The third question was then asked of the child. 'Can you explain to me how you figured out the character?' The participants were expected to self-report when they answered all the questions. We videotaped and recorded all participants' reading processes and answers.

During the recording, the participants were asked to elaborate on their answers. For example, when the author asked: 'Could you show me how you read the character?', the participant might answer: 'I just guess.' He or she was then asked: 'How do you guess its sound?' or 'Could you teach me how to guess the sound when you meet the unknown character?' These participants were encouraged to think aloud as they answered all the questions. These verbal reports were not timed.

RESULTS

The results of verbal reports were encoded into different categories as shown in Figure 1.

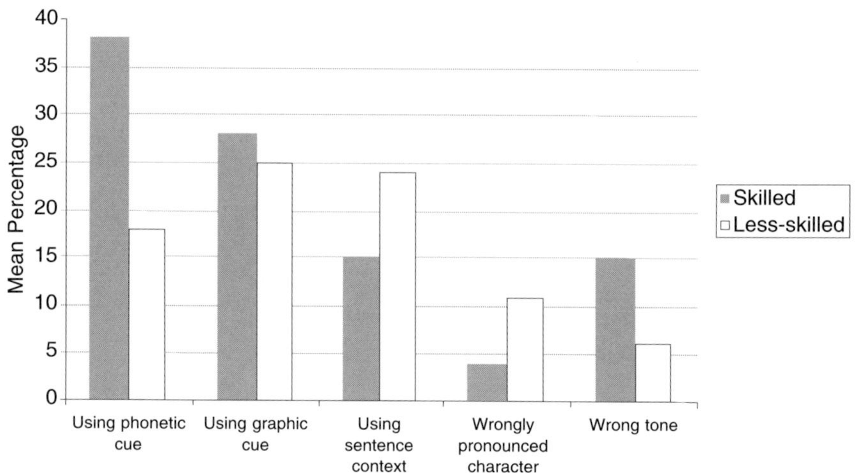

Figure 1. The mean percentage of errors for reading a story aloud by skilled and less-skilled readers.

The first category was labeled as *using phonetic cue* meaning that the participants identified the sound of an unknown character by reading the sound of the phonetic radical aloud (窸 → 悉). Second, the participants pronounced an unknown character by using graphic information of the unknown character as the parts of the character was similar to another character (嘎 → 夏). This identification might include the fact that children used semantic information of the unknown character to identify the sound of the character. Because it was uncertain whether these children knew the exact semantic feature of the character or just depended on its graphic feature, and the pronunciation was not the same as the semantic cue of the unknown character, we labeled this identification as *using graphic cue.* Third, the participants did not pay attention to the phonetic or graphic cues. They seemed to figure out the meaning of the unknown character from the context of the sentences; subsequently, they recalled a familiar character whose meaning was similar to the unknown character and gave this character the same pronunciation as that of the familiar character (狡 '獪' → 猾). This case was labeled as *using sentence context.* The fourth category was *wrongly pronounced character.* The participants would pay attention to the phonetic, graphic, and semantic cues of an unknown character. However, they made inaccurate inferences about the sound of the unknown character (蟲 → 轟), which were not related to the clues from the character. The participants finally pronounced the unknown character erroneously. The fifth category, *wrong tone*, refers to the name of an unknown character with a wrong tone in spite of correct spelling.

In this experiment, the total number of the errors of pronunciation during reading the story was calculated and attributed to different categories. The calculation of errors in each category was based on the results of participants' protocol reports. The categories represented the strategies children used to identify the unknown or unfamiliar characters. Each category showed the average rate of how often children used each strategy to pronounce the unknown or unfamiliar characters. The identification differences in this experiment between skilled and less-skilled readers are shown on Figure 1.

First, the rate for skilled readers using phonetic radicals to identify the sounds of the unknown characters was much higher (mean percentage = 38%) than for less-skilled readers (18%). Second, the mean percentage of using graphic cue to identify the sounds of the unknown characters by less-skilled readers (25%) was lower than that by skilled readers (28%). Third, less-skilled readers used sentence context to identify the sounds of the unknown characters (24%) more often than skilled readers (15%) did. This finding showed that less-skilled readers pay more attention to the context of the sentences in the story. Fourth, these less-skilled readers more often generated wrong pronunciations (11%) than did skilled readers

(4%). This indicates that students did not coordinate the phonetic cues, graphic cues and context clues to infer the sound of the unknown character. Fifth, skilled readers had a higher mean percentage (15%) of pronouncing the character with the wrong tone than did less-skilled readers (6%). A possible explanation for this result was that skilled readers focused on reading the story aloud and were careless on the character tones. In addition, only the less-skilled readers had a mean percentage (16%) in non-pronunciation; that is, they did not pronounce some unknown characters.

EXPERIMENT 2

The purpose of the second experiment was to examine the function of phonetic radicals in Chinese character identification. In Taiwan, when children first start to learn how to pronounce a character, they always follow a phonetic system known as *Zhuyin Fuhao* to read the character. Children have to be familiar with the skill of Zhuyin so that they can read any unknown characters with Zhuyin Fuhao. We were thus interested in evaluating the function of the phonetic system for Chinese children's character reading and the phonological processing of Chinese characters without phonetic clues. Three questions were investigated in this experiment. First, do children make significantly different representations of characters with phonetic clues as opposed to characters without phonetic clues? Second, when characters did not have phonetic clues, could children still identify the sound of the unknown character? Do the children have the concept of phonetic radicals? Can they use the phonetic radical of a character to acquire information about the character's sound? Third, what strategies do children use to recognize the pronunciation of an unknown character when they try to sound the unknown character without phonetic clues?

METHOD

Participants   Participants in this task were the same as in Experiment 1.

Materials   Two phonological lists were used in this experiment: one to be a non-phonetic list (NPL) without phonetic clues (Zhuyin Fuhao) and the other to be a phonetic list (PL) with phonetic clues (see Appendix A). Thirty characters were placed in each of the two phonological lists. The characters of each list were divided into two parts: (1) 15 characters were phonetic-logographic compounds composed of one phonetic radical and one semantic radical; and (2) the other 15 characters were logographic compounds composed of two or more semantic radicals. They were randomly arranged in the two lists. Both of the lists included 6 high-frequency characters, 6 medium-frequency characters and 16 low-frequency characters chosen from *A Study of Writing Vocabularies in Elementary School Children* (Chang & Chiu, 1972) and a Chinese dictionary.

Procedure   First, the NPL was administered to the 10 students. All students had to fill in Zhuyin Fuhao beside the 30 characters and leave no blanks for any character. We encouraged participants to infer the sounds of the unknown characters by means of reading the radicals of the characters. After they finished writing the NPL, the PL was administered to each participant. The child read each character aloud one by one to the researcher. The researcher then recorded the results of reading the phonetic list.

RESULTS

The analysis for NPL was based on the coding results. Figure 2 presents the mean percentage of errors in each category. The effectiveness of the phonetic system was evaluated by inspecting the mean differences in PL and NPL between skilled and less-skilled groups.

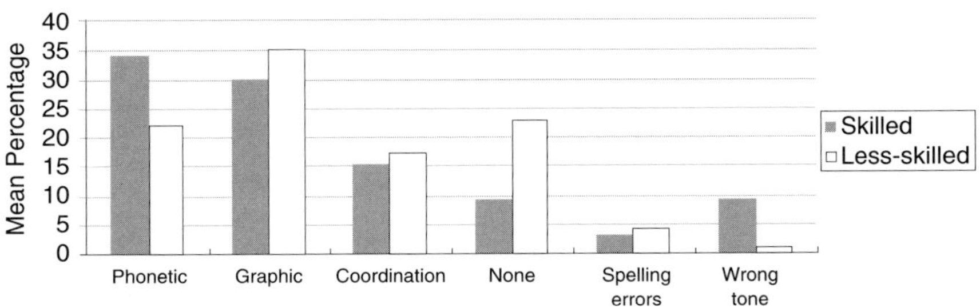

Figure 2.   The mean percentage of errors for the non-phonetic list by skilled and less-skilled readers.

The coding of NPL was arranged into six categories. First, the participants paid attention to the phonetic radical of an unknown character, and then identified the sound of the unknown character in accordance with the sound of the phonetic radical (怙 → 古). This strategy was labeled as *phonetic cue*. The second strategy was known as *graphic cue* which meant that the participants recognized the graphic cue of the unknown character was quite similar to the graphic cue of a known character so that they wrote the known character's Zhuyin for the unknown character (炙 → 炎). It was plausible that the children might focus on the semantic information of the unknown character to identify its pronunciation. However, they identified the pronunciation of the unknown character in relation to a similar graphic script instead of the sound of its semantic feature. Such identification was considered as a case of using graphic similarity. The third category was *coordination*. The participants had looked at the components of the unknown character, but did not associate the cues of the unknown character with the pronunciation of the unknown character, or they misidentified the cues of the unknown character so that they linked the unknown character to another lexical item (槃 → Li4). Fourth, the *none* category meant that the participants did not show any skill related to the unknown character identification. The Zhuyin symbols they wrote to the unknown character did not present any information from the context of the unknown character. Fifth, the unknown character should be pronounced with vowel sounds, but subjects might use the related consonant sounds instead of the vowel sounds during identification. This was labeled as *spelling errors*. The sixth category meant that the participants correctly spelled the sound of the unknown character, but put the wrong tone into the character.

The mean percentage of errors made by the ten subjects is given in Figure 2. For the NPL task, skilled readers were more likely to use phonetic cue to identify the sound of an unknown character (34%) than less-skilled readers (22%) were. This was consistent with the results of Experiment 1. The mean percentage of the errors on NPL in using graphic cue was higher (35%) for less-skilled readers, compared with the mean percentage (30%) for skilled readers. This result showed that less-skilled readers used graphic cue to identify the sound of an unknown character more than skilled readers did. The mean percentage of errors of coordination made by skilled readers was 15% and was 17% by less-skilled readers. There was no evidence that skilled readers coordinated the phonetic cue or graphic cue of an unknown character better than less-skilled readers did. Additionally, less-skilled readers made a much higher mean percentage (23%) in *none* than skilled readers with 9% of errors. The skilled and less-skilled groups made almost the same mean percentage on spelling errors (3% and 4%, respectively). Skilled readers still showed a higher error rate (9%) in using wrong tones to pronounce a character's sound than did less-skilled readers (0.8%). This was similar to the results of reading a story aloud in Experiment 1.

Table 1
Correct Answers in the Non-phonetic and Phonetic lists for Skilled and Less-Skilled Readers

Readers	*n*	NPL		PL	
		M	*SD*	*M*	*SD*
Skilled	5	18.2	2.59	29.4	.55
Less-Skilled	5	9.6	3.21	26.2	2.05

Note. NPL: Non-Phonetic List
         PL: Phonetic List

Children, either in the skilled group or in the less-skilled group, reported higher mean scores on attaining correct pronunciations on PL than on NPL (see Table 1). For PL, the skilled group had significantly higher mean score on correct naming ($M = 29.4$, $SD = .55$) than the less-skilled group ($M = 26.2$, $SD = 2.05$), $p < .01$. This indicates that skilled readers were likely to have better Zhuyin skills than less-skilled readers. For NPL, the mean score on correct answers for the skilled readers was 18.2 ($SD = 2.59$). This was significantly higher than the mean score of the less-skilled readers ($M = 9.6$, $SD = 3.21$) which was at .002 level. Skilled readers seem to have more effective strategy use in identifying the sounds of characters without phonetic clues than did less-skilled readers.

EXPERIMENT 3

In Experiment 2, children were asked to pay attention to the parts of the 30 characters. However, it did not account for the fact that children know the radicals and can coordinate them during character recognition. This study was also concerned with whether or not children can interrelate graphic information with phonetic and semantic information in identifying Chinese characters. The purpose of Experiment 3 was to investigate whether or not children can distinguish exactly the semantic and phonetic radicals of the 30 characters and understand the function of radicals in Chinese characters. For example, do the participants really recognize the parts of Chinese characters? Can the children coordinate the radicals of the characters for character identification? Which radicals do the children explicitly identify in the character during the recognizing process? This task asked the participants to discern the elements of Chinese characters according to the structure of Chinese characters. A component list served this purpose in Experiment 3.

METHOD

Participants   Participants in Experiment 3 were 40 fifth-grade students in Taiwan. The children were all enrolled in the same class, and included the 10 students from Experiment 1. In order to evaluate the coordinating ability and knowledge of cues, the 40 students were also divided into two groups: one of 20 skilled readers and the other of 20 less-skilled readers. The division of the students depended on the median number of total correct answers in the component list. The median number was six. The students with more than six correct answers were grouped as skilled readers, whereas the students with less than or equal to six were designated as less-skilled readers. The 10 participants in Experiments 1 and 2 went into their original groups as the range of correct answers for the five skilled readers ranged from 7 to 14 and 0 to 4 for the five less-skilled readers.

Materials   The component list consisted of thirty characters, the same as the phonological lists, and was designed as multiple-choice questions. Two variables, the semantic and phonetic radicals, were presented in the list. Each character was split into three parts, which were extracted from the strokes/radicals of a character and were assigned to each variable. A space item next to the radical variable served as a *none* choice. When participants were unable to identify the radicals of characters, or did not agree with the radical items, they had to mark this space (see Appendix B).

Procedure   The component list was administered to the 40 participants. This list included a sheet, which explained the operation of this task and a sample of how to do it. Before doing the task, the researcher clearly explained the operation of this experiment and difficult linguistic terms in the list, such as semantic radical and phonetic radical, to the participants. The participants were informed that they could pick more than one answer to one specific item if they agreed with the answers.

RESULTS

An independent two-sample t test was utilized to test the null hypothesis that there was no difference in mean scores of each dependent variable (errors of semantic radical and phonetic radical) between skilled and less-skilled readers in Experiment 3. First, the errors in both semantic and phonetic radicals of a character were calculated for each of the participants. The means of errors for skilled and less-skilled groups were 21.4 (SD = 3.41) and 26.35 (SD = 3.53) respectively, indicating that skilled readers showed a significantly higher mean score for accurately differentiating the phonetic and semantic radicals from graphic information of the characters than did less-skilled readers, t (38) = -4.512, p < .001. The null hypothesis was rejected. This suggested that skilled readers could coordinate the elements of a character, either a semantic radical or a phonetic radical, better than less-skilled readers. Second, the number of errors that participants misidentified, either semantic or phonetic radicals are presented in Table 2.

Table 2
Errors and Results of t *Tests for Skilled and Less-Skilled Readers*

Error type	Skilled readers		Less-skilled readers		
	M	*SD*	*M*	*SD*	*t* value
Semantic radical	18.4	3.62	21.35	3.63	-2.573*
Phonetic radical	8.6	2.98	19.05	7.78	-5.607***

* p < .05   *** p < .001

For the semantic radical, the means for the skilled and less-skilled groups were 18.4 (SD = 3.62) and 21.35 (SD = 3.63), respectively. There were significant differences between skilled and less-skilled readers, t (38) = -2.573, p < .05. For phonetic radicals, the results of t test showed that the mean score of skilled readers (M= 8.6, SD = 2.98) was significantly different from that of less-skilled readers (M = 19.05, SD = 7.78),

t (38) = -5.607, p < .001. Skilled readers showed a much lower error-rate in identifying phonetic radicals than did less-skilled readers. As shown in Table 3, the errors in identification of semantic radicals in phonetic-logographic compounds did not exhibit significant differences between the two groups, (M = 8.55, SD = 4.37 for skilled readers and M =10.6, SD = 2.7 for less-skilled readers, t (38) = -1.784, p > .05.

Table 3
Results of t *Tests Between Skilled and Less-Skilled Readers in the Component List*

Readers	*n*	Phonetic-logographic Compound			Logographic Compound		
		M	*SD*	*t* value	*M*	*SD*	*t* value
				Semantic radical			
Skilled		8.55	4.37	-1.784	9.85	6.29	-.514
Less-skilled	20	10.60	2.7		10.75	4.67	
				Phonetic radical			
Skilled	20	4.0	2.13	-4.677***	4.6	3.2	-4.324***
Less-skilled	20	9.1	4.39		9.95	4.51	

*** p < .001

The same result was also found for logographic compounds as the mean scores on semantic identification were 9.85 (SD = 6.29) for the skilled group and 10.75 (SD = 4.67) for the less-skilled group, t (38) = -514, p > .05, (see Table 3). The variance in semantic identification did not significantly explain the difference between the skilled and less-skilled groups. However, these two groups showed significant differences in processing the phonetic radicals. In Table 3, skilled readers had lower average error rates for phonetic-logographic compounds (M = 4.0, SD = 2.13) than did less-skilled readers (M = 9.10, SD = 4.39), t (38) = -4.677, p < .001. Skilled readers also had lower mean score on errors of phonetic radical for logographic compounds (M = 4.6, SD = 3.2) than those of less-skilled readers (M = 9.95, SD = 4.51), t (38) = -4.324, p < .001. These findings suggested that skilled readers were likely to better identify phonetic radicals in a Chinese character than did less-skilled readers.

GENERAL DISCUSSION

The results of this study showed that skilled and less-skilled readers used different strategies in identifying unknown characters. First, skilled readers, more than less-skilled readers, relied on phonetic cues to pronounce unknown characters. Less-skilled readers were more likely than skilled readers to use graphic similarity than phonetic cues during character recognition, although the mean percentage of graphic similarity was slightly different between skilled and less-skilled readers. Noticeably, less-skilled readers paid more attention to sentence context to infer the sounds of the unknown characters. This result was consistent with previous results that poor English readers used sentence context for word identification (West & Stanovich, 1978). In terms of an interactive-compensatory model, Stanovich (1980) assumed that if a poor reader was deficit in a word's lexical knowledge, he or she would rely heavily on other knowledge sources like contextual factors in order to identify the unknown word in sentences. This compensatory effect also appeared in Chinese character identification by the less-skilled readers in this study. Ku and Anderson (2001) supported the point that contextual support (characters placed in the text) is a significant factor that influences Chinese children to readily identify unfamiliar or unknown characters.

Second, another difference between skilled and less-skilled readers is likely related to their ability to integrate the cues of characters. The results of Experiments 1 and 2 supported the hypothesis that the two groups used different strategies in coordinating cues. Specifically, skilled readers in Experiment 1 had a higher mean percentage (81%) in using phonetic information, graphic information and sentence context during character identification than had the less-skilled readers (67%). Also, less-skilled readers had a higher error-rate (11%) in wrongly pronouncing the unknown characters than skilled readers (4%). These results suggest that less-skilled readers could not well interrelate the cues from characters and the meaning from context so that they made wrong inferences for the sounds of the unknown characters. In contrast, skilled readers were more able to employ the linguistic information of a low-frequency character and link the information to the meaning in order to decode the sound of the unknown characters (see also Chung, Cheng & Leong, 1988).

The results of Experiment 3 also provided supporting evidence in the skill of coordination in the skilled and less-skilled readers. Skilled readers had lower mean scores for incorrect answers than did less-skilled readers. This seems to show that skilled readers had better cue knowledge, both in semantic and phonetic radicals, than less-skilled readers had. In other words, skilled readers are more able to differentiate the cues of the characters and actually coordinate them as compared with less-skilled readers. Even though our results showed that skilled readers in this study represented better coordination in character identification than less-skilled readers, this needs to be further examined as the error rate of coordination in Experiment 2 showed just a slight difference between the two groups.

The third significant result was the phonological knowledge of children. This current study has found that skilled readers adopted phonological principles in character identification more frequently than did less-skilled readers. It seems that skilled readers might have better phonological knowledge than less-skilled readers. In Experiment 3, the error rate of identifying phonetic radicals for skilled readers was much lower than for less-skilled readers. Compared with mean difference in phonetic identification, the mean difference in semantic identification between the skilled and less-skilled groups was much closer, although these two mean scores were significantly different at .05 level. However, when the Chinese characters were classified into phonetic-logographic and logographic compounds, there was no significant difference in identifying semantic radicals between skilled and less-skilled readers. It is also noteworthy that Experiment 3 used phonetic-logographic compounds (phonograms) and logographic compounds (non-phonograms) to investigate whether or not children's phonological process is influenced by different character clues. The results show that children are likely to process phonological information regardless of phonogram or non-phonograms and this is consistent with the findings of Tan, Hoosain, and Peng (1995).

At this point, individual differences in Chinese character identification are related to the variation of knowledge about phonetic and semantic information in a character. The results of these three experiments indicated that phonological information is an important and necessary facilitator in character identification for Chinese children. Phonological processing 'at lexicality' is part of Chinese character identification (Perfetti, Zhang, & Berent, 1992; Perfetti & Tan, 1998; Perfetti & Zhang, 1991, 1995).

Given the differences in character identification between skilled and less-skilled readers, this study suggests three points for educational application. First, teachers can increase children's cue knowledge of Chinese characters and teach them how to coordinate the cues while identifying an unknown character. The three experiments suggest that skilled readers had better concepts of cues. Thus, teachers may guide their students to pay attention to the components of Chinese characters in terms of lexical context while learning new characters. This strengthens students' understanding of characters' mechanisms.

Second, instructors could teach children to use effective strategies in identifying unknown or unfamiliar characters. The results of this study suggest that children do use different strategies to identify characters and this produced different achievements in reading performance. Teachers should provide appropriate and useful methods to help students accurately process Chinese characters. Increasing children's fluency in character identification is likely to promote their ability to comprehend texts.

Third, teachers should encourage their students to read storybooks as well as their textbooks. In addition to the experimental tasks, the researcher interviewed the 10 participants in Experiment 1 after reading a story aloud. A main difference between skilled readers and less-skilled readers was their amount and breadth of reading. Each of the skilled readers said that they read books, either storybooks or their textbooks, at least one to two hours everyday. On the contrary, most of the less-skilled readers were less interested in reading storybooks and rarely spent their time in reading. When children read a lot, they also improve their knowledge of characters as much as they improve their reading skills (Cunningham & Stanovich, 1998). In turn, the richer a reader's prior knowledge of and experience with characters, the more automatic and rapid the identification may become.

These three experiments have provided consistent evidence that skilled readers excel in using phonological information to identify Chinese characters as compared with less-skilled readers who employed graphic and contextual information. However, as a very limited number of children participated in Experiments 1 and 2, the results of this study might not be generalized to all Chinese-speaking children. In Taiwan, children are not taught to distinguish semantic and phonetic radicals when they first start to learn the characters. They learn Zhuyin to name characters and usually learn the meanings of characters from teachers' explanations and their own memorization. Although the participating children showed lexical knowledge in character identification and used different strategies to solve problems in identification, the current study has not clarified why skilled readers were prominent in identifying phonetic radicals and the difference in semantic identification was moderate between the two groups. It seems that children are likely to store different lexical information and this is related to individual differences on reading achievement. Further research on children's character identification is needed, not only to verify these findings, but also provide theoretical bases for developing better teaching methods to facilitate children's character learning.

References

Chang, C. H., & Chiu, W. C. (1972). A study of writing vocabularies in elementary school children. *Bulletin of Research Institute of Education Taiwan Normal University* (Vol. 14, pp. 51–79). Taipei: Taiwan Normal University.

Chen, H. C. (1986). Component detection in reading Chinese characters. In H. S. R. Kao, & R. Hoosain (Eds.), *Linguistics, psychology and the Chinese language* (pp. 1–9). Hong Kong: University of Hong Kong.

Chen, M., Yung, Y. F., & Ng, T. W. (1988). The effect of context on perception of Chinese characters. In I. M. Liu, H. C. Chen, & M. J. Chen (Eds.), *Cognitive aspects of the Chinese language* (Vol. 1, pp. 27–39). Hong Kong: Asian Research Service.

Cheng, C. M. (1981). Perception of Chinese characters. *Chinese Journal of Psychology, 23,* 137–153.

Cheng, C. M. (1992). Lexical access in Chinese: Evidence from automatic activation of phonological information. In H. C. Chen, & O. J. L. Tzeng (Eds.), *Language processing in Chinese* (pp. 67–91). Amsterdam: North-Holland.

Cheng, C. M., & Shih, S. (1988). The nature of lexical access in Chinese: Evidence from experiments on visual and phonological priming in lexical judgment. In I. M. Liu, H. C. Chen, & M. J. Chen (Eds.), *Cognitive aspects of the Chinese language* (Vol.1, pp. 1–14). Hong Kong: Asian Research Service.

Chung, C. M., Cheng, S. C., & Leong, C. K. (1988). Interaction of reader and stimulus characteristics in children's recognition of Chinese. In I. M. Liu, H. C. Chen, & M. J. Chen (Eds.), *Cognitive aspects of the Chinese language* (Vol. 1. pp. 41–56). Hong Kong: Asian Research Service.

Cunningham, A. E., & Stanovich, K. E. (1998). The impact of print exposure on word recognition. In J. L. Metsala & L. C. Ehri (Eds.), *Word recognition in beginning literacy* (pp. 235–262). Hillsdale, NJ : Lawrence Erlbaum.

Daneman, M. (1991). Individual differences in reading skills. In R. Barr, M. L. Kamil, P. Mosenthal, & P. D. Pearson (Eds.), *Handbook of reading research* (Vol. 2, pp. 512–538). New York: Longman.

Ehri, C. L. (1994). Development of the ability to read words: Update. In R. B. Ruddell, M. R. Ruddell, & H. Singer (Eds.), *Theoretical models and processes of reading* (pp. 838–863). Delaware: International Reading Association.

Guthrie, J. T., & Tyler, S. J. (1976). Psycholinguistic processing in reading and listening among good and poor readers. *Journal of Reading Behavior, 8,* 415–426.

Hoosain, R. (1991). *Psycholinguistic implications for linguistic relativity: A case study of Chinese.* Hillsdale, NJ: Lawrence Erlbaum.

Hue, C. W. (1989). Word superiority and inferiority effect: A study of Chinese word recognition. *Chinese Journal of Psychology, 31,* 33–39.

Hue, C. W. (1992). Recognition processes in character naming. In H. C. Chen, & O. J. L. Tzeng (Eds.), *Language processing in Chinese* (pp. 93–107). Amsterdam: North-Holland.

Jorm, A. F., & Share, D. L. (1983). Phonological recoding and reading acquisition. *Applied Psycholinguistics, 4,* 103–147.

Ku, Y. M., & Anderson, R. C. (2001). Chinese children's incidental learning of word meanings. *Contemporary Educational Psychology, 26,* 249–266.

Peng, D. L., Guo, D. J., & Zhang, S. L. (1985). The retrieval of information of Chinese characters in making similarity judgment under recognition condition. *Acta Psychologica Sinica, 3,* 227–234.

Perfetti, C. A., Bell, L. C., & Delaney, S. M. (1988). Automatic (Prelexical) phonetic activation in silent word reading: Evidence from backward masking. *Journal of Memory and Language, 27,* 59–70.

Perfetti, C. A., Finger, E., & Hogaboam, T. (1978). Sources of vocalization latency differences between skilled and less skilled young readers. *Journal of Educational Psychology, 70,* 730–739.

Tzeng, O. J. L., & Hung, D. L. (1980). Reading in a nonalphabetic writing system: some experimental studies. In J. F. Kavanagh, & R. L. Venezky (Eds.), *Orthography, reading and dyslexia,* (pp. 211–226). Baltimore: University Park Press.

Tzeng, O. J. L., Hung, D. L., & Wang, W. S-Y. (1977). Speech recoding in reading Chinese characters. *Journal of Experimental Psychology: Human Learning and Memory, 3,* 621–630.

West, R. F., & Stanovich, K. E. (1978). Automatic contextual facilitation in readers of three ages. *Child Development, 49,* 717–727.

Author Note

We would like to thank Dr Che Kan Leong for his extensive and valuable review and editing of this paper.

Appendix A (Experiment 2)

I.   Directions: Write Zhuyin Fuhao in the spaces next to each character.

解		黔		妤		早		邃	
功		粟		獅		妃		吠	

履		恣		爸		但		茁	
做		辜		樂		炙		巍	

怙		竄		岳		皙		塵	
咆		搬		畋		槃		祝	

II.   Directions: Read each character aloud.

解	ㄐㄧㄝˇ	黔	ㄑㄧㄢˊ	妤	ㄩˊ	早	ㄗㄠˇ	邃	ㄙㄨㄟˋ
功	ㄍㄨㄥ	粟	ㄙㄨˋ	獅	ㄕ	妃	ㄈㄟ	吠	ㄈㄟˋ

履	ㄌㄩˇ	恣	ㄗˋ	爸	ㄅㄚˋ	但	ㄉㄢˋ	茁	ㄓㄨㄛˊ
做	ㄗㄨㄛˋ	辜	ㄍㄨ	樂	ㄌㄜˋ	炙	ㄓˋ	巍	ㄨㄟˊ

怙	ㄏㄨˋ	竄	ㄘㄨㄢˋ	岳	ㄩㄝˋ	皙	ㄓㄜˊ	塵	ㄔㄣˊ
咆	ㄆㄠˊ	搬	ㄅㄢ	畋	ㄊㄧㄢˊ	槃	ㄆㄢˊ	祝	ㄓㄨˋ

Appendix B (Experiment 3)

Directions: Choose the appropriate semantic and phonetic radicals of each character.

Characters	Semantic Radical			None	Phonetic Radical			None
解	角 ‾ 1	刀 ‾ 2	牛 ‾ 3		角 ‾ 1	刀 ‾ 2	牛 ‾ 3	
黔	黑 ‾ 1	今 ‾ 2	人 ‾ 3		黑 ‾ 1	今 ‾ 2	人 ‾ 3	
粟	西 ‾ 1	米 ‾ 2	木 ‾ 3		西 ‾ 1	米 ‾ 2	木 ‾ 3	
辜	十 ‾ 1	古 ‾ 2	辛 ‾ 3		十 ‾ 1	古 ‾ 2	辛 ‾ 3	
吠	口 ‾ 1	大 ‾ 2	犬 ‾ 3		口 ‾ 1	大 ‾ 2	犬 ‾ 3	

15

The Developing Lexicon: The Case of Hong Kong Secondary Students

Benjamin K. Y. T'sou, Anna S. F. Kwan and Godfrey K. F. Liu

The present study is a part of an ongoing Chinese vocabulary research, which seeks to investigate the lexical development of secondary and tertiary students in four Asian cities (Hong Kong, Taipei, Shanghai and Singapore) and to contribute to the setting of literacy benchmarks for Chinese language education in Hong Kong.

Vocabulary development is a crucial area of research because it relates closely to cognitive development (Anderson & Freebody, 1981; Terman, 1916; Wechsler, 1949) and academic achievement (Miller, 1988; Saville-Troike, 1984; Stanovich, 1986). In language development, vocabulary serves as basic building blocks in generating and understanding sentences (Miller, 1991) and in reading competence (Anderson & Freebody, 1981; Beck et al., 1987; Chall, 1958; Graves, 1986; Miller, 1988; Nagy & Anderson, 1984; Nagy & Herman 1987). Studies of vocabulary acquisition can therefore provide a window on the process of language acquisition as a whole (Clark, 1995).

A large number of teaching and learning strategies have been advanced to promote learners' lexical development, but few of them have given satisfying answers. In contrast to the large amount of published materials on vocabulary learning, little is known about how learners acquire and develop their vocabulary (Nation, 1990). Research into Chinese vocabulary has seen experiments examining aspects of words, such as characters and radicals, but studies into Chinese vocabulary acquisition are relatively under-developed.

Hong Kong educational reform has attracted considerable attention and gained mounting urgency in the last decade of the twentieth century because of the unprecedented political changes and their consequential impact on societal goals, education processes and their fulfilment. There is an urgent need to undertake investigations to determine the vocabulary benchmarks of students and to gain understanding on how they develop their vocabulary knowledge so as to benefit Chinese language education.

This study aims at helping to meet this need by providing empirical evidence on the lexical development of Hong Kong secondary students by assessing and comparing their word knowledge on the basis of newspaper and textbook corpuses.

Previous Studies

Vocabulary development

In describing vocabulary growth, researchers suggest that native speakers develop their vocabulary throughout their life span (e.g., Nation, 1990). Recent studies (Goulden, Nation & Read, 1990; Nagy & Anderson, 1984) demonstrate that an estimate of around 20,000 words for undergraduates is likely to be appropriate, suggesting that native speakers add about 1,000 to 2,000 of words per year (or three to seven words per day) to their vocabulary.

Carey (1978) distinguished between *fast mapping* and *extended mapping*, proposing that learners might quickly acquire the coarse meaning of a word (fast mapping) on the first exposure to the word, but it could take them years to acquire its full meaning (extended mapping).

Nation (1990), among others, identified two levels of vocabulary knowledge: *receptive* and *productive*. With receptive knowledge, learners are able to identify the 'what' aspects of the words (e.g., knowing what the word sounds like), whereas with productive knowledge, learners are able to master the 'how' aspects of the words (e.g., knowing how to pronounce the word). Learner's receptive vocabulary is much larger than their productive vocabulary and there are many words on the boundary. Most of the items in their receptive vocabulary are low frequency words.

Laufer and Nation (1995) studied the development of second language

(L2) lexis in the expression of the advanced learner and found that comprehensive input (exposure to the target language) was effective in enriching the active (productive) vocabulary of those learners whose vocabulary knowledge was below average. Thus, active vocabulary is determined by the functional needs of the learners rather than by comprehensive input. This finding leads Laufer and Nation (1995) to propose an *active vocabulary threshold hypothesis,* suggesting that the passive (receptive) and active (productive) vocabulary might follow different developmental paths. Passive vocabulary appears to develop through learners' lifetime, whereas productive vocabulary would stop growing when it reaches the average level of the group in which the learners are required to function.

Possible Factors Affecting Vocabulary Development

Important factors that affect the development of vocabulary include the nature of the vocabulary to be learned, the conditions of the learning process and the characteristics of the learners.

Nature of the vocabulary to be learned

Analysis of the attributes of words, which are more easily acquired by the learners, indicates that *frequency of occurrence* and *saliency* appear to be two of the major factors. Sternberg (1987) explained that 'multiple occurrences of an unknown word increase the number of available cues and can increase the usefulness of individual cues if readers integrate information obtained from cues surrounding the multiple occurrences of the word' (p. 92). Nagy and Herman (1987) claimed that even a single encounter of a word in context could help extent the learners' word knowledge. Although there has been some disagreement among researchers about the number of the encounters with a word to secure its acquisition, most of them agree 6 to 12 encounters would be reasonably sufficient (Jenkins & Dixon, 1983).

Saliency, the importance of a word, includes words that are: frequently occurring (Brown, 1993), having instructional focus (Brown & Payne, 1994), and needed by the learners in order to communicate (Hatch & Brown, 1995).

Related to frequency and saliency are studies of vocabulary learning (e.g., Anderson & Freebody, 1983; Carroll, Davies, & Richman, 1971; Nagy & Anderson, 1984). Those that can be found in the Hong Kong context include work in the last decade on academic vocabulary by Cheung and Lee (1986), Siu, Fan, Lee and Lai (1986) and more recently, vocabulary in printed media from the Linguistic Variation in Chinese Communities (LIVAC) corpus (1995–97).

In comparing the corpus by Siu et al. (1986) and the LIVAC corpus (1995–97) by the Language Information Sciences Research Centre, City University of Hong Kong, T'sou, Tsoi, Lai, Hu and Chan (2000) have found that there is only an overlap of 25% in the first 500 words of the two corpuses. Thus, using these two different sources, which focus on the words a learner needs to know well, to assess learners' knowledge should provide information on the important aspects of learners' vocabulary knowledge.

Conditions of learning

In any learning process, the *total time* devoted to learning is a major factor for the learning outcomes (Ebbinghaus, 1885). However, it is also the level of the mental processes operated on the materials to be learned that ascertains how well it will be retained (Craik & Lockhart, 1972; Craik & Tulving, 1975), thus stressing that the *depth of processing* is another important condition for learning.

Vocabulary learning can result from *intentional* or *incidental* learning or both. Intentional learning is learning as being planned for, or intended by the teachers or learners, whereas incidental learning is learning as a by-product of doing or learning something else. Research into native speakers (e.g., Beck et al., 1987; Calfee & Drum, 1986; Chall, 1987; Drum & Konopak, 1987; Graves, 1986, 1987; Mezynski, 1983; Stahl & Fairbanks, 1986) shows that intentional learning, particularly instruction, does facilitate the learning of words. However, other studies (e.g., Nagy & Anderson, 1984; Nagy & Herman, 1987) point out that in comparison with the enormous number of words a learner knows, only a very small proportion of words is a result of intentional learning. The vast bulk of our vocabulary is acquired by incidental learning. The big gap between what is taught and what is known suggests instruction alone cannot accomplish the prodigious task, and that more emphasis, research in particular, should be given to the incidental vocabulary learning.

Learners' characteristics

Explanations for vocabulary growth and reading comprehension have been discussed in L1 and L2 contexts (Hague, 1987; Kame'enui, Dixon, & Carnine, 1987). Four major hypotheses have been advanced: *aptitude hypothesis, knowledge hypothesis, instrumentalist hypothesis* and *access hypothesis*.

Aptitude hypothesis claims that vocabulary acquisition and reading skills are determined by learners' intellectual ability; that is, intelligent people know more words and have better reading comprehension. Knowledge hypothesis argues that vocabulary knowledge reflects learners' general knowledge which affects their reading ability, suggesting that learners who have more knowledge will learn more words and have better comprehension. Instrumentalist hypothesis claims that there is a direct relationship between the number of words known and reading comprehension, implying that learners who have more exposure to words will have their vocabulary expanded, which will in turn improve their reading comprehension. Access hypothesis states that words learned are not readily usable until their various meanings are acquired and easily accessible, stressing the needs for multiple exposure and practice.

Measuring Vocabulary Knowledge

When determining the lexical competence for knowing a word, lexical researchers (e.g., Cronbach, 1942; Nation, 1990; Richards, 1976) recommend that word knowledge should cover several dimensions. Nation (1990), for instance, lists the four general classification criteria proposed by George (1983), noting that knowing a word involves four important criteria: *form* (spoken and written), *position* (grammatical patterns and collocations), *function* (frequency and appropriateness) and *meaning* (concept and association).

Cronbach (1942) described five kinds of verbal behaviours which reflect the degree of increasing word knowledge: (a) *generalization*, being able to define the word; (b) *application*, selecting an appropriate use of the word, (c) *breadth of meaning*, recalling the different meanings of the word, and (d) *precision of meaning*, applying the word correctly to all possible situations, and (e) *availability*, being able to use the word productively.

Although it is useful to know what can be included in assessing word knowledge, there are problems to translate directly this idea into action. As noted by Wesche and Paribakht (1996) the majority of studies continue to focus on estimating vocabulary size (breadth of knowledge) rather than on assessing vocabulary knowledge (depth of knowledge). Few vocabulary tests have been conducted to look at the dimensions beyond meaning. There is a need to design tests to assess the depth of learners' vocabulary knowledge (Curtis, 1987; Nation, 1990; Palmberg, 1987; Read, 1988).

To assess learners' vocabulary knowledge, multiple-choice format still appears to be the most appropriate procedure for group testing, since this format can discriminate those who have no knowledge of a word and those who have some knowledge. However, to answer correctly typical multiple-choice items does not require precise knowledge of word meaning and thus provides little information on how well learners actually know the words they get correct (Cronbach, 1942, 1943; Curtis, 1987; Dolch & Leeds, 1953; Read, 1988, 1993). Other test formats, such as written production (Laufer & Nation, 1995) should be used along with multiple-choice items to assess different vocabulary knowledge levels.

The above review of the literature in this area should convince educators that vocabulary is a crucial area for research since it is of central importance in learners' cognitive and language development. Research into Chinese vocabulary knowledge thus deserves a high priority in Hong Kong language education as a part of quality culture. Individual students' receptive vocabulary and productive vocabulary seem to develop at different pace and might stop growing at different levels. Important factors for development were found with the nature of vocabulary and student characteristics. Vocabulary that is more frequent and salient tends to develop faster. Instructionally focused vocabulary (e.g., textbook) and non-instructionally focused (e.g., newspaper) vocabulary appear to develop at fast and differential speeds. Students' education level, general intellectual abilities and language proficiency are variables of vocabulary development.

Within this theoretical framework, this research aims to examine the Chinese vocabulary knowledge development among secondary students in Hong Kong. The following questions were formulated to focus the investigation:

1. To what extent do Hong Kong secondary students differ in their Chinese vocabulary knowledge with respect to: (a) recognition and production? (b) academic and general vocabulary?

2. What is the relationship between vocabulary knowledge and student characteristics, such as: (a) education levels (forms or grades), (b) Chinese proficiency, (c) general intellectual ability?

METHOD

Participants   The participants in Hong Kong were 856 students, approximately equal numbers of male and female, studying in Forms Two, Four and Six in two secondary schools. The distribution is indicated in Table 1.

Table 1
Sample Distribution

Form	n	School 1		School 2	
		Female	Male	Female	Male
2	415	100	111	102	102
4	331	96	94	69	72
6	110	37	20	32	21
Total	856	233	225	203	195

In Table 1, School 1 accommodates students who performed well (Band 1–2), whereas School 2 accommodates students who performed less well (Band 4–5) in their Secondary School Placement Assessment (SSPA).

In order to understand the students' Chinese language proficiency, the written part of the latest Chinese Attainment Test results for Form Two and Form Four students, and the Chinese results in School Certificate Examination for Form Six students were collected to indicate their general competence in Chinese language. Collected scores in descending order were divided into three groups of approximate size. Students whose marks located in the top group were categorized as 'high' level of proficiency, the middle group as 'middle' and the bottom group as 'low' level of proficiency. In this regard, School 1 was found containing students with relatively high Chinese proficiency, whereas School 2 containing students with relatively low Chinese proficiency. It should be stressed that there were great differences in Chinese proficiency among the Form Two and Four students in the two schools. These differences, however, were very small among the Form Six students, since all of them did well in their School Certificate Examinations the year before, prior to being selected for pre-university education.

Instruments   The major instrument employed in this study, the Chinese Vocabulary Knowledge Assessment Test (CVKAT), was developed by the researchers. Another instrument used to assess the students' general ability such as relating to reasoning by analogy was the Raven's Progressive Matrices (standard form) (Raven, 1960) since it fitted the purpose of this study and has been noted for its reliability and culture-fairness.

Corpuses

The lexical items in the Chinese Vocabulary Knowledge Assessment Test (CVKAT) and Translation Quiz (TQ) were drawn from two corpuses. The first was the Linguistic Variation in Chinese Communities (LIVAC) corpus established by the Language Information Sciences Research Centre, City University of Hong Kong, beginning in 1995, with a ten-year time span (refer to http://www.rcl.cityu.edu.hk/livac). This corpus simultaneously gathers every four days Chinese characters from newspapers published in Hong Kong, Taipei, Singapore and Shanghai. For 1995–1997, the corpus consisted of about 15 million characters. The CVKAT administered to Hong Kong students was based on the LIVAC-Hong Kong corpus.

The other corpus, containing about 800,000 Chinese characters, was established by Siu et al. (1986) at the School of Education, Chinese University of Hong Kong, which examined the frequency range and distribution of Chinese vocabulary among Hong Kong junior secondary school students. It includes both academic and extracurricular materials. The majority academic materials include a textbook on Chinese language and literature, two on Chinese history, two on mathematics, two on science and two on social studies. The remaining extracurricular materials contain sample texts selected for their educational relevance and interest to secondary school children: from five newspapers printed in 1983, 10 magazines published in the same year, and 10 fiction books.

A stratified sampling technique was used to sample 300 polysyllabic (mainly disyllabic) word tokens in each of the five different frequency bands from LIVAC-Hong Kong corpus and the local textbook corpus. Band 1 contains words of low frequency whereas Band 5 is of high frequency (see Appendix 1). These tokens were also categorized in terms of domains. With these 1,500 tokens, excluding proper nouns, a test to assess students' Chinese vocabulary knowledge was constructed.

In assessing learners' vocabulary knowledge, both multiple-choice and written production tests should be used to test word knowledge of different levels. Compared with dictionaries, well compiled word frequency lists on materials, such as learners' general vocabulary (as represented by newspapers) and academic vocabulary (as represented by textbooks) used by the learners are likely to be more appropriate sources for formulating vocabulary tests to assess learners' vocabulary knowledge.

Chinese Vocabulary Knowledge Assessment Test (CVKAT)

The vocabulary test contained 180 items, assessing students' vocabulary knowledge in the four dimensions (i.e., form, position, function and meaning) proposed by George (1983). Since the aim of this study was to investigate the use of vocabulary items, an emphasis was placed on the meaning (concepts and association) and position (grammatical patterns and collocation) dimensions. Items related to meaning were of several kinds: synonyms (definitions/equivalence), antonyms, componential elements and usage. For position, collocation and usage were the most typical.

In the test, students were assessed both vocabulary recognition and production. At the recognition level students were given items in a multiple-choice format whereas at the production level, students were required to give responses to the items of cloze procedures, correcting errors, and sentence completion. A sample of items is included in Appendix 2. Prior to the formal study, a four-phase pilot testing was administered to a total of 71 secondary and tertiary students to test the suitability of research design and testing instruments. The instruments were continually revised according to the pilot study results and students' opinions about the tests.

Data were collected from 856 secondary students from two schools. The Chinese Vocabulary Knowledge Assessment Test (CVKAT) and Raven's Progressive Matrices (RPM) were administered within a period of two weeks. Data gathered from individual students included also their age, sex, access to news from media, and their latest Chinese and English Attainment Test results (for Form Six students, their School Certificate Examination results).

All tests were marked according to the scoring procedures and double-checked by the research team members. Difficult cases in scoring were discussed and decisions made. The data were analysed using SPSS 7.0 for Windows. Tape recordings were made for the pilot studies and for specific tasks (as reported in Kwan & T'sou in this volume). The tapes were transcribed and students' response patterns were analysed.

Item analysis

Reliability was calculated for the 180 items in the CVKAT. An Alpha of .967 was obtained. From the Difficulty Index calculated for each item based on students' overall performance, 108 items with an Alpha of .958, were selected from the original set as an initial subset for further processing. Using a Discrimination Index calculated for each item with reference to students' Chinese proficiency levels, 100 items with an Alpha of .958 were further selected as a final subset for verifying trends found in the 180-item data set. Since the research hypotheses were built into the 180-item set, and the major purpose of the study was to set benchmarks for Hong Kong students, this 180-item set was used to report findings.

RESULTS

This section reports the analyses of the data obtained from secondary school students using CVKAT. This includes: (a) recognition tests versus production tests; (b) academic vocabulary versus general vocabulary, and (c) student characteristics and vocabulary knowledge.

Recognition tests versus production tests   Table 2 presents students' vocabulary test performance by parts in the two corpuses. Parts 1 to 3 were multiple-choice items, whereas Parts 4 to 6 were written production items. LIVAC included items selected from newspapers (general vocabulary) and Textbook from the textbook corpus (academic vocabulary). In Table 2, it can be seen that students performed better in Parts 1 to 3 (M = 68.00 and 65.37) than in Parts 4 to 6 (M = 53.85 and 60.65), indicating students' superior performance in lexical item recognition. Also, students were found having more homogeneous knowledge in word recognition than in production (SD = 13.06 and 15.08 vs. 22.24 and 22.14).

Table 2

Vocabulary Test Performance (%): by Parts and Corpuses

Corpus		Part		Overall
		1–3	4–6	
LIVAC	*M*	68.00	53.85	63.38
	SD	13.06	22.24	15.28
Textbook	*M*	65.37	60.65	63.09
	SD	15.08	22.14	17.25

n = 856

Academic vocabulary versus general vocabulary   Also indicated in Table 2, students' performances with LIVAC-Hong Kong and textbook items were comparable (M=63.38 vs. 63.09, SD 15.28 vs. 17.25). Using a paired sample t-test to compare the total mean scores for the two corpuses, no significant difference between the two corpuses was found.

However, when students' performances in recognition and written production were compared, it can be observed in Table 2 that students performed better in recognizing general lexical items (68.00 vs. 65.37) but did better with academic items in written production (53.85 vs. 60.64). Using a paired sample t-test to compare the means obtained for the two corpuses, it was found that there was a significant difference between recognition (t = 9.05, df = 855, p = .000) and written production (t = -32.01, df = 855, p = .000). This reveals that although students had similar overall scores with general and academic items, the gap between their recognition and production knowledge was much greater with general items than with academic items. This finding suggests that students' lexical knowledge of general items was likely to maintain at a recognition level, whereas that of the academic items had reached a production level.

Student characteristics and vocabulary knowledge   Tables 3 and 4 display students' performance in the vocabulary test by their education level.

It can be observed in Table 3 that there was a big gap between students' recognition and production knowledge in the general corpus. This gap became smaller as students had more educational experience.

Data in Table 3 also indicates students' general vocabulary development. Students gained substantial amount of knowledge (receptive 11.00%, productive 17.71%) between Form Two and Form Four. The gain between Form Four and Form Six was just about half of that of Form Two and Form Four (receptive 6.32%, productive 10.65%). This suggests that students develop rapidly their general vocabulary, in particular their productive knowledge in their junior secondary education. In their senior years of secondary education, this development appeared to slow down.

Table 4 displays the effects of students' education level on their test performance in the academic corpus. A gap was also found between the recognition and production items but this gap was much smaller than that in the general corpus. As students had more educational experience, the

Table 3
Vocabulary Test Performance: LIVAC by Education Level

		Form 2	Form 4	Form 6
Parts 1–3	*M*	61.52	72.52	78.84
	SD	13.39	09.47	6.72
Parts 4–6	*M*	43.36	61.07	71.72
	SD	21.36	19.24	11.29
Overall	*M*	55.58	68.78	76.51
	SD	15.17	11.73	6.83

n = 856

Table 4
Vocabulary Test Performance: Textbook Corpus by Education Level

		Form 2	Form 4	Form 6
Parts 1–3	*M*	58.38	69.92	78.06
	SD	14.19	12.95	10.04
Parts 4–6	*M*	50.41	67.74	77.95
	SD	21.75	18.64	11.81
Overall	*M*	54.53	68.86	78.01
	SD	16.53	14.26	8.68

n = 856

gap between their recognition and production knowledge was reduced. For Form Six students, this gap no longer existed.

Similar to that of general vocabulary, in the period from Form Two to Form Four, students also improved substantially their academic vocabulary (receptive 11.54% and productive 17.33%). The development of academic vocabulary appeared to slow down in their senior year of secondary education (receptive 8.14%, productive 10.21%).

Table 5 summarizes the effects of students' Chinese language proficiency on students' test performance by education level.

As expected, students with higher Chinese proficiency out-performed students with lower proficiency. This shows that students with higher education level and Chinese proficiency have acquired more vocabulary knowledge. The scores in Table 9 also validate the findings that students' vocabulary knowledge develops substantially in their junior secondary school years.

Table 6 presents briefly the correlation between the performance of vocabulary test and Raven's by forms.

Table 5
Vocabulary Test Performance: by Educational Level and Chinese Proficiency

| | Chinese proficiency levels | | | | | | | |
| | Low | | Middle | | High | | ANOVA[a] | |
Form	*M*	*SD*	*M*	*SD*	*M*	*SD*	*F*	Sig.
2	33.03	13.59	50.78	15.25	66.28	12.57	184.59	0.00
4	53.06	14.93	66.50	14.97	79.94	7.82	108.13	0.00
6	72.14	9.77	76.72	8.26	80.64	8.87	5.339	0.01
Overall	43.50	18.39	61.59	17.39	73.51	12.54	217.41	0.00

$n = 798$*
* 58 students' Chinese proficiency scores were not available.
[a] df = 2 for each form.

Table 6
Correlation Between Performance of Vocabulary Knowledge Test and Raven Test

Form	Pearson correlation
2	0.470**
4	0.351**
6	0.079

** Correlation is significant at the 0.01 level (2-tailed).

It can be observed in Table 6 that students' performance in the vocabulary knowledge test was positively correlated with their general ability as measured by Raven's Progressive Matrices. This correlation, however, became smaller and even not significant with students of higher forms, who had more educational experience and higher Chinese language proficiency.

To summarize, the present study has attempted to compare students' knowledge in general and academic vocabulary. Using different formats to assess different levels of vocabulary knowledge, students were found to have better Chinese vocabulary knowledge in recognition than in production. Although students obtained comparable overall scores for general and academic vocabulary, they showed slightly better knowledge in general receptive vocabulary, but more marked productive skills in academic productive vocabulary. During junior secondary school years, students appeared to develop rapidly their general and academic vocabulary, in particular their productive knowledge. Also during this period, students' Chinese vocabulary knowledge was found to correlate at varying degrees with their general intellectual ability.

DISCUSSION

Based on the data, it is possible to answer the research questions about secondary students' vocabulary knowledge and its relation to student characteristics.

The first question was to what extent do Hong Kong secondary students differ in their Chinese vocabulary knowledge, with respect to: (a) recognition and production and (b) academic vocabulary and general vocabulary?

Hong Kong secondary students, as other students in the world, display superior vocabulary knowledge in recognition than in written production. This supports the literature that students' receptive vocabulary is much larger than their productive vocabulary.

Students produced similar overall scores for academic and general vocabulary, showing a comparable breadth of knowledge in these two areas. However, further examining the knowledge level has revealed that there is a big gap (14% difference) between receptive and productive knowledge in general vocabulary but a much smaller gap (4.72% differences) in academic vocabulary. If productive knowledge is an important indicator for the depth of vocabulary knowledge, then we can conclude that students possess deeper knowledge in academic vocabulary.

Another question was: What is the relationship between vocabulary knowledge and student characteristics, such as: (a) education levels (forms) (b) Chinese language proficiency and (c) general ability such as reasoning by analogy?

Students' vocabulary knowledge can be predicted by their education levels, Chinese proficiency and, to a certain degree, general ability, as noted by Curtis (1987). She suggested that success in vocabulary learning may be determined by learners' prior knowledge of word meaning, which in turn affects their cognitive processes used to acquire new words. Alternatively, it is also true that students' vocabulary knowledge is a good predictor for their education level and Chinese proficiency, suggesting that a vocabulary test could be a substitute for language proficiency test.

Conclusion

Inspired initially by the small overlap of items found in general and academic corpuses, this study has attempted to explore students' knowledge in these two domains. The results from the research have yielded a description of Chinese vocabulary knowledge development among Hong Kong secondary students.

Using different formats to assess different levels of vocabulary knowledge among secondary students, it is found that they tend to acquire general vocabulary on a receptive level whereas that of academic vocabulary on a productive level. By checking students' vocabulary knowledge at different grades in secondary school, their vocabulary knowledge is found to increase both in breadth and in depth as they gain more educational experience. The development during the period from Form Two to Form Four is rapid.

This study has important implications for lexical development and assessment, as well as Hong Kong language education. The findings demonstrate that students' vocabulary appears to develop from receptive to productive. The critical conditions for this development are: *encounter, use* and *need. Encounter* is a prerequisite for formulating receptive knowledge. *Use* and *need* are critical for the elevation of receptive knowledge to productive knowledge. The academic vocabulary is introduced in the school context. Students are well motivated to learn this set of vocabulary well because it provides a measurement of their educational attainment. Thus, their academic vocabulary is elevated to the productive level at a much faster speed.

Students also have access to general vocabulary outside school, but the motivation and opportunities for them to use this vocabulary fully are more limited. There appears to be no pressing need for them to acquire full knowledge of this set of vocabulary. This might be the reason for slower development of productive skills in the general vocabulary, which is nonetheless important for the students after completion of formal education. Consequently, a significant divergence between the academic and general vocabularies should invite concern.

In terms of learning channels, general vocabulary appears to be acquired through incidental learning. This channel of learning seems to allow students to acquire a large amount of receptive vocabulary, which will be transferred to productive vocabulary as students mature. It takes a very long time, at least four years as observed in this study, for students to master this set of vocabulary at a productive level. Therefore, intervention, such as allocating time for vocabulary learning (Ebbinghaus, 1885) and engaging students in deeper mental process (Craik & Lockhart, 1972; Craik & Tulving, 1975) appears to be necessary for accelerating the process.

In assessing students' lexical knowledge, a variety of formats should be employed to test at the same time different levels of knowledge (Laufer & Nation, 1995). Multiple-choice format seems appropriate for assessing receptive vocabulary knowledge, whereas written production format seems suitable for productive knowledge.

While this study adds new information to the literature, it also raises a number of questions: (a) What constitutes lexical development? How does a receptive knowledge of vocabulary develop into productive vocabulary? (b) Should students' command of academic vocabulary be extended to include more items from the general vocabulary? (c) Should students' productive knowledge in general vocabulary be extended? (d) Should there be a common core vocabulary that students at the four Chinese speech communities should know? (e) If the response to (b), (c), and (d) are positive, how can we help our students to achieve these goals? (f) What are the consequential implications for the Hong Kong language curriculum? — its goals, objectives, content, teaching methodology, and the philosophy and methods of assessment?

These issues will be focused on in the subsequent studies of this project, and the results will, it is hoped, stimulate discussions leading to be beneficial reforms in Hong Kong language education.

References

Anderson, R. C., & Freebody, P. (1981). Vocabulary knowledge. In J. T. Guthrie (Ed.), *Comprehension and teaching: Research reviews* (pp. 77–117). Newark, DE: International Reading Association.

Anderson, R. C., & Freebody, P. (1983). Reading comprehension and the assessment and acquisition of word knowledge. In B. Hutson (Ed.), *Advances in reading/language research: A research annual* (pp. 231–256). Greenwich, CT: JAI Press.

Beck, I. L., McKeown, M. G., & Omanson, R. C. (1987). The effects and uses of diverse vocabulary instructional techniques. In M. G. McKeown & M. E. Curtis (Eds.), *The nature of vocabulary acquisition* (pp. 147–163). Hillsdale, NJ: Erlbaum.

Brown, C. (1993). Factors affecting the acquisition of vocabulary: Frequency and saliency of words. In T. Huckin, M. Haynes, & J. Coady (Eds.), *Second language reading and vocabulary learning* (pp. 263–286). Norwood, NJ: Ablex.

Brown, C., & Payne, M. E. (1994). *Five essential steps of processes in vocabulary learning*. Paper presented at the TESOL Convention, Baltimore, MD.

Calfee, R., & Drum, P. (1986). Research on teaching reading. In M. C. Wittrock (Ed.), *Handbook of research on teaching* (3rd ed., pp. 804–849). New York: Macmillan.

Carey, S. (1978). The child as word learner. In M. Halle, J. Bresnan & G. A. Miller (Eds.), *Linguistic theory and psychological reality* (pp. 264–293). Cambridge, MA: MIT Press.

Carroll, J. B., Davies, P., & Richman, B. (1971). *The American Heritage word frequency book*. New York: Houghton Mifflin.

Chall, J. S. (1958). *Readability: An appraisal of research and application*. Columbus: Ohio State University Press.

Chall, J. (1987). Two vocabularies for reading: Recognition and meaning. In M. G. McKeown & M. E. Curtis (Eds.), *The nature of vocabulary acquisition* (pp. 7–17). Hillsdale, NJ: Erlbaum.

Cheung, Y. S., & Lee, P. L. M. (1986). *A study of the English vocabulary in junior secondary textbooks in Hong Kong*. Hong Kong: Government Printer.

Clark, E. V. (Ed.). (1995). *Proceedings of the twenty-sixth annual child language research forum*. Stanford: Center for the Study of Language and Information.

Craik, F. I. M., & Lockhart, R. S. (1972). Levels of processing: A framework for memory research. *Journal of Verbal Learning and Verbal Behavior, 11,* 671–684.

Craik, F. I. M., & Tulving, E. (1975). Depth of processing and the retention of words in episodic memory. *Journal of Experimental Psychology: General, 104,* 268–684.

Cronbach, L. J. (1942). An analysis of techniques for systematic vocabulary testing. *Journal of Educational Research, 36,* 206–217.

Cronbach, L. J. (1943). Measuring knowledge of precise word meaning. *Journal of Educational Research, 36,* 538–534.

Curtis, M. E. (1987). Vocabulary testing and vocabulary instruction. In M. G. McKeown & M. E. Curtis (Eds.), *The nature of vocabulary acquisition* (pp. 37–51). Hillsdale, NJ: Erlbaum.

Dolch, E. W., & Leeds, D. (1953). Vocabulary tests and depth of meaning. *Journal of Educational Research, 47,* 181–189.

Drum, P. A., & Konopak, B. C. (1987). Learning word meanings from written context. In M. G. McKeown & M. E. Curtis (Eds.), *The nature of vocabulary acquisition* (pp. 73–87). Hillsdale, NJ: Erlbaum.

Ebbinghaus, H. (1885). *Uber das Gedachtnis. Untersuchungen zur Experimentellen Psychologie* (Memory. A Contribution to Experimental Psychology). Leipzig: Duncker & Humbolt.

George, H. V. (1983). *Classification, communication, teaching and learning.* English Language Institute: Victoria University of Wellington.

Goulden, R., Nation, I. S. P., & Read, J. A. S. (1990). How large can a receptive vocabulary be? *Applied Linguistics, 11,* 341–363.

Graves, M. F. (1986). Vocabulary learning and instruction. In E. Z. Rothkopf (Ed.), *Review of research in education* (Vol. 13, pp. 49–90). Washington, DC: American Educational Research Association.

Graves, M. F. (1987). The roles of instruction in fostering vocabulary development. In M. G. McKeown & M. E. Curtis (Eds.), *The nature of vocabulary acquisition* (pp. 165–184). Hillsdale, NJ: Erlbaum.

Hague, S. A. (1987). Vocabulary instruction: What L2 can learn from L1. *Foreign Language Annals, 20,* 217–225.

Hatch, E., & Brown, C. (1995). *Vocabulary, semantics, and language education.* New York: Cambridge University Press.

Jenkins, J. R., & Dixon, R. C. (1983). Vocabulary learning. *Contemporary Educational Psychology, 8,* 237–260.

Kame'enui, E. J., Dixon, R. C., & Carnine, D. (1987). Issues in the design of vocabulary instruction. In M. G. Mckeown & M. E. Curtis. (Eds.) *The nature of vocabulary acquisition* (pp. 129–145). Hillsdale, NJ: Erlbaum.

Laufer, B., & Nation, I. S. P. (1995). Vocabulary size and use: Lexical richness in L2 written production. *Applied Linguistics, 16,* 307–322.

Mezynski, K. (1983). Issues concerning the acquisition of knowledge: Effects of vocabulary training on reading comprehension. *Review of Educational Research, 53,* 253–279.

Miller, G. A. (1988). The challenge of universal literacy. *Science, 241,* 1293–1299.

Miller, G. A. (1991). *The science of words.* New York: Scientific American Library.

Nagy, W. E., & Anderson, R. C. (1984). How many words are there in printed school English? *Reading Research Quarterly, 19,* 304–330.

Nagy, W. E., & Herman, P. A. (1987). Depth and breadth of vocabulary knowledge: Implications for acquisition and instruction. In M. G. McKeown & M. E. Curtis (Eds.), *The nature of vocabulary acquisition* (pp. 19–35). Hillsdale, NJ: Erlbaum.

Nation, I. S. P. (1990). *Teaching and learning vocabulary.* Boston, MA: Heinle & Heinle.

Palmberg, R. (1987). On lexical inferencing and young foreign-language learner. *System, 15,* 69–76.

Raven, J. C. (1960). *Guide to using the Standard Progressive Matrices.* London: Lewis.

Read, J. (1988) Measuring the vocabulary knowledge of second language learners. *RELC (Regional Language Centre) Journal* 19(2), 12–25.

Read, J. (1993). The development of a new measurement of L2 vocabulary knowledge. *Language Testing, 10,* 355–371.

Richards, J. C. (1976). The role of vocabulary teaching. *TESOL Quarterly, 10*, 77–89.

Saville-Troike, M. (1984). What really matters in second language learning for academic achievement? *TESOL Quarterly, 18*, 199–219.

Siu, P. K., Fan, K., Lee, L. M., & Lai, T. C. (Eds.) (1986). *A study of Chinese vocabulary in Hong Kong junior secondary schools*. Hong Kong: Education Department Educational Research Establishment (in Chinese).

Stahl, S. A., & Fairbanks, M. M. (1986). The effects of vocabulary instruction: A model-based meta-analysis. *Review of Educational Research, 56*, 72–110.

Stanovich, K. E. (1986). Matthew effects in reading: Some consequences of individual differences in the acquisition of literacy. *Reading Research Quarterly, 21*, 360–407.

Sternberg, R. J. (1987). Most vocabulary is learned from context. In M. G. McKeown, & M.E. Curtis (Eds.), *The nature of vocabulary acquisition* (pp. 89–105). Hillsdale, NJ: Erlbaum.

Terman, L. M. (1916). *The measurement of intelligence*. New York: Houghton Mifflin.

T'sou, B. K. Y., Tsoi, W. F., Lai, T. B. Y., Hu, J., & Chan, S. W. K. (2000). LIVAC, A Chinese synchronous corpus, and some applications. *Proceedings of the International Conference on Chinese Language Computing* (pp. 223–238), Chicago.

Wechsler, D. (1949). *Manual for the Wechsler intelligence scale for children*. New York: Psychological Corporation.

Wesche, M., & Paribakht, T. S. (1996). Assessing second language vocabulary knowledge: Depth versus breadth. *Canadian Modern Language Review, 53*, 13–40.

Author Note

This research was supported in part by grant No. M027/95A from the Language Fund, Hong Kong. The authors are grateful for the co-operation of the participating schools and for advice from Peter Tung and C. K. Leong.

Appendix 1

Frequency bands in two corpuses

Band	Frequency*	Examples
1	1 – 3	自負，辯護權，靈機一觸
2	4 – 5	斷言，祝捷，急不及待
3	6 – 8	魄力，致哀，停滯不前
4	9 – 21	糾正，取決，以權謀私
5	> = 22	收容，成立，總額

Source: Linguistic Variation in Chinese Communities (LIVAC) 1995–97

Band	Frequency*	Examples
3	3	重申，浴血，居高臨下
4	4 – 8	自家，綵排，凝固
5	> = 9	風氣，康復，交流電

Source: Siu, Fan, Lee & Lai (1986)
* Occurrence within the entire corpus

Appendix 2

Sample of the Chinese Vocabulary Knowledge Assessment Test (CVCAT)

(一)　選出意義<u>最接近</u>的詞組 (*Select among the following the lexical item **closest in meaning** to the given one*)

示例：

序幕
A　落幕
B　程序
C　序列
D　開始　　　　　　　　　　　　　　　　　　答案是： D

(二)　　選出<u>最適當</u>的詞組 (*Select **the most suitable** lexical item*)
示例：

我們要養成早睡早起的 ＿＿＿＿＿。
A　習慣
B　訓練
C　態度
D　信念　　　　　　　　　　　　　　　　答案是： A

(三)　　找出<u>最不適當</u>的詞組 (*Identify **the least suitable** lexical item*)
示例：

「標榜」與下列哪一詞組意義不同？
A　突出
B　強調
C　重視
D　標記　　　　　　　　　　　　　　　　答案是： D

(四)　　填上適當的詞語（以四字為限）
(*Fill in the blank with a **suitable word** — maximum 4 characters*)
示例：

不要把雜物 ＿＿＿＿＿ 梯間，阻塞走火通道。　　答案是： 堆放

(五)　　改錯 (Error correction)
　　　　(a)　填上正確的字 (*Fill in the **correct character***)
示例：

距離〔孝〕試只有兩星期，我們要用功溫習。　　答案是： 考

　　　　(b)　填上正確的詞語 (*Fill in the **correct word***)
示例：

距離〔測試〕只有兩星期，我們要用功溫習。　　答案是： 考試

(六)　　續句〈續寫最少四個字，使成為意義完整的句子〉
(*Sentence completion — minimum four characters — to provide for a **meaningful sentence***)
示例：

疑犯口口聲聲＿＿＿＿＿＿＿。　　　　　答案是：説自己是冤枉的

16

Chinese Lexical Knowledge Development: Strategies for Decoding Unfamiliar Words

Anna S. F. Kwan and Benjamin K. Y. T'sou

This study is part of an international study on the Chinese lexical development of secondary and tertiary students in Hong Kong, Taipei, Shanghai and Singapore (T'sou, Kwan & Liu, 1997). The major aim of this paper is to explore the relationship between learners' lexical development and strategies used in decoding unfamiliar Chinese lexical items isolated from context. Research shows that vocabulary acquisition can result from *intentional* and *incidental* learning. Intentional learning is learning as being planned for, whereas incidental learning is a by-product of doing something else. Only a small proportion of our vocabulary is acquired by intentional learning (Anderson & Nagy, 1992; Anglin, 1993; Nagy & Anderson, 1984; Shu, Anderson & Zhang 1995).

To help students develop their vocabulary, both direct instructions and inferencing techniques are essential (Beck & McKeown, 1991). Direct instructions are important at the early stage of vocabulary development. As language teachers we should help students master frequently used words, aspects of which may include form (spoken and written), position (grammatical patterns and collocations), function (frequency and appropriateness) and meaning (concept and association) (e.g., Bai, 1991; George, 1983; Hatch & Brown, 1995).

Strategies to develop students as more effective independent word learners, such as inferencing strategies, should be introduced to students to empower them in their vocabulary development (Nagy, 1985). Learners should learn making use of information or cues available such as morphology of the word (Carton, 1971; Nagy & Anderson, 1984), cognate information (Carton, 1971; Haynes, 1984), grammatical class of the word (Carton, 1971; Clarke & Nation, 1980), semantic relationships between words (Alderson & Alvarez, 1978), rhetorical relationships (Alderson & Alvarez, 1978; Clarke & Nation, 1980), and knowledge of the world (Carton, 1971; Haastrup, 1985; Honeyfield, 1977). Also, learners should be encouraged to follow systematic procedures in the inferencing process. Typical steps include having learners first examining the prefix and or suffix of the unknown word to determine its part of speech, then looking at relationship between adjoining clauses or sentences and other sentences, guessing the meaning of the unknown word, and replacing the unknown word with the guess to check if it fits and makes sense (e.g., Bruton & Samuda 1981; Clarke & Nation, 1980; Fischer, 1994; Hatch & Brown, 1995; Nation, 1983).

However, it has been observed that in language classrooms, common practice in helping students develop their vocabulary seems to rely mainly on direct instruction, drill and practice, whereas the incidental learning of word meanings has been less emphasized (Anderson & Nagy, 1992; Shu & Anderson, 1997; Shu, Anderson & Zhang 1995). Incidental learning involves inferring meaning in the process, which requires inferencing skills at both context and word levels. Context level skills play a significant role in students' vocabulary knowledge development (de Glopper, van Daalen-Kapteijns & Schouten-van Parreren, 1996). If learners can find enough clues, they can infer the meaning of 80% of the unfamiliar words from context (Saragi, Nation & Meister, 1978). Word level inferencing is another important contributing factor to the rapid growth in vocabulary (Anglin, 1993). Mori and Nagy (1999) observed that students were more successful in inferring the meanings of novel kanji compounds when both words and contextual clues were provided.

While research emphasizes the usefulness of inferencing strategies, it has been found that successful lexical inferencing often depends on the language proficiency of the learners (Haastrup, 1991) and there appears to be a threshold level of proficiency that learners have to reach in order to be able to acquire and utilize the inferencing skills (Haastrup, 1991; Laufer, 1996; van Parreren & Schouten-van Parreren, 1981). Several researchers have analysed weaknesses in inferencing strategies employed by second language learners (Bensousan & Laufer, 1984; Haastrup, 1985; Haynes, 1984; Hosenfeld, 1977; Laufer & Sim, 1985; van Parreren & Schouten-van Parreren, 1981). The sources of wrong guesses made by the learners include:

basing the guess on morphology and false cognates, accessing the wrong word in lexical memory because of graphemic or phonemic similarity to the target word, selecting an inappropriate meaning of the polysemic words, and failing to identify the grammatical function of the words.

In Chinese language classroom, direct instructions are dominant and inferencing strategies less emphasized (Shu & Anderson, 1997; Shu, Anderson, & Zhang, 1995). A possible factor may be due to the uncertainty of the effectiveness of applying vocabulary research findings to learning Chinese language.

As learners and teachers of both Chinese and English languages, we believe that the strategies for inferencing unfamiliar words discussed above should be able to apply to learning Chinese. A strong reason for this is that similar conditions exist in Chinese language. For example, most complex Chinese characters are composed of a semantic radical and a phonetic radical (Li 1993; Yin & Rohsenow, 1994). Semantic radicals indicate the semantic category of morphemes corresponding to whole characters, whereas phonetic radicals suggest possible pronunciations. This structure creates the conditions, which make inferencing strategies applicable.

On the whole, the literature in learning vocabulary suggested that inferencing the meaning of unfamiliar words is an important means to extend learners' vocabulary. Word and context level strategies are independent and both should be introduced in language classrooms. However, common practice in language learning does not seem to follow this direction. One reason may be due to insufficient research in this area, in particular in Chinese vocabulary learning. There is an urgent need for more studies to look systematically into learners' inferencing strategies in a Chinese language context. As the first step of such a systematic investigation, we need to observe learners' performance in a natural process to obtain base line data, such as the types of strategies used, the types of knowledge and errors displayed in the decoding process. Also, there is a need to compare the performance of students with different lexical abilities to understand the relationships between learners' lexical abilities and their inferencing skill development in learning Chinese. It would be appropriate for this exploratory study to focus on students' decoding strategies at word and character levels.

Since this study aims to look at learners' natural decoding process, a grounded theory approach is appropriate in this regard. In order to bring a sharper focus to the investigation, three questions were formulated: (1) What types of strategies are used by students in decoding unfamiliar Chinese words? (2) What types of word knowledge and errors are demonstrated in the decoding process? (3) Are students' strategies, word knowledge and errors related to their Chinese lexical knowledge development?

METHOD

Participants   The participants of this study were 90 secondary school students of different lexical abilities from Form Two, Form Four and Form Six. They were selected from 856 secondary students participating in our Chinese lexical development study in which their Chinese lexical knowledge was assessed. The initial analysis of the study has been discussed in T'sou et al. (1997). The present analysis focuses on 12 students, half of them with high vocabulary scores (87.6%) and the rest with low vocabulary scores (36.5%) as indicated in a Chinese vocabulary test. These students are selected because they are typical cases that are able to represent the students in the sub groups.

Instrument   The instrument used in this study was the *Interview Schedule for Learner Guessing Strategies* (ISLGS), which was developed by the researchers to elicit students' guessing strategies for unfamiliar words.

The stimulus materials used in this study were 18 context independent multi-character words of low frequency, including 10 two-character words (e.g., 謦欬), 4 three-character words (e.g., 阿是穴) and 4 four-character words (e.g., 被堅執銳) of various morphological structures.

Procedure and data analysis   The students were interviewed individually using the ISLGS and the 18 unfamiliar multi-character words. Students were presented with the unfamiliar words one at a time and were asked if they had seen the word previously. If the student said the word was unfamiliar, the interviewer would encourage the student to read the word aloud and to provide a hypothetical meaning for the word and the reasons for determining that particular meaning. The interviewers would ask students questions to assist students in clarifying their responses, but would not provide guidance that could affect students' responses or the direction of the interview.

All the interviews conducted within one week were audio-recorded with the consent of the schools and the students. Data gathered from individual students also included their age, sex, access to news media, and their latest Chinese and English Attainment Test results (for Form Six students, their School Certificate Examination results). Interview data were transcribed and content analysed to identify students' strategies for decoding unfamiliar words. Within each segment, all strategies employed by the students in deriving the meaning of each unfamiliar word were coded according to sequence. A category system grounded from the data was then developed (see Table 1).

Table 1
Strategies for Inferring Meaning at Word and Character Levels

Code	Descriptions
	Word level
SW1	Use other familiar word(s) to replace the meaning of the target word
SW2	Use other familiar word(s) to assist decoding meaning
SW3	Use a known character to infer the meaning of an unknown character within a word
SW4	Analyse only parts of the components to derive a basic meaning
SW5	Analyse all components of the word to derive a basic meaning
SW6	Analyse all components of the word to derive a basic meaning then an extend meaning
SW7	Analyse all components of the word to derive a basic meaning then an associated meaning
SW8	Use morphological cues
SW8a	Analyse word structure
SW8b	Analyse prefixes and suffixes
SW9	Use phonological cues
SW10	Use orthographical cues
SW11	Other
	Character level
SC1	Use other familiar character(s) to replace the meaning of the unfamiliar character(s)
SC2	Use other familiar character(s) to assist decoding meaning of the unfamiliar character
SC3	Analyse only parts of the radicals in deriving a meaning
SC4	Analyse all radicals of the character, including sound and shape (meaning) symbols to derive a meaning
SC5	Analyse the meaning of all the radicals of the character to derive a global meaning
SC6	Analyse the meaning of all the radicals of the character to derive an associated meaning
SC7	Use phonological cues
SC8	Use orthographical cues
SC9	Other

Special word and character knowledge (knowledge not normally demonstrated by their fellow students in the interview), and linguistic errors were also identified (See Table 2 and 3). In the coding process, when an utterance involved more than one category, more than one code was assigned. In order to enhance the inter-coder reliability of the analysis, each interview transcription was coded separately by at least two researchers.

Since the emphasis of this paper is to examine students' decoding strategies and its relation to students' vocabulary knowledge development, the analysis here will focus on comparing students with strong and weak Chinese lexical knowledge.

Table 2
Word and Character Knowledge

Code	Descriptions
	Word level
KW1	Word meaning, but unable to explain it properly
KW2	Word meaning and able to explain it properly
KW3	Word formation
KW4	Word types (e.g., dialect, jargon, foreign)
KW5	Word parts
KW6	Collocation
KW7	Register
KW8	Phonology
KW9	Orthography
KW10	Morphology
KW11	Other
	Character level
KC1	The basic meaning of the character
KC2	The multi meaning of the character
KC3	Character formation
KC4	Phonology
KC5	Orthography
KC6	Morphology
KC7	Other

Table 3
Types of Errors

Code	Descriptions
	Word level
EW1	Word structure errors
EW2	Orthographically cueing errors
EW3	Phonologically cueing errors
EW4	Neglecting word components
EW5	Other
	Character level
EC1	Wrong rules for the formation of sound-shape characters (to assume that a character component can be both the sound and the meaning symbol)
EC2	Over-generalizing the rule for orthographical and semantic links
EC2a	Over-generalizing the rule for orthographical and phonetic links
EC3	Orthographical cueing errors
EC4	Neglecting character components
EC5	Other

RESULTS

The interview process and the data collected suggested that students used a common approach as well as word and character level strategies in the guessing tasks.

Common approach   When students were presented with a word, they would first search its meaning from their lexical memory. If it failed, they would access other familiar words to assist arriving at a meaning by using morphological, orthographical and phonological clues. When students felt uncertain about the meaning, they would analyse clues at word level or character level.

Word and character level strategies   The strategies (the category system is presented in Table 1) employed by the students can be categorized into word and character levels. Word level strategies involve analysing information at word level, such as word structure (e.g., 阿是穴, see Text 1). Character level strategies focus on information provided by a character such as radicals of a character (e.g., 署署, see Text 10 and 11). The frequency counts of word and character strategies for each student are indicated in Table 4.

Text 1

阿是穴 (Aa3 Si6 Yut9)

I.* 係咩嘢意思呢？

(What does it mean then?)

S. 唔，呢個係唔係人體嘅穴道嚟嫁。

(Well, does it refer to an acupuncture point of a human body?)

I. 人體嘅穴道，點解你咁估呢？

(The acupuncture point of the human body. What gave you that idea?)

S. 因為有個穴字。

(It is because the term contains the character 'Yut9'.)

*I = Interviewer   S = Student

Table 4

Strategy Counts at Word and Character Levels

Students	Word level	Character level	Total
Vocabulary knowledge			
Strong (SVK)	18.92 (83.46%)	3.75 (16.54%)	22.67 (100%)
Weak (WVK)	17.42 (80.38%)	4.25 (19.61%)	21.67 (100%)
All students	18.17 (81.96%)	4.00 (18.04%)	22.17 (100%)

n = 12

As shown in Table 4, all students used more word-level strategies than character-level strategies (81.96% vs. 18.04%). Students with strong vocabulary knowledge (SVK) used slightly more strategies than students with weak vocabulary knowledge (WVK) in decoding unfamiliar words (22.67 vs. 21.67). That is to say, a SVK student employed about 1.26 strategies to deal with an unfamiliar word, whereas a WVK student used about 1.20 strategies.

Compared with WVK students, SVK students utilized more word level strategies (18.92 vs. 17.42) and slightly fewer character level strategies (3.75 vs. 4.25). This seems to indicate that SVK students were more inclined to solve the problems by using word level clues.

Major strategy types   The major strategy types (over 10% in the total and demonstrated by at least 50% of the students in the group) used by most of the students are listed in Table 5.

Table 5
Major Strategy Types at Word and Character Levels

Students	Word level	Character level
Vocabulary knowledge		
Strong (SVK)	SW8 (33%)	SC3 (44%)
	SW5 (22%)	SC4 (41%)
Weak (WVK)	SW8 (28%)	SC4 (49%)
	SW4 (17%)	SC3 (39%)
	SW5 (14%)	

n = 12

There are similarities as well as differences in strategy types employed by SVK and WVK students. At word level, both SVK and WVK students employed extensively morphological clues (SW8) (see Text 1), particularly in analysing word structure.

SVK students were more analytical, they tended to analyse all components in a word (SW5) (see Text 2) before assigning a meaning to an unknown word, whereas WVK students tended to analyse only parts of information available (SW4) (see Text 3).

Text 2

深慶得人 (Sen1 Hing3 Dak7 Yan4)
I. 或者試吓解吓？
    (Would you mind making a guess of it?)
S. 好呀，我覺得係一啲賢能之士，尤其係啲君主，又或者係啲在高位之人，又或者係一啲有權力嘅人士，佢哋係外間又或者係一啲地方佢哋搵到一啲有賢能之士，幫得佢哋手嘅，咁佢哋好高興能夠搵到適當嘅人幫佢哋達到成功。
    (Well, I think it should mean some men of virtue, especially kings or people in high positions, or those securing power. They have found some capable persons somewhere who can help them secure their positions. These people feel so glad that they have found the right person to help them move up the ladder of success.)
I. 點解你會有咁嘅解釋呢？
    (Why did you give such an interpretation?)
S. 純粹字面解釋而已。
    (Well, I just based my guess on the literal context.)

Text 3

被堅執銳 (Pei 1 Gin1 Zap7 Joei6)
I.   知唔知點解呀？
      (Do you know the meaning of this term?)
S.   俾啲嘢打中。
      (Hit by something.)
I.   啊，俾嘢打中，點解你會咁估呢？
      (Oh, I see. How did you come up with such an interpretation?)
S.   又硬又銳吖嘛，所以，好合理地推論有人俾啲嘢打中囉。
      (It suggests something's very stiff and pointed, and thus, it is reasonable to deduce that someone is hit by something.)

Examining strategies at character level, similar to the trend found at word level, SVK students again tended to analyse all the possible radicals in a character (SC3), whereas WVK students were more inclined to arrive at a meaning by focusing on some of the radicals (SC4) although they were aware of the existence of other radicals.

Word and character knowledge   In the analysis, students' statements were coded for word and character knowledge, as well as errors. The coding systems are presented in Tables 2 and 3. The frequency counts and the major types of knowledge are detailed in Tables 6 and 7.

As expected, SVK students displayed significantly more knowledge at word and character levels than their WVK counterparts (10.66 vs. 4.00). Both SVK and WVK students demonstrated knowledge of word types such as identifying the target word as a jargon or a foreign word (KW4) (e.g., Text 4).

Table 6
Knowledge Counts at Word and Character Levels

Students	Word level	Character level	Total
Vocabulary knowledge			
Strong (SVK)	8.83 (82.83%)	1.83 (17.17%)	10.66 (100%)
Weak (WVK)	3.50 (87.50%)	0.50 (12.50%)	4.00 (100%)
All Students	6.17 (84.06%)	1.17 (15.94%)	7.34 (100%)

n = 12

Table 7
Major Knowledge at Word and Character Levels

Students	Word level	Character level
Vocabulary knowledge		
Strong (SVK)	KW2(35%)	
	KW4(19%)	KC3(67%)
	KW11(17%)	
Weak (WVK)	KW4(41%)	–

$n = 12$

Text 4

沙門 (Sa1 Mun4)

I. 係咩嚟嘅？咩意思？

(What's this? What does it mean?)

S. 人名。

(The name of a person.)

I. 人名，係咩人？

(The name of a person, what kind of person?)

S. 外國人，好似係譯名嚟嘅。

(Foreigner. It looks like a translation of the person's name.)

I. 肯定?

(Sure?)

S. 或者係地方名，我唔清楚。

(Or it might be the name of a place. I am not sure really.)

I. 你有冇曾經見過或者聽過佢？

(Have you ever come across or heard about anything related to it?)

S. 沙門氏菌。

(Salmonella.)

The notable characteristics of SVK students are: (a) they know the meaning of the unfamiliar words (KW2); (b) they are able to generate a wider range of potential meanings for the target words (KW11) (e.g., Text 5), and (c) their word knowledge appears to be broader and deeper.

At character level, SVK students presented statements concerning knowledge of character formation (KC3) (e.g., Text 6), whereas WVK students displayed very few character knowledge statements.

Text 5

阿是穴 (Aa3 Si6 Yut9)

I.　話俾我聽你諗到乜嘢。

(Tell me anything about this term?)

S.　或者係一個穴道, 即係人體一個穴道。又或者係一撻好出名嘅哋方，阿是可能係個名嚟嘅。個穴字呢，即係解山洞呀之類，或者解身上面啲穴道囉。

('Aa3 Si6' may be an acupuncture point, or more exactly, an acupuncture point of a human body, or it could be a very well known place. 'Aa3 Si6' would probably be a name, 'Yut9' would possibly be something like cavern, or it might just be an acupuncture point on the body.)

Text 6

坍塌 (Tan1 Tap8)

I.　點解讀坍塌？

(Why do you pronounce it as 'dan1 tap8').

S.　我本身識哩個塌字，另外一個讀 'd a n 1' 因為個字裏面有個「丹」字。

(I've come across the character '塌' before, the other one I pronounced 'dan 1', simply because the character '坍' carries the portion '丹' (dan 1).

Errors　Both the SVK and WVK students committed errors at word and character levels in their decoding. Tables 8 and 9 present their error counts and types.

Table 8

Error Counts at Word and Character Levels

Students	Word level	Character level	Total
Vocabulary knowledge			
Strong (SVK)	1.67 (47.71%)	1.83 (52.29%)	3.50 (100%)
Weak (WVK)	3.83 (74.22%)	1.33 (25.78%)	5.16 (100%)
All students	2.75 (63.51%)	1.58 (36.49%)	4.33 (100%)

n = 12

Table 9
Major Error Types at Word and Character Levels

Students	Word level	Character level
Vocabulary knowledge		
Strong (SVK)	EW1(60%)	EC1(39%)
	EW4(33%)	
Weak (WVK)	EW4(47%)	EC1(33%)
	EW3(34%)	EC2(33%)

$n = 12$

Not surprisingly, SVK students made fewer errors than WVK students (3.50 vs. 5.16) did. The major error types for both groups of students are slightly different. At word level, SVK students displayed more errors in word structure (EW1) (e.g., Text 7), whereas WVK students tended to neglect word components (EW4) (e.g., Text 8) and to commit phonologically cueing errors (EW3) (e.g., Text 9) in deriving meaning.

At character level, a common error for both groups of students is the wrong assumption about the formation of sound-shape character (形聲字), they tend to think that a character radical can be both the sound and the meaning symbol (EC1). Text 10 is a typical example of this.

Text 7

維管束 (Waai4 Gun2 Chuk7)

I.　呢個詞點解呢？

(What does that mean?)

S.　維管束。管束就即係抑制，限制啦，管住咁樣啦。維解維持住管制咁樣。

(Waai4 Gun2 Chuk7. 'Gun2 Chuk7' means to resist, to limit and to control. 'Waai4' means maintaining control over something, etc.)

Text 8

被堅執銳 (Pei1 Gin1 Zap7 Joei6)

I.　呢個詞語點解呢？

(Do you know the meaning of this term?)

S.　堅持執著，執著一啲嘢囉。

(Stick onto something and never let go of your stance, hold something till the end.)

Text 9

坍塌 (Tan1 Tap8)
I.   你有無見過呢個詞語呀？
(Have you ever come across this term?)
S.   係唔係糟蹋呀？
(Does it mean, 'spoil'?)
I.   唔，糟蹋，點解呀？
(What do you mean by 'spoil'?)
S.   唔會去珍惜一啲嘢咯。
(Taking something for granted.)

Text 10

詧詧 (Bou6 Bou6)
I.   點解讀「言言」呀？
(Why did you pronounce these two characters as 'Yin4 Yin4'?)
S.   下面果兩個言字。
(Simply because each of the two characters has the same character '言' at the bottom, which is pronounced as 'Yin4'.)
I.   你覺得係乜嚟嘅呢？
(Have you figured its meaning?)
S.   形容啲人好多嘢講啩。
(It may imply that someone's really talkative.)
I.   點解咁樣估呀？
(Why do you come up with such an idea?)
S.   都可能係個言字啦。
(Well, the inspiration comes also from the character '言'.)
I.   咁其他字嘅邊一部份話俾你聽好多嘢講吖？
(Are there further hints from other parts of the character prompting you to give such an interpretation 'talkative'?)
S.   可能個言字，佢重複兩次就即係好多嘢講。
(Well, the character '言' repeated twice in the word. This gives an impression of 'talkative'.)

Another error, mostly committed by WVK students, is the over-generalization of the rule for orthographical and semantic links (EC2) (e.g., Text 11).

Text 11

罾罾 (Bou6 Bou6)

I.　嗄，咁你覺得呢個詞點解呀？

(What is the meaning of this term?)

S.　點解呀？形容天上面啲嘢啩。

(What's the meaning? It might refer to things in the sky.)

I.　天上嘅咩嘢呀？

(What kind of things do you think are in the sky?)

S.　可能係雲呀，果啲嘢啦。

(It might be clouds, or things related.)

I.　啊，即係形容啲雲，即係形容啲雲嘅乜嘢？

(Oh, I see, you mean the clouds, in what way do you think the clouds are being described?)

S.　即係可能啲雲密麻麻，或者稀稀疏疏嗰啲。

(Well, it might describe clouds which are dense and close, or the reverse case, that is: clouds are thin and scattered.)

I.　咁點解你會覺得係形容啲雲嘅形狀大小呀？

(Why would you think that term actually refers to sizes of the clouds and things similar?)

S.　因為我覺得佢同個暮字有啲相似，咁暮字通常係指天上嘅雲和霧等。

(Because the character '罾' looks similar to the character '暮' (signifying 'evening'*), and this is supposed to belong to the same domain as '雲' (meaning 'clouds'), things etc.

*　The students misread the character '暮' (meaning 'evening') as '霧' (meaning 'fog').

To sum up, students used similar approaches in decoding unfamiliar words, first at the word level and then at the character level if necessary. They employed more word-level strategies than character-level strategies. There were no significant differences in strategy counts between SVK and WVK students, but SVK students used more word level strategies and fewer character level strategies than their WVK counterparts. In terms of strategy types, morphological cues, particularly analysing word structure, was the most employed strategy for both SVK and WVK students.

However, the most notable difference between the two groups of students was the thoroughness of the analysis in deriving a meaning for the target item. SVK students were able to pick up almost all the cues available in their analysis, whereas WVK students were able to make use of only partial information. The errors and word and character knowledge shown in the process indicated clearly that the WVK students were impeded by their lexical knowledge in the decoding process.

DISCUSSION

The present study has attempted to investigate, in a natural process, learners' strategies in decoding unfamiliar Chinese words isolated from context. At least two related phenomena were observed in students' decoding process. The first phenomenon was that SVK students were more thorough in their analysis. They tended to be able to pick up more cues and to use them to decode the unfamiliar words successfully, whereas the WVK students were found to analyse partial information to formulate meanings, which tended to lead to inaccurate interpretations.

Another phenomenon was that compared with SVK students, WVK students committed more errors and demonstrated less word knowledge in the decoding process. This seems to illustrate that students with different lexical knowledge appear to experience different processes in decoding unfamiliar words. SVK students had more access to information to facilitate their decoding process, whereas their WVK counterparts were found to be impeded by information deficit.

These two related phenomena suggest clearly that students' lexical knowledge is a crucial factor in successfully dealing with unfamiliar words. This is in line with researchers who propose that there is a lexical threshold for learners to benefit fully from word inferencing training (Haastrup, 1991; van Parreren & Schouten-van Parreren, 1981).

There are differences and similarities between the errors committed by L2 learners of English in other studies (Bensousan & Laufer, 1984; Haastrup, 1985; Haynes, 1984; Hosenfeld, 1977; Laufer & Sim, 1985; van Parreren & Schouten-van Parreren, 1981) and the students in this study. Like other L2 learners, both SVK and WVK students' errors are concerned with morphology, but most fall in the word structure category, which is a unique feature of the Chinese language. This shows clearly that students are not competent in this aspect of word knowledge. WVK students further indicate a lack of understanding of orthographical and semantic links at the character level. This type of errors is similar to L2 learners of English who search for the wrong item in lexical memory because of graphemic or phonemic resemblance to the target item. This reveals the weaknesses in WVK students' vocabulary learning resulting a vague visual and auditory image for the forms of the words.

These findings have important implications for lexical development, vocabulary teaching and research. The results show that the strategies demonstrated by both SVK and WVK students in decoding unfamiliar words were similar, but SVK students used more word level strategies and fewer character level strategies and were able to pick up more word level clues to arrive at word meaning. This seems to suggest that lexical knowledge and inferencing strategies are related but to different learning areas.

For language educators, the message seems clear. Learning inferencing strategies or developing learners' metacommunicative awareness may provide students with an analytical framework, which would help them deal with unfamiliar words. However, these strategies may not contribute drastically to the improvement of their lexical knowledge. To extend students' vocabulary size, strategies for learning unfamiliar words beyond inferencing are obviously needed.

As revealed in the data of this study, the weaknesses in students' word knowledge calls for a more systematic and thorough treatment during vocabulary learning which enables them to acquire a deeper word knowledge of the familiar vocabulary items beyond the semantic dimension (e.g., George, 1983). Some explicit instruction in syntactic and morphological analysis and certain linguistic knowledge such as rules for word and character structure should be addressed in Chinese language classrooms. Longitudinal research into the effects of teaching inferencing strategies and linguistic knowledge should also be conducted in schools to gain more understanding of the relationship between inferencing strategies and lexical knowledge.

References

Alderson, C., & Alvarez, G. (1978). *The development of strategies for the assignment of semantic information to unknown lexemes in text.* Mexico City: Centro de Ensenanza de Lenguas Extranjeras.

Anderson, R. C., Nagy, W. E. (1992). The vocabulary conundrum. *American*

Educator: The Professional Journal of the American Federation of Teachers, 16 (4), 14–18.

Anglin, J. M. (1993). Vocabulary development: A morphological analysis. *Monographs of the Society for Research in Child Development, 58* (10), Serial No. 238.

Bai, J. (1991). *Teaching Vocabulary: 8 faces of a word.* Paper presented at the Annual Meeting of the Chinese Language Teachers Association, Washington.

Beck, I. L., & McKeown, M. G. (1991). Social studies texts are hard to understand: Mediating some of the difficulties (Research directions). *Language Arts, 68,* 482–490.

Bensousan, M., & Laufer, B. (1984). Lexical guessing in context in EFL reading comprehension. *Journal of Research in Reading, 7* (1), 15–32.

Bruton, A., & Samuda, V. (1981). Guessing words. *Modern English Teacher, 8* (3), 8–21.

Carton, A. S. (1971). Inferencing: A process in using and learning language. In P. Pimsleur and T. Quinn (Eds.), *The psychology of second language learning* (pp. 45–58). Cambridge, UK: Cambridge University Press.

Clarke, D. F., & Nation, I. S. P. (1980). Guessing the meanings of words from context: Strategy and techniques. *System, 8* (3), 211–220.

De Glopper, van Daalen-Kapteijns, & Schouten-van Parreren, M. C. (1996). *Effects of training of a word learning strategy.* Paper presented at the Annual Conference of the American Educational Research Association, New York.

Fischer, U. (1994). Learning words from context and dictionaries: An experimental comparison. *Applied Psycholinguistics, 15* (4), 551–574.

George, H. V. (1983). *Classification, communication, teaching and learning.* English Language Institute: Victoria University of Wellington.

Haastrup, K. (1985). Lexical inferencing — a study of procedures in reception. *Scandinavian Working Papers on Bilingualism, 5,* 63–86.

Haastrup, K. (1991). Developing learners' procedural knowledge in comprehension. In R. Phillipson, E. Kellerman, L. Selinka, M. Sharwood Smith, & H. Swain (Eds.), *Foreign/ second language pedagogy research* (pp. 79–84). Clevedon: Multilingual Matters.

Hatch, E., & Brown, C. (1995). *Vocabulary, semantics, and language education.* New York: Cambridge University Press.

Haynes, M. (1984). Patterns and perils of guessing in second language reading. In J. Handscombe, R. A. Orem & B. P. Taylor (Eds.), *On TESOL '83: The question of control: Selected papers from the seventeenth annual convention of TESOL* (pp. 163–176). Washington, DC: TESOL.

Honeyfield, J. (1977). Word frequency and the importance of context in vocabulary learning. *RELC Journal, 8* (2), 35–42.

Hosenfeld, C. (1977). A preliminary investigation of the reading strategies of successful and non-successful language learners. *System, 5,* 110–123.

Laufer, B. (1996). The lexical threshold of L2 reading: where it is and how it relates to L1 reading ability. In K. Sajavaara & C. Fairweather (Eds.), *Approaches to Second Language Acquisition.* Jyvaskyla Cross Language Studies 17 (pp. 55–62) Jyvaskyla: Jyvaskyla University.

Laufer, B., & Sim, D. D. (1985). Taking the easy way out: Non-use and misuse of clues in EFL reading. *English Teaching Forum, 23* (2), 7–10, 20.

Li, D. (1993). *A study of Chinese characters.* Beijing: Peking University Press.

Mori, Y., & Nagy, W. (1999). Integration of information from context and word elements in interpreting novel kanji compounds. *Reading Research Quarterly, 34,* 80–101.

Nagy, W. E. (1985). *Vocabulary instruction: Implications of the new research.* Paper presented at the Annual Conference of the National Council of Teachers of English, Philadelphia.

Nagy, W. E., & Anderson, R. C. (1984). How many words are there in printed school English? *Reading Research Quarterly, 19 ,* 304–330.

Nation, I. S. P. (1983). Testing and teaching vocabulary. *Guidelines, 5* (1), 12–25.

Saragi, T., Nation, I. S. P., & Meister, G. F. (1978). Vocabulary learning and reading. *System, 6*(2), 72–78.

Shu, H., & Anderson, R. C. (1997). Role of radical awareness in the character and word acquisition of Chinese children. *Reading Research Quarterly, 32*(1), 78–89.

Shu, H., Anderson, R. C., & Zhang, H. (1995). Incidental learning of word meanings while reading: A Chinese and American cross-cultural study. *Reading Research Quarterly, 30,* 76–95.

T'sou, B. K. Y., Kwan, A. S. F., & Liu, G. K. F. (1997). *The developing lexicon: The case of Hong Kong secondary students.* Paper presented at the International Language in Education Conference.

Van Parreren, C. F., & Schouten-van Parreren, M. C. (1981). Contextual guessing: A trainable reader strategy. *System, 9*(3), 235–241.

Yin, B., & Rohsenow, J. S. (1994). *Modern Chinese characters.* Beijing: Sinolingua.

Author Note

This research was supported by a grant No: M027/95A from the Language Fund, Hong Kong.

Index